Romantics and Victorians

This book takes the reader not just to some of the key texts of the Romantic and Victorian periods, but also to the places that inspired them, and to current critical debates about them. It is a guidebook to reading historically which is – like all the best guidebooks – clear and easy to use. But its greatest achievement is that it never sacrifices complexity to clarity, and it repeatedly sends the reader back to the texts themselves, encouraging and supporting confident and active reading and re-reading. A practical book which is theoretically sophisticated but which wears its learning lightly and elegantly.

Clare Pettitt
Professor of Victorian Literature and Culture
King's College London

This admirably written and edited volume offers students an appealing, state-of-the-art introduction to male-authored Romanticism and ideas of the self, and the complex relationship of Victorian writers, both men and women, to concepts of 'home' and 'abroad' in a cosmopolitan and imperial age. Written with great flair and compression, each chapter addresses and integrates the social, formal and theoretical questions raised by its exploration of individual texts and writers, from the technologies of the self and the question of authorship in Romantic writing to issues of reading, audience and history in the Victorian period. Both the provocative questions for discussion and the suggested writing tasks highlight the wide-ranging ambitions of the editors and contributors to encourage students to think historically and read closely, inviting them to consider the responses of readers and critics within the nineteenth century itself in relation to recent critical and theoretical approaches.

Cora Kaplan
Honorary Professor in the School of English and Drama
Queen Mary, University of London

D1407075

Reading and Studying Literature

This book is part of the series *Reading and Studying Literature* published by Bloomsbury Academic in association with The Open University. The three books in the series are:

The Renaissance and Long Eighteenth Century (edited by Anita Pacheco and David Johnson)
ISBN 978-1-84966-622-0 (hardback)
ISBN 978-1-84966-614-5 (paperback)
ISBN 978-1-84966-634-3 (ebook)

Romantics and Victorians (edited by Nicola J. Watson and Shafquat Towheed)
ISBN 978-1-84966-623-7 (hardback)
ISBN 978-1-84966-624-4 (paperback)
ISBN 978-1-84966-637-4 (ebook)

The Twentieth Century (edited by Sara Haslam and Sue Asbee)
ISBN 978-1-84966-620-6 (hardback)
ISBN 978-1-84966-621-3 (paperback)
ISBN 978-1-84966-620-4 (ebook)

This publication forms part of the Open University module A230 *Reading and studying literature*. Details of this and other Open University modules can be obtained from the Student Registration and Enquiry Service, The Open University, PO Box 197, Milton Keynes MK7 6BJ, United Kingdom (tel. +44 (0)845 300 60 90, email general-enquiries@open.ac.uk).

www.open.ac.uk

Romantics and Victorians

Edited by Nicola J. Watson and Shafquat Towheed

BLOOMSBURY ACADEMIC

Published by

Bloomsbury Academic
an imprint of Bloomsbury Publishing Plc
36 Soho Square
London W1D 3QY
United Kingdom
and
175 Fifth Avenue
New York
NY 10010
USA
www.bloomsburyacademic.com

In association with

The Open University
Walton Hall
Milton Keynes MK7 6AA
United Kingdom

First published 2012

Edited and designed by The Open University.

Printed and bound in the United Kingdom by Latimer Trend & Company, Estover Road, Plymouth PL6 7PY.

CIP records for this book are available from the British Library and the Library of Congress.

ISBN 978-1-84966-623-7 (hardback)
ISBN 978-1-84966-624-4 (paperback)
ISBN 978-1-84966-637-4 (ebook)

1.1

Contents

Preface

Romantics and Victorians is the second book in the three-volume series *Reading and Studying Literature,* which aims to provide a chronological overview of the major literary periods. The other two books in the series are *The Renaissance and Long Eighteenth Century* (edited by Anita Pacheco and David Johnson) and *The Twentieth Century* (edited by Sara Haslam and Sue Asbee). Together, these three books form the core teaching material for the Open University undergraduate module *Reading and studying literature* (Open University module code A230).

Romantics and Victorians provides a thought-provoking overview of the development of English literature in the period from the French Revolution in 1789 to the death of Queen Victoria in 1901, an era in which the British overseas empire expanded inexorably, even while ideas about individual liberty were taking hold at home. The first part of the book, 'Romantic lives', explores the literature of the Romantic period (*c.*1789–1832) through the life and work of three great British writers (William Wordsworth, Percy Bysshe Shelley and Thomas De Quincey) and an influential European writer (E.T.A. Hoffmann). Focusing on the figure of the author, the chapters draw out the close connections between the inner mental lives of these writers, the natural world around them, and the idea current at the time of the 'Romantic life' as one lived in constant aesthetic and political engagement. Offering guided readings of a range of poetry and prose works, including Wordsworth's 'I wandered lonely as a cloud' (1807), De Quincey's *Confessions of an English Opium Eater* (1821) and Hoffmann's 'The Sandman' (1816), these four chapters develop the skills of close reading and analysis.

The second part of the book, 'Home and abroad in the Victorian age', looks at works by three great Victorian novelists through their representations of 'home' and 'abroad'. We often associate the Victorian period with conservative social values, but these chapters show that the Victorians were also affected by events in the wider world, and the literature of the age often contested simplistic ideas about the home. The books examined here are Emily Brontë's Gothic-tinged novel of doomed love on the Yorkshire moors, *Wuthering Heights* (1847); Arthur Conan Doyle's London-based but India-entangled detective novel, *The Sign of Four* (1890), featuring the world's most famous consulting detective, Sherlock Holmes; and Robert Louis Stevenson's experimental Pacific-Island tale, 'The Beach of Falesá' (1892–3). While the first part of the book centres on the figure of the Romantic author, the second part gives attention to the Victorian reader. The chapters develop close reading skills and an awareness of different types of prose writing, and also provide a wealth of information about how the Victorians acquired and read literature. Together, the two parts of *Romantics and Victorians* offer readers a detailed insight into how literature was written and read in Britain in the nineteenth century, as well as providing a thorough investigation into the cultural values of the time.

Open University modules and text books are the products of extensive collaboration and involve the labour of numerous people. Sincere thanks are due to members of the A230 module team who did not write for this volume, but contributed generously to the discussions that helped to shape it: Sue Asbee, Richard Danson Brown, Jessica Davies, Suman Gupta, Sara Haslam, David Johnson, Anita Pacheco, Steve Padley and Dennis Walder; to the curriculum manager Rachel Pearce; the editors Hannah Parish and Richard Jones; and the external assessor Michael Baron.

List of contributors

Richard Allen is Professor of Literature at The Open University, and was for a number of years Dean of Arts. He is author of the chapter 'Heritage and nationalism' in Rodney Harrison (ed.) *Understanding the Politics of Heritage* (2009), and edited with Harish Trivedi *Literature and Nation: Britain and India 1800–1990* (2001).

Delia da Sousa Correa is a Senior Lecturer in the Department of English at The Open University. Her research centres on connections between literature and music in the Victorian and Modernist periods. She is the author of *George Eliot, Music and Victorian Culture* (2003) and editor of *The Nineteenth-Century Novel: Realisms* (2000), *Phrase and Subject: Studies in Literature and Music* (2006), and, with W.R. Owens, *The Handbook to Literary Research* (2010). She is General Editor of the *Katherine Mansfield Studies* journal.

Clare Spencer is an Associate Lecturer with The Open University in Wales; her teaching specialism is in poetry. She has tutored OU English Literature modules since the mid-1980s, and was the recipient of an OU Teaching Award in 2007. She is co-author of the *Study Companion* (2008) for the module *The Arts Past and Present*.

Shafquat Towheed is a Lecturer in the Department of English at The Open University. He is the editor of *The Correspondence of Edith Wharton and Macmillan, 1901–1930* (2007), *New Readings in the Literature of British India, c.1780–1947* (2007) and the Broadview edition of Arthur Conan Doyle's *The Sign of Four* (2010). He is the co-editor of *Publishing in the First World War: Essays in Book History* (2007); *The History of Reading: A Reader* (2010); *The History of Reading, Vol.1: International Perspectives, c.1500–1990* (2011) and *The History of Reading, Vol. 3: Methods, Strategies, Tactics* (2011).

Nicola J. Watson is a Senior Lecturer in the Department of English at The Open University. A specialist in the Romantic period and in reception studies, she has published three books (*Revolution and the Form of the British Novel 1790–1825* (1994), *England's Elizabeth: An Afterlife in Fame and Fantasy* (2002, co-authored with Michael Dobson); *The Literary Tourist: Readers and Places in Romantic and Victorian Britain* (2006)), two edited collections (*At the Limits of Romanticism* (1994, with Mary Favret) and *Literary Tourism and Nineteenth-Century Culture* (2009)), an edition of Sir Walter Scott's *The Antiquary* (2003), and many essays on the poetry and fiction of the Romantic period.

Required reading

You will need to read the following texts in conjunction with this book:

Part 1

The required reading for Chapters 1–4 can be found in 'Readings for Part 1'.

Part 2

For Chapters 5 and 6: Emily Brontë (2009 [1847]) *Wuthering Heights* (ed. Ian Jack; introduction and additional notes Helen Small), Oxford World's Classics, Oxford, Oxford University Press.

For Chapter 7: Arthur Conan Doyle (2010 [1890]) *The Sign of Four* (ed. Shafquat Towheed), Peterborough ON, Broadview. Additional reading for this chapter can be found in 'Readings for Part 2'.

For Chapter 8: Robert Louis Stevenson (2008 [1892–3]) 'The Beach of Falesá' in *South Sea Tales* (ed. Roslyn Jolly), Oxford, Oxford University Press. Additional reading for this chapter can be found in 'Readings for Part 2'.

Part 1
Romantic lives

Aims

The first part of this book will:

- introduce you to a selection of poetry and prose from the Romantic period
- compare and contrast these writings' depictions of Romantic lives
- use the author's life and compositional choices and practices as a context for reading individual texts.

Introduction to Part 1

Nicola J. Watson

Welcome to 'Romantic lives', the first part of *Romantics and Victorians*. This part of the book concentrates on literature written in Europe between 1789 and the 1820s. The French Revolution and the Napoleonic Wars together gave birth to a self-consciously modern and revolutionary pan-European movement across all the arts which, by the late nineteenth century, had come to be called, with the benefit of hindsight, 'Romanticism'. Given limited space, we have chosen to focus on a single but very important aspect of Romanticism: its emphasis upon the powers and terrors of the inner imaginative life. Not everyone living in the period conceived of themselves as living a 'Romantic' life; nor did everyone approve of living in that way, some regarding it as dangerously self-indulgent. Nor did all or even most of the writing of the period concentrate upon the inner life. Nonetheless, it is possible to trace a change in conceptions of the inner life which tended to give it primacy and prominence. The period saw the rapid rise, expansion and evolution of modes of writing associated with exploration of the self: lyric poetry, autobiography, biography and the confessional essay. Equally, contemporary writings, whether fictional or non-fictional, were shot through with anxieties about the Romantic self, often expressed in the Gothic, a non-realist mode of exploring the darkest and innermost human passions, drives and fears.

Starting with the English poet William Wordsworth (1770–1850), we consider how he represented his inner life and poetic vocation in relation to the landscape of the Lake District, which lies in the north-west of England. The following chapter turns to explore how the life of the younger English poet Percy Bysshe Shelley (1792–1822) came to be identified as quintessentially Romantic by the Victorians, and contrasts this construction with his own depictions of the work of the Romantic poet in a group of lyrics from the 1820s. The third chapter focuses on *Confessions of an English Opium-Eater* (1824) by Thomas De Quincey (1785–1859) to consider an example of Romantic prose autobiography. The last chapter in this part examines a short story by E.T.A. Hoffmann (1776–1822), 'The Sandman', as a Gothic description of the disintegration of the Romantic self.

This exploration of Romantic lives is governed intermittently by an exploration of the concept of 'the author'. This is, first, because our sense of what an 'author' is was forged in this period. Second, thinking about texts in terms of 'the author' produces some interesting ways of reading texts (and potential pitfalls). Indeed, the idea of the author is so useful and so commonplace in popular culture and literary criticism that it is hard to stand back and examine it. However, if we do so, it becomes apparent that modern Western culture is heavily invested in authors and their lives. Readers are interested enough, for example, to visit all sorts of places associated with writers, including their graves. The ways in which these graves are marked suggest the different ways in which the Romantic author has been imagined. Consider, for example, these images of the graves of Wordsworth (in Grasmere churchyard), Shelley (in the Protestant Cemetery, Rome), De Quincey (in St Cuthbert's, Edinburgh) and Hoffmann (in Berlin-Kreuzberg) (Figures 1 and 2).

Not all these graves demonstrate a contemporaneous interest in these people as authors. De Quincey's memorial itself doesn't identify him as a writer at all (giving details only of his dates and places of birth and death), though the later, supplementary notice suggests his importance. Wordsworth's grave locates him as a member of his family. In contrast, the inscription on Shelley's grave in the Protestant Cemetery in Rome was evidently interested in myth-making around the poet from the very start; the quotation from Ariel's song 'Full fathom five / Thy father lies' in Shakespeare's play *The Tempest* alludes to Shelley's death by drowning when his boat was overwhelmed by a storm, a death which would be central to Victorian conceptions of him. Hoffman's gravestone is also interested in making claims for him as a genius. The inscription reads 'Born in Konigsberg in Prussia [now Kalingrad in Russia]/on 4 January 1776/ Died Berlin on 25 January 1822/Supreme Court Justice/Exceptional in his career/as poet/as musician/as painter/Dedicated by his friends'.

We'll be coming back to the question of how these writers conceived of themselves as authors later. Meanwhile, it is instructive to notice how useful we find the idea of the author as readers and critics. We conventionally use the author's name to refer to a body of literary work, with the clear if inexplicit understanding that because, say, a set of poems is by Wordsworth, they can all be usefully related one to another. Literary biography is based on much the same principle – that an author's texts can be related to one another as an evolution or progression; literary biography also takes for granted that narrating the writer's life will 'explain', or at any rate usefully contextualise, his or her texts. Editors (as we will see in the cases of Wordsworth and Shelley)

Figure 1 The Wordsworth family plot, St Oswald's Church, Grasmere, Cumbria. Photographed by Peter Titmuss. Photo: © Peter Titmuss/Alamy.

Figure 2 The graves of Shelley, De Quincey and Hoffman. Left: Grave of Percy Bysshe Shelley, Protestant Cemetery, Rome, 2008. Photographed by Elio Lombardo. Photo: © CuboImages srl/Alamy. Centre: Tombstone of Thomas De Quincey, St Cuthbert's churchyard, Edinburgh. Photo: © The Scotsman Publications Ltd. Licensor: www.scran.ac.uk. Right: Gravestone of E.T.A. Hoffmann, Berlin. Photographed by Markh.

have organised manuscripts as a way of reconstituting successive moments of a writing life, without much questioning this as an enterprise. A sense of the interpenetration of life and works is especially strong around authors who have created autobiographical personae within their writings, which have then been elaborated after their deaths through biography, editing and memorialisation.

The power of the idea of the author has been challenged in the twentieth century by literary critics who regarded efforts to 'explain' or 'fix' a literary text by reference to the author's life as suspect. The 'New Criticism' (an American critical movement) or 'Practical Criticism' (the English variant) of the 1950s insisted that readers engage solely with the words on the page, ignoring the author altogether. Psychoanalytic theories of the self deriving from the work of Sigmund Freud, and in particular from his notion of 'the unconscious' as a necessary repository of repressed desires, meant that human beings were no longer conceived as being fully known to themselves. These theories were influential in fostering the idea that an author was not in control of his or her 'intention'. A number of left-wing theorists working in the 1960s, 1970s and 1980s argued further that any text was perpetually on the threshold of escaping the intention of the author, even if she or he, or we, could really know what that was. This was either because it was readers (rather than the author) who conferred meaning upon the text (this was argued by the French critic Roland Barthes, 1915–1980) or because of ambiguities inherent in language itself (this was argued by the French-Algerian critic-philosopher Jacques Derrida, 1930–2004). These arguments, challenging the perceived authority of the author, were part of a generally anti-authoritarian philosophical and political stance.

Barthes' important essay arguing that it was not the author, but the reader, who conferred meaning upon a text was provocatively entitled 'The death of the author' (1968). However, that was not quite the end of the author. Rather, other ways of thinking about what the idea of the author was 'for' in Western culture opened up as a result. It became possible, for instance, to think more carefully about how and why individual texts produce a sense of the author. Critics began to explore how and why authors adopt different personae in their writings and to think about how the author has been represented. In an influential essay entitled 'What is an author?' (1969), the French philosopher, sociologist and historian of ideas Michel Foucault (1926–1984) suggested asking further questions about the author, such as how and why it became important to identify the author of a piece of literary writing; how and why the author acquired cultural status; when and why 'authenticity' and originality became acid-tests for genius; when authors' lives had become interesting; and when it was that writing had started to be read in terms of an author's life. Scholars since have enquired into the nature of literary careers and into how writers have dealt with publishers, booksellers, reviewers and each other, an enquiry that has reached into the histories of copyright, censorship, collaborative authorship, plagiarism, parody, forgery, biography, autobiography, pseudonymity and anonymity (see Bennett, 2005).

These theoretical questions about authorship are of particular interest here because the idea of the writer as an original genius, an exceptional man ahead of his time, possessed by inexplicable, spontaneous, visionary inspiration, first became dominant in the Romantic period (Bennett, 2005, pp. 58–60). Around the turn of the nineteenth century the modern sense of the author – as a professional producer of original written material for which she or he expected to be paid – emerged. This was the result of a number of factors. Systems of literary patronage (where an author expected to be supported by an aristocratic patron) had been in sharp decline throughout the later part of the eighteenth century, and were being replaced by the emergence of a market-based publishing industry. There was now a fixed period of authorial copyright from which authors could benefit financially from their writing. By the end of the century, there was a boom in publishing, which was becoming cheaper due to technological innovations, and more profitable due to an expanding reading audience. The literary marketplace was filled with newly aggressive genres such as the novel. At the same time, a new class of industrialists, bureaucrats and scientists was emerging, increasing their power to shape culture in distinctively utilitarian ways.

Under these pressures, most contemporary poets and many prose writers began in self-defence to construct themselves in opposition to popular culture as powerful legislators of high culture. The critic Marlon Ross describes how poetry therefore came to be seen as 'above' mere popularity:

> The romantic poets come to believe … that the greatness of a poet has no direct relation to the reading public who either buys or does not buy his work; that poets' influence in politics and history may not be palpable but is nonetheless more real than the

influence of utilitarians who engineer, oversee, and operate the machinery of society; and that great poetry can be written only by powerful men capable of reaching grand visionary heights.

(Ross, 1989, p. 22)

While, as we'll see, different writers developed many and various models of Romantic authorship, they were all responding to the same contemporary pressures. But as we read Romantic writings in the light of individual writers' conceptions of the Romantic author's vocation, it is important to remember that this idea of the author is a fiction, open to analysis and criticism.

References

Barthes, R. (2002 [1968]) 'The death of the author', in Finkelstein, D. and McCleery, A. (eds) *The Book History Reader*, London and New York, Routledge, pp. 221–4.

Bennett, A. (2005) *The Author*, New York and Oxford, Routledge.

Foucault, M. (2002 [1969]) 'What is an author?', in Finkelstein, D. and McCleery, A. (eds) *The Book History Reader*, London and New York, Routledge, pp. 225–30.

Ross, M.B. (1989) *The Contours of Masculine Desire: Romanticism and the Rise of Women's Poetry*, New York and Oxford, Oxford University Press.

Chapter 1
William Wordsworth: poet in a landscape

Nicola J. Watson

Aims

This chapter will:

- explore how Wordsworth conceived himself as a Romantic poet
- introduce a selection of Wordsworth's poetry, ranging from lyric to pastoral to epic
- explore how we can use the author's life and compositional choices and practices as a way into reading individual texts.

Introduction

Beside the road that runs alongside the lake of Grasmere in the north-west region of England known as the Lake District, there stands a small whitewashed cottage, set back a little from what is now the main road.

Figure 1.1   Dove Cottage, Grasmere. The Wordsworth family home, now a museum. Photo: Dove Cottage, The Wordsworth Trust.

This is Dove Cottage. From 1799 to 1808, it was the home of the poet William Wordsworth (1770–1850), his sister Dorothy (1771–1855) and (from 1802) his wife, Mary Hutchinson (1770–1859). Although Wordsworth is today regarded as of such cultural importance that two other houses in the Lake District with which he is associated are also preserved as museums – his birthplace in Cockermouth, and Rydal Mount, the house in which he lived from 1813 until his death in 1850 – Dove Cottage remains the most popular tourist destination. This is because Dove Cottage chimes with the modern sense of what 'Wordsworth' stands for today. It's worth pausing to think what that might be before setting off to study Wordsworth's poetry.

Activity 1

Look at Figure 1.2, a postcard recently for sale in the gift shop attached to the house-museum.

Dove Cottage

Figure 1.2   Postcard of Dove Cottage. Photo: Dove Cottage, The Wordsworth Trust.

1   What does this image convey about the cottage and its location?

2   How does it position the viewer?

3   What does it imply about the relation between the cottage and the poet?

Discussion

1   This image describes the cottage as a country idyll.

2   It positions the viewer as an insider walking in through the back garden, rather than as a tourist let through the front door for an entrance fee.

3   The relation between the cottage and the poet is described by the relation between the photograph and the facsimile signature of Wordsworth, which connects the house with the act of writing. The signature additionally suggests that the writing done in this cottage is associated especially with the work of self-inscription and self-making – or, to put it another way, with the autobiographical.

This sense of Wordsworth at home in the Lake District, whether in Dove Cottage itself or in the landscape around it, is of long standing. It first became entrenched within the popular imagination when Wordsworth was still alive with the publication of some important pieces of periodical journalism: an essay by the journalist and critic William Hazlitt (1778–1830) entitled 'My first acquaintance with poets' (1823), and a series of essays by a fellow journalist Thomas De Quincey (1785–1859) published as 'Reminiscences of the English Lakes and the Lake Poets' between 1834 and 1840. In the wake of late nineteenth-century scholarly work on Wordsworth after his death, the importance of the Dove Cottage years became ever clearer, and Dove Cottage was established as a museum in the summer of 1890 by a cleric and literary enthusiast, Sir Stopford Augustus Brooke (1832–1916). As the critic Polly Atkin notes, by 1893 visitors from as far away as Massachusetts, Montreal and Singapore had arrived to pay their sixpence, peep inside, and sign their names in the visitors' book (Atkin, 2009, p. 85). To raise the necessary funds, Brooke wrote a pamphlet which promoted a myth of the Wordsworths' life in Dove Cottage. Brooke describes the cottage and the region generally as the place that both generated and witnessed the poetry:

> There is no place … which has so many thoughts and memories as this …; none at least in which they are so closely bound up with the poet and the poems; almost everything in this garden has

been written of beautifully; almost every flower has been planted by his or his sister's hands; in almost every tree some bird has built of which he has sung. In every part of this little place he has walked with his sister or his wife or talked with [his friend and fellow-poet] Coleridge. And it is almost untouched.

(Brooke quoted in Atkin, 2009, p. 89)

Dove Cottage and the surrounding landscape are still conceived as places where you can get closer to the poetry through getting closer to the poet's life. A postcard recently sold at the museum (Figure 1.3) makes this claim by juxtaposing a photograph of the lake of Ullswater with the poem known to scholars as 'I wandered lonely as a cloud' and popularly as 'Daffodils' or 'To Daffodils'.

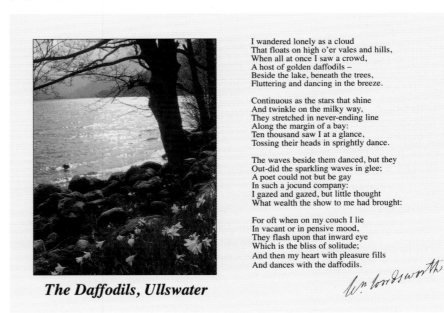

I wandered lonely as a cloud
That floats on high o'er vales and hills,
When all at once I saw a crowd,
A host of golden daffodils –
Beside the lake, beneath the trees,
Fluttering and dancing in the breeze.

Continuous as the stars that shine
And twinkle on the milky way,
They stretched in never-ending line
Along the margin of a bay:
Ten thousand saw I at a glance,
Tossing their heads in sprightly dance.

The waves beside them danced, but they
Out-did the sparkling waves in glee;
A poet could not but be gay
In such a jocund company:
I gazed and gazed, but little thought
What wealth the show to me had brought:

For oft when on my couch I lie
In vacant or in pensive mood,
They flash upon that inward eye
Which is the bliss of solitude;
And then my heart with pleasure fills
And dances with the daffodils.

Wm Wordsworth

The Daffodils, Ullswater

Figure 1.3   Postcard, 'The daffodils, Ullswater'. Photo: Dove Cottage, The Wordsworth Trust.

In what follows, we are going to explore how Wordsworth developed his poetic voice, **persona** and project over the years in which he lived in Dove Cottage, looking at a cross-section of the poetry he was writing. We'll start with 'I wandered lonely as a cloud', probably the most famous poem that Wordsworth ever wrote. Certainly it is the poem that most visitors to Dove Cottage seem expected to recognise, to judge by the museum's logo that combines a quill pen with a daffodil to form a stylised 'W', the claim on the notice outside that these are the most famous lines in the English language and were written in Dove Cottage, and the sheer quantity of daffodil-themed merchandise for sale in the gift shop.

Reading a poem: formal aspects

We will begin with the poem's formal aspects, looking at how form generates meaning. We'll focus on some technical characteristics of the poem: **voice** (who seems to be speaking), **diction** and **vocabulary** (what sort of language the poem is using); **metre** and rhythm; **rhyme**; and linguistic enhancements such as **alliteration** (beginning adjacent or near-adjacent words with the same consonants) and **assonance** (repeating vowel sounds across words). Attending to technical detail in this fashion is a way of describing how the poem works to compact meaning into memorable language. But it can also tell us what sort of poem this is claiming to be – whether a grand, ambitious piece, or something simple and artless.

If you don't feel confident about reading poetry, here are some tips to help. Because of the necessities of metre and rhyme, words in poems are not always in the order in which you would find them in prose, so it often helps to do the following:

1 Read the poem aloud to get the general sense and rhythm of it.

2 Then, it helps to look for the full stop. (In the poem in Activity 2 below, the first one comes at the end of the first stanza.)

3 Then look for the main verb or verbs. (In the first stanza below, this would be 'wandered' and 'saw'.)

4 Then mentally discard sub-clauses to get the broad shape of the main sentence. (Sub-clauses are short sections that can be subtracted from the sentence and still leave it grammatically complete. They themselves do not make complete sentences.)

Activity 2

Read Wordsworth's poem 'I wandered lonely as a cloud' (reproduced below), and consider the following questions:

1 Who is speaking? What sort of voice is this? Consider the diction, vocabulary and sentence structure – are they simple or sophisticated?

2   Have a go at marking up technical features of the poem, such as rhyme, metre, alliteration and assonance.

Identify the rhyme scheme by marking the first rhyme sound 'a' at the end of the first line, the second 'b' and so on. Then mark the metrical stresses by reading the lines aloud and marking where the rhythmic beat seems to fall. (When we analyse a line of poetry in this way we are said to scan the line. Indicate the stresses by a slash mark (/) over the relevant word or syllable and the unstressed sounds by a cross (x) in the same way.) Then highlight repeated sounds within the lines (alliteration and assonance). Here is an example of how you might begin to mark up the first stanza (or verse):

```
x   /    x   / x / x    /
I wandered lonely as a Cloud                    a
  x   /    x   /  x  /   x    /
That floats on high o'er Vales and Hills,       b
  x    / x  / x / x   /
When all at once I saw a crowd                  a
  x / x / x  / x /
A host of dancing Daffodils;                    b
x /  x  /   x  / x   /
Along the Lake, beneath the trees,              c
  x  /   x   /  x / x  /
Ten thousand dancing in the breeze.             c
```

3   Once you've done this, consider what you've found out about what the poem claims to be.

4   Finally, can you state what you take to be the argument of each stanza and of the poem as a whole?

I wandered lonely as a Cloud
That floats on high o'er Vales and Hills,
When all at once I saw a crowd
A host of dancing Daffodils;
Along the Lake, beneath the trees,
Ten thousand dancing in the breeze.

The waves beside them danced, but they
Outdid the sparkling waves in glee: –
A Poet could not but be gay
In such a laughing company:
I gazed – and gazed – but little thought
What wealth the shew to me had brought:

For oft when on my couch I lie
In vacant or in pensive mood,

They flash upon that inward eye
Which is the bliss of solitude,
And then my heart with pleasure fills,
And dances with the Daffodils.

(1807 version in Gill, 1990, pp. 303–4)

Discussion

1 This poem is voiced by an 'I', who is eventually identified as a poet, but otherwise is not provided with much social context. The diction, vocabulary and sentence structure is simple and direct.

2 You should have discovered that each line is organised as a series of stressed and unstressed syllables – here, in four sets of paired unstressed and stressed syllables. (These sets are known as 'feet' and this particular type of pairing of stresses is called '**iambic**'.) The rhyme scheme is ababcc. The paired lines that end with c rhymes that complete the stanza are known as rhyming **couplets**. This means that both metre and rhyme are relatively and consciously simple. Highlighting similar sounds and repeated words within the poem makes clear the way that preponderating sounds tie the lines and subject matter tightly together within individual stanzas and across the poem as a whole.

3 We have, then, a poem that is claiming to be a simple poem. It is a **lyric** – that is, a short poem devoted to expressing a single mood or moment of consciousness, usually foregrounding the poet as speaker.

4 The poem's argument is organised in three stages, corresponding to the three stanzas. The first stanza describes the experience; the second the poet's immediate reaction to it; and the third the way in which the experience has continued to work within the poet's memory and consciousness. This doesn't exactly tell us what the poem argues, but we might surmise that the poem offers the poet's experience as a model for the reader's own – it describes how experiences of natural beauty can enter, work within and are beneficial to individual minds. The clarity and compactness of the language contributes to the poem's claim that this experience has a clarity and simplicity of outline as it has impressed itself within the poet's memory and as it revives itself within his consciousness.

Underlying this attention to the formal aspects of a poem (often known as close reading or textual analysis, and derived from the critical priorities of what is called the New Criticism or Practical Criticism) is a particular idea of what a poem is: that is, something which is designed to generate a stable and perfected meaning and affect, remaining reliably itself whoever reads it, and whenever they read it. The idea is that the poem can be read without any extra contextual information. This technique of reading is very useful but in the end rather limited; in practice, there is no such thing as reading without context – if only because a reader automatically brings their own contexts to the experience of reading. In fact, this poem has often been read biographically, as a transcription of the experience of 'William Wordsworth'. Biographical reading identifies the 'I' as Wordsworth, the lake as Ullswater, when this experience took place (in 1802, according to Dorothy Wordsworth's journal), and when and where the poem was composed and published (composed between March 1804 and April 1807, at Dove Cottage, and published in a collection entitled *Poems in Two Volumes*, 1807). Most importantly, it makes the experience described in this short poem more powerful culturally by ascribing it to an important poet. In fact, the postcard we began with effectively reads the poem biographically. It should be said, however, that although this chapter will explore ways of reading Wordsworth's poetry in relation to his life, you should always be cautious of assuming that when a poet writes in the first person there is always an autobiographical dimension, even when that first person is closely identified with the poet. This is because even where there is verifiably an autobiographical element present it will often be transmuted in the writing.

Reading a poem: biographical aspects

In this section, we're going to look at ways of reading this poem in its biographical context through looking at Dorothy Wordsworth's journal. In composing this poem, Wordsworth used (as he did on other occasions) his sister's account of the original experience as an aid to his memory.

Activity 3

Turn to Reading 1.1 at the end of this part of the book. This is an extract from Dorothy Wordsworth's journal for Thursday 15 April 1802. Read it through and compare her account with her brother's poem (reproduced in Activity 2 above).

1   How do the two accounts tally or differ?

2   What difference does reading the journal entry make to your understanding of the poem?

Discussion

1   Both accounts clearly refer to the same experience of seeing a mass of daffodils in flower growing along the margins of a lake under the trees and being blown about by a high wind. They share, too, some of the same ways of describing the experience, in particular the tendency to think of the daffodils as behaving like people (**personification**) in describing them as 'dancing' and 'gay'.

On the other hand, these are very different *types* of account. Dorothy's account is in prose, and conforms to the genre and function of a journal – to recount the events and experiences of the day more or less in the order in which they happened, for the purposes either of maintaining a record for oneself, or, in Dorothy's case, explicitly to please her brother. It is an essentially private form of writing, and was never designed to be published. The journal is full of everyday detail, information and observation which is not evidently ranked by importance – it relates where they were (walking from Eusemere along the shores of Ullswater and so eventually home over the Kirkstone Pass), who they were visiting, what they managed to get to eat and drink, their physical comforts and discomforts, and what they were reading. The description of seeing the daffodils begins as botanical and seasonal observation (compare her remarks about the hawthorn, or her interest in how the daffodils came to self-seed), before changing into a description of a more evidently intense and personal experience – it's the first moment in the entry for that day that she uses the word 'I'.

Comparing the journal entry to the poem makes it clear by contrast what the poem is, and is not, interested in doing (and, of course, what the journal is, and is not, interested in doing). The first thing to say about the poem is, of course, that it *is* a poem – a lyric. More importantly, as a poem it is meant to be published – it is a public form. Wordsworth's account also displays some very striking divergences from Dorothy's. Most notably it writes out her presence, and, for that matter, all the people, buildings and animals with which the vale is otherwise populated. While Dorothy describes this as a shared experience, the poem foregrounds a Romantic 'I' who wanders alone and disconnected, more cloud than human body, and who is identified as a poet. The one-off immediacy of the experience Dorothy recounts is changed in the poem to the stored-up 'wealth' that the poet repeatedly realises through being able to revivify the scene through memory.

2   The effect of reading the poem against the journal can be rather ambiguous. On the one hand, the journal certifies the poem as 'true' – it all really happened. On the other hand, it invalidates the claim to immediacy and memorability that the poem apparently makes

on behalf of the experience – Wordsworth seems to have needed to be reminded of this experience when he came to draft the poem at least two years after the journal entry was made. The comparison with the journal entry throws into sharp relief what are probably the two most important and most 'Wordsworthian' things about the poem: its interest in dramatising the figure of the poet, and its interest in the workings and solace of memory as a foundation of identity. At the same time the comparison shows that the figure of the solitary poet-genius is a fiction – the making of the poem was in fact a collaborative enterprise.

In comparing these two pieces of writing, it is important to remember that *both* of them are acts of crafted writing. This is obvious in the case of the poem, but less so in the case of the journal. It is tempting to think of Dorothy's journal simply as the ground or source material for the poem, but there is plenty of evidence to show that even though the journal was written hastily and whenever time served, Dorothy consciously revised her writing for maximum effect (Woof, 1991; Woof, 1992). That said, the difference between the two forms of writing is the difference between private writing by a woman living at the turn of the nineteenth century and the public, conscious and ambitious self-inscription of a Romantic male poet. The idea of authorship in the period is conditioned both by the genres a writer works in and by the gender position within which and from which a writer operates; as a gross generalisation, the male poet was (and is) more 'Romantic' than the female prose writer. However, the way in which the Romantic poet describes the self as private and inward explains why today's culture has come increasingly to allow the female privacies and inwardnesses of Dorothy's journal equal status as 'Romantic'. Another postcard recently on sale at Dove Cottage glossed the photograph of daffodils at Ullswater with *Dorothy's* words.

It is possible to contextualise this poem in relation to other biographical material. We might note, for example, that two of the most famous lines in the poem – 'They flash upon that inward eye / Which is the bliss of solitude' – are known to have been written not by Wordsworth but by his wife (Burton, 1958, p. xvii). Or we might go to an early notebook full of notes made by Wordsworth and his brother, Christopher, dating from the early 1790s, in which Christopher writes out an outline for a poem 'descriptive of the lakes etc. Febry 1792'. This includes a mention of Gowbarrow Park and, specifically, of the daffodils: 'Daffodils, early in the spring. vast numbers of them by Ullswater Side' (Fink, 1958, p. 65). What this suggests is that Wordsworth's sight of daffodils by Ullswater was not, as the poem implies, a one-off experience. The trickiness of taking the poem's stance literally is also highlighted by the possibility of reading the poem in contexts wider than the biographical: contemporary guidebooks to the Lakes make it clear that this great body of flowers was a famous sight at the time.

Still, reading Dorothy's journal alongside the poem seems one way of getting very close to the poet himself; as Pamela Woof puts it, 'where the same experience informs both journal and poem there is for us the fascination of coming closer to the imagination at work' (Woof, 1991, p. xvii). To what extent, however, is trying to get closer to the poet's imaginative life at Dove Cottage really a sensible way of reading the poetry? With many poets and writers this may not be an especially fruitful approach, but in the case of Wordsworth it happens to be more appropriate. This is for three reasons. The first is that, as we'll see, Wordsworth himself conceived of living in this remote part of the Lake District as an experiment in the imaginative life of a poet. The second is that in much of his most important poetry Wordsworth took his own life, imagination and consciousness as his central poetic subject matter. The third reason is that Wordsworth subjected his poems to continual acts of revision and reorganisation throughout his life, which means that they exist in many different manuscript and print versions. Reading the successive variants of the poems embodied in those manuscripts is to engage intimately with the poet's own processes of composition.

You may have noticed, for example, that the version of 'I wandered lonely as a cloud' reproduced on the postcard is not the same as the version provided above. The most critical difference is that a stanza appears to be missing – this is because, in 1815, Wordsworth added the stanza beginning 'Continuous as the stars that shine', and made other more minor but significant revisions. Comparing the 1807 poem with the version of 1815, it becomes evident that the earlier version is less repetitive and less deliberately 'poetic'. Deciding *which* version to take as the 'proper' version entails making an aesthetic decision which, put crudely, entails deciding when Wordsworth was most truly Wordsworthian. Over the last thirty years or so, that decision has been made by scholars in favour of the work Wordsworth did at Dove Cottage and in the couple of years before that, while he was resident in Nether Stowey and then travelling in Germany. This has meant privileging the shorter version of 1807. But more importantly, attending to Wordsworth's practice of revision in this way subjects the governing fiction of the poem – which characterises itself as a spontaneous effusion by a uniquely sensitive Romantic genius – to considerable stress and qualification. Constructing a complete biographical reading of this poem reminds us, paradoxically, that 'I wandered lonely as a cloud' is *not* the simple act of autobiographical recollection it might appear to be at first, nor is it even the less simple act of recollecting multiple acts of recollection.

Strangers and locals

The fame of 'I wandered lonely as a cloud' may be ascribed to the way it condenses the 'Wordsworthian'. This may be summed up as the concentration upon the poet's solitary, imaginatively intense experience within a natural landscape which results in profound and permanent, if unquantifiable, spiritual benefit to the poet's inner life. Apparently autobiographical, the poem functions as a philosophical and generalisable statement of the value of recollecting natural landscape within urban modernity.

This vision of a spiritually therapeutic relationship between human and landscape had by the end of the nineteenth century not only resulted in the establishment of Dove Cottage as a museum, but in the formation of the National Trust to conserve the Lake District in its entirety (Gill, 1998). The postcards we've been looking at dramatise the sense of Wordsworth's poetry having stamped itself upon the landscape of the Lake District. In turn, the landscape comes to dramatise the Romantic poet's inner life, and, by extension, arguably, *everyone's* inner life. To put it another way, the modern urban self has learned from Wordsworth how to recollect natural beauties.

This sense of the poet as 'lonely as a cloud', disconnected, alone, self-absorbed, is very much the dominant version of the Wordsworthian within the popular cultural imagination. However, Wordsworth himself was not uncritical of the social, moral and political implications of such a stance. This is the subject of a much less well-known poem, known as 'Point Rash-Judgment', written and published in 1800.

Activity 4

Read the poem 'Point Rash-Judgment', reproduced as Reading 1.2. (If you find the sentence structure difficult, return to the general tips provided in the section 'Reading a poem: formal aspects' above. Don't worry about any references you don't understand at this stage – concentrate on getting a general understanding of the poem.)

Is there anything that strikes you as similar to 'I wandered lonely as a cloud'? Are there any strong divergences? Consider the following:

1   the form of the poem

2   the way the poet is represented in relationship to the landscape

3   the moral of the poem.

Discussion

This poem is clearly similar to 'I wandered lonely as a cloud' in its celebration of the pleasure of wandering and its focus on looking at the natural world. It begins by describing the poet sauntering along the edge of a lake in a pleasantly 'vacant mood', which seems very like the mood described in the last stanza of the previous poem.

There are, however, striking differences:

1   In the place of the rhyming stanzas of 'I wandered lonely as a cloud', we have **blank verse**, unrhymed lines of **iambic pentameter**. This verse form is automatically grander because of its associations with Shakespeare and Milton than the deliberately naive lyric form of the first poem.

2   Whereas in 'I wandered lonely as a cloud' the poet is first of all alone in the landscape and then alone on his 'couch' and the poem as a whole is enamoured of 'solitude', in 'Point Rash-Judgment' the poet is accompanied by two friends, and can hear the reapers and see the fisherman. If 'wandering' in the first poem is clearly felt to be the physical equivalent to 'musing', the parallel 'sauntering' described in the second poem is thrown into sharp and critical focus as the product of a gentleman's unthinking privilege of leisure. If 'vacancy' in the first poem is presented as a state of receptivity, here it is presented as privileged idleness. The aesthetic view of the landscape the relatively wealthy can indulge – admiring the 'dead calm' lake and amusing themselves with literary allusions to classical mythology or medieval romance – is quite different from the mortally sick fisherman's view of it, as he tries to wrest something to eat from the bosom of what is consequently transformed into something that really is 'dead' to him and 'unfeeling' towards his predicament. While 'I wandered lonely as a cloud' asserts that the poet is

unproblematically at one with the natural landscape, this poem is troubled by the way that the landscape means something very different to gentlemen and labourers.

3   The moral that the poem draws only imperfectly resolves the difficulty of who owns and benefits from the landscape by describing how the chastened companions name the landscape (which presumably already had a perfectly good name given to it by the locals), in much the same way that European colonial explorers named places they 'discovered'. They name it 'Point Rash-Judgment', so giving it 'a memorial name, uncouth indeed / As e'er by Mariner was giv'n to Bay / Or Foreland on a new-discover'd coast' (ll. 83–5). The poet and his companions may name the landscape as a memorial to their class guilt, but that naming is still an act of appropriation. The 'wealth' they gain from the experience is different from that acquired by the poet in 'I wandered lonely as a cloud', but the idea of gaining moral wealth remains.

'Point Rash-Judgment' begins to describe some of the moral, political and intellectual problems that run through Wordsworth's poetry of 1800. They all stem from the problem of how to claim Grasmere as a fit 'home' for a poet.

It could be said that the Wordsworths took up residence in Dove Cottage in the bleak December of 1799 pretty much by accident. It was an empty house by the side of the road that happened to catch Wordsworth's eye as he and his friend and poetic collaborator Samuel Taylor Coleridge (1772–1834) came down through Grasmere vale earlier that year on a walking tour. But to say this would be to underplay a number of determining circumstances. William and Dorothy had spent much of their early lives in the Lake District. They were short of money, and it was a cheap place to live. They had long dreamed of a more permanent home. The collapse of political idealism after the apparent failure of the French Revolution and the repressive conservatism of wartime England meant that, like many other radical sympathisers at the time, the disillusioned Wordsworths were urgently in search of a refuge from mainstream society, and the Lake District's remoteness offered it. It represented a society free from both the horrors of industrialisation and urbanisation and the miseries produced by the new large-scale farming. In poetic terms, the Lake District's economy, dependent for the most part on sheep, approximated to that depicted in the popular eighteenth-century genre of **pastoral** poetry derived from classical antecedents, which took as its subject the idyllically leisured life of the shepherd. Finally, the landscape was famous in late eighteenth-century culture for its remote beauty.

As the critic James Butler has noted, it is possible to read Wordsworth's poems of 1800 through a biographical lens, noting that they are shot through with an anxiety about how, arriving as a tourist and a stranger, the poet can lay claim to being a native, a person who has simply returned (see Butler, 1996). 'Point Rash-Judgment' clearly does that by (re)naming places. Other poems, such as 'The Brothers', visit and revisit problematic scenes of homecoming.

Activity 5

Read the poem 'The Brothers' (reproduced as Reading 1.3). It is a fairly lengthy narrative that takes the form of a verse dialogue between a vicar and a stranger, to whom the vicar tells the story of a local tragedy. As you read, consider these questions:

1   How does the poem dramatise homecoming?

2   What might it say about Wordsworth's own anxieties over making a home with his sister in Grasmere?

Discussion

1   The drama of this homecoming turns on the way that the returning brother is not recognised in his home village. Instead, twelve years older than when he left, he is misrecognised by the priest as a stranger – as a tourist, idle and well-heeled, with nothing better to do than drive through the district, sit about sketching picturesque places, or dawdle in a churchyard collecting picturesque stories of the locality.

The poem draws a strong contrast between the priest sitting securely at home, with his wife, family and domestic work around him, and the wandering Leonard, homesick, solitary, returning with the intention of resuming a shepherd's life and being reunited with his only brother, and uncertain as to whether he has remembered the number of graves in the churchyard correctly.

Leonard's problem is that in many ways he *is* a stranger. 'Accidents and changes' (l. 144) mean that he finds it hard to recognise the place itself: 'he lifted up his eyes, / And looking round he thought that he perceiv'd / Strange alteration wrought on every side / Among the woods and fields, and that the rocks, / And the eternal hills, themselves were chang'd.' (ll. 92–6) – and he is no longer up to date with the 'history' of the place. He has to be told of both by the local priest.

Leonard's homecoming is a dream both of his own and of the locals (ll. 303–19) but it is destroyed by the story he is told by the priest concerning the fate of his brother, who dies sleep-walking in search of him: 'his cherish'd hopes, / And thoughts which had been his an hour before, / All press'd on him with such a weight, that now, / This vale, where he had been so happy, seem'd / A place in which he could not bear to live' (ll. 418–22).

2 Of course Leonard is not Wordsworth, nor is he in a simple way a poetic persona for Wordsworth in the way that the 'I' of 'I wandered lonely as a cloud' is. Yet 'The Brothers' can be read as expressing Wordsworth's anxieties about the feasibility of making a home in Grasmere. It asks whether it is possible for wanderers truly to come home. It asks whether fond memories of your birthplace as a location of timeless pastoral pleasure are inevitably doomed to painful correction by the hard facts. And it asks whether it is possible, or desirable, to re-establish childhood sibling intimacy. If we are reading the poem in relation to the author's situation at the time of composition, we can see that, although the poem is in no sense 'about' the Wordsworths, all the questions posed in 'The Brothers' arguably derive from Wordsworth's thinking about returning to Grasmere both in terms of his personal affections and in terms of his proper subject matter as a poet.

Ambitions and projects

In 1800 Wordsworth was engaged both in a major re-evaluation of his work to date (in the shape of re-editing, greatly expanding and prefacing a second edition of the *Lyrical Ballads*, the collection of poems he and Coleridge had originally put together in 1798) and in addressing himself to a major work also conceived in conversation with his friend during the winter of 1797–8. This was to be a vast 'philosophic poem' of anything between 10,000 and 33,000 lines entitled *The Recluse, or Views of Nature, Man, and Society*. This project was to include or organise large sections of Wordsworth's existing poetry, including 'The Brothers'. As Beth Darlington puts it:

> The grand design proposed to synthesize mankind's philosophical, scientific, historical, and political knowledge and experience in poetry that would move man to realize on earth the Utopian vision confined for centuries to his hopes and dreams. To this awesome task Wordsworth was to consecrate his full powers and energies;

for this, he believed, he had been singled out by Nature, reared and schooled to be a poet.

(Darlington, 1977, p. 4)

In the event, Wordsworth proved unable to put this poem together from its component parts, publishing only what was originally projected as merely its second book under the title *The Excursion* in 1814. During 1800, he wrote a poem to serve as a prospectus to this project, elaborating a myth of his arrival and domicile in Grasmere. Shaped in 1806, but never fully finished or published in his lifetime, it exists in a number of versions, but readers have known it since its first publication in 1888, long after Wordsworth's death, as *Home at Grasmere*. We are going to take a look at its opening and its ending.

Activity 6

Turn to Reading 1.4 at the end of this part of the book. Read lines 1–53. This is the earliest version of *Home at Grasmere* (Manuscript (MS) B). How does the boy Wordsworth perceive Grasmere? How does his relationship with it as an adult promise to be different?

Discussion

To the boy, Grasmere seemed to be a 'seclusion' (l. 6), a 'paradise' (l. 12), a whole 'World' (l. 43), and a bowl-shaped arena of air enclosed by lake and hills, filled with the movement of cloud, breezes and 'winged Creatures' (l. 32). It seemed a vision of 'liberty' (l. 35) for the spirit and has served since as a powerful and consoling memory. There are notes, however, of anxiety – almost the first thought that occurs to the boy as he views this paradise is of death. To the adult, it is suggested, it may be all that it seemed to the boy and yet a little more – now it will be 'mine for life' (l. 52).

Later lines describe homecoming as the fulfilment of a long-held dream:

> The boon is absolute; surpassing grace
> To me hath been vouchsafed; among the bowers
> Of blissful Eden this was neither given
> Nor could be given – possession of the good
> Which had been sighed for, ancient thought fulfilled,

And dear Imaginations realized
Up to their highest measure, yea, and more.

(ll. 122–8)

Grasmere is insistently represented as somewhere blessed and perfect, an Eden or a paradise, a 'termination and a last retreat, / A Centre, come from wheresoe'er you will, / A Whole without dependence or defect, / Made for itself and happy in itself, / Perfect Contentment, Unity entire' (ll. 166–70). This reiterates the boy's sense of paradisial seclusion in adult – and political – terms as refuge from 'the common world' and 'these unhappy times':

A promise and an earnest that we twain,
A pair seceding from the common world,
Might in that hallowed spot to which our steps
Were tending, in that individual nook,
Might even thus early for ourselves secure,
And in the midst of these unhappy times,
A portion of the blessedness which love
And knowledge will, we trust, hereafter give
To all the Vales of earth and all mankind.

(ll. 248–56)

If you read on, you will see that the poem goes on to veer between the celebration of Grasmere as a blessed place of seclusion and retirement and the expression of pervasive anxieties about whether withdrawal from the world is self-indulgent or socially responsible. The poem eventually resolves in a grand statement of poetic vocation and ambition.

Activity 7

Turn back to *Home at Grasmere* (Reading 1.4) and read from 'A Voice shall speak, and what will be the Theme?' to the end (lines 958–1048). Consider the following questions:

1   What does Wordsworth say his subject matter will be?

2   How does he conceive the poet's work and the poet's readership?

3   How does his choice of form and language convey his sense of the ambition of his project?

Discussion

1   Wordsworth lays out his projected subject matter as 'the mind of Man, / My haunt and the main region of my song' (ll. 989–90) and the relationship of the mind of man to nature and vice versa.

2   He conceives of the poet as a 'mighty' prophet of a more perfect state of society. His work can be carried out from an 'inviolate retirement' (l. 970) both as man and as poet which will 'Express the image of a better time' (l. 1045). His readership may be 'few' now but will extend to 'Mankind in times to come' (l. 1034).

3   He conveys the ambition of his project in the conscious grandeur of his form and language. The form he chooses, blank verse, is associated with **epic poetry**. Epic is the 'highest', and supposedly most ambitious, poetic form. Employing classical conventions derived from Homer's *Odyssey* and Virgil's *Aeneid* (such as the episode describing a descent into the underworld), and alluding to John Milton's Christian epic *Paradise Lost* (1667), Wordsworth sets up his projected poem as an epic for his times, and identifies himself as an epic poet, in command of the grandest subject and commensurate poetic language. His language is elevated, abstract, Latinate (derived from Latin roots), and sometimes archaic ('thy' and 'thou', for example). The poem is characterised by long and complicated sentence structures typical of epic as in the lines following 'Come, thou prophetic Spirit …' (l. 1026).

In the event, Wordsworth expended his efforts on what he came to describe as 'the portico' to his otherwise mostly unwritten epic. This was a thirteen-book poem that was eventually posthumously entitled and published in 1850 by his widow Mary Wordsworth as *The Prelude: or, Growth of a Poet's Mind/An Autobiographical Poem*. Its subject was Wordsworth's youth up to 1799, and it was about the making of the poet who would write *The Recluse*. *The Prelude* was a poem that Wordsworth wrote and rewrote from 1799 for most of his life. Although he himself felt he had failed to write his epic, with hindsight it is clear that he did indeed write an epic for and of his times – an epic in the form of autobiography. We turn to this poem next.

Writing the self

Why did autobiography seem to Wordsworth an appropriate mode for epic? Or, to put it another way, why was it possible and even important at this historical juncture to describe the self in such grand terms? One answer to this question concerns the thinking of the philosopher John Locke (1632–1704). Locke held that human consciousness was constructed from data provided by external sensations. Much of eighteenth-century thinking was subsequently devoted to elaborating, debunking or solving the problems inherent in this theory of human consciousness. In particular, theories of memory were evolved to explain how human consciousness could experience itself as continuous selfhood, rather than as a discontinuous bundle of evanescent sense impressions. As the critic Anne Mellor has put it, 'Wordsworth attempted to represent a unitary self that is maintained over time by the activity of memory, and to show that this self or "soul" is defined, not by the body and its sensory experience, but by the human mind, by the growth of consciousness' (Mellor, 1993, p. 145). *The Prelude* celebrates the enduring coherence of the self despite

> The vacancy between me and those days
> Which yet have such self-presence in my mind
> That sometimes when I think of them I seem
> Two consciousnesses – conscious of myself,
> And of some other being.
>
> (Wordsworth, 1979 [1805], Book Second, ll. 29–33)

This accounts for the insistence throughout the poem not so much upon memories, as upon the *act* of remembering.

A second possible answer to this question is that the late eighteenth century had seen the publication of the *Confessions* (1782), the monumental prose autobiography of the philosopher Jean-Jacques Rousseau (1712–1778). Published after his death, its introspective and astonishingly frank account of Rousseau's inner life exerted a profound influence upon Romantic writers, most especially and inescapably upon those engaged in autobiographical writing. Rousseau's interest in the way in which adult behaviour seems to be related to traumatic experiences in childhood and adolescence finds echoes in Wordsworth's interest in the continuing power of childhood memory within the man.

Before we look at part of *The Prelude* in more detail, we have to tackle the problem that there is, in a sense, no such poem. There is no one established text of *The Prelude*. The poem known by this title evolved over many years and has continued to evolve until the present day (Gill, 2006, p. 4). It had its origins in 1798 as an intention, became a short manuscript in 1798–9, developed into a two-part poem by the end of 1799, developed further into a five-book poem by March 1804, and had expanded to thirteen books by the summer of 1805. Extensive revisions were made in 1819 and a final revision in 1839; in 1850 the poem was published in fourteen books edited by Mary Wordsworth (Gill, 2006, pp. 16–17). The poems we're going to be looking at are derived from manuscripts in preference to the published version the Victorians knew. In choosing to study them we are making a major critical choice – choosing to read *The Prelude* more according to when it was composed rather than according to when it was published. This decision in its turn depends upon making an aesthetic judgement against the older, Victorian Wordsworth, retrieving his first thoughts from the overlay of his second thoughts and his post-1850 legacy.

By looking at successive manuscript revisions, we can look at Wordsworth's acts of composition and re-composition as a form of continuous autobiographical self-making. We are going to compare two versions of the same episode in *The Prelude*, the first written *c*.1799, the second *c*.1805, in which Wordsworth tells the story of his memory of a drowning in Esthwaite Lake (for an extended version of this exercise, see Wolfson, 1997, pp. 100–32). Wandering along the lake shore, the boy notices a heap of clothes on the shore and assumes they belong to a swimmer. Evening falls, but the clothes are still there; the next day, he watches as the lake is dragged and a corpse recovered.

Activity 8

Read the two versions of this story, reproduced as Readings 1.5 and 1.6 at the end of this part of the book. Reading 1.5 is the entire 'First Part' of the earliest version of *The Prelude* (written in two parts in 1799): for this activity you only need to read lines 250–96. Reading 1.6 is an extract from Book Five of the thirteen-book version of 1805, ll. 389–557.

As you read, ask yourself: What remains the same between the earlier and later versions? What small changes does Wordsworth make? Are there any major changes, and if so, what are their implications?

Discussion

Perhaps the most important thing that remains the same between the versions is the abrupt juxtaposition of the twilight vigil and the next day's search within a single line, balanced across a full stop ('The breathless stillness. The succeeding day', line 274 in the 1799 version and line 466 in the 1805 version). This requires the reader to fill in the blank in a way that a child does – or does not, and is responsible for the 'breathless' feeling of the episode.

There are a series of small changes within the account itself: the **apostrophe** to Hawkshead in line 261 of the 1799 version vanishes; there are small changes in syntax and punctuation; more narrative motivation is provided (explaining why the company come, for example, in l. 467 of the 1805 version); and the language positions the poet further from his child-self (for instance the replacement of the simplicity of 'iron hooks' in the 1799 version (l. 276) with the more technical 'grappling-irons' in the 1805 version (l. 469)).

The really major change that Wordsworth makes, however, is to how he places this episode within the poem's narrative as a whole. This change means that Wordsworth's sense of what this episode might mean in telling the story of the growth of a poet's mind has also changed.

In the first version, the story is introduced as a possible exception to the argument Wordsworth has been making, which, put briefly, is that his child-self was at one with a largely beneficent Nature who exerted a 'ministry' throughout his boyhood adventures, an educating power, making 'The surface of the universal earth / With meanings of delight, of hope and fear, / Work like a sea' (1799 version, ll. 191, 196–8). The adult poet-narrator says that despite the horror of the scene this is just one of many memories that exist for him in the form of abiding images. He claims that such visual impressions become as real and permanent within the mind as the original landscape (their 'archetypes' (l. 287)) and assume new significance and power with the passage of time. He claims that the impressions from these 'spots of time' (l. 288) are the mysteriously resistant sites and reservoirs of poetic imagination – a version of the claim made with much less anxiety in 'I wandered lonely as a cloud'.

In the second version, however, these lines are relocated and organised within a book entirely devoted to the poet's education by nature, books and school. The commentary that follows upon the episode is very different. Although it is equally anxious to assert that the experience was *not* terrifying, but valuable, this is explained by reference to the child's distancing sense of the experience as akin to fairy tale and romance.

In both versions, however, this episode is flanked by other tales of loss, fear and death. In the first version, it is almost immediately followed by the child's experience of losing his guide near the site of a wife-murderer's execution and then by the story of the unexpected death of his father. In the second version, the lines are placed so as to follow a passage beginning 'There was a boy' (l. 389), which concludes with yet another death. This was originally drafted as a separate poem in the first person, and did not finish with the death of the boy; here, however, the poet-narrator casts himself as an adult mourner for the dead child – as apt a **metaphor** as any for the autobiographer pondering vanished childhood. What the two versions have in common, then, is a sense that the intensity of such memories tends to be connected with loss, guilt and death even as that is disavowed by the poem. Even more strikingly, taken together these two passages describe the problematic of autobiography – the way that it dramatises the present self trying to recapture and interpret past experience. Studying Wordsworth's revisions allows the reader to track the way that the older man revisions, rereads and rewrites his past self in full consciousness that it is probably impossible to retrieve it:

> As one who hangs down-bending from the side
> Of a slow-moving boat upon the breast
> Of a still water, solacing himself
> With such discoveries as his eye can make
> Beneath him in the bottom of the deeps,
> Sees many beauteous sights—weeds, fishes, flowers,
> Grots, pebbles, roots of trees—and fancies more,
> Yet often is perplexed and cannot part
> The shadow from the substance, rocks and sky,
> Mountains and clouds, from that which is indeed
> The region, and the things which there abide
> In their true dwelling; now is crossed by gleam
> Of his own image, by a sunbeam now,
> And motions that are sent he knows not whence,
> Impediments that make his task more sweet;
> Such pleasant office have we long pursued
> Incumbent over the surface of past time –
> With like success.

(Wordsworth, 1979 [1805], Book Fourth, ll. 247–64)

Conclusion

This chapter has been exploring very different ways of reading Wordsworth's poetry through his life. In reading 'I wandered lonely as a cloud', we considered how a poem could be read in the light of biographical information supplied in other texts. We read 'Point Rash-Judgment', 'The Brothers', and *Home at Grasmere* as poems that meditate either explicitly or implicitly upon Wordsworth's decision to settle in Grasmere and devote himself to poetry. We glanced back at *The Prelude* to get a flavour of how Wordsworth describes his own life in an effort to explain how he became a poet. We also subjected *The Prelude* to a biographical reading by examining the ways in which Wordsworth repeatedly revised it over his lifetime. Different though these approaches are, they have in common an investment in the idea of the author as a subjectivity which can make sense of and connect these otherwise disparate poems. The practice of reading poetry biographically is actively encouraged by Wordsworth's foregrounding of himself as subject-matter.

Yet reiterating a note of caution about reading biographically is in order here. This is because all biographical representation is itself inevitably a fiction. To illustrate this, we might finish by comparing two representations of Wordsworth as poet, made when he was much older and had achieved substantial fame. The first (Figure 1.4), a watercolour by Margaret Gillies painted in 1839, depicts him at home with his wife, Mary Hutchinson. Although he is not looking at his wife, the bond between them is emphasised by her dependent and attentive look. The pen she is holding suggests that she is acting as his amanuensis, taking down dictation at a table covered with books and manuscripts. By contrast, the second (Figure 1.5), an oil painting by Benjamin Robert Haydon executed in 1842, depicts the poet in a sublime outdoor setting, standing alone on the summit of Helvellyn, the highest mountain in the Lake District. It dramatises the poet as a solitary, dominating the landscape with the power of his thought and imagination, remote from home, collaboration, and the business of publication. The first is true to the biographical information supplied by diaries, letters and contemporary accounts. The second is true to Wordsworth's sense of himself (shared by the Victorians) as epic Romantic genius. While the first picture hangs in Dove Cottage, reinforcing its local story of collaborative domesticity, the second hangs in the National Gallery in

Figure 1.4   Margaret Gillies, *Portrait of William and Mary Wordsworth*, 1839. Dove Cottage, Grasmere. Photo: © Dove Cottage, The Wordsworth Trust/The Bridgeman Art Library.

Figure 1.5   Benjamin Robert Haydon, *Portrait of William Wordsworth*, 1842, oil on canvas, 125 × 99 cm. National Portrait Gallery, London. Photo: © Giraudon/The Bridgeman Art Library.

London and certifies Wordsworth's pre-eminence in the national canon. Both depictions are 'biographical', but they suggest very different ways we might read and value the poet's endeavour.

References

Atkin, P. (2009) 'Ghosting Grasmere: the musealisation of Dove Cottage' in Watson, N.J. (ed.) *Literary Tourism and Nineteenth-Century Culture*, Houndmills, Palgrave, pp. 84–94.

Burton, M.E. (1958) *The Letters of Mary Wordsworth 1800–1855*, Oxford, Clarendon Press.

Butler, J.A. (1996) 'Tourist or native son: Wordsworth's homecomings of 1799–1800', *Nineteenth-Century Literature*, vol. 51, no. 1, pp. 1–15.

Darlington, B. (ed.) (1977) *Home at Grasmere: Part First, Book First, of The Recluse*, Ithaca and London, Cornell University Press.

Fink, Z.S. (1958) *The Early Wordsworthian Milieu*, Oxford, Clarendon Press.

Gill, S. (ed.) (1990) *William Wordsworth*, Oxford, New York, Oxford University Press.

Gill, S. (1998) *Wordsworth and the Victorians*, Oxford, Clarendon Press.

Gill, S. (2006) *William Wordsworth's The Prelude: A Casebook*, Oxford, Oxford University Press.

Mellor, A. (1993) *Romanticism and Gender*, New York, Routledge.

Wolfson, S. (1997) *Formal Charges: The Shaping of Poetry in British Romanticism*, Stanford, CA, Stanford University Press.

Woof, P. (ed.) (1991) *Dorothy Wordsworth: The Grasmere Journals*, Oxford, Oxford University Press.

Woof, P. (1992) 'Dorothy Wordsworth's Grasmere journals: the patterns and pressures of composition' in Brinkley, R. and Hanley, K. (eds) *Romantic Revisions*, Cambridge, Cambridge University Press, pp. 169–90.

Wordsworth, W. (1979 [1805]) *The Prelude* in Wordsworth, J., Abrams, M.H. and Gill, S. (eds) (1979) *The Prelude 1799, 1805, 1850: Authoritative Texts; Context and Reception; Recent Critical Essays*, New York, W.W. Norton and Company.

Further reading

Heinzelman, K. (1988) 'The cult of domesticity: Dorothy and William Wordsworth at Grasmere' in Mellor, A. (ed.) *Romanticism and Feminism*, Bloomington, IN, Indiana University Press, 1988, pp. 52–78.

Johnston, K.R. (1984) *Wordsworth and The Recluse*, New Haven, Yale University Press.

Chapter 2
Percy Bysshe Shelley: inner and outer lives

Richard Allen with Clare Spencer

Aims

This chapter will:

- introduce you to a selection of Shelley's shorter poems, ranging in form from ode to sonnet, and in preoccupation from the personal to the political

- explore how multiple, fragmented versions of Shelley's identity as a poet are constructed in the writing, editing and reception of his work

- explore how the poet's life and compositional choices and practices provide contexts for reading and understanding individual poetic texts.

Introduction

In this second chapter we continue to investigate the persona of the Romantic poet, ideas about the poetic vocation, and how the author has been represented by studying the work of another major poet of the period – Percy Bysshe Shelley (1792–1822). To remind yourself of one way in which Shelley's Romantic life has been mythologised and invested with iconic status, you might like to look back at the inscriptions on the poet's gravestone in Rome (see Figure 2 in the introduction to this part of the book). Here you will see how Shelley's sudden death by drowning is elevated through an **allusion** to Ariel's song in Shakespeare's play *The Tempest* (1611). The full text of the song conveys its atmosphere of mystery, fluidity and mutability:

> Full fathom five thy father lies.
>   Of his bones are coral made;
> Those are pearls that were his eyes;
>   Nothing of him that doth fade
> But doth suffer a sea-change
> Into something rich and strange.
>   Sea-nymphs hourly ring his knell:
>   Ding dong.
> Hark, now I hear them.
>   Ding-dong bell.
>
> (Shakespeare, 1997 [1611], Act 1, Scene 2, ll. 400–9)

The Shakespearean allusion thus memorialises the author as a figure who himself participated in the 'rich and strange'. Where Wordsworth's gravestone evokes notions of home, simplicity and rootedness in nature, Shelley's conveys contrasting ideas of exile, the heart, mysteriousness, and classical affinities (this last suggested by the Latin inscription). This may tell us something about the character of the poet's life itself.

Unlike Wordsworth, Shelley did not attempt in his poetry to project what we have seen in Chapter 1 as a grand, unified 'self', described through conscious, autobiographical acts of recollection. Instead, the versions of the poet we will encounter in Shelley's work are varied, elusive, often accusatory and sometimes prophetic in tone; they are dramatised rather than recollected, and shifting rather than stable.

The keynotes of Shelley's Romantic life as voiced in the poetry were its kaleidoscopic and rootless nature.

This chapter begins by considering how the act of editing a poet's output can itself involve constructing a particular version of the author's life. We'll then analyse two of Shelley's celebrated lyric poems, written more than a year after he had left England for Italy in March 1818. 'To a Skylark' and 'Ode to the West Wind' both explore the centrality of the imagination to the vocation of the poet. From these famous **odes** (poems of direct address), we'll turn to Shelley's life as a radical intellectual, and to two poems composed in Italy in 1819 – a year of political turbulence for Britain. 'England in 1819' and 'To the Lord Chancellor' feature the figure of the poet in the voice of the accuser; they offer a coruscating satire of the establishment. In 'Ozymandias' (composed near London in 1817) and 'Written on Hearing the News of the Death of Napoleon' (1821), the stance of political protester modulates into that of historical observer. Both poems arguably demonstrate a consciousness of the Romantic period itself as involving a historical turn in the tide. Finally, we'll consider the complex ode 'Mont Blanc', an earlier piece written during a tour of Switzerland in 1816, which features the younger Romantic poet's characteristically heroic quest for truth and the ideal through an encounter with the awe-inspiring landscape of the Alps.

This small selection of poems does not claim to be representative of Shelley's work as a whole. He is equally well known for his long narrative poems, verse dramas and Romantic allegories drawing on classical mythology. But the fact that these shorter poems may elicit only a fragmentary understanding of Shelley's poetic life is not necessarily a disadvantage. Writers and artists of the Romantic period believed that the human mind and imagination could aspire at best to momentary and transitory self-insight and grasp of life's ultimate truths. Shelley's abruptly curtailed lifespan (he died before his thirtieth birthday) did not allow him the retrospective reassessment of his own writing undertaken by Wordsworth, which, as Nicola Watson says in Chapter 1, 'allows the reader to track the way that the older man revisions, rereads and rewrites his past self' (p. 33). Where it was for the most part Wordsworth himself who reassembled the fragments of memory and experience that enabled him to describe (and to some extent reinvent) his Romantic life, it is up to readers to assemble their own versions of Shelley the poet: versions which will always be fluid and subject to change.

A life 'edited by Mrs Shelley'

For readers of the late nineteenth century, Shelley was consecrated as the archetypal Romantic poet: his idealised image guarded and perpetuated by early exponents of English literature as an academic discipline. What were the defining features of this authorial archetype?

Activity 1

Consider the comments below from a review article written in 1904 by John C. Bailey – later Chairman of the English Association, an organisation founded in 1906 to promote the teaching of literature:

> the gulf between us and Shelley lies in the fact that we are of the earth earthy and he is airy of the air. His landscape is not our well-loved trees and flowers, not so much even our worshipped sea and mountains; it is night and day, dark and dawn, winds and clouds and the movements of elemental air, the stars in their courses, the sun and the moon, not as givers of earthly light, but as circling worlds, immeasurably distant, solitary, and aloof.
>
> (Bailey, 1911, p. 164)

What version of Shelley the author does Bailey offer us here? What would you expect the poetry to be like from reading this description? What aspects of Shelley's life might have been omitted? List some of the qualities that Bailey ascribes to the poet and his work, and keep your list to one side to test against the evidence of the poems we'll be reading later.

Discussion

Bailey's Shelley is an elevated being who exists on another level from the rest of us: an almost ethereal creature, not unlike the spirit Ariel in Shakespeare's play *The Tempest* – the source of the epitaph on his gravestone. This 'airy' figure has access to the higher powers of the cosmos: the stars, moon and 'circling worlds' of other planets. And the implication is that he shares the elusive quality of those worlds: 'distant, solitary and aloof'. From reading this description, we might expect to encounter nature poetry, but the kind of nature poetry which deals with the elements, perhaps even with science, rather than the local world of the particular place. There is no sense here of Shelley as a poet who engages with the contemporary issues of his day, or as a poet who writes about himself and his life experience.

Figure 2.1   Attributed to Edwin Beyerhaus, *Portrait of Percy Bysshe Shelley – the Eton Atheist*, 1820. Photo: © Getty Images.

A visual equivalent of Bailey's Shelley can be seen in the portrait by Edwin Beyerhaus (Figure 2.1). This image of Shelley as the elevated and almost other-worldly Romantic genius was promoted and sustained by the editor of the first comprehensive and accurate collection of his work, his second wife, Mary Wollstonecraft Shelley (née Godwin; 1797–1851). Published in 1839, after Shelley's death, the collection was entitled *The Poetical Works of Percy Bysshe Shelley. Edited by Mrs. Shelley.* We'll see below how the act of editing and annotating the poems was for Mary Shelley also an act of 'editing' Shelley's life: assembling its fragments into a Romantic reputation which would endure long into the future, effacing the memory of Shelley's notoriety in his own day.

Shelley's public reputation in his own lifetime was not that of the sensitive, other-worldly creature evoked by Beyerhaus and the late Victorians. His first attempt at a substantial poem, *Queen Mab*, contained the kinds of attacks on the monarchy and religion bound to upset the establishment. Initially printed and circulated privately in 1813, some surplus copies of the poem found their way onto the market via the publisher William Clark in 1821. Clark was prosecuted by the Vice-Suppression Society. *The Times* of the day reported that the indictment was based chiefly on the blasphemous nature of the text: one example judged fit to be reprinted was 'the opinion that as, like other systems, Christianity has arisen and augmented, so, like them, it will decay and perish' (*The Times*, 11 December 1821, p. 2). The prosecution was successful, but the poem itself went on to acquire an underground fame among radicals. Pirate editions published in subsequent years – often omitting the most contentious passage – were read almost as an alternative Bible by the radical movements of the 1830s and the Chartists (1840s political reformers who adopted a 'People's Charter') who succeeded them.

Shelley fully intended his poem to shock an orthodox public, and his own open advocacy of atheism and free love furthered the reputation it earned him. Even after his death in 1822, Shelley was cited in a custody case as an earlier example of bad paternal behaviour: 'The children of Percy Bysshe Shelley had also been taken from their father because he had intended to bring them up in the belief, or should we say the profession of atheistical doctrines' (*The Times*, 25 February 1826, p. 3). The scandal attached to his son's public image horrified Shelley's respectable father; and Sir Timothy Shelley did everything possible to suppress his memory after his death. For Mary Shelley, dependent on a small allowance from Sir Timothy, this was a problem. She wanted to publish Shelley's work and write a memoir of him, not only to glorify his memory, but also for her own financial benefit. But she could not afford to antagonise her conservative benefactor.

In an eventual compromise, Sir Timothy agreed to the publication of an edition of the poems, on condition that there would be no accompanying memoir. The *Collected Poems* of 1839 nonetheless present a clear version of the author's life and imaginative experience, not least because the shorter poems at the end of the four volumes are organised year by year, with Mary Shelley's notes forming a kind of diary of Shelley's Romantic life. At key points, Mary's own feelings colour the account, and almost constitute a dual biography in which events increasingly foreshadow Shelley's death and her widowhood. In the notes on the poems of 1820–1, for example, she wrote:

> My task becomes inexpressibly painful as the year draws near which sealed our earthly fate; and each poem and each event it records has a real or mysterious connection to the final catastrophe.
>
> (Shelley quoted in Allen, 2000, p. 85)

In the notes on the poems of Shelley's final year, she expresses her 'burning desire to impart to the world, in worthy language, the sense I have of the virtues and genius of the Beloved and the Lost' (Shelley, 1904 , p. 761) and writes of the way her work was leading her to 'recurrence to the past – full of its own deep and unforgotten joys and sorrows' (1904, p. 761). Such comments provide the foundation stones of the mythology of Shelley the tragic genius.

Mary Shelley does acknowledge the poet's competing reputation as a radical elsewhere in her commentary, noting for example that the poem *Alastor* 'ought rather to be considered didactic than [merely] narrative' (1904, p. 33); but generally she remakes Shelley to a different and more inwardly focused pattern. Her Shelley is far less political than the Shelley who had been feted by radicals in the circulation of *Queen Mab*. It is perhaps not surprising, then, that one of the most striking aspects of her life story of Shelley comes in a note to *Queen Mab* itself, in which she writes:

> Shelley did not expect sympathy or approbation from the public; but the want of it took away a portion of the ardour that ought to have sustained him while writing … [his] mind could not be bent

from its natural inclination … he loved to shelter himself rather in the airiest flights of fancy forgetting love and hate, and regret and lost hope, in such imaginations as borrowed their hue from sunrise and sunset.

(Shelley quoted in Allen, 2000, p. 87)

In keeping with this, Mary Shelley's note to *Alastor*, cited at the start of this paragraph, continues:

It [*Alastor*] was the outpouring of his emotions, embodied in the purest form he could conceive, painted in the ideal lines which his brilliant imagination inspired.

(Shelley quoted in Allen, 2000, p. 84)

Here, surely, we have the source of the archetype of Shelley the Romantic poet recycled by Bailey sixty-five years later. Mary Shelley's edition of the poems, with her accompanying annotations, remained the authoritative Shelley text until the beginning of the twentieth century. And that text constructs an author whose 'brilliant imagination' lent itself to 'airiest flights of fancy' – a poet who aspired to 'ideal lines' and 'the purest form'. In the next section we'll look for evidence of this airy version of Shelley in the form and language of two of his lyric poems.

A life of the imagination

'To a Skylark'

'To a Skylark' was written and published in 1820, and is arguably the poem which best conveys the image of the poet that Mary Shelley wanted preserved. She recalled that the piece was written on or about 7 July, when the Shelleys were living near Pisa in Italy: 'It was on a beautiful summer evening, while wandering among the lanes whose myrtle-hedges were the bowers for the fireflies, that we heard the carolling of the skylark which inspired one of the most beautiful of his poems' (quoted in Holmes, 1987, p. 599).

Activity 2

You should now read Shelley's 'To a Skylark', which is reproduced as Reading 2.1 at the end of this part of the book. Take a few moments to note your first impressions of how the poem captures Mary's image of her husband.

Discussion

In your first reading of the poem, you can probably pick out examples of what Mary Shelley calls the 'airiest flights of fancy' in which the poetic imagination transcends the constraints of everyday existence. The imagery in which the skylark is compared to 'a cloud of fire' (l. 8), 'a star of Heaven' (l. 18), and even to a poet-figure 'hidden / In the light of thought' (ll. 36–7) contributes to that airy, cosmic frame of reference we have already come to associate with the mythologised Shelley.

The contrasts between the Shelleys' real life at this time and the joyous raptures imagined in the poem are stark. Richard Holmes, author of the definitive biography of Shelley, refers to this as a period of 'domestic difficulties and secret gloom' (1987, p. 599). Shelley was struggling to find a London publisher for the outpouring of political poetry he had produced during the previous year. He and Mary were pursued by demands for money from Mary's father William Godwin (1756–1836). And above all, Shelley was anxious about the health of his daughter, Elena Adelaide Shelley. Elena is something of a mystery: Shelley registered himself as her father when she was born in 1818, but Mary Shelley was not her mother. One conjecture is that her mother was Claire Clairmont (1798–1879), Mary Shelley's half-sister who travelled with the couple to Italy. Another speculation is that the Shelleys' servant, Elise Foggi, gave birth to the child: her husband Paolo Foggi had subsequently threatened Shelley with blackmail. Within a day or so of the evening walk that inspired 'To a Skylark', the sad news arrived that Elena had died on 9 June.

Does this poem therefore represent an escape from reality? Does the life of the imagination involve turning away from this difficult world? And can attending to the shape and movement of the poem along with its biographical context help us to answer these questions?

Activity 3

Turn back to the poem for a second time. Concentrate on the first three stanzas, and try to scan them by marking up the stressed syllables. What patterns, and disruptions of pattern, can you detect? You may find that it helps to speak the poem aloud, or listen to a spoken version (try using an online search engine to find one on the internet).

Discussion

This very unusual stanza form, with its four centred, compact lines followed by one much longer line, establishes an underlying metrical pattern sustained throughout the poem, though it is interrupted by irregularities. It is possible to mark up the first stanza like this:

On the whole, each of the short lines has three stressed syllables organised in a fairly regular **trochaic metre** – where the stressed syllable precedes the unstressed one. (To fit the trochaic pattern, the word 'heaven' is pronounced as just one syllable. Line 4, however, does not quite work to pattern because it is clear that 'thy' could be either stressed or unstressed, while the sense of the line demands that 'full' be stressed. 'Profuse' is strictly stressed here in an archaic fashion, though read aloud with modern pronunciation the stresses would reverse.) The last line unexpectedly shifts into iambic metre and contains twice as many stresses. One interpretation is that the rhythm soars up and away in the final line to create the impression of a bird rising and singing in the sky. Shelley has apparently discovered the 'purest form' to capture the image of flight and compare it with the liberating impetus of poetic creativity.

Points of irregularity and tension within this pattern, however, suggest that the unease of Shelley's real-world life is never entirely transcended, regardless of what Mary Shelley says about him 'forgetting … regret and lost hope' through his poetry. Look at these two lines from the second stanza, for example (again, with stressed syllables marked):

$$x \quad / \quad / \quad x \quad / \quad x$$

The blue deep thou wingest,

$$x \quad / \quad x \quad / \quad x \quad / \quad x \quad / \quad x \quad / \, x \quad / \quad x$$

.And singing still dost soar, and soaring ever singest.

The soaring motif is unsettled here, both by the heavy consecutive stresses on the phrase 'blue deep', and by the unstressed syllable which ends the final line with an awkwardly descending cadence. For all the escapist identification with the skylark, the reality of earthly loss and pain seems to make itself felt as a subtle rhythmic undercurrent in the poem.

Speaking or hearing the poem spoken aloud demonstrates how its attractiveness and power depend on the interplay between such patterns of sound and movement and their variation. What makes poetry interesting is often the disjunction between how the speaking voice would naturally sound the words, and what the metrical pattern invites it to do. Similarly, while the poem's rhyme scheme follows a regular pattern of ababb, it is varied by the introduction of the occasional **half-rhyme**. In lines 67–9, for example, the phrases 'triumphal chant', 'empty vaunt' and 'hidden want' provide half-rhymes. The fact that we are denied the satisfaction of a full rhyme here perhaps enacts the sense of lack in the stanza itself: human song can never aspire to 'match' that of the skylark.

On reading the entire poem, you'll have seen that its argument develops as it proceeds, with one key shift in direction, and a changing role for the voice of the first-person poet-speaker. From line 61 onwards the airy, fanciful comparisons gradually give way to contrasts between the transcendent perfection of the birdsong and the shortcomings of human existence. In lines 77–80, we are told that the skylark is free from 'langour', 'annoyance' and the 'sad satiety' of worldly love. And lines 86–90 might well remind us of the 'difficulties and secret gloom' which, according to Holmes, characterised Shelley's life at this time:

> We look before and after,
>   And pine for what is not:
>   Our sincerest laughter
>   With some pain is fraught;
> Our sweetest songs are those that tell of saddest thought.

(ll. 86–90)

The skylark itself, of course, soars so high that it disappears from view, though the joy of its song continues to echo throughout the poem. The focus of the final stanza, however, is not so much the birdsong as the poet himself and his vocation: note the use of the pronouns 'me', 'my' and 'I' at this critical moment. There is a poignant appeal from the speaker to his audience in the phrase 'The world should listen then' (l. 105). And this takes us back to Mary Shelley's comment about want of sympathy from the public for Shelley's work. A poem which might initially have seemed to turn away from the real world thus returns us forcibly to it.

'Ode to the West Wind'

We'll now consider the 'Ode to the West Wind'. This poem was written earlier than 'To a Skylark' – on 25 October 1819 – and according to Shelley, it was again composed in a moment of direct inspiration, when he and Mary were living in Florence. In a note included with the first publication in 1820, Shelley wrote:

> This poem was conceived and chiefly written in a wood that skirts the Arno … on a day when that tempestuous wind, whose temperature is at once mild and animating, was collecting the vapours which pour down the autumnal rains. They began, as I foresaw, at sunset with a violent tempest of hail and rain, attended by that magnificent thunder and lightning peculiar to the Cisalpine regions.
>
> (Leader and O'Neill (eds), 2003, p. 762)

Activity 4

Read 'Ode to the West Wind' now (you'll find this reproduced as Reading 2.2). If you're in a position to read it aloud, be prepared for its exclamatory, high-pitched style. Don't hesitate to dramatise!

After you've read the poem once, look back carefully at the first and final stanzas. Are there similarities and differences in comparison with 'To a Skylark'? Focus this time on the imagery, the tone of the first-person voice, the rhyme scheme and the pace of the lines. What kind of version of Shelley are we offered here?

Discussion

Of course you'll have noticed the similar focus on the elements of nature, though this time in more turbulent form. The 'pale purple even' (l. 16) and 'rainbow clouds' (l. 33) of the previous poem are replaced here by a wind which is 'wild' (l. 1), 'fierce' (l. 61) and 'impetuous' (l. 62). The imagery remains airy, however, with the west wind compared to breath and fleeing ghosts; and the motif of music and song is also shared with 'To a Skylark'. In this case, however, instead of a 'rain of melody' (l. 35) and notes which flow like a 'crystal stream' (l. 85), we have the summoning call of 'clarion' (l. 10) and 'trumpet' (l. 69). The tone of the poet-speaker is urgent, even demanding, when compared with the rapturous wonderment and reflection evoked by the song of the skylark. You may have spotted the accumulation of imperative verbs in the final stanza: 'drive', 'scatter' and the repeated 'be'. The second-person address which is characteristic of the ode as a form is here more insistent; the voice of the poet-speaker demands to be heard.

The rhyme scheme is more intricate than that of 'To a Skylark'. The middle line of each three-line unit (or **tercet**) rhymes with the first and third lines of the next, making a tightly interlocked structure for each fourteen-line stanza: aba bcb cdc ded ee. If you have already studied (or written) poetry, you'll probably realise that these fourteen line units, with their use of iambic pentameter, adopt the approximate shape of a **sonnet**. One effect of this rhyme scheme is to invest the poem with a driving forward momentum in which each tercet anticipates the sound of the next. In combination with a frequent use of **enjambement** (lines which run on into the next without punctuation), this lends the poem a rapid, almost frantic pace which matches its insistent tone. The listening persona of 'To a Skylark', inspired by an animated nature, is replaced here by a more intensely personal voice which becomes almost self-dramatising in its anxiety to be heard, not only by the wind but by 'mankind' (1.67) and even 'the universe' (1.63). This is hardly the remote voice of Bailey's Shelley, reaching us from worlds 'distant … and aloof'.

What you may not have registered at this stage is the literary self-consciousness of the ode, though its nod to the sonnet form may have alerted you to some of its continuities with an elite tradition in poetry. The three-line units used here are technically known as terza rima, a form which Shelley borrowed from *The Divine Comedy* (1308–21) by the Florentine poet, Dante Alighieri (*c.*1265–1321). Later allusions can also prompt us to recognise that what is apparently a nature poem is in fact shot through with references to literature, history and culture. Thus, in the second stanza, there is a reference to Greek mythology in 'some fierce Maenad' (l. 21); and in the third stanza Roman history is alluded to in the mention of 'Baiae's bay' (l. 32). Returning to the opening stanza, the imagery of the leaves echoes the description of the fallen angels in Milton's *Paradise Lost* (Milton, 1971 [1667] ll. 299–304), and 'Destroyer and Preserver' evokes the Hindu Gods Shiva and Vishnu. While many of these allusions may not be familiar to today's casual reader, they are evidence that the speaker of this ode is constructed as an educated, consciously literary figure in a way that the 'Skylark's' speaker is not.

Both of these poems, therefore, seem at some level to conform in their imagery, **lexicon** (word choice) and subject matter to the version of the Romantic life constructed by Mary Shelley: 'he loved to shelter himself rather in the airiest flights of fancy forgetting love and hate, and regret and lost hope, in such imaginations as borrowed their hue from sunrise and sunset' (Shelley quoted in Allen, 2000, p. 87). But in other respects there are signs of something more in keeping with the vehement, publicly engaged Shelley who was less admired by the general readership of the nineteenth century: an undercurrent of metrical unease; an urgent, perhaps even hectoring tone; a voice eager for literary recognition.

In 'Ode to the West Wind', the earlier of the two poems, this kind of poetic ambition appears, at least at first, to be energetic and hopeful: the storm unleashes forces which 'surge' (l. 19), 'waken' (l. 29) and 'fly' (l. 44). The winds from the Atlantic may hint at the revolutionary change which had led to the creation of the United States of America in 1776. And the 'old palaces and towers' (l. 33) of long-institutionalised power are submerged beneath the waves of transition. There is a sense here of the forward-looking poet anticipating a regenerated society. But the hint of gloom and inadequacy we've already noted in 'To a Skylark' intrudes into stanza 4:

> Oh! lift me as a wave, a leaf, a cloud!
> I fall upon the thorns of life! I bleed!
>
> A heavy weight of hours has chained and bowed
> One too like thee: tameless, and swift, and proud.

(ll. 53–6)

This surely conditions our reading of the final stanza and invites us to interpret the energy and optimism there as infused with an element of personal desperation. The 'airiest fancy' of both poems, in the final analysis, is inextricably linked through the imagination to the real world of 'regret and lost hope'.

The political radical

What about the protesting Shelley, the free-thinking radical who satirised and scandalised the establishment of his day, offending propriety with poems like *Queen Mab*? This political persona came to dominate the poet's reputation in the twentieth century, decisively replacing the Victorian mythology. To commemorate the two hundredth anniversary of Shelley's birth, in July 1992 the left-wing journalist Paul Foot wrote an article on the poet in the magazine *The Socialist Review*. There he depicts a 'resolutely revolutionary' Shelley who 'developed a passionate hatred and contempt for the class society in which he found himself' and wrote 'diatribe[s] against the social order' (Foot, 1992, p. 18). In these comments, Foot reiterates the version of Shelley he had researched for his polemical biography *Red Shelley*, published in 1980.

The Mask of Anarchy and 'Sonnet: England in 1819'

Foot's focus in his commemorative article is Shelley's famous poem *The Mask of Anarchy*, written in **broadsheet ballad** form in September 1819. Britain in 1819 was in the grip of an economic recession which had begun after the end of the Napoleonic Wars. Hardship led to civil unrest which the Government responded to vigorously: a mass popular demonstration (calling for parliamentary reform) at Peterloo near Manchester had been violently suppressed in August, leading to eighteen deaths and hundreds of serious injuries among the demonstrators. The event is portrayed in *The Mask of Anarchy* in terms like those below. (The poem is printed in full as Reading 2.8 if you would like to read more of it, but it is not essential that you do so at this point.)

> And at length when ye complain
> With a murmur weak and vain
> 'Tis to see the Tyrant's crew
> Ride over your wives and you –
> Blood is on the grass like dew.

(ll. 188–92)

After a series of direct attacks on the repressive legislators of its day, unambiguously named, the poem concludes with a rousing call for the oppressed populace to stir into revolutionary action:

> And that slaughter to the Nation
> Shall steam up like inspiration,
> Eloquent, oracular;
> A volcano heard afar.
>
> …
>
> 'Rise like lions after slumber
> In unvanquishable number –
> Shake your chains to earth like dew
> Which in sleep had fallen on you –
> Ye are many – they are few'.

(ll. 360–4, 368–72)

You will notice here the compelling, thumping rhythm of **ballad metre** (trochaic feet, with four stresses in each line), with its pronounced emphasis on the first syllable of the lines. This is a poem which strives for a popular, accessible and dramatised voice to carry its political opinions.

This accusatory, polemical persona recurs in another of Shelley's 1819 poems which was unpublishable in his own lifetime, this time a sonnet. The English sonnet conventionally adopts one of two rhyme schemes, and typically involves a 'turn' from the argument of the first eight lines to the final six which generate a conclusion. The Petrarchan scheme (abba abba cde cde) ends with a pair of tercets, whereas the Shakespearean scheme (abab cdcd efef gg) ends with a clinching couplet. English sonnets traditionally use the metre called iambic pentameter.

Activity 5

Read the poem 'Sonnet: England in 1819' (Reading 2.3) now. In what ways does the poem conform with, or break away from, traditional sonnet conventions as described above? What might Shelley's distinctive employment of the sonnet form tell us about the political persona constructed here?

Discussion

'Sonnet: England in 1819' breaks with convention in both its use of rhyme and its organisational structure. The rhyme scheme abababcdcdccdd allows for only four rhyming sounds in total, lending a particularly emphatic tone to what are predominantly single-syllable rhymes. And the poem lacks an obvious turn, consisting not so much of an argument as of a list of those accused: the monarch; the unreformed parliament; the army; the law.

The lines may be scanned as superficially conforming to the rules of iambic pentameter, with five stressed syllables alternating with unstressed ones:

$$x \quad / \quad x \quad / \quad x \quad / \quad x \quad / x \quad /$$
An old, mad, blind, despised, and dying King;

But their sense and punctuation drives us to add additional stresses, for example on the word 'mad' and perhaps even on the first syllable of 'despised'. Again, the effect is to construct the poetic voice as a loud and insistent one, pausing between words for maximum rhetorical effect.

The poet-figure is clearly an angry one, pouring scorn on the 'leechlike' politicians who govern the country, and bursting through the constraints of the sonnet form in a declamatory, public invective. But all this rule-breaking culminates in the expected final couplet whose vision of a 'glorious phantom' of freedom may well remind us of the other, airier Shelley.

Shelley's depiction of England in 1819 is realistic in some respects. King George III had been declared insane in 1810 and was to die in January 1820. His sons, condemned here as 'the dregs of their dull race', were notoriously dissolute. Similar attacks against royalty and corrupt and repressive public figures motivated a whole sequence of political poems Shelley composed in Italy in 1819, and might certainly lead us to conclude that political revolution was part of his Romantic agenda. Shelley is plainly an advocate of change and liberty, writing through personae who – as it were – see things from below and sympathise with the working people 'starved and stabbed in th'untilled field' (l. 8) of Peterloo. But equally the poem bears out Paul Foot's complaint that what he calls Shelley's 'hate-songs' of 1819 often end 'with vaporous appeals, so common among demagogues who duck the real issues' (1980, p. 157).

'To the Lord Chancellor'

A more personal manifestation of Shelley's political self appears in the poem 'To the Lord Chancellor', originally titled 'To Lxxd Exxxn'. Even a rapid reading of the poem – which you can undertake now by referring to Reading 2.4 – will register the directness of its attack. It is addressed to Lord Eldon, Lord Chancellor in the British Government from 1801 to 1827. Eldon was caricatured in *The Mask of Anarchy* as the figure of Fraud, weeping crocodile tears which turn to stone and, as they do so, knock out the brains of innocent children. 'To the Lord Chancellor' opens by cursing the politician on behalf of the country to which he has allegedly done so much damage. And in this case it is perhaps the relentless repetition of that word 'curse' which threatens to rupture and overwhelm a rather more conventional iambic pentameter and regular stanzaic form. In the third and fourth stanzas, the address becomes more intimate: the curse is now that laid by 'a father', motivated by 'a parent's outraged love' (ll. 13, 17). Here the attack takes on an individual and literal force: the 'tyrant' Eldon had made a court judgment three years before which in an important way changed the tenor of Shelley's own life.

In 1816 the poet had left his first wife, Harriet Westbrook, and their two children, and was living with Mary (still Mary Wollstonecraft Godwin at this stage). In December of that year, Harriet unexpectedly committed suicide. Shelley was deeply shocked, but saw that this event left the way open to marriage with Mary and custody of his two children, Ianthe and Charles. But the custody claim was disputed by Harriet's parents, and was eventually heard in the Court of Chancery by Lord Eldon. Neither side won. Shelley was successfully labelled as dangerous and morally unsound, unfit to be a father. But the children were placed with a foster family rather than with their grandparents. Reading this poem in the light of this information, the figure of the political radical fighting for freedom and against the tyranny of the law is overlaid by a picture of a distraught father deprived of the rightful care of his children.

Reading these two poems in a biographical context, therefore, may make them look less revolutionary than they initially seemed: the first ending on a note of evasion; the second motivated by a personal grudge. The apparently spontaneous political anger of 'England in 1819' is in fact channelled through the distance of geographic exile; and in fact the poem was composed at a time when reactionary rather than revolutionary forces were in the ascendant in both Britain and the rest of Europe. 'To the Lord Chancellor' is also less spontaneous and ingenuous than it would seem, whether regarded as a primarily political or personal outburst. It was written retrospectively, two and a half years after the court hearing in March 1817, and Eldon's judgement had in reality given Shelley some rights of access to his children, though – as Shelley's biographer, Richard Holmes, observes – there is no evidence that he ever used them (1987, p. 775).

What this reveals is the element of myth-making in the management of Shelley's reputation, both on his own part or the part of his executors and publishers. The persona of the bitter, despairing father is a version of himself which Shelley constructed well after the direct impact of the court hearing. Mary Shelley would build on this image in her 1839 notes on 'To the Lord Chancellor', inviting us to read the poem as articulating the emotion of tragic loss: 'No words can express the anguish he felt when his elder children were torn away from him' (Leader and O'Neill (eds), 2003, p. 775). Our understanding of the politics of this poem and others is modified by a sense of their history – not just their compositional history, but the history of constructing Shelley the Romantic poet.

A witness to history

In the next two poems we will study, Shelley's political concerns take on a wider historical scope. In their approach to the lives of the great figures of the past, Romantic writers and artists often seemed to be in search of imaginative equivalents for the factual accounts being written by historians. And Shelley in particular demonstrates a consciousness of his own period as one in which the tide of history was turning. As he wrote in the 'Preface' to his poem *Laon and Cythna*, published in 1817:

> There is a reflux in the tide of human things which bears the shipwrecked hopes of men into a secure haven, after the storms are past. Methinks those who now live have survived an age of despair.
>
> (Leader and O'Neill (eds), 2003, p. 132)

'Ozymandias' (written in 1817) and the later poem 'Written on the News of Hearing of the Death of Napoleon' (1821) combine these two aspects of the Romantic awareness of history, and construct a new role for the poet as witness to historical process.

'Ozymandias' and 'Written on Hearing the News of the Death of Napoleon'

'Ozymandias' takes its inspiration from Shelley's encounter with a giant piece of Egyptian sculpture, the head and shoulders of Emperor Ramses II, dating from *c*.1250 BCE. The fragment was moved to London from Egypt in 1817 and presented to the British Museum, where it remains to this day (see British Museum, 2010). As an object of imperial origins, the sculpture's display in London reminded viewers both of Napoleon's imperial ambitions, and of British imperial power now in the ascendancy across the world. The first Egyptian objects to appear in London had been originally destined for one of Napoleon's pet projects, the Louvre in Paris, but were seized from the French as the spoils of war. And the fact that British-funded collectors could now commandeer and import Egyptian objects with impunity was testimony to renewed British power in the Mediterranean.

Activity 6

Read 'Ozymandias' (Reading 2.5) and 'Written on Hearing the News of the Death of Napoleon' (Reading 2.6). Think about the poems in relation to the photograph of the sculpture in Figure 2.2.

What images of power do the poems and photograph present? How is the poet-speaker positioned in the poems? How do you think Shelley conceived of their function?

Discussion

Both the poems and the sculpture itself represent a figure of immense worldly stature. The size of the statue, hard to conceive unless you are standing in front of it, is colossal. This fragment alone is 2.5 metres high and weighs over seven tons. Ramses' unbending gaze, unconventionally sculpted 'so that the eyes appear to look down towards the viewer' (British Museum, 2010), conveys a sense of domination and control. The two poems look back on emperors whose rule was marked by terror: Napoleon's 'fierce spirit rolled' (l. 34) in wealth and bloodshed; Ozymandias governed with a 'sneer of cold command' (l. 5). But in each case the image of power is linked to ideas of ruin, fragmentation and erasure of past grandeur. The sculpture of Ramses is obviously damaged (the hole on the right shoulder was

Figure 2.2   Ramses II, the 'Younger Memnon', British Museum, London.
Photo: © The Trustees of the British Museum.

made by Napoleon's army when they attempted unsuccessfully to remove the sculpture from its Egyptian tomb). The face of the statue of Ozymandias lies 'shattered' on the sand. And Napoleon's rule is metaphorically labelled as 'a torrent of ruin' (l. 36). The deliberate discrepancy of scale between 'Ozymandias' as a conspicuously short poem and the vastness of the inspiring sculpture is dramatised as an ironic inscription within the sonnet: 'Look on my Works, ye Mighty, and despair!' (l. 11).

In both poems, the first-person speaker plays a marginal, almost journalistic role. The 'I' in 'Ozymandias' is presented simply as a listener, hearing the traveller's tale. 'Written on Hearing the News of the Death of Napoleon' is constructed as an interview, in which the personified figure of Earth responds in this final stanza to earlier questions from the poet-speaker. Again, therefore, the narrating voice of the poem is confined at this stage to a passive, listening role. The function of the poems seems to be to represent power on a grand scale, but at the same time take a wide historical view of that power, and record its limits. Shelley places his fragments of Ozymandias in an imaginary landscape of long vistas and a lost past: 'Nothing beside remains' (l. 12).

The erasure of these omnipotent figures is, of course, not complete in either the poems or the sculpture itself. The finely carved contours of Ramses' face are sharply preserved. The statue of Ozymandias may be reduced to decay, its fragments almost lost in the desolate landscape as the 'lone and level sands stretch far away' (l. 14), but the 'passions' of the ruler still survive in his sculpted expression. And while Napoleon's empire may have disappeared, those who follow him are invited by Earth to 'mould' his memory so that its hopes remain interwoven with its shame. Intermixed with the poems' vision of political ambition as tyrannical and transitory is a kind of admiration for the 'glory' of powerful figures whose memory will never be entirely effaced.

We noted at the start of this section that Shelley may have been striving through poetry of this sort to achieve an imaginative equivalent for the work of historians. The poems themselves consciously record and comment upon two world-historical events – the collapse of empires. And the attitudes they express quite possibly resonated in the minds of their original readers with one of the major historical works of the late eighteenth century, Edward Gibbon's *The Decline and Fall of the Roman Empire* (1776–89), still very widely read in Shelley's own time. It has been argued, for example, that Gibbon's 'final verdict on the Western [Roman] Empire was that "the story of its ruin is simple and obvious … the natural and inevitable effect of immoderate greatness"' (quoted in Pocock, 1977, p. 290). Equally, for Gibbon, 'no theory of human progress could be constructed which did not carry the negative implication that progress was at the same time decay … that what multiplied human capabilities also fractured the unity of human personality' (Pocock, 1977, pp. 292–3).

Gibbon's ideas about how an empire's 'immoderate greatness' and progress led to inevitable fracture and decay reverberate through the vocabulary of the two poems. In this context, Shelley may have been suggesting in poetic terms that the political disruption in Europe in the years around 1820 was taking place in a historical period in which heroism and a search for ideals coexisted with crisis and the end of an era.

How do these poems represent the role of the poet, therefore? Is it necessarily a less political role than the one we've met in the radical poems of 1819? Rather than adopting a strategy of direct attack, 'Ozymandias' offers a detached and seemingly objective scrutiny. The sonnet employs three nested levels of narration, with Ozymandias's own words nesting inside the traveller's story, which itself nests inside the words of the narrating 'I'. The effect is one of distancing, with – unusually – no sense of Shelley himself as a dramatised presence in the poem. In 'Written on Hearing the News of the Death of Napoleon' both voices are more fully characterised. The narrator begins by challenging Earth, demanding to know if the world can continue now Napoleon is gone: 'canst thou move, Napoleon being dead?' (l. 8). There is a hint of the insistent, rhetorical version of Shelley we've heard before here. But it is the voice of Earth which is invested with real vigour, its language taking on a remarkable energy in heavy rhymes and monosyllables:

> 'Still alive and still bold,' shouted Earth,
>   'I grow bolder and still more bold.
>   The dead fill me ten thousand fold…'

(ll. 25–8)

In this and the preceding stanza, Earth speaks through metaphors of renewal, which might remind us of the qualified optimism of 'Ode to the West Wind': 'the quick spring like weeds out of the dead' (l. 24); 'by the spirit of the mighty dead / My heart grew warm' (ll. 31–2). And we can't overlook the fact that the words 'hopes' and 'glory' appear in the final line of this poem about a fallen dictator. So there is some space in this narrative for the idealism which underpins the radical politics that surface openly in poems like 'Sonnet: England in 1819'.

The agency of the poet in these examples, however, is largely unacknowledged: the 'I' in 'Ozymandias' listens silently to the tale of fallen glory; and Earth shouts down the speaker's peremptory questions about Napoleon: 'It is thou who art overbold' (l. 19). In his emphatic conclusion to his essay *A Defence of Poetry*, written in 1821, Shelley claimed that this witnessing role for the poet, at a critical moment in English history, was the most important of all:

> our own will be a memorable age, and we live among such philosophers and poets as surpass beyond comparison any who have appeared since the last national struggle for civil and religious liberty. The most unfailing herald, companion, or follower of the awakening of a great people to work a beneficial change in opinion or institution, is poetry. ... Poets are the hierophants of an unapprehended inspiration; the mirrors of the gigantic shadows which futurity casts upon the present; the words which express what they understand not; the trumpets which sing to battle and feel not what they inspire; the influence which is moved not, but moves. Poets are the unacknowledged legislators of the world.
>
> (Leader and O'Neill (eds), 2003, p. 701)

As we have seen earlier, Shelley's political reputation is bound up in myth-making; and he is certainly mythologising the role of the poet here. But the evidence of these two poems has shown that it is not necessarily when the voice of the poet as speaker is heard most loudly that this 'awakening', legislative role Shelley conceived for poetry is at its most effective. And you may well conclude – along with many other readers – that 'Ozymandias' is among the most successful of Shelley's political poems.

A life in pursuit of the ideal

Our investigation of Shelley's diverse explorations of the poet's role will conclude with a poem which once again underpins his nineteenth-century reputation as the poet of extreme landscapes. 'Mont Blanc' explores those extremes in search of something beyond the ordinary, political or historical world: a pursuit of the ideal. The irony of the poem is that the imaginative endeavour of the archetypal Romantic quester may well be the end in itself: the ideal is not necessarily attained.

'Mont Blanc'

'Mont Blanc' was written in 1816, after the Shelleys visited the Vale of Chamouni (also known as Chamonix) on 23 July, en route for Lake Geneva. The River Arve spills down the ravines of this valley towards the lake. This first encounter with the Alps foreshadowed one of the settings for Mary Shelley's novel *Frankenstein* (1818), as she recorded: 'Never was a scene more awfully desolate … the vast expanse of snow was chequered only by … gigantic pines, and the poles that marked our road' (quoted in Holmes, 1987, p. 323). And the mountains themselves exceeded the reach of Shelley's own imagination, as he wrote:

> Pinnacles of snow, intolerably bright, part of the chain connected with Mont Blanc shone through the clouds at intervals on high. I never knew I never imagined [*sic*] what mountains were before. The immensity of these ariel summits excited when they burst suddenly upon the sight, a sentiment of extatic [*sic*] wonder, not unallied to madness.
>
> (Shelley quoted in Holmes, 1987, p. 339)

Shelley's emotional reaction here is framed in the terms of the **sublime**, a key concept for eighteenth- and nineteenth-century thinking about the imagination. The sublime involves landscapes or situations which elicit from the observer a state of awareness combining fear, admiration and awe. Shelley's contemporary, the Romantic poet Byron (1788–1824), explained the concept in Canto 3 of his narrative poem *Childe Harold's Pilgrimage* (composed in the summer of the same year, and inspired by a similar trip within the Alps). Sublimity, Byron tells us, 'expands the spirit, yet appals'; and the observer who is sensitive enough to experience it learns 'how earth may pierce to Heaven, yet leave vain man below' (Byron, 2000, p. 123).

The first-person speaker of 'Mont Blanc' is constructed as just such a sensitive observer: the raw experience of the mountains he evokes in the first three verse paragraphs prompts his mind to the insights which then dominate the final two sections.

Activity 7

'Mont Blanc' has been reproduced as Reading 2.7 at the end of this part of the book. Shelley wrote more than one version of this poem, and it is Version A we are using here. Read it now, trying to let its breakneck momentum carry you through any passages which may seem complex or obscure.

Focus on the opening verse paragraph of the poem and consider the following questions:

1 How would you characterise the syntax (the sentence structure) of these eleven lines? What are its effects?

2 The first six lines do not so much describe the landscape of the River Arve as use it as a metaphor. To what is the river compared?

3 What does this combination of syntax and metaphor suggest about the relationship of the perceiving mind to the extreme landscape of the external world?

Discussion

1 You probably spotted that these lines form a single, fast-moving sentence, broken by one or two pauses marked by colons or semi-colons. Rarely do these pauses occur at the ends of lines. Thus, you can see how the tumultuous flow of the language imitates the flow of the turbulent river.

2 In the first six lines, the river is compared to the fluid and changeable impressions of the outer world which 'flow through the mind'. Their impact is alternately depressing and uplifting. A second metaphor is introduced from line 4 onwards, where 'human thought' is likened to a 'feeble brook' which takes on the sound of its dramatic Alpine surroundings.

3 There is a sense that the human mind, conceived at this stage in abstract terms, is carried away by the force of the world around it, just as the syntax whirls us on past the line endings. The power of thought is at risk of being overwhelmed and dwarfed by the immensity of the external universe it seeks to grasp: the landscape of the 'rapid waves' and vast, bursting river.

The intensity and immediacy of feeling here are characteristic of the discourse of the sublime, as are vocabulary items like 'vast', 'wild' and 'splendour'. In the second and third sections of the poem, too, the strength of feeling generates a syntax which seems on the verge of losing control. The ravine as the main subject of the exceptionally long sentence, which extends from line 12 to the exclamation mark in line 34, is hard to keep track of. And the idea that the first-person speaker is gaining knowledge and insight from this experience is qualified by the bewildering quality of this syntax: a linguistic equivalent, perhaps, of Shelley's 'ecstatic wonder, not unallied to madness' quoted earlier.

Activity 8

Now consider the second and third verse paragraphs of 'Mont Blanc' in more detail, focusing your attention on those sections which feature the first-person 'I'. In what terms is the poet-speaker represented here, and how and what does the landscape teach him? What happens when his eye turns from the river to the summit of the mountain?

Discussion

Initially the condition of the speaker appears to be one of trance-like self-absorption. He muses in an 'unforeseeing' way on his own 'wild thoughts' and 'separate fantasy' (ll. 41 and 36). And at the start of the third section, the 'gleams' of the ideal world he seeks are clouded by a death-like state of sleep and dream to the extent that 'the very spirit fails' (l. 57). Poetry is capable of rendering only a 'faint image' of the greater truth, confined as it is like a witch in a 'still cave' (ll. 44 and 47).

In line 60, the clouds disperse to reveal the mountain peak: 'Far, far above, piercing the infinite sky', and described again in terms of the 'unearthly', 'unfathomable' sublime (ll. 62 and 64). Unlike the whirling chaos of the river in its ravine, the pinnacle of the mountain represents an ideal which compels attention and stabilises the imaginative perception of the speaker: 'all seems eternal now' (l. 75). The language of the high peaks teaches a 'simple' and 'serene' faith in nature: a faith which arguably displaces that of religious systems:

> Thou hast a voice, great Mountain, to repeal
> Large codes of fraud and woe; not understood
> By all, but which the wise, and great, and good
> Interpret, or make felt, or deeply feel.

> (ll. 80–4)

The Shelley notorious for his atheism and political radicalism perhaps makes an appearance in the reference to repealing 'large codes of fraud and woe'. But more important is the unspoken implication that Romantic poets themselves are among the 'wise and good' who can understand and interpret the voice of the mountain. They have the power not only to 'feel' its inspiring message, but to make the message felt by others. You can see how the views later expressed in *A Defence of Poetry* have begun to take shape here.

These opening sections of the poem seem to show Shelley consciously creating a difficult and fragmented poetry, to embody the difficulty of the quest for the ideal. The experience of the ravine and the mountain peak convey a sense of the mutually coexisting chaos, extreme possibilities and potential rewards of the Romantic life. Such concerns re-emerge in the final verse paragraph, where the attention turns from the 'secret strength' of the mountain to the 'imaginings' of the poet-figure's mind:

> And what were thou, and earth, and stars, and sea,
> If to the human mind's imaginings
> Silence and solitude were vacancy?

> (ll. 142–4)

The speculation here is that the enigma of Mont Blanc depends in the last analysis not on the mountain itself, but on the receptive mental state of those who experience it. The grandeurs of nature are conferred by the human mind itself, responding actively to silence and solitude. 'Mont Blanc' thus seems to conclude that the poet's role is to quest after extremes of mental experience, and uncover for others the ideals and ultimate truths inherent in them. This vision of the Romantic vocation suggests that such intellectual pinnacles exist to be scaled, through the creative power of the poetic imagination.

Conclusion

Shelley and his poet-speakers have featured in this chapter in a wide range of guises. Along with the ethereal spirit, the political protester, the angry father and the literary intellectual, we've encountered the witness to history, the angst-ridden creative artist, and the quester after ideals. All have their origins in Shelley's life, whether projected in his own voice through letters or notes or verse, or recounted by others such as his friends, wife or literary executors. But none renders his Romantic life into a single coherent story. The edited image of that life which survived for the whole of the nineteenth century was readily redrawn in the twentieth.

At times, as in 'Ode to the West Wind', these shifting poetic selves intermix in an individual poem. At other times, as in 'England in 1819', one version clearly predominates. But rarely do the many manifestations of Shelley the poet coalesce into an instant of wholeness. It is perhaps too soon to predict what the twenty-first century Shelley will look like. Possibly a green Shelley will emerge from the investigative work of eco-criticism (Morton, 2006, p. 203), with the vegetarian author re-versioned as an early environmentalist. But then, as now, there will always be multiple Shelleys for you to negotiate and enjoy.

References

Allen, R. (2000) 'Mary Shelley as editor of the poems of Percy Shelley' in Bellamy, J., Laurence, A. and Perry, G. (eds) *Women, Scholarship and Criticism: Gender and Knowledge 1790–1900*, Manchester, Manchester University Press, pp. 77–90.

Anonymous correspondent (1821) 'Queen Mab', *The Times*, 11 December, issue 11,426, p. 2.

Anonymous correspondent (1826) 'Court of Chancery, Friday, Feb. 24 Wellesley V. The Duke of Beaufort', *The Times*, 25 February, issue 12,900, p. 3.

Bailey, J.C. (1911) *Poets and Poetry: Being Articles Reprinted from the Literary Supplement of 'The Times'*, Oxford, Clarendon Press.

British Museum (2010) 'Colossal bust of Ramesses II, the "Younger Memnon"' [online], London, British Museum, http://www.britishmuseum.org/explore/highlights/highlight_objects/aes/c/colossal_bust_of_ramesses_ii.aspx (Accessed 21 September 2010).

Byron, Lord G. (2000 [1986]) *Byron: The Major Works* (ed. J. McGann), Oxford, Oxford University Press.

Foot, P. (1984 [1980]) *Red Shelley*, London, Bookmarks Publications.

Foot, P. (1992) 'Poetry of protest', *Socialist Review*, no. 155, pp. 18–20.

Holmes, R. (1987) *Shelley: The Pursuit*, London, Penguin.

Leader, Z. and O'Neill, M. (eds) (2003) *Percy Bysshe Shelley: The Major Works*, Oxford, Oxford University Press.

Milton, J. (1971 [1667]) *Paradise Lost* (ed. A. Fowler), Harlow, Longman.

Morton, T. (2006) 'Nature and culture' in *The Cambridge Companion to Shelley*, *Cambridge Collections Online* [online], Cambridge University Press, http://cco.cambridge.org.libezproxy.open.ac.uk/uid=1060/extract?id= ccol0521826047_CCOL0521826047A014 (Accessed 18 September 2010).

Pocock, J.G.A. (1977) 'Gibbon's decline and fall and the world view of the late enlightenment', *Eighteenth Century Studies*, vol. 10, no. 3, pp. 287–303.

Shakespeare, W. (1997 [1611]) *The Tempest* in Greenblatt, S. et al. (eds) *The Norton Shakespeare*, London, Norton, pp. 3055–107.

Shelley, M. (1904 [1839]) 'Preface and notes to the Complete Poetical Works of Percy Bysshe Shelley', in Hutchinson, T. (ed.) *Poetical Works of Shelley*, Oxford, Clarendon Press.

Further reading

Chandler, J. (1998) *England in 1819: The Politics of Literary Culture and the Case of Romantic Historicism*, Chicago, Chicago University Press.

Honour, H. (1991) *Romanticism*, London, Penguin.

Chapter 3
Thomas De Quincey: journalist in the city

Nicola J. Watson

Aims

This chapter will:

- introduce you to ways of reading the Romantic non-fictional prose essay
- explore the representation of the Romantic self and life through an autobiographical prose text, *Confessions of an English Opium-Eater*
- discuss this text in relation to the professionalisation of the Romantic author within the periodical culture of the 1820s.

Introduction

In 1821, one year before Shelley was drowned, the thirty-six-year-old Thomas De Quincey (1785–1859), debt-ridden and drug-dependent, was sitting in a London coffee house, drafting and redrafting an essay on odd bits and pieces of coffee-stained paper. What purported to be the autobiographical 'Confessions of an English Opium-Eater' subsequently appeared in two instalments in one of the leading periodicals of the day, *The London Magazine* (see Figure 3.1). So sensationally successful were these essays with the *London*'s readership that De Quincey was pressed to bring out a third instalment. Instead, in the following year, he published the first two episodes in a collected and slightly expanded form (with an appendix explaining 'the non-appearance of a third Part') as a small free-standing book. Like the initial instalments, this was brought out anonymously. The *Confessions* would subsequently undergo revision, expansion and elaboration for publication in 1856 in De Quincey's fourteen-volume compilation of his essays, *Selections Grave and Gay* (1853–60). This later, much longer, version amounts to a Victorian reflection on a late Romantic text; so, in keeping with our emphasis upon authorship in the Romantic period, we are going to concentrate here on the 1821 version, reproduced in its entirety as Reading 3.1. You can either choose to read this all in one sitting now, or to stage your reading of it as you work through the sections of this chapter.

The *Confessions of an English Opium-Eater* would in fact be the only free-standing book De Quincey himself ever published. It launched him on a long career as a professional journalist on a wide variety of subjects literary, philosophical and scientific, first with *The London Magazine* and, later, with *Blackwood's Magazine*, once he moved to Edinburgh in 1830. The persona that he created in them of 'the Opium-Eater' would define De Quincey's autobiographical writing from then on; he would publish 'Notes from the Pocket book of a late Opium-Eater' in 1823, 'Sketches … from the Autobiography of an English Opium-Eater' as 'Autobiographic Sketches' between 1834 and 1841, a sequel or extension to the *Confessions*, 'Suspiria de Profundis' in 1845, and finally, the essay 'The English Mail-Coach' in 1854.

In considering the *Confessions*, it seems at first as though we are in a completely different world from that of Wordsworth and Shelley. With the poets we have been exploring a rarefied world of consciously elevated poetic and philosophic ambition and vocation, expressed in 'high' forms such as the blank verse epic and the ode. With them we have been frequenting places felt by those poets to be particularly beautiful and powerful, one of them exemplifying a sense of national pastoral, the other a European sublime. Both Wordsworth and Shelley in their different ways consciously, explicitly and defiantly refused to write to the taste of the contemporary public, insisting either that their work would 'create the taste by which they were to be judged' (Wordsworth, 1974 [1815], p. 80) or that it would have power in the future – this is the force of Shelley's claim in his *A Defence of Poetry* that poets were 'the unacknowledged legislators of the world' (Shelley, 1965 [1840; written 1821], p. 140) and effectively the argument of his 'Ode to the West Wind' (1820). Neither Wordsworth nor Shelley, moreover, were dependent upon their writing to earn their livings: Shelley had a gentleman's independent income at his disposal and, as for Wordsworth, as De Quincey rather bitterly remarked in his 1838 biographical essay on his former idol and acquaintance for *Tait's Magazine*, his financial luck was phenomenal and rendered him independent from the approval of the public: 'at measured intervals throughout the long sequel of his life … a regular succession of … God-sends have fallen in, to sustain his expenditure, duly as it grew with the growing claims upon his purse' (1970 [1834–9], p. 194). In striking contrast, De Quincey was not, despite his early ambitions to be one, a poet. This ambition was what had drawn him to solicit the acquaintance of Wordsworth and his family in 1803 and eventually to move (with a due sense of discipleship) into Dove Cottage itself in 1809, bringing with him a library of 5,000 books and an intention to live as a gentleman scholar. Instead, having run through his own slender patrimony, he was forced into the inadequately paid profession of a hack journalist for the magazine market of the 1820s, based in the twin centres of writing and publishing throughout the entirety of the nineteenth century, Edinburgh and London. Although he had hoped to emulate Wordsworth's retirement in Grasmere, he ended up commuting between the Lake District and the metropolis in order to scrape a living. Studying De Quincey's periodical journalism thus provides a perspective on the nature and function of Romantic authorship that strongly contrasts with that imagined by either Wordsworth or Shelley.

The Romantic author and the marketplace

In the 1820s, contemporaries felt that the literary marketplace was changing dramatically. It now seemed particularly 'fast' and ephemeral, obsessed with celebrity and sensation. Much of this feeling arose from the expansion of periodical culture, which was rapidly building new reading audiences. Particularly influential were the two monthly literary magazines, *Blackwood's Edinburgh Magazine*, published from 1817 onwards in Edinburgh, and *The London Magazine*, which was revived in 1820 in conscious rivalry to *Blackwood's*. The struggle between these two publications was so intense and acrimonious that in 1821 it led to a duel in which the editor of the *London*, John Scott, was killed.

Writers had, since at least the late 1780s, been anxious about changes in the relation between writer and readership, a change driven largely by a large-scale shift from a system of patronage to a market-driven system. A particular focus of this anxiety had long been the novel, which was perceived as written mostly by women for women, and which was distributed to its ever-widening readership through the circulating libraries. Reviews from the 1780s onwards are filled with anxious references to the factory production of formula fiction. Indeed, the efforts of Wordsworth and Shelley, among others, to define the nature of the poet and the work of poetry were energised by their sense of a vastly expanded reading public with dubious taste formed by novel-reading. In the 1820s this sense of unease over the debasement of literature accelerated strongly, and can be found expressed even in those publications most intent on catering to their audience's likes and dislikes from month to month.

Activity 1

Read the following passage drawn from an anonymously authored essay entitled 'Fugitive literature'. This was published in the same issue of *The London Magazine* as the first instalment of the *Confessions*. It narrates how the author (who signs himself 'Thurma') meets a baronet in the streets of London and is invited home to view his 'Literary Museum' housed in 'An apartment of very goodly dimensions, elegantly furnished with carpeting of the first manufacture; chairs, tables, sofas etc; and the walls hung round with handsome wooden frames, partially gilt'. The passage describes what he sees in those frames. As you read, consider what it has to say about the state of modern literature.

On examining the frameful of rarities, I certainly did pronounce it one of the greatest curiosities I had ever beheld. Fragments of letters in various hands, and on various subjects, remnants of marriage settlements, wills, memorials, verse and blank verse, all arranged in admirable order, and carefully pasted on canvas, formed at once the strangest medley of style and subject … Indeed, whatever tended to awaken merriment, sympathy, amazement – in fine, every native emotion slumbering in the breast, was to be met with amongst this wonderful assemblage of originals.

(Anon., 1821, p. 50)

Discussion

There is perhaps an anxiety being expressed here about the flattening out of any hierarchy between types of writing in the marketplace – so private letters and legal documents (marriage settlements and wills) seem to have the same status as 'verse and blank verse', traditionally, as we've already seen, 'higher' forms of literature. You may have noticed, also, that the idea of the author as controlling genius is conspicuously absent; instead, the focus is on the activity of the *reader* as consumer, collector and connoisseur.

The essay goes on to make it clear that these scraps have not been acquired directly from their authors or even from a publisher or bookseller. In fact, they are recycled waste paper, rescued from having been used as mere wrapping paper by a variety of tradesmen, to become designated as 'literature' again. The papers that 'Thurma' excavates from one of the baronet's drawers of waste paper sourced from a trunk-maker include, much to his chagrin, one of Thurma's own early poems, 'an epistle from a fellow travelling the country with a dancing bear', a ballad in the manner of best-selling poet and novelist Sir Walter Scott (1771–1832), and a letter supposedly from an apprentice-poet to his father which tends to prove 'beyond the possibility of a doubt, that a certain class of men, hitherto deemed untameable as the wild ass's colt, have at length been reduced by the manufacturing system, and fairly brought under the yoke':

Master employs no less than fifteen hands, – nine of them ballad-makers – the rest attached to the dying-speech and elegy departments. ... Figure to yourself fifteen men of sublime genius, pacing to and fro on the factory floor; holding up the semblance of nether garments with one hand, a sketch-book in the other, – all of them 'rapt in meditation high'.

(Anon., 1821, p. 51)

This essay may be seen as a meditation upon the professionalised production of literature, which clearly stands in very ambivalent relation to poets, 'men of sublime genius' such as the Scottish ploughman poet Robert Burns, whose poem 'The Brigs of Ayr' (1786), describing a Bard 'rapt in meditation high', is quoted above. Poets here work to order, on an industrial scale. Nothing could be further from the self-depictions of Wordsworth and Shelley musing and enthusing in natural landscapes.

In imagining this literary museum, this essay also describes the nature of the contemporary periodical. The periodical was, after all, a compilation of various types of pieces, gaining power from the miscellaneousness and piquancy of their juxtapositions, aiming precisely at 'the strangest medley of style and subject' tending 'to awaken merriment, sympathy, amazement', and recycling private manuscripts for public consumption. *The London Magazine* offered just such a miscellany.

Activity 2

Look at Figure 3.1 (the title page of *The London Magazine* for October 1821). What does this list of contents suggest about what the editors of *The London Magazine* thought their readership would like?

Discussion

Two things strike me about this list of contents. The first is the sheer variety of *types* of writing included – ranging from the essay through to information on stocks and shares and an almanac (although, despite this variety, you might have noticed that no fictional prose is included). The second is that the bulk of this writing is anonymous or pseudonymous. It is branded not to authors, but to the magazine.

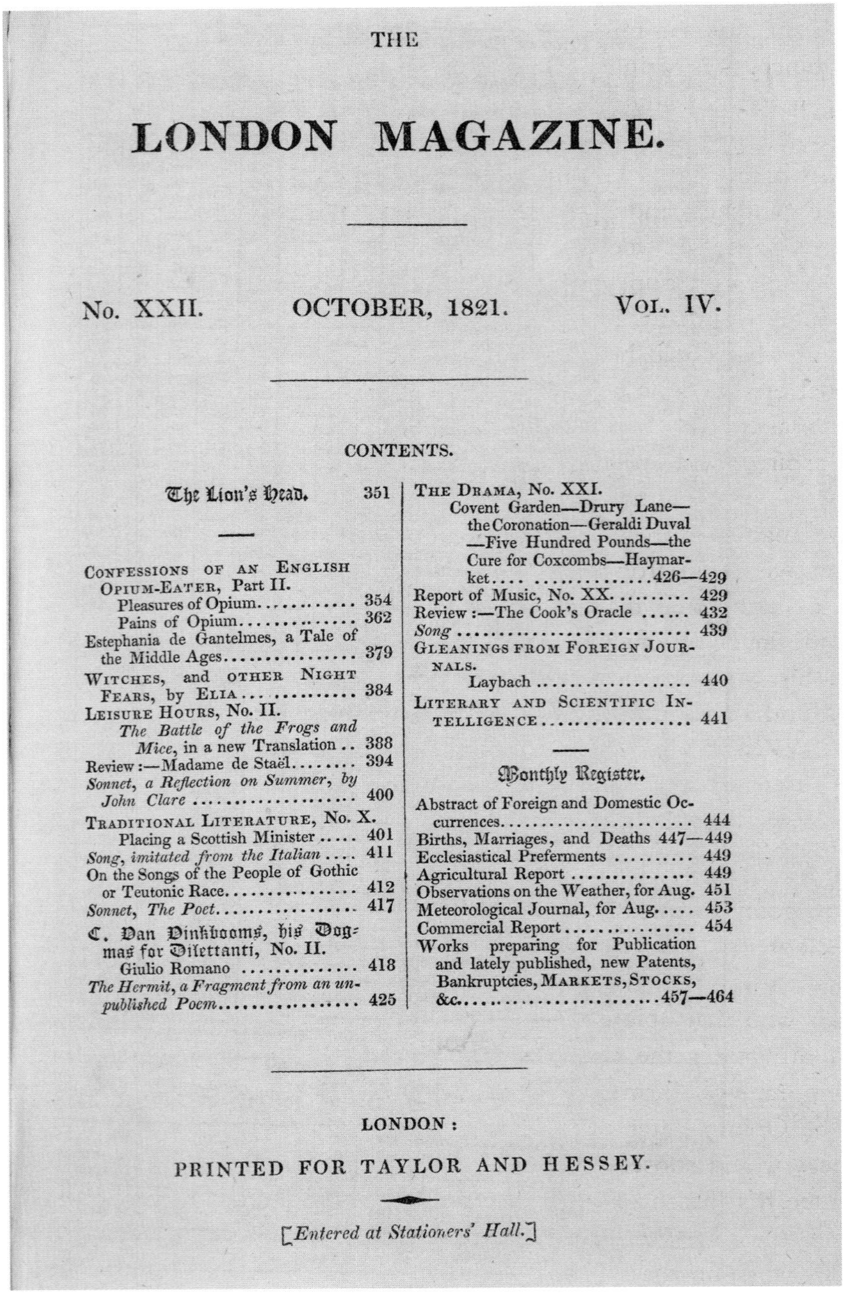

THE

LONDON MAGAZINE.

No. XXII.   OCTOBER, 1821.   VOL. IV.

CONTENTS.

LONDON :

PRINTED FOR TAYLOR AND HESSEY.

[Entered at Stationers' Hall.]

Figure 3.1   Table of contents, listing Part 2 of the *Confessions of an English Opium-Eater, The London Magazine*, vol. 4, no. 22, October 1821. Bodleian Library, Oxford per 3977 e. 215/4. Photo: Bodleian Libraries.

This, then, was the milieu within which the would-be Romantic poet De Quincey was writing. Although this milieu professionalised the writer, it did not automatically grant him celebrity status, certainly did not grant him status as a man of genius, and it did not pay well either. Charles Lamb (1775–1834), known as 'Elia', author of the essay entitled 'Witches; and other Night-Fears' that also appears on this contents page, was very celebrated as a periodical essayist but was never able to give up his income from his day job as a clerk at the East India Company. Moreover, the periodical medium dictated the form of what could be written for it. The *London* did not publish national epic or lyric ode. Rather, its writers specialised in the occasional essay. ('Occasional' in this usage does not mean 'infrequent' but 'inspired by a specific occasion'.) The essay form was perceived as 'lower', unstably hybrid, deliberately 'curious' or unusual in subject matter, more consciously ephemeral, explicitly experimental, and, above all, metropolitan. The periodical medium also dictated the form of authorship that the writer could occupy; while Wordsworth, after the initial anonymous publication of the *Lyrical Ballads*, wrote under his own increasingly well-respected name, De Quincey here writes under the alias of 'the Opium-Eater' and signs himself only 'XYZ'.

The Opium-Eater introduced

We are going to make a start on reading the *Confessions* by looking at the persona that De Quincey constructs in 'the Opium-Eater', and how it relates to his audience. It is important not to mix up De Quincey as **author** with the Opium-Eater as **first-person narrator** (the 'I' who is apparently telling the story). This is tempting, of course, because the autobiographical form of the text can seem to claim that De Quincey and the Opium-Eater are one and the same person and because De Quincey would subsequently use 'The Opium-Eater' as a byline. It is also true that much of this material verifiably finds its roots in De Quincey's own experience. But I suggest that for the sake of clarity, as in your work on the self-projections of both Wordsworth and Shelley, you think of the Opium-Eater as a constructed persona, and of De Quincey as the author who constructs that persona, and gets paid for doing so.

Activity 3

If you have not already done so, read the opening section of De Quincey's *Confessions* (reproduced in Reading 3.1), beginning 'To the Reader'. Stop when you get to the heading 'Preliminary confessions'. As you read, make notes on the following questions:

1   What does the Opium-Eater assert and imply about his imagined reader?

2   What information does the Opium-Eater convey about himself both directly (through statement) and indirectly (through implication)?

3   What sort of text does the Opium-Eater suggest this is going to be?

Discussion

1   The Opium-Eater begins by addressing his reader directly and formally ('To the Reader') and describes the reader as 'courteous'. In selling his story to the magazine readership, he flatteringly implies that the reader is desirous of the 'interesting', the 'useful', and the 'instructive' (p. 230). Even as he actually appeals to mere prurient curiosity in the trailing of 'the public exposure of our own errors and infirmities' (p. 230), he also suggests pleasingly that the reader will have such delicate sensibilities, such an especially English sense of 'propriety', and be so 'decent and self-respecting', as to revolt from the mere sensationalism of an account (which actually turns out not to be) of '[g]uilt and misery' (p. 230). By including numerous and various allusions and quotations, he intimates that he expects his reader will be of a high level of education – indeed, by including classical quotations, he more than half suggests that his ideal reader is a man, because the generality of women did not have access to a classical education.

2   The Opium-Eater represents himself as 'English', and as 'a scholar'. In distancing himself from 'demireps, adventurers, or swindlers' (p. 230), more usual authors of 'confessions', he by implication classes himself as a gentleman, a 'philosopher' and an intellectual, not a hack (a writerly analogue to a prostitute or conman) writing for money. Under the guise of describing 'the whole class of opium-eaters' (pp. 231–2), he shamelessly name-drops, claiming acquaintance with the great and the good. As he cites his evidence and statistics, he also represents himself as a scholar of and expert in the phenomenon of his own addiction and of opium addiction generally, an investigative journalist even, rather than a mere anecdotalist. You may have noticed, too, his extensive use of quotation and allusion, which proves his familiarity with the poetry of Wordsworth and suggests he can read French, German and ancient

Greek. What the Opium-Eater doesn't do (and will continue not to do), is provide himself with a name, retaining a teasing anonymity.

3   The Opium-Eater is concerned to make plain what these 'confessions' are *not* going to be: they are not going to be 'gratuitous acts of self-humiliation' in a 'French' or 'German' style (p. 230), and they are not going to be like the money-making confessions of 'demireps, adventurers or swindlers'. Instead, the *Confessions* are going to be discreet (this is just 'an extract'), scientific, and, crucially, useful and instructive – they will have 'a moral'.

With this last statement, De Quincey sets up a space for his writing that carefully distances it from two sorts of writing to which it is undoubtedly allied. The first is the autobiography of the French philosopher Jean-Jacques Rousseau, simply entitled his *Confessions*, published in 1782. We've already come across this text in connection with Wordsworth. In it Rousseau famously described his youthful amatory experiences with unprecedented candour and in brilliant and fervid language. The influence of the *Confessions*, together with Rousseau's novel about forbidden love, *Julie; ou, La Nouvelle Héloïse* (1761), inspired a vogue for the display of 'passion' in fiction and in real life. In the 1790s such Rousseauistic self-indulgence was widely blamed by conservative writers for both the outbreak and the failure of the French Revolution. By the 1820s Rousseau could seem both unprincipled and out of date – hence perhaps De Quincey's disavowal. The second sort of writing that De Quincey is distancing himself from is a class of writings which was selling well in London at the time; a representative sample of this might be the *Memoirs* published by the courtesan Harriette Wilson (1786–1845) a little later and very lucratively in 1825, which exposed her various affairs with the good and the great (including Arthur Wellesley, the Duke of Wellington (1769–1852)) to fascinated public scrutiny. De Quincey promises his readers, then, that *his* confessions will be more modern than previous scandalous types of memoirs, suggests that they may pleasingly outdo earlier works for sensation, and provides a fig-leaf for the pleasures of sensationalist reading in the shape of a moral pay-off.

In the next section of De Quincey's *Confessions*, entitled 'Preliminary confessions', the Opium-Eater begins by amplifying this description of what his confessions will do: they will provide an autobiographical narrative of how he came to be addicted to opium; they will provide a 'key' to his later dreams; and they will create 'some previous interest of a personal sort in the confessing subject ... which cannot fail to render the confessions themselves more interesting' (p. 234). Of these, the last justification is especially interesting, because it suggests the way in which De Quincey begins to craft a celebrity persona in the Opium-Eater.

Activity 4

Continue your reading of De Quincey's *Confessions* (Reading 3.1) by reading the section entitled 'Preliminary confessions' on p. 233 (stopping when you get to the heading 'Part 2' on p. 262). Make some notes on how 'the Opium-Eater' characterises himself.

Discussion

The Opium-Eater

1   'boasteth himself to be a philosopher' (p. 234). This sort of 'philosopher' combines the analytical abilities of someone like Samuel Taylor Coleridge, whom he explicitly cites, and something more akin to the poet Wordsworth's abilities: 'such a constitution of the *moral* faculties, as shall give him an inner eye and power of intuition for the vision and the mysteries of our human nature: *that* constitution of faculties, in short, which (amongst all the generations of men that from the beginning of time have deployed into life, as it were, upon this planet) our English poets have possessed in the highest degree ...' (pp. 234–5). This constitution means that 'the phantasmagoria of *his* dreams (waking or sleeping, day-dreams or night-dreams)' is exceptional, not mundane ('of oxen') (p. 234).

2   describes himself as serially abandoned and intermittently oppressed by his guardians, and (eventually) by all subsequent households through which he passes; he presents himself as an intellectually precocious 'scholar' – compounded of irritable class pride in his status (the son of a merchant) and social connections, and pride in his ability to converse with men and women of all classes; he seems oppressed by an obscure sense of guilt, crime and sin, although this appears in the shape of his continuous self-exculpations; he appears sexually susceptible if not sexually active, obsessed with a series of lost and conjecturally dead women ranging from the portrait at school which he kisses in farewell, through to the ten-year-old girl whom he befriends, to Ann, the Oxford Street prostitute.

3   describes himself as deeply nostalgic, preoccupied by the relation and contrast between past and present selves, as his description of revisiting the house off Oxford Street pinpoints:

> For myself, I never fail to visit it when business draws me to London; about ten o'clock, this very night, August 15, 1821, being my birth-day – I turned aside from my evening walk, down Oxford-street, purposely to take a glance at it: it is now occupied by a respectable family. … Marvellous contrast in my eyes to the darkness – cold – silence – and desolation of that same house eighteen years ago, when its nightly occupants were one famishing scholar, and a neglected child (p. 248).

Note also his revisiting of places associated with Ann (p. 249).

4   describes himself as an object of the reader's curiosity and speculation. He engages in a conversational flirtation with the implied reader: 'Here let me stop for a moment to check my reader from any erroneous conclusions …' (p. 259).

To sum up, so far De Quincey has been setting up a relationship between author and reader that is particularly flattering to both. In fact, throughout the piece, De Quincey will pique the reader's curiosity about the Opium-Eater, making confessional gestures and then withholding his identity. Nowhere is this plainer than in this later passage in which he commissions an imaginary painter to paint the interior of his cottage:

> I admit that, naturally, I ought to occupy the foreground of the picture; that being the hero of the piece, or (if you choose) the criminal at the bar, my body should be had into court. This seems reasonable: but why should I confess, on this point, to a painter? or why confess at all? If the public (into whose private ear I am confidentially whispering my confessions, and not into any painter's) should chance to have framed some agreeable picture for itself, of the Opium-eater's exterior, – should have ascribed to him, romantically, an elegant person, or a handsome face, why should I barbarously tear from it so pleasing a delusion – pleasing both to the public and to me? No: paint me, if at all, according to your own fancy …
>
> (p. 288)

Figure 3.2   Sir John Watson Gordon, *Thomas De Quincey*, 1846, oil on canvas, 76 × 64 cm. Scottish National Portrait Gallery, PG 1116.

If you still wish, after this sort of teasing, to know what the real De Quincey actually looked like, his portrait is shown in Figure 3.2.

In the passage above, De Quincey can be seen constructing his readership, a necessity in the face of a large and anonymous paying audience. This is a situation quite different from that which, for example, Wordsworth postulates in all the versions of *The Prelude* and *The Recluse*, which are explicitly and conversationally addressed to a single close poet friend and equal, Samuel Taylor Coleridge. Confessing one's past life to a close friend requires much less justification than baring all to a paying public – hence De Quincey's self-imaging in the passage above as the subject of a painting on public exhibition, or as a criminal in court, only to erase these images in favour of an image of himself whispering confidentially into the private ear of, paradoxically, 'the public'. Confessions here are laundered as sufficiently 'private' by the physical invisibility offered by writing and the authorial anonymity enforced by the culture of the periodical. But the passage also suggests that it is very tricky indeed to attempt a 'character-sketch' of 'the Opium-Eater' because he is composed of all the things he says he might be, but perhaps is not (is he the 'hero of the piece'? Is he a 'criminal at the bar'? Is he 'handsome'?). His identity metamorphoses all the time. As we read through the later sections of the text, this flirtation and speculation slowly reveals its nightmare side, the progressive disintegration of a stable sense of the self.

As our reading of the text so far might suggest, the persona of the Opium-Eater is as much a matter of style as substance. In the next activity we are going to take a closer look at De Quincey's style.

Activity 5

Now turn to 'Part 2' of De Quincey's *Confessions* (Reading 3.1). Read the first paragraph, and consider the following questions:

1 How would you characterise the length and structure of De Quincey's sentences?

2 How would you describe De Quincey's choice of voice, diction and vocabulary?

Discussion

You might have come up with some of the following observations:

1 De Quincey's sentences are very long (this entire paragraph is composed of only four sentences). They are structurally complicated – developed to that length by the use of semi-colons and colons, dividing the sentence up into statement and further repetition and elaboration (e.g. 'the storm which I had outlived seemed to have been the pledge of a long fair-weather; the premature sufferings which I had paid down, to have been accepted as a ransom for many years to come' (p. 262)). They are also extended by parallel clauses (e.g. 'with a fortitude more confirmed, with the resources of a maturer intellect, and with alleviations from sympathising affection' (p. 263)).

2 The voice is mostly grandiose. You might have noticed that to produce his grandiose effects De Quincey adopts archaic diction and

rhythms meant to be reminiscent of the King James Bible; an example of this would be 'thou that listenest to the sighs of orphans, and drinkest the tears of children' (p. 262). His vocabulary tends to the emotionally extreme: 'sighs', tears', 'anguish', 'pangs', 'calamities', 'groans', 'storm', 'sufferings', 'sorrow', 'noxious'; these are strongly contrasted, often in the same sentence, with images of 'fair-weather', 'immunity', 'serenity' and 'peace of mind' and 'ransom'.

De Quincey's style is characterised by grandeur and sensationalism. It employs rhetorical strategies more commonly found in poetry than in prose such as apostrophe and personification ('So then, Oxford-street, stony-hearted step-mother!' (p. 262)). It deploys sensationally violent juxtapositions of tone, subject and image. It switches between the humorous, the sentimental, the reportorial, the satiric, the conversational, the suspenseful, the bawdy, the teasing, the refined and the sublime. Reproducing the schizoid miscellany of the periodical form, it was calculated to engage an audience, who, in modern terms, might be regarded as having a shorter attention span than the reader of epic verse.

The persona that De Quincey creates through this style is a world away from that of the writer he most admired, Wordsworth. The difference can be brought into sharp relief by trying to imagine how very differently De Quincey would have written up the episode of the drowned man in *The Prelude* that we looked at in Chapter 1. The *Confessions* are nevertheless deeply engaged with *The Prelude*. In particular, they are concerned with the conversation that *The Prelude* represented between Wordsworth and Coleridge. Indeed, it could be said that the *Confessions* represents a belated effort to crash that conversation between poets as an equal interlocutor. The subject of the next section is the significance of the Opium-Eater's earlier claims to be a poet like Wordsworth in relation to his autobiographical project in the *Confessions*.

Rethinking Romantic autobiography

In claiming to be both philosopher and poet, De Quincey, in his persona of the Opium-Eater, is making new and large claims for the scope of his prose. The claim removes him from being merely an anonymous hack writing for the periodicals to being a colleague of the older Wordsworth and Coleridge.

The *Confessions* are reticent about De Quincey's youthful relations with Wordsworth. The Opium-Eater notes that his intention on running away from school was originally 'to proceed to Westmorland, both from the love I bore to that county, and on other personal accounts' (p. 240). What he has left out here was that De Quincey's intention was to make the acquaintance of Wordsworth himself, whom he had long passionately admired – indeed, the volume of 'a favourite poet' in the Opium-Eater's pocket was the *Lyrical Ballads*. The second coded reference to this admiration comes at the opening of Part 2:

> oftentimes on moonlight nights, during my first mournful abode in London, my consolation was (if such it could be thought) to gaze from Oxford-street up every avenue in succession which pierces through the heart of Marylebone to the fields and the woods; for *that*, said I, travelling with my eyes up the long vistas which lay part in light and part in shade, '*that* is the road to the North, and therefore to __, and if I had the wings of a dove, *that* way I would fly for comfort'.
>
> (p. 263)

Eventually, De Quincey did introduce himself to the Wordsworths and subsequently became an intimate. It might seem surprising that he is so reticent in the *Confessions* about his relations with the Wordsworths, especially since while he was writing his essays in London, De Quincey's family were actually living in Dove Cottage, just down the road from the Wordsworths at Rydal Mount. But the two households had become estranged largely owing to De Quincey's anger at the Wordsworth women's refusal to pay calls on his wife, Margaret Simpson, something that they found socially awkward because she was the daughter of a local farmer.

Yet although Wordsworth is mentioned explicitly only once in Part 1 and once in Part 2, the text of the *Confessions* is saturated with references to Wordsworth's poetry. The critic Grevel Lindop has detailed and analysed these references, concluding that taken together they amount to a complicated and ambivalent argument with Wordsworth even as they draw on Wordsworth's poetry to provide a model of visionary writing (see Lindop, 1995). De Quincey's formulation of the idea of a 'literature of power' (which first appears in the series of *Letters to a Young Man Whose Education Has Been Neglected* published in *The London Magazine* in 1823) would depend on a Wordsworthian model: the literature of power was concerned with 'the infinity of the life within' and was that writing which makes us 'feel vividly, and with a vital consciousness, emotions which ordinary life rarely or never supplies occasions for exciting' (De Quincey, 2000 [1823], p. 71). This was, according to De Quincey, the province of Wordsworthian poetry, but it also, crucially, could be achieved by what he called 'impassioned prose', a description of his own *Confessions*. The function of writing was to organise and actualise inert and sleeping modes of feeling within the reader.

More generally and pervasively, the *Confessions* rethinks the autobiographical project and narrative model of *The Prelude*, a poem with which De Quincey was familiar in manuscript (in the thirteen-book version of 1805) from very early on. Like Wordsworth, but in prose rather than poetry, De Quincey endeavours to trace the nature and the continuity of the self through the mechanisms of memory; and he places an equal, if less optimistic, value upon the powers of imagination to effect visionary transformation in the relation between the self and the perceived world. In parallel to Wordsworth's idea that there are important 'spots of time' which, *The Prelude* argues, vivify the adult poet's imagination, De Quincey postulates what he would later come to call (in a sequel to the *Confessions*, *Suspiria de Profundis*) 'involutes'. These 'involutes' he described as 'perplexed combinations of *concrete* objects' which encode 'compound experiences incapable of being disentangled'; these carry and conserve 'our deepest thoughts and feelings' (De Quincey, 1998 [1845], p. 104). The dreams and nightmares he narrates in the *Confessions* work as 'involutes' preserving emotion, in something like the same way that Wordsworth's emotions are embodied in childhood memories.

However, the *Confessions* also functions as a critique, even as a parody, of the Wordsworthian model of the Romantic self (see North, 1994). We can see this if we compare statements by Wordsworth and De Quincey on the nature and import of childhood memories.

Activity 6

Compare the two passages below: the first is from the 1799 *Prelude*, and the second from De Quincey's *Confessions*. To what extent does De Quincey's thinking seem to reiterate Wordsworth's? How does it differ?

> There are in our existence spots of time,
> Which with distinct pre-eminence retain

A fructifying virtue, whence, depressed
By trivial occupations and the round
Of ordinary intercourse, our minds –
Especially the imaginative power –
Are nourished and invisibly repaired;
Such moments chiefly seem to have their date
In our first childhood.

(Wordsworth, 1979 [1799], First Part, ll. 288–96)

The minutest incidents of childhood, or forgotten scenes of
later years, were often revived [in dreams]: I could not be said
to recollect them; for if I had been told of them when waking,
I should not have been able to acknowledge them as parts of
my past experience. But placed as they were before me, in
dreams like intuitions, and clothed in all their evanescent
circumstances and accompanying feelings, I *recognised* them
instantaneously. ... Of this at least, I feel assured, that there is
no such thing as *forgetting* possible to the mind; a thousand
accidents may, and will interpose a veil between our present
consciousness and the secret inscriptions on the mind ... but
... the inscription remains for ever.

(pp. 295–6)

Discussion

Wordsworth offers a fiction of poetic self-possession and nourishment
through the voluntary activation and consideration of childhood
memories. By contrast, De Quincey describes childhood memories as
accessed involuntarily through his opium dreams, and there is a
suggestion that 'forgetting' might be desirable.

To put it another way, in place of the power of the Wordsworthian
poet, De Quincey offers the powerlessness of the opium-addict. In
Part 2, De Quincey's critique is played out in the way in which opium-
dreams infect and infiltrate the healthy, national and Wordsworthian
pastoral of Grasmere and Dove Cottage. As the opening of Part 2 has
it, 'even in that very northern region it was, even in that very valley, nay,
in that very house to which my erroneous wishes pointed, that this

second birth of my sufferings began … There it was, that for years I was persecuted by visions as ugly, and as ghastly phantoms as ever haunted the couch of an Orestes' (p. 263). In this way, the *Confessions* are related to, and anticipate, De Quincey's biographical sketches of Wordsworth and his family at Dove Cottage in the series of essays he produced for *Tait's Magazine* and republished as *Recollections of the Lakes and the Lake Poets* which, brilliantly written and very unwelcome to the Wordsworths themselves, at once critiqued, created and exploited the cult of Dove Cottage.

We'll be coming back to De Quincey's description of Dove Cottage in the *Confessions*, but before that, we are going to take a look at the ways in which the *Confessions* are structured.

Activity 7

Now turn back to the beginning of 'Part 2' of the *Confessions*. So far, you have looked at the first paragraph. If you have not already done so, read through the rest of 'Part 2' to the end of the *Confessions*. Once you have finished, try to make sense of how the *Confessions* as a whole is structured. De Quincey's own subdivisions and signposts should help you; you may also find it useful to note flashbacks, flashforwards and repetitions.

Discussion

At its simplest, the architecture of the *Confessions* falls into six sections across two parts:

Part 1

1   The section starting with 'To the Reader' (the introductory address to the reader).

2   'Preliminary confessions' (autobiographical account of youth pre-1804).

Part 2

1   The introductory section to Part 2

2   'The pleasures of opium' (1804 in Grasmere)

3   'Introduction to the pains of opium' (1816 in Grasmere)

4   'The pains of opium'

Overall, the *Confessions* offers an account of how the narrator came to take up opium (which, according to him, necessitates an account of his youthful adventures), followed by an account of how he came, more or less, to give up opium.

You might agree with me, though, that the piece seems a good deal less tidy in structure than this suggests when you're actually in the middle of reading it. This is because the separate sections are intricately interconnected by flashbacks and flashforwards, by memories, and, in the final section, by dream repetitions and combinations of memories. The repetition effects that De Quincey goes in for, which he would much later in his career describe as a 'fugue' (after the musical form in which multiple musical lines invert and repeat each other in a complex and prescribed mathematical sequence), are confusing and disorienting. The description of the Piranesi engraving of flight upon flight of 'unfinished stairs' as possessing a 'power of endless growth and self-reproduction' is the most apt evocation of the structure as a whole (p. 297).

If one structuring principle is this repetition, another one may also be at work. Grevel Lindop argues that the piece as a whole is organised by the Biblical (and Miltonic) story of 'the Fall' (Lindop, 1998, p. x). Part 1 supposedly describes a condition of 'innocence', and Part 2 a fallen condition of 'experience', separated by the fatal ingesting of opium. Opium serves as a modern version of the apple featured in the story told in the first book of the Bible, Genesis, when Adam and Eve disobey God by eating the forbidden fruit of the Tree of Knowledge, and as a result are cast out of Eden and become subject to pain and death. Whether this is so or not, Milton's reworking of this myth in *Paradise Lost* certainly informs the *Confessions*. The two final dreams are both reminiscent of Milton. The first is a narrative of redemption with an evangelical tinge, a story of paradise regained; it is Easter Sunday, and Ann has been promoted from London to the heavenly Jerusalem. The second is an apocalyptic dream described in Miltonic terms:

> at last, with the sense that all was lost... and but a moment allowed, – and clasped hands, and heart-breaking partings, and then – everlasting farewells! and with a sigh, such as the caves of hell sighed when the incestuous mother uttered the abhorred name

of death, the sound was reverberated – everlasting farewells! and again, and yet again reverberated – everlasting farewells!

(pp. 303–4)

(The 'incestuous mother' is Milton's figure of Sin, who breeds with her son Death.) Milton also supplies De Quincey with the quotation that appears within his final lines:

my sleep is still tumultuous, and, like the gates of Paradise to our first parents when looking back from afar, it is still (in the tremendous line of Milton) –

With dreadful faces throng'd and fiery arms.

(p. 306)

Seductive and useful though this schema is, there are difficulties in setting out to describe the structure of the *Confessions* as though the text had a hidden but perfect structure that one could fathom with enough time and patience, or as though it would be possible to trace out De Quincey's authorial intention in structuring it. This is because, to put it at its simplest, this version of the *Confessions* is avowedly unfinished; the third instalment was never written owing to De Quincey's relapse into ill health and addiction over the next two years. More nebulously, though, as with *The Prelude*, this sort of Romantic autobiography, dependent as it is upon representing the action of the present mind reflecting back upon the past, is never, and *can* never be finished. For Wordsworth this meant, optimistically, that the past remained a quarry for poetry. For De Quincey, the necessarily interminable labours of memory are anxiously imaged in the sufferings of 'poor Piranesi' as he climbs infinite aerial flights of 'unfinished stairs'. To put it another way, the *Confessions* puts a **Gothic** twist on the Wordsworthian project of Romantic autobiography.

Opium and the Romantic imagination

Let's now take a closer look at how the text characterises opium; after all, the narrator goes so far as to remark that not 'the opium-eater, but the opium, is the true hero of the tale' (p. 304). Part 2 details the Opium-Eater's first taking of opium in the form of laudanum in the autumn of 1804, in which it was dissolved in port wine. At the time, opium was commonly taken in this fashion as a standard form of pain relief. However, opium in the contemporary cultural imagination was more than simply a medical drug. It could serve as a metaphor for the Romantic imagination as in Coleridge's preface to his celebrated poem 'Kubla Khan' (published in the first edition of the *Lyrical Ballads*, 1798) in which he describes how the poem is an imperfect transcript of a dream vision he had while under the influence of opium. Opium might carry a third meaning; it had ever-increasing political resonance during the century as a marker of empire, speaking as it did of trade with the Far East, especially India and China.

Activity 8

Return to the text of the *Confessions* and reread the section 'The pleasures of opium' as far as the paragraph ending '... and over all is the great light of the majestic intellect' (pp. 265–9).

How are opium and its effects characterised?

Discussion

The characterisation of opium is complicated by the retrospection of the narrator. His past self had heard of it as a mythic substance like 'manna' or 'Ambrosia' (p. 265); his present self is divided between a sense of its pleasures and its pains, between condescension to, and pity for, his former self's ignorance.

That said, opium is described as a paradoxical compound of the corporeal and commercial on the one hand and the divine and moral on the other. The account of the visit to the druggist near the Pantheon contrasts the dull and mundane realities of the London street, the dullness, stupidity, mortality, physicality and mere commercialism of the druggist, with the infinite, the divine, the spiritual, the immortal, the apocalyptic, and the paradisial effects of opium in 'the world within me' (p. 266). Opium is described at once as a commodity and 'the secret of happiness, about which philosophers had disputed for so many ages': 'happiness might now be bought for a penny, and carried in the waistcoat pocket: portable ecstacies might be had corked up in a pint bottle: and peace of mind could be sent down in gallons by the mail coach' (p. 266).

In particular, the claim is made that opium produces not just happiness but full self-possession. It introduces among the 'mental faculties' 'the most exquisite order, legislation, and harmony', 'invigorates' a man's 'self-possession', communicates 'serenity and equipoise', and 'with respect to the temper and moral feelings in general, it gives simply that sort of vital warmth which is approved by the judgment, and which would probably always accompany a bodily constitution of primeval or antediluvian health' (p. 268). It 'gives an expansion to the heart and benevolent affections' (p. 268) and tends to 'compose what had been agitated, and to concentrate what had been distracted' (p. 269). In short, the Opium-Eater 'feels that the diviner part of his nature is paramount; that is, the moral affections are in a state of cloudless serenity; and over all is the great light of the majestic intellect' (p. 269).

The Opium-Eater then turns to considering the effects of opium-eating upon his pleasures – the pleasure of opera-going, and of walking the streets of London. One of the things you might have noticed is the Opium-Eater's detachment from the social world in which he is taking his pleasures. The music displays to him only his own life; he listens only to the Italian chat that he can't understand; he sees the poor among whom he wanders not as in distress but in terms of aesthetic groupings; and opium seems to conduce to solitude, silence, reveries and trance rather than to engaged sociability: 'I stood at a distance, and aloof from the uproar of life' (p. 276). Lindop argues that this solipsism is an effect of his 'fall' (1998, p. xi) but the text seems to value this isolation. The pleasures described seem something like an urban version of 'I wandered lonely as a cloud'. The section concludes with the astonishing prose aria to the healing effects of opium which soothes sorrow, anger and guilt with oblivion and dream, retrieving even the dead: 'Thou only givest these gifts to man; and thou hast the keys of Paradise, oh, just, subtle, and mighty opium!' (p. 277).

As we read on about the pains of opium, however, it seems that if in one aspect opium may 'legislate and harmonise', in the other it disorders, confuses and disintegrates. If opium in its consoling first aspect seems very like the Wordsworthian version of the romantic imagination, in the second it is certainly a demonic variant.

Dreaming Dove Cottage

I want now to return to the *Confessions'* representation of Dove Cottage. In the long pictorial evocation of domestic happiness at the cottage (pp. 285–8), the Opium-Eater places, at the centre of the composition, not himself, but opium: 'a quart of ruby-coloured laudanum' (p. 288).

This part of the chapter explores the meaning of the Opium-Eater's positioning of opium at the heart of Dove Cottage by paying attention to the episode of the visit of the Malay to whom he gives opium (pp. 283–4). This episode is one of the places in the text where De Quincey's rewriting of the Wordsworthian myth of the poetic self is at its most prominent. You may wish to re-read this passage now before proceeding (from 'Now, then, I was again happy …', on p. 282, to 'brought other Malays with him worse than himself, that ran "a-muck" at me, and led me into a world of troubles', on p. 284).

One possible reading of this incident, provided by the critic Charles Rzepka, is that it crystallises many of De Quincey's anxieties about being an author, and perhaps especially about his relations with Wordsworth. At this time, De Quincey was a thirty-six-year-old failed writer occupying the cottage in which his 'idol' had produced much of the work which De Quincey knew and admired; a cottage which was already the focus of literary pilgrimage as early as 1816 when a young Cambridge student came to the door, much as the younger De Quincey had done, to make the acquaintance of Wordsworth. Rzepka argues that the Malay has a 'multiply encrypted identity' (1993, p. 185). On the one hand he seems to be a version of De Quincey's younger self arriving at Dove Cottage to worship Wordsworth as an idol. On the other, he seems to be a version of his present-day self, as a fellow opium-eater. But the Malay also seems to be there to critique De Quincey's fragile pretensions; he explodes De Quincey's masquerade as a scholar and linguist, because he alone is aware that De Quincey is speaking gibberish to him in the effort to preserve his reputation as a linguist with his household and the locals.

Another way of viewing this episode, however, is to note that it reworks a recurrent feature of Wordsworth's verse. It recalls the many stories in Dorothy Wordsworth's journals of persons encountered on the road or beggars who came to the cottage, and the various poems that Wordsworth wrote centred on encounters with local people, including 'Point Rash-Judgment' and the poem 'Resolution and Independence', the story of Wordsworth's encounter with a leech-gatherer, which De Quincey quotes in the *Confessions*. Wordsworth's poems after 1800 have a tendency to celebrate the poet's dialogue with locals and travellers, however imperfect, as something that imparts sociable benefit to the poet. By contrast, the Opium-Eater describes his encounter with the foreign as a failure of communication between cultures. Arguably

De Quincey constructs himself as a dark double to Wordsworth, and his prose as a critique of Wordsworth's poetic stances.

The tableau foregrounds the Malay's foreignness in strong contrast to the 'Englishness' of the cottage-setting and its inhabitants:

> In a cottage kitchen ... stood the Malay – his turban and loose trowsers of dingy white relieved upon the dark panelling: he had placed himself nearer to the girl than she seemed to relish; though her native spirit of mountain intrepidity contended with the feeling of simple awe which her countenance expressed as she gazed upon the tiger-cat before her. And a more striking picture there could not be imagined, than the beautiful English face of the girl, and its exquisite fairness, together with her erect and independent attitude, contrasted with the sallow and bilious skin of the Malay, enamelled or veneered with mahogany, by marine air, his small, fierce, restless eyes, thin lips, slavish gestures and adorations. Half-hidden by the ferocious looking Malay, was a little child from a neighbouring cottage who had crept in after him, and was now in the act of reverting its head, and gazing upwards at the turban and the fiery eyes beneath it, whilst with one hand he caught at the dress of the young woman for protection.
>
> (p. 283)

The critics John Barrell and Nigel Leask among others have pointed out the ways in which the story of the Malay, and especially De Quincey's guilt and anxiety over having possibly poisoned him with his gift of opium, distilled contemporary English anxieties about empire, and it's worth recalling here that the full title of the book is *The Confessions of an English Opium-Eater* (Barrell, 1991; Leask, 1992). (This episode is only one of De Quincey's anxious depictions of the east, and it was not peculiar to him alone; in Chapter 7, you will encounter another version of this anxiety in Arthur Conan Doyle's *The Sign of Four*.) The Malay imports into Dove Cottage everything that potentially disintegrates English domesticity and, by extension, the Romantic self. This effect will be repeated and amplified in dream form.

Activity 9

In the *Confessions*, reread the section starting '*May*, 1818. The Malay has been a fearful enemy for months …' to '… in the mighty and sudden revulsion of mind, I wept, and could not forbear it, as I kissed their faces' (pp. 299–301). In what ways could this opium-dream be said to attack Englishness?

Discussion

The 'Orient', conceived as an undifferentiated concatenation or association of Malaya, China, southern Asia, India and Egypt, is accessed here through its product, opium. But far from providing a pleasurable experience, here its effects are described as inimical to the Englishman's self, waking or dreaming. Opium's version of the Orient disperses the dreaming self of the English Opium-Eater across multiple subject-positions – 'I was the idol; I was the priest; I was worshipped; I was sacrificed' (p. 300) – and subjects the English self to an alien religious economy which punishes him for sins that he does not own: 'I had done a deed, they said, which the ibis and the crocodile trembled at' (p. 300). Above all, it functions as the alien obverse to the happy cottage home in England to which the distressed Opium-Eater awakes in 'broad noon' to find that 'my children were standing, hand in hand, at my bed-side; come to show me their coloured shoes, or new frocks, or to let me see them dressed for going out' (p. 301).

Conclusion

As the Opium-Eater's self is undone through the tormenting agency of a series of dreams, the structure of the narrative symptomatically begins to break down, similarly disjoined from ordinary chronological assumptions; as the Opium-Eater remarks:

> I have not been able to compose the notes for this part of my narrative into any regular and connected shape. I give the notes disjointed as I find them, or have now drawn them up from memory. Some of them point to their own date; some I have dated; and some are undated. Whenever it could answer my purpose to transplant them from the natural or chronological order, I have not scrupled to do so. Sometimes I speak in the present, sometimes in the past tense.
>
> (p. 289)

The Opium-Eater is thus a dysphoric version of the Romantic self postulated by Wordsworth. Wordsworth's self is sustained through the action of memory. De Quincey's, by contrast, is haunted and destroyed by the involuntariness of memory reconstituted as dream. In place of Wordsworth's assertion of Romantic poetic vision, De Quincey gives us visionary addiction. In place of Wordsworth's sense of the disembodied self sublime, De Quincey supplies a sick body. In place of Wordsworth's depiction of strong domesticity within a national and health-giving landscape, De Quincey shows a domestic idyll blotted out by the apocalyptic inner landscape of the mind, haunted by terrors associated with the far-flung British Empire. But the kinship of the two versions of Romantic vision is marked by the appearance of Dove Cottage at the heart of both.

Figure 3.3   Blue plaque commemorating where Thomas De Quincey wrote *Confessions of an English Opium-Eater,* 4 York Street (now 36 Tavistock Street), London. Photographed by George Redgrave. Photo: © George Redgrave.

That said, the Opium-Eater clearly represents a very different model of Romantic authorship and the power and function of literature from that postulated either by Wordsworth or by Shelley. Both Wordsworth and Shelley aspired, in their different ways, to lofty and health-giving poetic, political and moral 'prophecy', whether developed in parochial seclusion or cosmopolitan exile, whether directed at the nation or towards some supranational world order. De Quincey's writing by contrast offers not so much prophecy as a prophetic nightmare of the urban and imperial masses, and a persona conceived as metropolitan, imperial, consumerist and ephemeral. So it is perhaps not surprising that, if you visit Dove Cottage today, you will find that although De Quincey's twenty-odd years' residence there is extensively acknowledged, it does not set the tone for the interpretation and enjoyment of the cottage. The London coffee houses in which De Quincey scribbled the *Confessions* may be long gone, but he is remembered in the city all the same. The (misspelt) blue plaque set above a small and pleasant Turkish restaurant at 36 Tavistock Street, London WC2 marking where De Quincey wrote the *Confessions* seems an altogether more appropriate memorial to his Romantic autobiographical project which, though it reflected upon the seclusion of Grasmere, was conceived in and about the imperial metropolis.

References

Anon. (1821) 'Fugitive literature', *The London Magazine*, vol. 4 (July–December), pp. 49–56.

Barrell, J. (1991) *The Infection of Thomas De Quincey: A Psychopathology of Imperialism*, New Haven and London, Yale University Press.

De Quincey, T. (1998 [1821]) *Confessions of an English Opium-Eater and Other Writings* (ed. G. Lindop), Oxford, Oxford University Press.

De Quincey, T. (2000 [1823]) 'Letters to a young man whose education has been neglected' in Burwick, F. (ed.) *The Works of Thomas De Quincey*, vol. 3, London, Pickering & Chatto.

De Quincey, T. (1970 [1834–9]) *Recollections of the Lakes and of the Lake Poets* (ed. D. Wright), Harmondsworth, Penguin.

De Quincey, T. (1998 [1845]) *Suspiria de Profundis* in *Confessions of an English Opium-Eater and Other Writings* (ed. G. Lindop), Oxford World's Classics, Oxford, Oxford University Press.

Leask, N. (1992) *British Romantic Writers and the East: Anxieties of Empire*, Cambridge, Cambridge University Press.

Lindop, G. (1995) 'De Quincey's Wordsworthian quotations', *Wordsworth Circle*, vol. 26, no. 2, pp. 58–65.

North, J. (1994) 'Opium and the romantic imagination: the creation of a myth' in Vice, S., Campbell, M. and Armstrong, T. (eds) *Beyond the Pleasure Dome: Writing and Addiction from the Romantics*, Sheffield, Sheffield Academic Press, pp. 109–17.

Rousseau, J.-J. (1977 [1781–8]) *The Confessions* (trans. and introduction J.M. Cohen), Harmondsworth, Penguin.

Rzepka, C. (1993) 'De Quincey and the Malay: Dove Cottage idolatry', *Wordsworth Circle*, vol. 24, no. 3, pp. 180–5.

Shelley, P.B. (1965 [1840]) *A Defence of Poetry* in Ingpen, R. and Peck, W.E. (eds) *The Complete Works of Percy Bysshe Shelley*, 10 vols, vol. 7, pp. 109–42.

Wordsworth, W. (1974 [1815]) 'Essay supplementary to the preface' in Owen, W.J.B. and Worthington Smyser, J. (eds) *The Prose Works of William Wordsworth*, 3 vols, Oxford, Clarendon Press, vol. 3, pp. 62–84.

Wordsworth, J., Abrams, M.H. and Gill, S. (eds) (1979) *William Wordsworth, The Prelude 1799, 1805, 1850: Authoritative Texts; Context and Reception; Recent Critical Essays*, New York and London, W.W. Norton and Company.

Further reading

Cafarelli, A.W. (1991) *Prose in the Age of Poets: Romanticism and Biographical Narrative from Johnson to De Quincey*, Philadelphia, University of Pennsylvania Press.

Hayter, A. (1969) *Opium and the Romantic Imagination*, London, Faber.

Morrison, R. (1997) 'Opium-eaters and magazine wars: De Quincey and Coleridge in 1821', *Victorian Periodicals Review*, vol. 30, no. 1, pp. 27–40.

St Clair, W. (2004) *The Reading Nation in the Romantic Period*, Cambridge, Cambridge University Press.

Chapter 4
E.T.A. Hoffmann: fantasy lives

Richard Allen with Clare Spencer

Aims

This chapter will:

- introduce you to short prose fiction of the Romantic period
- continue exploring how Romantic writers depicted themselves and how this fed into subsequent representations of them as Romantic geniuses
- continue the discussion of the dark side of the Romantic imagination as associated with the extremes of madness and delusion
- consider the depiction of women in relation to Romantic genius.

Introduction

In this chapter, we pursue the theme of Romantic lives through a tale, 'The Sandman' (1816), by one of the greatest European Romantic writers, E.T.A. Hoffmann.

Over the last three chapters we have been exploring three writers' avowedly autobiographical depictions of their lives, considering in particular their representations of themselves as Romantic writers, and subsequent representations of them as Romantic authors. With this chapter we jump back a decade to the breathless and uncertain moment just after Napoleon's fall, in 1816, and we turn our eyes away from England and Scotland, to the war-scarred territories of what would become Germany. We turn away from autobiographical versions of the Romantic life to experimental fictive representations. From writers who each exploited versions of a single persona, we turn to look at a writer who adopted a dizzying succession of personae.

Hoffmann's work is often said to represent the culmination of German Romanticism. The period of his life corresponds broadly with that of the writers whose work we have explored so far. Born in Prussia in 1776 (an area composing parts of modern Germany, Poland and Lithuania and Russia), Hoffmann died in 1822, the same year as Shelley. His experience of the changes brought about by the Napoleonic Wars was arguably, however, more immediate than that of any of the British writers. He was forced to flee back and forth across Europe according to the fortunes of war. In 1805 Prussia came under the control of Napoleon, and the Prussian Civil Service was disbanded; Hoffmann's already erratic career as a civil servant collapsed and he was forced to exploit his interests in musical composition and music journalism to make his living in Warsaw. In 1807 he was deported to Berlin by the French authorities, where he nearly starved to death, and in 1808 he went to Bamberg as theatre musical director. In 1813, when he went first to Dresden and then to Leipzig in pursuit of posts in opera companies, Hoffmann found himself more or less on the battlefield of the Battle of Dresden (August 1813) and was then caught up in the Battle of the Nations (October 1813) in which 500,000 men fought for three days close to Leipzig. Oscillating between Dresden and Leipzig, Hoffmann began to produce a substantial amount of writing, publishing his first collection of short stories, *Fantasiestücke*, in 1813. Recalled to Berlin to a post in the judiciary, Hoffmann continued to support himself until his death largely by producing fiction and criticism.

Author of two novels, seven literary fairy tales (including the one on which Tchaikovsky's ballet *The Nutcracker*, 1892, is based), and sixty other 'tales' or 'pieces' along with a large body of important music criticism, Hoffmann was extensively read both in German and in French translation across Europe and America in his own lifetime. He did not appear in English translation until the middle of the nineteenth century. His work exerted considerable influence on the subsequent development of the short form of the 'tale of mystery and imagination' as practised, for example, by the Scots novelist Walter Scott (1771–1832) and the American writers Nathaniel Hawthorne (1804–1864) and Edgar Allan Poe (1809–1849). His influence may also be traced within the tradition of Russian fiction as it stretches from Alexander Pushkin (1799–1837) to Fyodor Dostoyevsky (1821–1881). His posthumous celebrity, however, has probably been most strongly shaped by a French play, *Les Contes d'Hoffmann* (1851), which subsequently formed the basis of the libretto by Jules Barbier and Michel Carré used by Jacques Offenbach for his opera *Les Contes d'Hoffmann*, first performed in 1881 and a mainstay of the operatic repertoire ever since. The play is also the source for Michael Powell and Emeric Pressburger's film *The Tales of Hoffmann* (1951).

The 1851 play took three of Hoffmann's tales – 'A New Year's Eve Adventure' ('Die Abenteuer der Silvester-Nacht', 1815), 'The Sandman' ('Der Sandmann', 1816) and 'Councillor Krespel' ('Rat Krespel', 1818) – and framed them as stories about three past love affairs described by Hoffman during a drinking-bout in a bierkeller with his friends. This biographical emphasis required a fair amount of adaptation of the stories, because they are structurally complex and resist simple biographical reading of this kind. This is particularly true of 'The Sandman', the focus of this chapter; it is by no means straightforward to identify the character Nathanael – the **protagonist** of 'The Sandman' – with Hoffman himself. Nevertheless, the play remains fundamentally faithful in its depiction of Hoffmann's life as a man and as a writer. It preserves the author's arguably well-deserved reputation as a heavy-drinking genius. It replicates his habit of framing up his stories collectively and internally as tales told to and discussed with a band of male friends, whom he fictionalised as the 'Serapiontic brotherhood' or 'die Serapionsbrüder'. Finally, it pays homage to a habit of recasting unhappy amours in thinly disguised fictional form to the great annoyance and embarrassment of everyone else concerned. 'A New Year's Eve Adventure', for example, was transparently an account, first in realist and then in fantastical vein, of Hoffmann's unrequited infatuation for his sixteen-year-old music pupil Julia Marc, a potentially scandalous situation which her father dealt with by marrying her off to another man in 1812.

Play, opera and film suggest the extent to which Hoffmann's tales have been seen to dramatise their author; but a reading of the tales shows that though they may in some ways solicit biographical reading, they also bewilder it. Hoffmann had a habit of crafting personae for himself. As a music critic, he adopted the persona of one Johannes (Kapelmeister) Kreisler (Figure 4.1), an imaginary violinist and conductor and a persona of enough glamour to be appropriated by the composer Robert Schumann in his *Kreisleriana* (1838). Hoffmann also tried to borrow some of Mozart's celebrity by adopting 'Amadeus' as a middle name. Within his stories, he repeatedly appears as a character under his own name as either 'Theodore' or 'Hoffmann'. A single brief example of the way that 'Hoffmann' flickers through so many of the tales will have to suffice here. 'A New Year's Eve Adventure' (published in 1815 in the fourth volume of a collection of Hoffmann's 'fantasy pieces') is supplied with a foreword presenting Hoffmann as the 'editor' of the journals of a man called 'the travelling enthusiast'. These journals are themselves addressed to Hoffmann as their first reader: 'You can see, my dear Theodore Amadeus Hoffmann, that a strange dark power manifests itself in my life too often, steals the best dreams away from sleep, pushing strange forms into my life' (Hoffmann, 1967, p. 129). Hoffmann-as-editor maintains a sceptical distance by commenting that the enthusiast 'has apparently not separated the events of his inner life from those of the outside world; in fact we cannot determine where one ends and the other begins'. However he also says that editing this narrative is what he can do by way of homage to one 'who has encountered so much strangeness and madness, everywhere and at all times, but especially on New Year's Eve in Berlin' (Hoffmann, 1967, p. 129). Hoffmann's tales are throughout characterised by an oscillation between voices located in the real world of contemporary Berlin and voices prey to dreams and visions and living in 'a strange magical realm' (Hoffmann, 1967, p. 104).

Figure 4.1   E.T.A. Hoffmann as Kreisler, 1822, pencil. Coll. Archiv f.Kunst & Geschichte. Photo: © akg-images. Design for the cover of a planned third volume of *The Life and Opinions of Tomcat Murr*, which was never completed.

The tales were published under titles such as *Fantasiestücke* (Fantasy-pieces) and *Nachtstücke* (Night-pieces), titles calculated to evoke ideas of darkness, obscured vision and the world of dreams. In particular, they evoke **fantasy** and the fantastic – which may be defined briefly as literature which is interested in portraying events that could not happen in real life. In this sense, fantasy and the fantastic are the opposite of realism, which specialises in portraying the everyday in faithful detail. 'The Sandman' was first published along with other stories in 1816 in *Nachtstücke*. Hoffmann's stories have since come to be known as *kunstmärchen* (literary tales), to signal their kinship with another kind of story, the *Kinder- und Hausmärchen* (children's and household tales)

Figure 4.2   Unknown engraver, after A. Deleraud, *E.T.A. Hoffmann, c.*1850, chalk lithograph. From L'Artiste. Coll.Archiv F.Kunst & Geschichte. Photo: © akg-images.

published in 1812 by the Brothers Grimm (Jacob, 1785–1863 and Wilhelm, 1886–1859). If you are familiar with any of Grimms' fairy tales, you may recognise parallels with Hoffmann's Gothic fantasies as you work through this chapter. But *märchen* also had an important pre-history within literature in German as allegorical tales set inside longer stories. A recent editor of Hoffmann's works, Everett Bleiler, notes that 'these often appeared as symbolic kernels or germs within the larger context of a story, offering in frankly poetic and mythical form the point offered more or less realistically in the full story. The *märchen* was thus a microcosm within a macrocosm' (Hoffmann, 1967, p. xx). This suggests a structural complexity of doubling and parallelism; and it also suggests a juxtaposition of the supernatural with the everyday. This legacy appears very clearly in the structure of 'A New Year's Eve Adventure'. A realistic story of going to an evening party, being cold-shouldered by the beloved and getting drunk afterwards serves as a frame to a supernatural tale which recasts the beloved as a witch. Subsequent tales, including 'The Sandman', similarly insist that the real world and the fantastical are contiguous and simultaneous. It is the nature of Romantic vision to apprehend this simultaneity, but this seeing is not necessarily benign. The little girl at the end of Hoffmann's experiment in the literary fairy tale, 'Nutcracker and the King of Mice', seems still to live in a child's visionary world of perpetual Christmas Eve: 'Marie is to this day the queen of a realm where all kinds of sparkling Christmas Woods, and transparent Marzipan Castles – in short, the most wonderful and beautiful things of every kind – are to be seen – by those who have eyes to see them' (Hoffmann, 1967, p. 182). But Hoffmann's adult protagonists, vouchsafed or apparently vouchsafed a vision of a world beyond the ordinary, are very often tormented and even destroyed by the memory.

In 'A New Year's Eve Adventure', Hoffmann-as-editor does not entirely explicate the strangeness of the tale the travelling enthusiast tells, instead exhibiting it for the sophisticated pleasure of his readers:

> The Geisterseher [spirit-seer] may beckon you to his side, and before you are even aware of it, you will be in a strange magical realm where figures of fantasy step right into your own life, and are as cordial with you as your oldest friends. I beg of you – take them as such, go on with their remarkable doings, yield to the shudders and thrills that they produce, since the more you go along with them, the better they can operate.
>
> (Hoffmann, 1967, p. 104)

Bearing this in mind as a manifesto for how readers might approach Hoffmann's tales, let's turn to 'The Sandman'. You will be invited to read the full story, reproduced as Reading 4.1, after completing an initial activity based on its opening sections.

Three Romantic writers

'The Sandman' opens with letters ostensibly written by two of the story's central characters, Nathanael and Clara. These precede a long section of narration in the voice of a fictionalised authorial persona: the 'Hoffmann' figure we encountered above. This narrating persona, as we will see below, begins by addressing the reader directly in the first person, though his overt use of 'I' disappears as his narrative gains momentum. What confronts us here are three fictive versions of the Romantic writer, with each of the three providing their own perspective on events. The effect is not only to produce a fragmented structure, but also to demonstrate the difficulty of obtaining any definitive account of reality.

Activity 1

Before reading 'The Sandman' in its entirety, consider the three extracts reprinted below, and make some notes in response to the following questions. The first extract is from Nathanael's opening letter to Lothar; the second is from Clara's reply to this misdirected letter; and in the third the fictionalised author explains his motivation for telling the story.

1 How is each of these Romantic narrators characterised? Attend to their style of expression, as well as to what they tell us about themselves.

2 What similarities do you detect between these three narrators?

3 What resemblances can you identify between the personae of these three fictional Romantic writers and any of the Romantic selves we have encountered in the preceding chapters of this book?

Extract 1

Something appalling has entered my life! Dark forebodings of a hideous, menacing fate are looming over me like the shadows of black clouds, impervious to any kindly ray of sunlight. It is time for me to tell you what has befallen me. I realize that I must, but at the very thought mad laughter bursts from within me. Oh, my dear Lothar, how am I ever to convey to you that what happened to me a few days ago has indeed managed to devastate my life so cruelly! If only you were here, you could see for yourself; but now you must undoubtedly consider me a crack-brained, superstitious fool. To cut a long story short, the appalling event that befell me, the fatal memory of which I am vainly struggling to escape, was simply this: a few days ago, at twelve noon on 30 October to be precise, a barometer-seller entered my room and offered me his wares. Instead of buying anything, I threatened to throw him downstairs, whereupon he departed of his own accord.

(p. 307)

Extract 2

It is the phantom of our own self which, thanks to its intimate relationship with us and its deep influence on our own minds, casts us down to hell or transports us to heaven. You see, my darling Nathanael, that Lothar and I have talked at length about dark powers and forces, and now that I have with some labour, written down the main points, it seems to me quite profound. I don't quite understand Lothar's last words, I only have a dim idea of what he means, and yet it all sounds very true. I beg you to forget all about the hateful advocate Coppelius and the barometer-man Giuseppe Coppola. Be assured that these alien figures have no power over you; only your belief in their malevolent power can make them truly malevolent to you. If every line of your letter did not reveal the deep perturbation of your spirits, if your state of mind did not cause me pain in my very soul, then, indeed, I could make jokes about the advocate Sandman and the barometer-seller Coppelius. Keep your spirits up!

(pp. 315–16)

Extract 3

I must confess, kind reader, that nobody has actually asked me to tell the story of young Nathanael; you are aware, however, that I belong to the curious race of authors, who, if they are filled with such a vision as I have just described, feel as though everyone who approaches them, and all the world besides, were asking: 'Whatever's the matter? Tell me everything, my dear fellow!' Thus I felt powerfully impelled to tell you about Nathanael's calamitous life. Its strange and wondrous character absorbed my entire soul; but for that very reason, and because, dear reader, I have to put you in the right mood to endure an odd tale, which is no easy matter, I racked my brains to find a portentous, original, and arresting way of beginning Nathanael's story. ... Unable to find words that seemed to reflect anything of the prismatic radiance of my inner vision, I decided not to begin at all. Be so good, dear reader, as to accept the three letters, kindly communicated to me by my friend Lothar, as the sketch for my portrayal; as I tell the story, I shall endeavour to add more and more colour to it.

(pp. 318–19)

Discussion

1   Nathanael presents himself as the victim of extreme feelings, and of events beyond his control. His exclamatory **register** betrays the heightened emotional sensitivity of a mind troubled by 'dark forebodings' and the compulsive rehearsing of a 'fatal memory'. At the same time, his account of the occasion which sparked this reaction is matter-of-fact and draws on the conventions of **realism**: the exact specification of time and date authenticate his memory as an accurate one. Clara's voice, by contrast, strikes us as one of commonsense reassurance: she explains away Nathanael's fears as the product of a 'phantom' self and of his misguided 'belief' in malevolent powers, and comfortingly urges him to 'Keep your spirits up'. Underlying her pragmatic dose of therapy though is a hint of anxious uncertainty: 'I don't quite understand'; 'I only have a dim idea'. The fictionalised author-figure in the third extract adopts a confidential and conversational tone, but portrays himself as a Romantic visionary: 'absorbed' by the tale he has to relate and 'powerfully impelled' to tell it. That single-minded absorption might be something his readers too have experienced, but the Romantic writer credits his particular insight with a 'prismatic radiance' which is all his own.

2   Despite the evident differences between the anguished turmoil of Nathanael, Clara's rational concern to calm him, and the author-figure's highly self-conscious account of how he sought to open his story in a striking way, these three fictional Romantic writers display

some similarities. They declare themselves in tones of intense passion (even the apparently sensible Clara refers to 'the pain in my very soul'). They share a characteristically Gothic vocabulary of 'menacing fate', 'dark powers and forces', and 'strange' and 'portentous' stories. They each exhibit a confusing mix of obsession and detachment. And, interestingly, all three writers refer to the difficulty of communicating what they want to say: 'how am I ever to convey to you'; 'I have with some labour, written down'; they are 'unable to find words'. There is a sense here of a crisis in the Romantic vocation: a suspicion that language may be inadequate to the enormity of the Romantic visionary's endeavour to both capture and transcend reality.

3   No doubt you spotted the continuities between the troubled figure of Nathanael depicted here and De Quincey's depiction of 'a self undone by its dreams' (see Chapter 3, p. 95). And you may also have noticed how the direct way in which the authorial persona discusses his writing dilemmas with the reader resembles the Opium-Eater's remarks about his inability to compose his narrative into a connected shape. You may have registered too how the theme of inescapable memory connects back to the autobiographical persona of Wordsworth's *The Prelude*. And the image of the Romantic writer as a visionary unsure of his own expressive powers might remind us of the figure of the poet articulated in Shelley's 'Ode to the West Wind'.

In each of these three fictional personae we have a construct of the Romantic writer whose imagination has in some way exceeded their control. Nathanael is 'vainly struggling' to escape from the imagined threat posed by the barometer-seller. Clara's inclination to turn the story into a joke is thwarted by her anxiety about what she imagines as Nathanael's 'deep perturbation of spirits' and 'state of mind'. And the authorial persona, with more than a hint of irony, declares 'the prismatic radiance' of his own imagination to be beyond his power as a writer to convey. As he goes on to explain not long after the extract we've been examining: 'the poet can do no more than capture the strangeness of reality, like the dim reflection in a dull mirror' (p. 319).

Please read 'The Sandman' in its entirety now if you have not already done so. Bear in mind that what you are reading is a translation. This means that it is more difficult to offer authoritative readings of the detail and rhythm of the text, although the plot, narrative voice, narrative structure and imagery still come through strongly. As you read, notice how the authorial persona inserts himself into the story as an eyewitness, and claims acquaintance with its characters. Try to stay alert to any judgements this persona offers through the more knowing viewpoint of **irony** and with the benefit of hindsight. And be aware of the ways in which this fictionalised version of Hoffmann-the-writer channels and subtly manipulates the story's complex and unstable mix of common-sense explanation and the Gothic horrors generated by an imagination out of control.

Ways of seeing: eyes and 'I's

In your study of the three extracts in Activity 1 above, you may have registered that seeing, sight and vision form a prominent strand of connecting imagery. Nathanael wishes fervently that Lothar 'could see for yourself'. Clara employs the words 'dark' and 'dim' to refer to forces beyond her understanding. And the authorial figure not only repeats the word 'vision', but also refers to the 'prismatic radiance' of his own creative impulse. At the moment when the fictionalised 'Hoffmann' takes over the narration, he steps back from recounting events and instead describes the mood of obsessive inspiration in terms of vision. It prompts, he says, 'a strange, fixed stare as though you were trying to make out forms, invisible to other eyes, in empty space' (p. 318).

The idea that there is more than one way of seeing, and that the Romantic artist might be equipped with a special and privileged way of seeing, is thus explored in 'The Sandman' through the recurring pattern of references to sight, vision, and above all to eyes. In the next activity we are going to explore how these different ways of seeing are depicted.

Activity 2

Reread the two sections of the story which focus on the doubled figure of Coppelius/Coppola. The first is in Nathanael's opening letter, from 'On seeing Coppelius now' (on p. 311) to 'I felt nothing more' (on p. 312). This is the scene in which he recalls his childhood eavesdropping and discovery during one of his father's mysterious experiments with Coppelius. The second features the scene in which Coppola sells the spyglass to Nathanael, from 'Now, however, Coppola came ...' (on p. 324) to 'laughing loudly as he went downstairs' (on p. 326). How do the motifs of eyes and seeing function in these episodes?

Discussion

In the first of these scenes, eyes and the fear of their loss are at the core of the remembered nightmare of the child Nathanael: 'It seemed to me that human faces were visible on all sides, but without eyes, and with ghastly, deep, black cavities instead' (p. 311). Neither child nor reader is clear at this stage about the nature of the experiment taking place in the father's study; but reading retrospectively we realise that the eyes are the last and most difficult additions to the dolls, who can only plausibly be animated if the eyes are taken from another, living figure. Being able to see thus becomes a symbol of existence: to see is to be. Thus when the Sandman throws a handful of sand (or in this case 'fragments of red-hot coal') into your eyes and you are forced to close them, you are cut off from feeling and thinking. Existence returns only when you awake and see again.

The scene in which Coppola brings spectacles and spyglasses for sale to Nathanael's lodgings provides a key point in this pattern of imagery. At first Nathanael is baffled by Coppola's cry 'I 'ave beautiful eyes-a to sell you'; but then he sees the spectacles piling up and instantly imagines them as 'flaming eyes' which 'flickered and winked and goggled' at him (p. 325). The spectacles take on a life of their own, the multiple versions of reality they offer leaving Nathanael disorientated and overwhelmed. The spyglass, on the other hand (which in fact magnifies rather than corrects the version of reality that we see), seems to bring 'objects before one's eyes with [the] clarity, sharpness, and distinctness' (p. 325) of accurate and single vision. It seems that Hoffmann is establishing two ways of seeing here: the spyglass way in which vision is apparently unproblematically improved; and the spectacles way, which renders reality subject to countless subjective and bewildering perspectives.

These ways of seeing, then, can be understood as metaphors for different Romantic ways of perceiving reality. The distorting lenses of the multiple pairs of spectacles demonstrate how perception is vulnerable to the vagaries of individual subjectivity: the 'eyes' of the spectacles represent the innumerable 'I's who see the world in different ways. But on the other hand, like the wonderful telescopes which the German astronomer William Herschel (1738–1822) was creating in Britain at around this time, and like the creative faculty of the Romantic artist, the spyglass can in theory provide privileged access to a single truth. What the events of 'The Sandman' demonstrate is that even this heightened perceptive faculty of the Romantic imagination can render the truth obscure and inaccessible, and even fatal, when it is misapplied.

Why should Coppola (whose name means 'eye-sockets' in Italian) be introduced initially as a barometer-seller, if this pattern of eyes and seeing is so important? We might perhaps interpret selling barometers as a front, concealing Coppola's darker secrets. But it is possible to detect a further level of meaning in Hoffmann's linking of barometer and spyglass. Both of these instruments mediate between ourselves and the external world. We tap the barometer and that conditions our sense of the weather. We use a spyglass – a man-made invention – to see a distant object, and that conditions our sense of the reality of the object. When viewed through the spyglass, Olimpia's 'eyes seemed to sparkle more and more vividly' (p. 325). In both cases, perception depends on a scientific instrument which may not be entirely reliable. And through the deft exercise of irony, the spyglass, which ought to enable Nathanael to see more clearly, becomes the instrument of his blindness to Olimpia's true status as a mechanical doll.

The scene of Olimpia's 'death', when Nathanael comes upon Spalanzani and Coppola tearing apart his beloved, brings the recurring theme of eyes and sight to a powerful climax, and demonstrates how ways of seeing are fundamental to self-identity. Coppola and Spalanzani argue their competing claims to have given 'life' to Olimpia through respectively providing the eyes and the clockwork mechanism: 'I made the eyes … I made the clockwork' (p. 332). Olimpia's own terrible fate is symbolised by the tearing out of her eyes: she has 'no eyes, just black caverns where eyes should be' (p. 332) – exactly like the figures in the child's earlier nightmare vision. When Spalanzani picks up the eyes and hurls them at Nathanael 'so that they struck him on the chest' (p. 332), it is plain that in his estimation the eyes, and the 'life' they gave to the doll, belong most properly to Nathanael. The story indicates that Nathanael has invested everything – his whole way of seeing life – in his idealising love for Olimpia and what she represents: passion, transcendence, poetry. When that way of seeing fails, the coherence of the 'I' fractures, and he loses his mind and his sense of identity.

Childhood trauma and Romantic subjectivity

The crisis of the unified self we encountered above in relation to failed perception has been interpreted differently in another reading of 'The Sandman', that offered by the famous founder of psychoanalysis, Sigmund Freud (1856–1939). Freud's discussion of 'The Sandman' appears in an article written in 1919 on 'the uncanny' (in German, *'das unheimlich'*), where he treats the story of Nathanael and his nightmare fate as if it were one of his own case studies. At the heart of Freud's thinking is the idea that the experiences we have as a child shape our adult identities, and in particular our sexual selves. The notion that childhood experience is a significant shaping influence on the adult self is, of course, one that you have already met in relation to Wordsworth's handling of the memory of a drowning in *The Prelude*: one of the 'spots of time' which act as reservoirs for the poetic imagination. You'll perhaps remember Nicola Watson's observation in Chapter 1 that the philosopher Rousseau's 'interest in the way in which adult behaviour seems to be related to traumatic experiences in childhood and adolescence finds echoes in Wordsworth's interest in the continuing power of childhood memory within the man' (p. 30).

Activity 3

Compare the adult Nathanael's assessment of his formative childhood memories with the adult Wordsworth's 1799 reflection on his memory of the drowning, both reproduced below. How does each of the speakers sum up the remembered event? And how do they explain its impact on them?

> Why should I weary you, my dear Lothar? Why should I dwell on minute details, when so much remains to be told? Suffice it to say that I was caught eavesdropping and was roughly treated by Coppelius. Fear and terror brought on a violent fever, with which I was laid low for several weeks. 'Is the Sandman still there?' These were my first coherent words and the sign that I was cured, that my life had been saved. Now I need only tell you about the most terrifying moment of my early life; you will then be convinced that it is not the weakness of my eyesight that makes everything appear colourless, but that a sombre destiny has indeed veiled my life in a murky cloud, which perhaps I shall not penetrate until I die.

(p. 312)

… I might advert
To numerous accidents in flood or field,
Quarry or moor, or 'mid the winter snows,
Distresses and disasters, tragic facts
Of rural history, that impressed my mind
With images to which in following years
Far other feelings were attached – with forms
That yet exist with independent life,
And, like their archetypes, know no decay.

(Wordsworth, 1979 [1799], ll. 279–87)

Discussion

Nathanael of course associates the remembered episode in his father's study with 'fear and terror', but sums it up in terms which are unexpectedly matter-of-fact and dismissive: 'I was caught eavesdropping and was roughly treated by Coppelius'. The memory serves as a prelude to 'the most terrifying moment' of his father's death – the next episode in the story he is so eager to tell.

The autobiographical narrator of *The Prelude* reflects as an adult on his memory of the recovery of the drowned man, describing it as just one among many 'tragic facts of rural history' that he remembers from his childhood. He remarks that such memories in retrospect evoke 'far other feelings' than those experienced at the time. And he notes how the 'independent life' of the imagination has invested the memories with abiding significance – a significance he later goes on to describe as nourishing.

The creative 'mind' of Wordsworth's autobiographical narrator has thus allowed him to distance and absorb a traumatic childhood memory of loss, guilt and death, into a story of the maturing of his poetic imagination. As we saw in Chapter 1, the memory is valued for what it might mean for the coherent story of the growth of the poet's mind. By contrast, the effect of memory on Nathanael is much less benign. Nathanael initially notes the immediate physical impact of his traumatic encounter: he was laid low with a 'violent fever', from which he was subsequently cured. In the longer term, however, the disturbing episode in the study is mapped onto the occasion of his father's death, with the superimposed memories producing a sense that 'a sombre destiny has indeed veiled my life in a murky cloud, which perhaps I shall not penetrate until I die'. The impact of Nathanael's memory is to burden him with feelings of unresolved loss and inescapable fate, and with a poetic imagination driven by compulsion: 'So much remains to be told'.

Wordsworth's tale of the drowned man appears not long before the section in the 1799 *Prelude* in which the narrator recounts the death of his own father, an event which he says 'corrected' the kind of youthful desires he often experienced as an intense 'anxiety of hope' (ll. 360 and 357). For this narrator, the sense of loss attached to the death of the father provides him with a kind of steadying perspective. And the moment of Gothic trauma involved in watching in twilight for the reappearance of the missing man is similarly contained by the thought that memories can be sustaining. For Nathanael, however, the memory of his father's loss does not supply perspective but further distorts it. The death of the father has apparently stunted his growth from childhood to adulthood, and he finds himself in a 'colourless' adult present in which the anxiety of childhood trauma remains unprocessed and undiluted.

Freud explains this impact of childhood memory in 'The Sandman' in relation to his concept of the 'uncanny' or '*unheimlich*'. In German, this term gains most of its meaning as the opposite of '*heimlich*', which usually means 'homely' or 'familiar' (or 'family-ar'). Freud draws on a quotation from the German philosopher Friedrich Wilhelm Joseph Schelling (1775–1854) to explain the term: '*unheimlich* is that which ought to have remained hidden, but has nonetheless come to light' (quoted in Freud, 1955, p. 241). Later, when discussing 'The Sandman' he provides a further definition, couched in psychological terms:

> An uncanny experience occurs either when infantile complexes which have been repressed are once more revived by some impression, or when primitive beliefs which have not been surmounted seem once more to be confirmed.
>
> (Freud, 1955, p. 249)

The sudden appearance of the barometer seller revives a repressed memory in Nathanael which is a composite of the story of the Sandman, and Coppelius's threat that his eyes will be pulled out. In Nathanael's retelling the repressed memory links his experience in the room that seems both workshop and torture chamber, the return of Coppelius a year later, and the death of his father.

The particular 'infantile complex' that Freud refers to above is the fear of castration: a fear which, in his psychological theory, is associated with the male child's developing sense of rivalry with his father for the affections of his mother. Without dealing with this fear of castration by deferring to his father's prior claims, a boy cannot develop as an adult and independent personality. Freud reads 'The Sandman' as a case study of Nathanael – a man marked by a boyhood failure to pass beyond and repress the fear of castration, encapsulated in his horrified remembering of Coppelius's threat to pull out his eyes. Nathanael suffers from unresolved guilt, feeling that he is in some way responsible for his father's death, and from an unresolved fear of Coppelius who seems to be a double for his father.

Clara and Olimpia

The relationship between the 'homely' and the 'uncanny', the familiar and the strange, is equally important for the story's treatment of its two female characters. There are of course many parallels between them; in fact, they double one another. Clara's first attempt at describing herself through Nathanael's eyes tells us of her characteristic 'calm and deliberation' in the face of crisis (p. 314). Our first view of Olimpia reveals her as a similarly composed and balanced figure: 'a tall, very slim woman, beautifully proportioned and magnificently dressed, was sitting in front of a small table on which she was leaning, with her hands folded' (p. 317). Clara is subject to criticism for being 'unresponsive and prosaic' (p. 319), and in parallel, at Spalanzani's ball 'criticism was levelled particularly at the rigid and silent Olimpia' (p. 329). Both women are repeatedly described as cold. Nathanael's indignant riposte to Clara's rejection of his poem is to call her 'You accursed lifeless automaton', in a **proleptic** allusion to his later discovery about Olimpia; in the climactic scene on the tower, he will actually mistake Clara for Olimpia.

These women both exemplify the *heimlich* in that they fulfil the socially approved role for women as the passive, modest exemplars of domestic virtue. The main difference between the two is that Clara is allowed a voice and a measure of agency in the action of the story, whereas Olimpia is 'entirely passive and taciturn' (p. 331). Clara sees, Olimpia is seen. Clara's role is to contain the flights of Nathanael's imagination by opposing them, and thus anchor him back to reality; whereas Olimpia's compliant responses indulge his extremes of fantasy. What is perhaps of most interest about these two women, however, is the fact that both are presented as the direct or indirect products of masculine creative endeavour.

Activity 4

Reread the following two passages from *The Sandman*: first, from 'I might now go on cheerfully with my story ...', on p. 319, to '... and all his irritation vanished', on p. 320; second, from 'Observing his friend's state of mind' to '... and I'm wasting my words', on p. 330. Compare the narrator's introductory description of Clara, in the first passage, with Siegmund's account of the general opinion of Olimpia and Nathanael's response to it, in the second, by answering the following questions:

1   What strike you as the similarities and differences between these descriptions?

2   How do the descriptions convey that both women are, in their different ways, constructed as the artificial creations of men?

3   How are we invited to respond to these efforts of artificial creation?

Discussion

1   The narrator's assessment of Clara is tempered by the detachment of humour. We learn little about her physical attributes other than that the way they might be conventionally described is 'a lot of nonsense'. We are, however, told twice about her 'sly, ironic smile'; and the narrator offers apparently sincere praise for her 'warm-hearted' tenderness, and 'acute, discriminating mind'. He seems to be providing a balanced judgement of a woman who, he implies, should be valued for her internal personal qualities rather than her external beauty. In Siegmund's and Nathanael's descriptions of Olimpia, we are given two starkly opposing views of the woman which can't be reconciled: views which can't be reconciled. Siegmund focuses on her physical body, finding her face and figure 'regular' but her gaze and movement uncannily lifeless. Nathanael on the other hand lauds the depths of Olimpia's 'soul', recognising himself in the 'inner world' of her love. Both descriptions draw on opposing imagery of cold and warmth. The main difference between these descriptions relates to their reliability: the reader is persuaded by the author-figure's view of Clara, and unsurprised by Siegmund's assessment of Olimpia; but we register conclusively that Nathanael's view of Olimpia is deluded because he is the only one who holds it.

2   The description of both women is framed by reference to art. Hoffmann's description of Clara is interrupted by a telling digression on some of the ways in which painters, poets and other creative workers have attempted to render female beauty in artistic form. Architects and sculptors focus on making the female figure 'perfectly proportioned'. Painters use line and 'colouring techniques' to idealise the female form. Poets use imagery or 'comparisons' with the

landscape as an indirect means of capturing the 'vivifying' effects of feminine allure. Musicians locate their creative inspiration in the 'penetrating' gaze of the female muse. Siegmund's description of Olimpia, by contrast, credits her appearance of beauty to the creative work of craft rather than art. Her movement is 'produced by some mechanism like clockwork'; and her singing, playing and dancing exhibit the 'soulless timing of a machine'. Her 'regular', 'measured' and 'perfect' qualities are attributed to an all-too-evident artifice which betrays her as 'only pretending to be a living being'. Both women are thus described in terms of forms of masculine idealisation.

3   Hoffmann's comic jibes at the devices and pretensions of painters and poets invite unambiguous scepticism towards the artistic idealisation of the female form. The satire aimed at the 'very odd comparison' made between Clara's eyes and a Ruysdael landscape painting exposes the sort of easy and unoriginal artistic **trope** whereby female fertility is equated with the productivity of the land. The creative imagination is dismissed by both Clara and the narrator as the product of 'muddle-headed enthusiasts' who mistake 'shifting, shadowy images' for the real thing. The attempt at using science to manufacture the ideal woman is subjected to similar ridicule: we are invited to share Siegmund's reaction to Olimpia as 'weird' and 'strange'. Ultimately the tale suggests a critique of the efforts of both artists and scientists to reconstruct the feminine ideal in imaginary form.

Both women, then, in different ways, act as a critique of the masculine Romantic imagination. Clara's clear-sighted but rational sensibility would seem to throw into sharp relief the distortion and sickness of Nathanael's vision. Olimpia, as a mere mechanical doll, equally reveals his idealising vision as creative but deluded.

Art and automata

This sceptical assessment of creative genius, whether artistic or scientific, has continuities with other Romantic texts, including Mary Shelley's *Frankenstein, or the Modern Prometheus* published two years later in 1818. Frankenstein, an enthusiastic student of science, sets about creating another human being, by galvanising inanimate body parts with electricity. At a later point in the novel, he goes on to destroy the female companion that he makes for his monster. Nathanael's creative project is literary rather than scientific, but is equally associated with a project of animating the inanimate: we learn that his 'Poems, fantasies, visions, novels, stories, were supplemented daily by all manner of incoherent sonnets, *ballades*, and *canzoni*, which he read to Olimpia for hours on end without ever wearying' (p. 330). Nathanael here is the embodiment of the Romantic imagination, which becomes self-devouring in its excess of aspiration. Like Frankenstein, Nathanael is ultimately destroyed by the paradox of the Romantic artist's condition as the critic Röder describes it: 'to remain subject to the constraints of the temporal world while his imagination makes him yearn for the higher realm of the ideal' (Röder, 2003, p. 15). His poems are not brilliant inventions so much as literary versions of automata. His love for the automaton Olimpia is itself parodic of the love of the invisible world of transcendence. You might have noticed that Nathanael's misguided response to her is couched in an exaggerated parody of the language of transcendent Romanticism: 'an inner world filled with love and lofty awareness of the spiritual life led in contemplation of the everlasting Beyond' (p. 330).

To further explore this idea that Nathanael represents a distorted version of the Romantic author, we can usefully consider the fine line between imagination and delusion drawn in the context of his earlier attempt at writing poetry. The narrator informs us that 'in the past Nathanael had shown a special gift for composing charming and vivid stories' (p. 321): this belief that the Romantic writer has some 'special' quality is of course familiar from our discussion of ways of seeing above. Nathanael's 'special gift' has, however, been warped by the introspective mood which leads him to dwell on 'dreams and premonitions' (pp. 320 and 322). It results, moreover, in compositions which have become 'gloomy, unintelligible and formless' and infected by what Clara perceives as 'dismal, obscure, tedious mysticism' (p. 320).

Activity 5

Now focus on the section of 'The Sandman' in which Nathanael writes his fantasy narrative poem about the impending destruction of his relationship with Clara, and then reads it out to her. The passage begins with the sentence: 'Finally he conceived the plan of writing a poem' on p. 321, and ends with Clara's injunction to 'Throw the crazy, senseless, insane story into the fire' on p. 322.

1 What effect does the act of writing the poem have on Nathanael?

2 What is the effect of its content when he reads it aloud, both to himself and later to Clara?

Discussion

The exercise of the imagination involved in creative writing appears on the surface to have a therapeutic effect. Nathanael is 'calm and collected' when absorbed in the process of composition, and sufficiently detached to revise his work and submit it 'to the constraints of metre'. While he is writing the poem, he is able to converse with Clara 'in a lively, cheerful manner about pleasant matters'. All of his real-world fears and nightmarish forebodings have been channelled into the act of literary creation; and for a moment it seems as if Nathanael, like Wordsworth in *The Prelude*, might be able to contain the darker side of his imagination by subjecting it to the distancing and control of the writing process.

The content of the poem and Nathanael's reaction to it reveal, however, that writing poetry has simply become a means for the fictional Romantic author to indulge his wildest fantasies. The 'black hand', the recurring 'circle of flames', and the violent waves which 'rear up like black giants with white heads' are visions of a hallucinatory quality which culminate in the final delusory perception that 'what looks at him from Clara's kindly eyes is death'. And on reading the poem to Clara, Nathanael is again 'entirely carried away' from reality by the force of the imaginary world which possesses him. Perhaps most significantly, when Nathanael first reads the poem out loud, he experiences a splitting of the self: the words he has written do not seem to be his own: 'whose hideous voice is this?' When the ironic voice of the narrator tells us of Nathanael's later decision 'that it was a highly successful poem', it doesn't take much for the reader to be convinced that this assessment is entirely deluded.

Hoffmann's story shows us, then, how a fervent authorial imagination allowed to run riot can too easily mutate into destructive delusion. Nathanael's imagination is his undoing, figuratively symbolised in the child's memory of Coppelius dislocating his hands and feet and trying to fit them back into the wrong sockets (p. 312).

The story, however, also offers us an alternative, apparently healthier, version of the imagination, and an analysis of where Nathanael's approach to the creative Romantic life has gone wrong. Clara, we are told, in spite of the prosaic and clear-sighted qualities which make her unresponsive to fantasy literature, 'had the vivid imagination of a cheerful, ingenuous, child-like child' (p. 320). You might want to think about how this relates to the failure of the two to relate to each other on the basis of compromise. Is Hoffmann endorsing this kind of imagination, or suggesting that it too has limitations? What exactly are we meant to think of Clara's destiny as reported in the last paragraph of the story in which she finds 'the quiet domestic happiness which suited her cheerful, sunny disposition, and which she could never have enjoyed with the tormented, self-divided Nathanael' (p. 336)?

But Nathanael is not the only figure in this story who seems to embody the equivocal nature of Romantic art and the Romantic imagination. An alternative, more powerful figure for the Romantic artist might rather be Dr Coppelius. A diabolical seducer, who possesses the power of enduing his automaton with apparent life, and who is capable of appearing in multiple forms, Coppelius is just one version of an ambiguously demonic figure who appears repeatedly in Hoffmann's fiction. Very frequently, such figures appear in connection with technology, and especially with automata, which particularly fascinated Hoffmann. Let's take a look at two passages from a story entitled 'Automata' (written in 1814 but published in the collection *Die Serapions-Brüder* in 1819) connected with a mysterious figure called Professor X—, so as to dig more deeply into Hoffmann's exploration of the proper vocation of the Romantic artist.

Activity 6

Read the two extracts from 'Automata' reproduced below. The first deals with a formal visit that two friends pay to Professor X— , celebrated for his connection with a particularly mysterious automaton, the 'Talking Turk', who appears to be able to read the very soul of his questioner. They ask to see his famous collection of automata. The second describes their discovery, while on a walk beyond the town, of the Professor wandering in his garden, which another friend describes as 'his mysterious laboratory' (Hoffmann, 1967, p. 101). Compare what these two extracts have to say about the nature of art and Romantic genius.

Extract 1

He fetched his keys with a great clatter, and opened the door of a tastefully and elegantly furnished hall, where the automata were. There was a piano in the middle of the room on a raised platform; beside it, on the right, a life-sized figure of a man, with a flute in his hand; on the left, a female figure, seated at an instrument somewhat resembling a piano; behind her were two boys with a drum and a triangle. In the background our two friends noticed an orchestrion … and all around the walls were a number of musical clocks. The Professor passed in an offhand way close by the orchestrion and the clocks, and just touched the automata, almost imperceptibly; then he sat down at the piano, and began to play, pianissimo, an andante in the style of a march. He played it once through by himself; and as he commenced it for the second time the flute player put his instrument to his lips, and took up the melody; then one of the boys drummed softly on his drum in the most accurate time, and the other just touched his triangle. … Presently the lady came in with full chords sounding something like those of a harmonica, which she produced by pressing down the keys of her instrument; and then the whole room kept growing more and more alive; the musical clocks came in one by one, with the utmost rhythmical precision; the boy drummed louder; the triangle rang through the room, and lastly the orchestrion set to work, and drummed and trumpeted fortissimo, so that the whole place shook. This went on till the Professor wound up the whole business with one final chord, all the machines finishing also, with the utmost precision. Our friends bestowed the applause which the Professor's complacent smile (with its undercurrent of sarcasm) seemed to demand of them. …

'Most interesting and ingenious, wasn't it?' said Ferdinand; but Lewis's anger, long restrained, broke out.

'Oh! Damn that wretched Professor!' he cried. 'What a terrible, terrible disappointment! Where are all the revelations we expected?

(Hoffmann, 1967, p. 94)

Extract 2

What was their astonishment to see Professor X— standing in the middle of the garden, beneath a lofty ash-tree! Instead of the repellent ironic grin with which he had received them at his house, his face wore an expression of deep melancholy

earnestness, and his gaze was fixed upon the heavens, as if
he were contemplating that world beyond the skies, of which
these marvellous tones, floating in the air like the breath of a
zephyr, were telling. He walked up and down the central path,
with slow and measured steps; and, as he passed along,
everything around him seemed to waken into life and
movement. In every direction crystal tones came scintillating
out of the dark bushes and trees, and, streaming through the
air like flame, united in a wondrous concert, penetrating the
inmost heart, and waking in the soul the most rapturous
emotions of a higher world. Twilight was falling fast; the
Professor disappeared among the hedges, and the tones died
away in pianissimo. At length our friends went back to town in
profound silence ...

(Hoffmann, 1967, pp. 99–100)

Discussion

The first passage describes the Professor as a man of the utmost
ingenuity in producing musical machines, but also a charlatan, showman
and ironist; the second describes him as a true Romantic artist who
produces music which, though possibly using some sort of technology,
seems to transcend it. The 'revelations' that the friends had hoped from
the first display are provided by the second. The story is concerned to
distinguish true art from fake. True art channels the transcendent,
however imperfectly, and is associated with the natural; fake art may be
perfect but is merely mechanical. You might have noticed in the extracts
above that while the first musical performance has a distinct beginning,
middle and climax, conducted within the formalities of a polite visit,
the second is a case of unintentional eavesdropping, and the musical
performance 'wakens' and 'dies away' through the garden like a
living thing.

Hoffmann, like other Romantic contemporaries, experimented
constantly to try to find an appropriate form and language through
which to convey an apprehension of the transcendent – and its dark
double, madness and delusion. Typically therefore, and like the second
instance of music in the garden, the structure of Hoffmann's stories
embodies uncertainty and open-endedness, an open form that will be

dreamlike or visionary, filled with repetition and yet fragmentary. The language will draw attention to its own limitations. The entire story will poise in a delicate balance the rational and the unexplained, or even supernatural. Hoffmann offers many descriptions of this aesthetic in his tales, but one will have to do here. This is part of the concluding conversation between 'Theodore' and his friends Lothair and Ottmar from 'Automata'. Ottmar notes that

> 'Theodore used to take a delight in exciting people's imaginations by means of the most extraordinary – nay, wild and insane – stories, and then suddenly break them off. Not only this, but everything he did at that time was a fragment. He read second volumes only, not troubling himself about the firsts or thirds; saw only the second and third acts of plays; and so on.'
>
> 'And,' said Theodore, 'I still have that inclination; to this hour nothing is so distasteful to me as when, in a story or a novel, the stage on which the imaginary world has been in action is swept so clean by the historic broom that not the smallest grain or particle of dust is left on it; when you go home so completely sated and satisfied that you have not the faintest desire left to have another peep behind the curtain. On the other hand, many a fragment of a clever story sinks deep into my soul, and the continuance of the play of my imagination, as it goes along on its own swing, gives me an enduring pleasure ...'
>
> (Hoffmann, 1967, pp. 102–3)

Of all of Hoffmann's 'Tales', 'The Sandman' is probably the least imperfect in form or inconclusive in story. It is also the most inclined to ascribe the supernatural to psychological disturbance. Yet it conforms to this description of the Romantic aesthetic to the extent that it does not fully resolve the tensions between what its three narrating voices perceive as reality. The fantastic finds a precarious lodging-place in the hesitation between their different versions of events. Or, to put it another way, at the end the quasi-supernatural figure of Dr Coppelius remains unassimilated within the realist account offered by the ironic voice of Hoffmann-as-narrator.

Conclusion

We have seen in this chapter how the multiple personae Hoffmann crafted for his professional life are paralleled in 'The Sandman' by a fictional recasting of the narrating 'Hoffmann' figure. We have also seen how the treatment of Nathanael offers a sceptical view of the tendency of the Romantic artist to fantasise and idealise. Hoffmann's stories juxtapose the *heimlich* with the uncanny, the deluded with the rational, the unified with the divided self, and the idea of crafted fakery with that of true creative genius. For this author, the vocation of the Romantic artist is to find a form and language which will accommodate such oppositions in an open and unresolved co-existence.

References

Freud, S. (1955 [1919]) 'The uncanny' in *An Infantile Neurosis and Other Works 1917–1919*, vol. 17 of *The Complete Psychological Works of Sigmund Freud* (trans. J. Strachey), London, Hogarth Press, pp. 217–52.

Hoffmann, E.T.A. (2008) 'The Sandman' in *E.T.A. Hoffmann: The Golden Pot and Other Tales* (trans. R. Robertson), Oxford, Oxford University Press, pp. 85–118.

Hoffmann, E.T.A. (1967) *The Best Tales of Hoffmann* (ed. E.F. Bleiler), New York, Dover Publications.

Röder, B. (2003) *A Study of the Major Novellas of E.T.A. Hoffmann*, Woodbridge, Camden House.

Shelley, M.W. (1982 [1818]) *Frankenstein, or the Modern Prometheus: The 1818 Text* (ed. J. Rieger), Chicago, Chicago University Press.

Wordsworth, W. (1979 [1799]) *The Prelude* in Wordsworth, J., Abrams, M.H. and Gill, S. (eds) *The Prelude 1799, 1805, 1880: Authoritative Texts; Context and Reception; Recent Critical Essays*, New York, W.W. Norton and Company, pp. 1–13.

Further reading

Beutin, W., et al. (1993) *A History of German Literature* (trans. C. Krojzl) London, Routledge.

Brown, H.M. (2006) *E.T.A. Hoffmann and the Serapiontic Principle*, Rochester, NY, Camden House.

Dutchman-Smith, V. (2009) *E.T.A. Hoffmann and Alcohol: Biography, Reception, and Art*, London, MHRA and Institute of Germanic and Romance Studies, School of Advanced Study, University of London.

Kropf, D.G. (1994) *Authorship as Alchemy: Subversive Writing in Pushkin, Scott, Hoffmann*, Stanford, Stanford University Press.

Todorov, T. (1975) *The Fantastic: A Structural Approach to a Literary Genre*, Ithaca, NY, Cornell University Press.

Ziolkowski, T. (1990) *German Romanticism and its Institutions*, Princeton, Princeton University Press.

Conclusion to Part 1

Nicola J. Watson

The last four chapters have been concerned with the ways in which Romantic writers have written (and been written into) Romantic lives. One peculiarity that binds much writing of the Romantic period together is an unprecedented interest in the interior life. Romantic writing is often preoccupied with making claims both for the importance of the interior life, and for the social importance of writers' efforts to represent 'the mind of man'.

We looked first at the way that Wordsworth came to conceive of the poet's work as describing the interior life of the individual and, by extension, the sympathies that bind man to man in a regenerate society. Wordsworth carried out his poetic experiment on himself, using a great range of genres, from epic, in his autobiographical poem *The Prelude*, to lyric, in short poems exploring episodes of intense remembered emotion. By way of contrast, we have considered the multiple and shifting ways in which Shelley conceived the poet's work, concentrating on his lyrics. His sometimes anxious self-scrutiny is intermixed with a fervent engagement with the public, political world, and the poet's role within it. In both cases, we have seen how the poets' claims for the importance of poetry and the poet solicit and reward interpretation rooted in the biographical. With De Quincey's *Confessions*, we turned to look at a distinctively urban and Gothic take on representing the Romantic inner life, especially the operations of memory. Rather than being empowered, as the Wordsworthian self is, by the resources of memory, the writer describes himself as victimised by memories transformed into monstrous dreams. De Quincey's narrative displays strongly Gothic tendencies: a sense of the self fragmented and victimised, of nightmare repetition and suffocating enclosure, of meaning deferred and occluded rather than revealed and resolved. Hoffmann, writing in the new short form of the literary tale, also described the Romantic life in Gothic terms. 'The Sandman' describes a self not in control of itself, its perceptions or its self-expression, which falls victim to its own only half-understood desires and drives.

While both Wordsworth and Shelley, in their grandest statements, fuse the real of the natural landscape with the real of the poet's mind into a sublime vision of poetic power, the prose writers typically describe a more uncertain negotiation of the writer with the real, in which it is not clear what is real and what is merely subjective. Each writer develops his own language to describe this; De Quincey concentrates on the distortions of dreams that infect domestic bliss, while Hoffmann describes the distortions of vision that Nathanael experiences. Accordingly, where the autobiographical form is adopted, it tends to be truncated or contested, as in the diary form of the later parts of the *Confessions* or the opening and strongly contrasting letters of 'The Sandman'. Along with this uncertainty about the truth of poetic vision or imagination, we can read an uncertainty about its power and efficacy in the modern world. Both texts seem to argue that poetic vision is inimical to everyday domestic heterosexual happiness; they also, however, glamorise as well as deplore this heightened state of imagination.

This change of emphasis in the representation of the Romantic self may well reflect world events. These chapters bracket the Romantic period, from the years immediately following the French Revolution to the establishment across Europe of autocracies after the fall of Napoleon. Wordsworth's exploration of the poetic self evidently tends to the optimistic, as does that of Shelley, albeit in a more qualified vein. It is probably not coincidental that Wordsworth's formative years coincided with the optimism of the French Revolution, and although he later turned against revolutionary politics, his faith in the power of the individual remained of its time. Equally, Shelley consciously held to his own version of revolutionary optimism against the grain of his own formative years, the aftermath of the Napoleonic wars, a period of economic hardship, social unrest, and general cultural uncertainty right across Europe. Hoffmann and De Quincey are more characteristic of their era in their pessimistic explorations of the delusive and self-destructive power of the imagination.

Readings for Part 1

Contents

Reading 1.1 Dorothy Wordsworth, *The Grasmere Journals*

Source: Dorothy Wordsworth (1993 [1802]) *The Grasmere Journals* **(ed. P. Woof), Oxford, Oxford University Press, pp. 84–6 and 215. Footnotes are by the editor of this edition.**

Thursday 15th. It was a threatening misty morning – but mild. We set off after dinner from Eusemere – Mrs Clarkson went a short way with us but turned back. The wind was furious & we thought we must have returned. We first rested in the large Boat-house, then under a furze Bush opposite Mr Clarksons, saw the plough going in the field. The wind seized our breath the Lake was rough. There was a Boat by itself floating in the middle of the Bay below Water Millock – We rested again in the Water Millock lane. The hawthorns are black & green, the birches here & there greenish but there is yet more of purple to be seen on the Twigs. We got over into a field to avoid some cows – people working, a few primroses by the roadside, woodsorrel flowers, the anemone, scentless violets, strawberries[1], & that starry yellow flower which Mrs C calls pile wort[2]. When we were in the woods beyond Gowbarrow park[3] we saw a few daffodils close to the water side, we fancied that the lake had floated the seeds ashore & that the little colony had so sprung up – But as we went along there were more & yet more & at last under the boughs of the trees, we saw that there was a long belt of them along the shore, about the breadth of a country turnpike road. I never saw daffodils so beautiful they grew among the mossy stones about & about them, some rested their heads upon these stones as on a pillow for weariness & the rest tossed & reeled & danced & seemed as if they verily laughed with the wind that blew upon them over the Lake, they looked so gay ever glancing ever changing. This wind blew directly over the Lake to them. There was here & there a little knot & a few

[1] Strawberries and the 'scentless violets' are an added insertion.
[2] Mrs Clarkson was not alone in calling the 'starry yellow flower', or Lesser Celandine, 'pile wort'; (William Withering, *An Arrangement of British Plants according to the latest Improvements of the Linnean System and an Introduction to the Study of Botany*, vol. ii (Birmingham, 1796), p. 504) also offers 'Common Pilewort' as an alternative name.
[3] Walking the length of Ullswater (9 miles) on its western shore, D and W, when beyond Gowbarrow Park, were closer to Patterdale than to Pooley Bridge. Gowbarrow Park comprised the lower slopes of Gowbarrow Fell and was a deer park belonging to the Duke of Norfolk. It was noted by every Lakes writer from Gilpin in 1772 to Green in 1819. The daffodils were to be celebrated in W's poem, 'I wandered lonely as a cloud', of 2 years later. They were not, of course, the large, garden daffodils that we know today but the smaller, paler, wild daffodils, pseudo-narcissi.

stragglers a few yards higher up but they were so few as not to disturb the simplicity & unity & life of that one busy highway – We rested again & again. The Bays were stormy & we heard the waves at different distances & in the middle of the water like the Sea – Rain came on, we were wet when we reached Luffs but we called in. Luckily all was chearless & gloomy so we faced the storm – we *must* have been wet if we had waited – put on dry clothes at Dobson's. I was very kindly treated by a young woman, the Landlady looked sour but it is her way. She gave us a goodish supper, excellent ham & potatoes. We paid 7*l* when we came away. William was sitting by a bright fire when I came downstairs he soon made his way to the Library piled up in a corner of the window. He brought out a volume of Enfield's Speaker, another miscellany, & an odd volume of Congreve's plays. We had a glass of warm rum & water – we enjoyed ourselves & wished for Mary. It rained & blew when we went to bed. NB deer in Gowbarrow park like to skeletons.

Reading 1.2 William Wordsworth, 'Point Rash-Judgment'

Source: James Butler and Karen Green (eds) (1992) *Lyrical Ballads, and Other Poems, 1797–1800*, **New York, Cornell University Press, pp. 247–50**.

A narrow girdle of rough stones and crags,
A rude and natural causeway, interpos'd
Between the water and a winding slope
Of copse and thicket, leaves the eastern shore
Of Grasmere safe in its own privacy.   5
And there, myself and two beloved Friends,
One calm September morning, ere the mist
Had altogether yielded to the sun,
Saunter'd on this retir'd and difficult way.
– Ill suits the road with one in haste, but we   10
Play'd with our time; and, as we stroll'd along,
It was our occupation to observe
Such objects as the waves had toss'd ashore,
Feather, or leaf, or weed, or wither'd bough,
Each on the other heap'd along the line   15
Of the dry wreck. And in our vacant mood,
Not seldom did we stop to watch some tuft
Of dandelion seed or thistle's beard,
Which, seeming lifeless half, and half impell'd
By some internal feeling, skimm'd along   20
Close to the surface of the lake that lay
Asleep in a dead calm, ran closely on
Along the dead calm lake, now here, now there,
In all its sportive wanderings all the while
Making report of an invisible breeze   25
That was its wings, its chariot, and its horse,
Its very playmate and its moving soul.
– And often, trifling with a privilege
Alike indulg'd to all, we paus'd, one now
And now the other, to point out, perchance   30
To pluck, some flower or water-weed, too fair
Either to be divided from the place
On which it grew, or to be left alone
To its own beauty. Many such there are,
Fair ferns and flowers, and chiefly that tall plant   35

So stately, of the Queen Osmunda nam'd,
Plant lovelier in its own retir'd abode
On Grasmere's beach, than Naid by the side
Of Grecian brook, or Lady of the Mere
Sole-sitting by the shores of old Romance.   40
– So fared we that sweet morning: from the fields
Meanwhile, a noise was heard, the busy mirth
Of Reapers, Men and Women, Boys and Girls.
Delighted much to listen to those sounds,
And in the fashion which I have describ'd   45
Feeding unthinking fancies, we advanc'd
Along the indented shore; when suddenly,
Through a thin veil of glittering haze, we saw
Before us on a Point of jutting land
The tall and upright figure of a Man   50
Attir'd in peasant's garb, who stood alone
Angling beside the margin of the lake.
That way we turn'd our steps; nor was it long
Ere making ready comments on the sight
Which then we saw, with one and the same voice   55
We all cried out, that he must be indeed
An idle man, who thus could lose a day
Of the mid-harvest, when the labourer's hire
Is ample, and some little might be stor'd
Wherewith to chear him in the winter time.   60
Thus talking of that Peasant we approach'd
Close to the spot where with his rod and line
He stood alone; whereat he turn'd his head
To greet us – and we saw a Man worn down
By sickness, gaunt and lean, with sunken cheeks   65
And wasted limbs, his legs so long and lean
That for my single self I look'd at them,
Forgetful of the body they sustain'd. –
Too weak to labour in the harvest field,
The man was using his best skill to gain   70
A pittance from the dead unfeeling lake
That knew not of his wants. I will not say
What thoughts immediately were ours, nor how
The happy idleness of that sweet morn,
With all its lovely images, was chang'd   75
To serious musing and to self-reproach.
Nor did we fail to see within ourselves
What need there is to be reserv'd in speech,
And temper all our thoughts with charity.
– Therefore, unwilling to forget that day,   80

My Friend, Myself, and She who then receiv'd
The same admonishment, have called the place
By a memorial name, uncouth indeed
As e'er by Mariner was giv'n to Bay
Or Foreland on a new-discover'd coast,   85
And POINT RASH-JUDGMENT is the name it bears.

Reading 1.3 William Wordsworth, 'The Brothers'

Source: James Butler and Karen Green (eds) (1992) *Lyrical Ballads, and Other Poems, 1797–1800*, **New York, Cornell University Press, pp. 142–59. Footnotes are by William Wordsworth.**

'These Tourists, Heaven preserve us! needs must live
A profitable life: some glance along,
Rapid and gay, as if the earth were air,
And they were butterflies to wheel about
Long as their summer lasted; some, as wise,   5
Upon the forehead of a jutting crag
Sit perch'd, with book and pencil on their knee,
And look and scribble, scribble on and look,
Until a man might travel twelve stout miles,
Or reap an acre of his neighbour's corn.   10
But, for that moping son of Idleness
Why can he tarry *yonder?* – In our church-yard
Is neither epitaph nor monument,
Tomb-stone nor name, only the turf we tread,
And a few natural graves.' To Jane, his Wife,   15
Thus spake the homely Priest of Ennerdale.
It was a July evening, and he sate
Upon the long stone seat beneath the eaves
Of his old cottage, as it chanced, that day,
Employ'd in winter's work. Upon the stone   20
His Wife sate near him, teasing matted wool,
While, from the twin cards tooth'd with glittering wire,
He fed the spindle of his youngest child,
Who turn'd her large round wheel in the open air
With back and forward steps. Towards the field   25
In which the parish chapel stood alone,
Girt round with a bare ring of mossy wall,
While half an hour went by, the Priest had sent
Many a long look of wonder, and at last,
Risen from his seat, beside the snowy ridge   30
Of carded wool which the old Man had piled
He laid his implements with gentle care,

This Poem was intended to be the concluding poem of a series of pastorals the scene of which was laid among the mountains of Cumberland and Westmoreland. I mention this to apologise for the abruptness with which the poem begins.

Each in the other lock'd; and, down the path
Which from his cottage to the church-yard led,
He took his way, impatient to accost   35
The Stranger, whom he saw still lingering there.

   'Twas one well known to him in former days,
A Shepherd-lad who ere his thirteenth year
Had changed his calling, with the mariners
A fellow-mariner, and so had fared   40
Through twenty seasons; but he had been rear'd
Among the mountains, and he in his heart
Was half a Shepherd on the stormy seas.
Oft in the piping shrouds had Leonard heard
The tones of waterfalls, and inland sounds   45
Of caves and trees: and when the regular wind
Between the tropics fill'd the steady sail
And blew with the same breath through days and weeks,
Lengthening invisibly its weary line
Along the cloudless main, he, in those hours   50
Of tiresome indolence would often hang
Over the vessel's side, and gaze and gaze,
And, while the broad green wave and sparkling foam
Flash'd round him images and hues, that wrought
In union with the employment of his heart,   55
He, thus by feverish passion overcome,
Even with the organs of his bodily eye,
Below him, in the bosom of the deep,
Saw mountains, saw the forms of sheep that graz'd
On verdant hills, with dwellings among trees,   60
And Shepherds clad in the same country grey
Which he himself had worn.[1]

               And now at length,
From perils manifold, with some small wealth
Acquir'd by traffic in the Indian Isles,
To his paternal home he is return'd,   65
With a determin'd purpose to resume
The life which he liv'd there, both for the sake
Of many darling pleasures, and the love
Which to an only Brother he has borne
In all his hardships, since that happy time   70
When, whether it blew foul or fair, they two
Were brother Shepherds on their native hills.

---

[1] This description of the Calenture is sketch'd from an imperfect recollection of an admirable one in prose, by Mr. Gilbert, author of the Hurricane.

– They were the last of all their race; and now,
When Leonard had approach'd his home, his heart
Fail'd in him, and, not venturing to inquire   75
Tidings of one whom he so dearly lov'd,
Towards the Church-yard he had turn'd aside,
That, as he knew in what particular spot
His family were laid, he thence might learn
If still his Brother liv'd, or to the file   80
Another grave was added. – He had found
Another grave, near which a full half-hour
He had remain'd, but, as he gaz'd, there grew
Such a confusion in his memory,
That he began to doubt, and he had hopes   85
That he had seen this heap of turf before,
That it was not another grave, but one
He had forgotten. He had lost his path,
As up the vale he came that afternoon,
Through fields which once had been well known to him: 90
And oh! what joy the recollection now
Sent to his heart! he lifted up his eyes,
And looking round he thought that he perceiv'd
Strange alteration wrought on every side
Among the woods and fields, and that the rocks,   95
And the eternal hills, themselves were chang'd.

By this the Priest who down the field had come
Unseen by Leonard, at the church-yard gate
Stopp'd short, and thence, at leisure, limb by limb
He scann'd him with a gay complacency.   100
Ay, thought the Vicar, smiling to himself,
'Tis one of those who needs must leave the path
Of the world's business, to go wild alone:
His arms have a perpetual holiday,
The happy man will creep about the fields   105
Following his fancies by the hour, to bring
Tears down his cheek, or solitary smiles
Into his face, until the setting sun
Write Fool upon his forehead. Planted thus
Beneath a shed that overarch'd the gate   110
Of this rude church-yard, till the stars appear'd
The good man might have commun'd with himself
But that the Stranger, who had left the grave,
Approach'd; he recogniz'd the Priest at once,
And after greetings interchang'd, and given   115

By Leonard to the Vicar as to one
Unknown to him, this dialogue ensued.

LEONARD.

You live, Sir, in these dales, a quiet life:
Your years make up one peaceful family;
And who would grieve and fret, if, welcome come   120
And welcome gone, they are so like each other,
They cannot be remember'd. Scarce a funeral
Comes to this church-yard once in eighteen months;
And yet, some changes must take place among you,
And you, who dwell here, even among these rocks   125
Can trace the finger of mortality,
And see, that with our threescore years and ten
We are not all that perish. — I remember,
For many years ago I pass'd this road,
There was a foot-way all along the fields   130
By the brook-side — 'tis gone — and that dark cleft!
To me it does not seem to wear the face
Which then it had.

PRIEST.

                   Why, Sir, for aught I know,
That chasm is much the same —

LEONARD.

                        But, surely, yonder —

PRIEST.

Ay, there indeed your memory is a friend   135
That does not play you false. — On that tall pike
(It is the loneliest place of all these hills)
There were two Springs which bubbled side by side,
As if they had been made that they might be
Companions for each other: ten years back,   140
Close to those brother fountains, the huge crag
Was rent with lightning — one is dead and gone,
The other, left behind, is flowing still. —
For accidents and changes such as these,
Why we have store of them! a water-spout   145
Will bring down half a mountain; what a feast
For folks that wander up and down like you,
To see an acre's breadth of that wide cliff
One roaring cataract — a sharp May storm
Will come with loads of January snow,   150
And in one night send twenty score of sheep
To feed the ravens, or a Shepherd dies

By some untoward death among the rocks:
The ice breaks up and sweeps away a bridge –
A wood is fell'd: – and then for our own homes!   155
A child is born or christen'd, a field plough'd,
A daughter sent to service, a web spun,
The old house-clock is deck'd with a new face;
And hence, so far from wanting facts or dates
To chronicle the time, we all have here   160
A pair of diaries, one serving, Sir,
For the whole dale, and one for each fire-side.
Yours was a stranger's judgment: for historians
Commend me to these vallies.

LEONARD.

                  Yet your church-yard
Seems, if such freedom may be used with you,   165
To say that you are heedless of the past.
An orphan could not find his Mother's grave.
Here's neither head nor foot-stone, plate of brass,
Cross-bones or skull, type of our earthly state
Or emblem of our hopes: the dead man's home   170
Is but a fellow to that pasture field.

PRIEST.

Why, there, Sir, is a thought that's new to me.
The Stone-cutters, 'tis true, might beg their bread
If every English church-yard were like ours:
Yet your conclusion wanders from the truth.   175
We have no need of names and epitaphs,
We talk about the dead by our fire-sides.
And then for our immortal part, *we* want
No symbols, Sir, to tell us that plain tale:
The thought of death sits easy on the man   180
Who has been born and dies among the mountains.

LEONARD.

Your dalesmen, then, do in each other's thoughts
Possess a kind of second life: no doubt
You, Sir, could help me to the history
Of half these Graves?

PRIEST.

                For eight-score winters past   185
With what I've witness'd and with what I've heard
Perhaps I might, and, on a winter's evening,
If you were seated at my chimney's nook,
By turning o'er these hillocks one by one,

We two could travel, Sir, through a strange round,   190
Yet all in the broad high-way of the world.
Now there's a grave – your foot is half upon it,
It looks just like the rest, and yet that man
Died broken hearted –

                    LEONARD.

                    'Tis a common case,
We'll take another: who is he that lies   195
Beneath yon ridge, the last of those three graves; –
It touches on that piece of native rock
Left in the church-yard wall –

                    PRIEST.

                         That's Walter Ewbank.
He had as white a head and fresh a cheek
As ever were produc'd by youth and age   200
Engendering in the blood of hale fourscore.
For five long generations had the heart
Of Walter's forefathers o'erflow'd the bounds
Of their inheritance, that single cottage,
You see it yonder, and those few green fields.   205
They toil'd and wrought, and still, from sire to son,
Each struggled, and each yielded as before
A little – yet a little – and old Walter,
They left to him the family heart, and land
With other burthens than the crop it bore.   210
Year after year the old man still preserv'd
A chearful mind, and buffeted with bond,
Interest and mortgages; at last he sank,
And went into his grave before his time.
Poor Walter! whether it was care that spurr'd him   215
God only knows, but to the very last
He had the lightest foot in Ennerdale:
His pace was never that of an old man;
I almost see him tripping down the path
With his two Grandsons after him – but you,   220
Unless our Landlord be your host tonight,
Have far to travel, and in these rough paths
Even in the longest day of midsummer –

                    LEONARD.

But these two orphans?

                    PRIEST.

         Orphans! such they were –
Yet not while Walter liv'd – for, though their Parents   225

Lay buried side by side as now they lie,
The old Man was a father to the boys,
Two fathers in one father: and if tears
Shed when he talk'd of them where they were not,
And hauntings from the infirmity of love,   230
Are aught of what makes up a mother's heart,
This old Man in the day of his old age
Was half a mother to them. – If you weep, Sir,
To hear a stranger talking about strangers,
Heaven bless you when you are among your kindred! –   235
Ay. You may turn that way – it is a grave
Which will bear looking at.

              LEONARD.

                    These Boys – I hope
They lov'd this good old Man –

              PRIEST.

                    They did, and truly,
But that was what we almost overlook'd,
They were such darlings of each other. For   240
Though from their cradles they had liv'd with Walter,
The only kinsman near them in the house,
Yet he being old, they had much love to spare,
And it all went into each other's hearts.
Leonard, the elder by just eighteen months,   245
Was two years taller: 'twas a joy to see,
To hear, to meet them! from their house the School
Was distant three short miles, and in the time
Of storm and thaw, when every water-course
And unbridg'd stream, such as you may have notic'd   250
Crossing our roads at every hundred steps,
Was swoln into a noisy rivulet,
Would Leonard then, when elder boys perhaps
Remain'd at home, go staggering through the fords,
Bearing his Brother on his back – I've seen him,   255
On windy days, in one of those stray brooks,
Ay, more than once I've seen him, mid-leg deep,
Their two books lying both on a dry stone
Upon the hither side: – and once I said,
As I remember, looking round these rocks   260
And hills on which we all of us were born,
That God who made the great book of the world
Would bless such piety –

              LEONARD.

It may be then –
PRIEST.

Never did worthier lads break English bread:
The finest Sunday that the Autumn saw,   265
With all its mealy clusters of ripe nuts,
Could never keep these boys away from church,
Or tempt them to an hour of sabbath breach.
Leonard and James! I warrant, every corner
Among these rocks and every hollow place   270
Where foot could come, to one or both of them
Was known as well as to the flowers that grow there.
Like roe-bucks they went bounding o'er the hills:
They play'd like two young ravens on the crags:
Then they could write, ay and speak too, as well   275
As many of their betters – and for Leonard!
The very night before he went away,
In my own house I put into his hand
A Bible, and I'd wager twenty pounds,
That, if he is alive, he has it yet.   280

LEONARD.

It seems, these Brothers have not liv'd to be
A comfort to each other. –

PRIEST.

             That they might
Live to that end, is what both old and young
In this our valley all of us have wish'd,
And what, for my part, I have often pray'd: 285
But Leonard –

LEONARD.

      Then James still is left among you –

PRIEST.

'Tis of the elder Brother I am speaking:
They had an Uncle, he was at that time
A thriving man, and traffic'd on the seas:
And, but for this same Uncle, to this hour   290
Leonard had never handled rope or shroud.
For the Boy lov'd the life which we lead here;
And, though a very Stripling, twelve years old,
His soul was knit to this his native soil.
But, as I said, old Walter was too weak   295
To strive with such a torrent; when he died,
The estate and house were sold, and all their sheep,

A pretty flock, and which, for aught I know,
Had clothed the Ewbanks for a thousand years.
Well — all was gone, and they were destitute,   300
And Leonard, chiefly for his Brother's sake,
Resolv'd to try his fortune on the seas.
'Tis now twelve years since we had tidings from him.
If there was one among us who had heard
That Leonard Ewbank was come home again,   305
From the great Gavel[2], down by Leeza's Banks,
And down the Enna, far as Egremont,
The day would be a very festival,
And those two bells of ours, which there you see
Hanging in the open air — but, O good Sir!   310
This is sad talk — they'll never sound for him
Living or dead — When last we heard of him,
He was in slavery among the Moors
Upon the Barbary Coast — 'Twas not a little
That would bring down his spirit, and, no doubt,   315
Before it ended in his death, the Lad
Was sadly cross'd — Poor Leonard! when we parted,
He took me by the hand and said to me,
If ever the day came when he was rich,
He would return, and on his Father's Land   320
He would grow old among us.

LEONARD.

If that day
Should come, 't would needs be a glad day for him;
He would himself, no doubt, be then as happy
As any that should meet him —

PRIEST.

Happy, Sir —

LEONARD.

You said his kindred all were in their graves,   325
And that he had one Brother —

PRIEST.

That is but
A fellow tale of sorrow. From his youth

---

[2] The great Gavel, so called I imagine, from its resemblance to the Gable end of a house, is one of the highest of the Cumberland mountains. It stands at the head of the several vales of Ennerdale, Wastdale, and Borrowdale. The Leeza is a River which flows into the Lake of Ennerdale: on issuing from the Lake, it changes its name, and is called the End, Eyne, or Enna. It falls into the sea a little below Egremont.

James, though not sickly, yet was delicate,
And Leonard being always by his side
Had done so many offices about him,   330
That, though he was not of a timid nature,
Yet still the spirit of a mountain boy
In him was somewhat check'd, and when his Brother
Was gone to sea and he was left alone
The little colour that he had was soon   335
Stolen from his cheek, he droop'd, and pin'd and pin'd:

LEONARD.

But these are all the graves of full-grown men!

PRIEST.

Ay, Sir, that pass'd away: we took him to us.
He was the child of all the dale – he liv'd
Three months with one, and six months with another   340
And wanted neither food, nor clothes, nor love;
And many, many happy days were his.
But, whether blithe or sad, 'tis my belief
His absent Brother still was at his heart.
And, when he liv'd beneath our roof, we found   345
(A practice till this time unknown to him)
That often, rising from his bed at night,
He in his sleep would walk about, and sleeping
He sought his Brother Leonard – You are mov'd,
Forgive me, Sir: before I spoke to you,   350
I judg'd you most unkindly.

LEONARD.

But this youth,
How did he die at last?

PRIEST.

One sweet May morning,
It will be twelve years since, when spring returns,
He had gone forth among the new-dropp'd lambs,
With two or three companions whom it chanc'd   355
Some further business summon'd to a house
Which stands at the Dale-head. James, tir'd perhaps,
Or from some other cause, remain'd behind.
You see yon precipice – it almost looks
Like some vast building made of many crags,   360
And in the midst is one particular rock
That rises like a column from the vale,
Whence by our Shepherds it is call'd, the Pillar.
James, pointing to its summit, over which

They all had purpos'd to return together, 365
Inform'd them that he there would wait for them:
They parted, and his comrades pass'd that way
Some two hours after, but they did not find him
At the appointed place, a circumstance
Of which they took no heed: but one of them, 370
Going by chance, at night, into the house
Which at this time was James's home, there learn'd
That nobody had seen him all that day:
The morning came, and still he was unheard of:
The neighbours were alarm'd, and to the Brook 375
Some went, and some towards the Lake; ere noon
They found him at the foot of that same Rock
Dead, and with mangled limbs. The third day after
I buried him, poor Lad, and there he lies.

LEONARD.

And that then *is* his grave! – Before his death 380
You said that he saw many happy years?

PRIEST.

Ay, that he did. –

LEONARD.

       And all went well with him –

PRIEST.

If he had one, the Lad had twenty homes.

LEONARD.

And you believe then, that his mind was easy –

PRIEST.

Yes, long before he died, he found that time 385
Is a true friend to sorrow, and, unless
His thoughts were turn'd on Leonard's luckless fortune,
He talk'd about him with a chearful love.

LEONARD.

He could not come to an unhallow'd end!

PRIEST.

Nay, God forbid! You recollect I mention'd 390
A habit which disquietude and grief
Had brought upon him, and we all conjectur'd
That, as the day was warm, he had lain down
Upon the grass, and, waiting for his comrades
He there had fallen asleep, that in his sleep 395
He to the margin of the precipice

Had walk'd, and from the summit had fallen headlong –
And so no doubt he perish'd: at the time,
We guess, that in his hands he must have had
His Shepherd's staff; for midway in the cliff　　　　400
It had been caught, and there for many years
It hung – and moulder'd there.

　　　　　　　　　　　The Priest here ended –
The Stranger would have thank'd him but he felt
Tears rushing in; both left the spot in silence,
And Leonard, when they reach'd the church-yard gate,　　405
As the Priest lifted up the latch, turn'd round,
And, looking at the grave, he said, 'My Brother'.

The Vicar did not hear the words: and now,
Pointing towards the Cottage, he entreated
That Leonard would partake his homely fare:　　　　410
The other thank'd him with a fervent voice,
But added, that, the evening being calm,
He would pursue his journey. So they parted.

It was not long ere Leonard reach'd a grove
That overhung the road: he there stopp'd short,　　　415
And, sitting down beneath the trees, review'd
All that the Priest had said: his early years
Were with him in his heart: his cherish'd hopes,
And thoughts which had been his an hour before,

All press'd on him with such a weight, that now,　　　420
This vale, where he had been so happy, seem'd
A place in which he could not bear to live:
So he relinquish'd all his purposes.
He travell'd on to Egremont; and thence,
That night, address'd a letter to the Priest　　　　425
Reminding him of what had pass'd between them,
And adding, with a hope to be forgiven,
That it was from the weakness of his heart
He had not dared to tell him who he was.

This done, he went on shipboard, and is now　　　　430
A Seaman, a grey-headed Mariner.

Reading 1.4 William Wordsworth, *Home at Grasmere*

Source: William Wordsworth (1977 [1888]) *Home at Grasmere*
(ed. B. Darlington), Ithaca and London, Cornell University Press,
pp. 38–106. Footnotes are by the editor of this edition.

Once on the brow of yonder Hill I stopped,[1]
While I was yet a School-boy (of what age
I cannot well remember, but the hour
I well remember though the year be gone),
And with a sudden influx overcome   5
At sight of this seclusion, I forgot
My haste – for hasty had my footsteps been,
As boyish my pursuits – [and sighing said],[2]
'What happy fortune were it here to live!
And if I thought of dying, if a thought   10
Of mortal separation could come in
With paradise before me, here to die.'
I was no Prophet, nor had even a hope,
Scarcely a wish, but one bright pleasing thought,
A fancy in the heart of what might be   15
The lot of others, never could be mine.[3]

The place from which I looked was soft and green,
Not giddy yet aerial, with a depth
Of Vale below, a height of Hills above.
Long did I halt; I could have made it even   20
My business and my errand so to halt.
For rest of body 'twas a perfect place;
All that luxurious nature could desire,
But tempting to the Spirit. Who could look
And not feel motions there? I thought of clouds   25

---

[1]   The hill that William Wordsworth (WW) refers to here is Loughrigg Terrace, at the southern end of Grasmere Lake.

[2]   This line was left incomplete in the original transcription; it is printed here as revised.

[3]   The sensation that WW attributes to his younger self on first viewing Grasmere, and the special serenity he later claims for the vale, are not a unique response. As early as 1769, Thomas Gray found an unusual sense of 'repose' in 'this little unsuspected paradise,' where 'all is peace, rusticity, & happy poverty in its neatest most becoming attire' (*Correspondence of Thomas Gray*, ed. Paget Toynbee and Leonard Whibley [3 vols.; Oxford, 1935], III, 1099). Guide books echo and amplify this description, and private journals surpass them in subtlety and detail. See, for example, Daphne Foskett, *John Harden of Brathay Hall* 1772–1847 (Kendal, 1974), p. 8. For WW's prose description of Grasmere, see *Prose*, II, 163, 271n–272n.

That sail on winds; of breezes that delight
To play on water, or in endless chase
Pursue each other through the liquid depths
Of grass or corn, over and through and through,
In billow after billow evermore;   30
Of Sunbeams, Shadows, Butterflies, and Birds,
Angels, and winged Creatures that are Lords
Without restraint of all which they behold.
I sate, and stirred in Spirit as I looked,
I seemed to feel such liberty was mine,   35
Such power and joy; but only for this end:
To flit from field to rock, from rock to field,
From shore to island, and from isle to shore,
From open place to covert, from a bed
Of meadow-flowers into a tuft of wood,   40
From high to low, from low to high, yet still
Within the bounds of this huge Concave; here
Should be my home, this Valley be my World.

From that time forward was the place to me
As beautiful in thought as it had been   45
When present to my bodily eyes; a haunt
Of my affections, oftentimes in joy
A brighter joy, in sorrow (but of that
I have known little), in such gloom, at least,
Such damp of the gay mind as stood to me   50
In place of sorrow, 'twas a gleam of light.
And now 'tis mine for life: dear Vale,
One of thy lowly dwellings is my home!

Yes, the Realities of Life – so cold,
So cowardly, so ready to betray,   55
So stinted in the measure of their grace,
As we report them, doing them much wrong –
Have been to me more bountiful than hope,
Less timid than desire. Oh bold indeed
They have been! Bold and bounteous unto me,   60
Who have myself been bold, not wanting trust,
Nor resolution, nor at last the hope
Which is of wisdom, for I feel it is.

And did it cost so much, and did it ask
Such length of discipline, and could it seem   65
An act of courage, and the thing itself
A conquest? Shame that this was ever so,
Not to the Boy or Youth, but shame to thee,
Sage Man, thou Sun in its meridian strength,

Thou flower in its full blow, thou King and crown   70
Of human Nature; shame to thee, sage Man.
Thy prudence, thy experience, thy desires,
Thy apprehensions – blush thou for them all.
But I am safe; yes, one at least is safe;
What once was deemed so difficult is now   75
Smooth, easy, without obstacle; what once
Did to my blindness seem a sacrifice,
The same is now a choice of the whole heart.
If e'er the acceptance of such dower was deemed
A condescension or a weak indulgence   80
To a sick fancy, it is now an act
Of reason that exultingly aspires.
This solitude is mine; the distant thought
Is fetched out of the heaven in which it was.
The unappropriated bliss hath found   85
An owner, and that owner I am he.
The Lord of this enjoyment is on Earth
And in my breast. What wonder if I speak
With fervour, am exalted with the thought
Of my possessions, of my genuine wealth   90
Inward and outward? What I keep have gained,
Shall gain, must gain, if sound be my belief
From past and present rightly understood
That in my day of childhood I was less
The mind of Nature, less, take all in all,   95
Whatever may be lost, than I am now.
For proof behold this Valley and behold
Yon Cottage, where with me my Emma dwells.[4]

  Aye, think on that, my Heart, and cease to stir;
Pause upon that, and let the breathing frame   100
No longer breathe, but all be satisfied.
Oh, if such silence be not thanks to God
For what hath been bestowed, then where, where then
Shall gratitude find rest? Mine eyes did ne'er
Rest on a lovely object, nor my mind   105
Take pleasure in the midst of [happy] thoughts,[5]
But either She whom now I have, who now
Divides with me this loved abode, was there
Or not far off. Where'er my footsteps turned,
Her Voice was like a hidden Bird that sang;   110

---

[4] Emma or Emmeline is the name by which WW occasionally refers to Dorothy
  Wordsworth (DW) in his poems.
[5] 'happy' was supplied to fill a gap left in transcription.

The thought of her was like a flash of light
Or an unseen companionship, a breath
Or fragrance independent of the wind;
In all my goings, in the new and old
Of all my meditations, and in this   115
Favorite of all, in this the most of all.
What Being, therefore, since the birth of Man
Had ever more abundant cause to speak
Thanks, and if music and the power of song
Make him more thankful, then to call on these   120
To aid him and with these resound his joy?
The boon is absolute; surpassing grace
To me hath been vouchsafed; among the bowers
Of blissful Eden this was neither given
Nor could be given – possession of the good   125
Which had been sighed for, ancient thought fulfilled,
And dear Imaginations realized
Up to their highest measure, yea, and more.

   Embrace me then, ye Hills, and close me in;
Now in the clear and open day I feel   130
Your guardianship; I take it to my heart;
'Tis like the solemn shelter of the night.
But I would call thee beautiful, for mild
And soft and gay and beautiful thou art,
Dear Valley, having in thy face a smile   135
Though peaceful, full of gladness. Thou art pleased,
Pleased with thy crags and woody steeps, thy Lake,
Its one green Island and its winding shores,
The multitude of little rocky hills,
Thy Church and Cottages of mountain stone–   140
Clustered like stars, some few, but single most,
And lurking dimly in their shy retreats,
Or glancing at each other cheerful looks,
Like separated stars with clouds between.
What want we? Have we not perpetual streams,   145
Warm woods and sunny hills, and fresh green fields,
And mountains not less green, and flocks and herds,
And thickets full of songsters, and the voice
Of lordly birds – an unexpected sound
Heard now and then from morn to latest eve   150
Admonishing the man who walks below
Of solitude and silence in the sky?
These have we, and a thousand nooks of earth,
Have also these; but nowhere else is found –

No where (or is it fancy?) can be found – 155
The one sensation that is here; 'tis here,
Here as it found its way into my heart
In childhood, here as it abides by day,
By night, here only; or in chosen minds
That take it with them hence, where'er they go. 160
'Tis (but I cannot name it), 'tis the sense
Of majesty and beauty and repose,
A blended holiness of earth and sky,
Something that makes this individual Spot,
This small abiding-place of many men, 165
A termination and a last retreat,
A Centre, come from wheresoe'er you will,
A Whole without dependence or defect,
Made for itself and happy in itself,
Perfect Contentment, Unity entire. 170

    Long is it since we met to part no more,
Since I and Emma heard each other's call
And were Companions once again, like Birds
Which by the intruding Fowler had been scared,
Two of a scattered brood that could not bear 175
To live in loneliness; 'tis long since we,
Remembering much and hoping more, found means
To walk abreast, though in a narrow path,
With undivided steps. Our home was sweet;
Could it be less? If we were forced to change, 180
Our home again was sweet; but still, for Youth,
Strong as it seems and bold, is inly weak
And diffident, the destiny of life
Remained unfixed, and therefore we were still

Lines 185–191 are missing.

[We will be free, and, as we mean to live
In culture of divinity and truth,
Will choose the noblest Temple that we know.
Not in mistrust or ignorance of the mind 195
And of the power she has within herself
To enoble all things made we this resolve;
Far less from any momentary fit
Of inconsiderate fancy, light and vain;
But that we deemed it wise to take the help 200
Which lay within our reach; and here, we knew,
Help could be found of no mean sort; the spirit
Of singleness and unity and peace.
In this majestic, self-sufficing world,

This all in all of Nature, it will suit,   205
We said, no other [   ] on earth so well,
Simplicity of purpose, love intense,
Ambition not aspiring to the prize][6,7]
Of outward things, but for the prize within —
Highest ambition. In the daily walks   210
Of business 'twill be harmony and grace
For the perpetual pleasure of the sense,
And for the Soul — I do not say too much,
Though much be said — an image for the soul,
A habit of Eternity and God.   215

   Nor have we been deceived; thus far the effect
Falls not below the loftiest of our hopes.
Bleak season was it, turbulent and bleak,
When hitherward we journeyed, and on foot,
Through bursts of sunshine and through flying snows,   220
Paced the long vales — how long they were, and yet
How fast that length of way was left behind,
Wensley's long Vale and Sedbergh's naked heights.
The frosty wind, as if to make amends
For its keen breath, was aiding to our course   225
And drove us onward like two Ships at sea.
Stern was the face of nature; we rejoiced
In that stern countenance, for our souls had there
A feeling of their strength. The naked trees,
The icy brooks, as on we passed, appeared   230
To question us. 'Whence come ye? To what end?'
They seemed to say. 'What would ye?' said the shower,
'Wild Wanderers, whither through my dark domain?'
The Sunbeam said, 'Be happy.' They were moved,
All things were moved; they round us as we went,   235
We in the midst of them. And when the trance
Came to us, as we stood by Hart-leap Well —
The intimation of the milder day
Which is to come, the fairer world than this —
And raised us up, dejected as we were   240
Among the records of that doleful place
By sorrow or the hunted beast who there
Had yielded up his breath, the awful trance —
The Vision of humanity and of God
The Mourner, God the Sufferer, when the heart   245

[6] Lines 192–208 are supplied from MS. A to fill part of the gap left in MS. B.
[7] WW wrote 'prize' over 'praise' in MS. A, apparently correcting an error in transcription.

Of his poor Creatures suffers wrongfully –
Both in the sadness and the joy we found
A promise and an earnest that we twain,
A pair seceding from the common world,
Might in that hallowed spot to which our steps   250
Were tending, in that individual nook,
Might even thus early for ourselves secure,
And in the midst of these unhappy times,[8]
A portion of the blessedness which love
And knowledge will, we trust, hereafter give   255
To all the Vales of earth and all mankind.[9]

Thrice hath the winter Moon been filled with light[10]
Since that dear day when Grasmere, our dear Vale,
Received us. Bright and solemn was the sky
That faced us with a passionate welcoming   260
And led us to our threshold, to a home
Within a home, what was to be, and soon,
Our love within a love. Then darkness came,
Composing darkness, with its quiet load
Of full contentment, in a little shed   265
Disturbed, uneasy in itself, as seemed,
And wondering at its new inhabitants.
It loves us now, this Vale so beautiful
Begins to love us! By a sullen storm,
Two months unwearied of severest storm,   270
It put the temper of our minds to proof,
And found us faithful through the gloom, and heard
The Poet mutter his prelusive songs
With chearful heart, an unknown voice of joy
Among the silence of the woods and hills,   275
Silent to any gladsomeness of sound
With all their Shepherds.

                          But the gates of Spring
Are opened; churlish Winter hath given leave
That she should entertain for this one day,
Perhaps for many genial days to come,   280
His guests and make them happy. They are pleased,

---

[8] 'These' is an editorial correction for 'those,' which fails to make sense in context.
[9] For a more detailed description of the journey referred to here (lines 218–256), see
WW's letter to Samuel Taylor Coleridge (STC), 24 and 27 December 1799, *Early Years*,
pp. 273–280. In her Grasmere journal for 4–6 October 1802, DW describes the journey
she made with WW and MW, following their wedding, along the same route, and her
account recalls incidents from the earlier journey; see *Journals*, pp. 157–161.
[10] In early 1800 the moon was full on 10 January, 9 February, and 10 March; these dates
help to fix the period to which WW alludes here.

But most of all, the birds that haunt the flood,
With the mild summons, inmates though they be
Of Winter's household. They are jubilant
This day, who drooped or seemed to droop so long;   285
They show their pleasure, and shall I do less?
Happier of happy though I be, like them
I cannot take possession of the sky,
Mount with a thoughtless impulse, and wheel there,
One of a mighty multitude whose way   290
And motion is a harmony and dance
Magnificent. Behold them, how they shape,
Orb after orb, their course, still round and round,
Above the area of the Lake, their own
Adopted region, girding it about   295
In wanton repetition, yet therewith –
With that large circle evermore renewed –
Hundreds of curves and circlets, high and low,
Backwards and forwards, progress intricate,
As if one spirit was in all and swayed   300
Their indefatigable flight. 'Tis done,
Ten times, or more, I fancied it had ceased,
And lo! the vanished company again
Ascending – list again! I hear their wings:
Faint, faint at first, and then an eager sound,   305
Passed in a moment, and as faint again!
They tempt the sun to sport among their plumes;
They tempt the water and the gleaming ice
To show them a fair image. 'Tis themselves,
Their own fair forms upon the glimmering plain,   310
Painted more soft and fair as they descend,
Almost to touch, then up again aloft,
Up with a sally and a flash of speed,
As if they scorned both resting-place and rest.
Spring! for this day belongs to thee, rejoice!   315
Not upon me alone hath been bestowed –
Me, blessed with many onward-looking thoughts –
The sunshine and mild air. Oh, surely these
Are grateful; not the happy Quires of love,
Thine own peculiar family, Sweet Spring,   320
That sport among green leaves so blithe a train.

    But two are missing – two, a lonely pair
Of milk-white Swans. Ah, why are they not here?
These above all, ah, why are they not here
To share in this day's pleasure? From afar   325

They came, like Emma and myself, to live
Together here in peace and solitude,
Choosing this Valley, they who had the choice
Of the whole world. We saw them day by day,
Through those two months of unrelenting storm,   330
Conspicuous in the centre of the Lake,
Their safe retreat. We knew them well – I guess
That the whole Valley knew them – but to us
They were more dear than may be well believed,
Not only for their beauty and their still   335
And placid way of life and faithful love
Inseparable, not for these alone,
But that their state so much resembled ours;
They also having chosen this abode;
They strangers, and we strangers; they a pair,   340
And we a solitary pair like them.
They should not have departed; many days
I've looked for them in vain, nor on the wing
Have seen them, nor in that small open space
Of blue unfrozen water, where they lodged   345
And lived so long in quiet, side by side.
Companions, brethren, consecrated friends,
Shall we behold them yet another year
Surviving, they for us and we for them,
And neither pair be broken? Nay, perchance[11]   350
It is too late already for such hope;
The Shepherd may have seized the deadly tube
And parted them, incited by a prize
Which, for the sake of those he loves at home
And for the Lamb upon the mountain tops,   355
He should have spared; or haply both are gone,
One death, and that were mercy given to both.

    I cannot look upon this favoured Vale
But that I seem, by harbouring this thought,
To wrong it, such unworthy recompence   360
Imagining, of confidence so pure.
Ah! if I wished to follow where the sight
Of all that is before my eyes, the voice
Which is as a presiding Spirit here
Would lead me, I should say unto myself,   365
They who are dwellers in this holy place[12]

---

[11] 'be broken' was written over 'divided' in transcription.
[12] 'in' was written over 'of' in transcription.

Must needs themselves be hallowed. They require
No benediction from the Stranger's lips,
For they are blessed already. None would give
The greeting 'peace be with you' unto them,   370
For peace they have; it cannot but be theirs.
And mercy and forbearance – nay, not these;
There is no call for these; that office Love
Performs and charity beyond the bounds
Of charity – an overflowing love,[13]   375
Not for the creature only, but for all
Which is around them, love for every thing
Which in this happy Valley we behold!

    Thus do we soothe ourselves, and when the thought
Is passed we blame it not for having come.   380
What if I floated down a pleasant stream
And now am landed and the motion gone –
Shall I reprove myself? Ah no, the stream
Is flowing and will never cease to flow,
And I shall float upon that stream again.   385
By such forgetfulness the soul becomes –
Words cannot say how beautiful. Then hail!
Hail to the visible Presence! Hail to thee,
Delightful Valley, habitation fair!
And to whatever else of outward form   390
Can give us inward help, can purify
And elevate and harmonize and soothe,
And steal away and for a while deceive
And lap in pleasing rest, and bear us on
Without desire in full complacency,   395
Contemplating perfection absolute
And entertained as in a placid sleep.

    But not betrayed by tenderness of mind
That feared or wholly overlooked the truth
Did we come hither, with romantic hope   400
To find in midst of so much loveliness
Love, perfect love, of so much majesty
A like majestic frame of mind in those
Who here abide, the persons like the place.
Nor from such hope or aught of such belief   405
Hath issued any portion of the joy
Which I have felt this day. An awful voice,
'Tis true, I in my walks have often heard,

---

[13] 'an overflowing' was written over 'a heart delighting' in transcription.

Sent from the mountains or the sheltered fields,
Shout after shout – reiterated whoop   410
In manner of a bird that takes delight
In answering to itself or like a hound
Single at chase among the lonely woods –
A human voice, how awful in the gloom
Of coming night, when sky is dark, and earth   415
Not dark, not yet enlightened, but by snow
Made visible, amid the noise of winds
And bleatings manifold of sheep that know
That summons and are gathering round for food –
That voice, the same, the very same, that breath   420
Which was an utterance awful as the wind,
Or any sound the mountains ever heard.

    That Shepherd's voice, it may have reached mine ear
Debased and under prophanation, made
An organ for the sounds articulate   425
Of ribaldry and blasphemy and wrath,
Where drunkenness hath kindled senseless frays.
I came not dreaming of unruffled life,
Untainted manners; born among the hills,
Bred also there, I wanted not a scale   430
To regulate my hopes; pleased with the good,
I shrink not from the evil in disgust
Or with immoderate pain. I look for man,
The common creature of the brotherhood,
But little differing from the man elsewhere   435
For selfishness and envy and revenge,
Ill neighbourhood – folly that this should be –
Flattery and double-dealing, strife and wrong.

    Yet is it something gained – it is in truth
A mighty gain – that Labour here preserves   440
His rosy face, a Servant only here
Of the fire-side or of the open field,
A Freeman, therefore sound and unenslaved;
That extreme penury is here unknown,
And cold and hunger's abject wretchedness,   445
Mortal to body and the heaven-born mind;
That they who want are not too great a weight
For those who can relieve. Here may the heart
Breathe in the air of fellow-suffering
Dreadless, as in a kind of fresher breeze   450
Of her own native element; the hand
Be ready and unwearied without plea

From task too frequent and beyond its powers,
For languor or indifference or despair.
And as these lofty barriers break the force   455
Of winds – this deep vale as it doth in part
Conceal us from the storm – so here there is
A Power and a protection for the mind,
Dispensed indeed to other solitudes
Favoured by noble privilege like this,   460
Where kindred independence of estate
Is prevalent, where he who tills the field,
He, happy Man! is Master of the field
And treads the mountain which his Father trod.
Hence, and from other local circumstance,   465
In this enclosure many of the old
Substantial virtues have a firmer tone
Than in the base and ordinary world.

    Yon Cottage, would that it could tell a part
Of its own story. Thousands might give ear,   470
Might hear it and blush deep. There few years past
In this his Native Valley dwelt a Man,
The Master of a little lot of ground,
A man of mild deportment and discourse,
A scholar also (as the phrase is here),   475
For he drew much delight from those few books
That lay within his reach, and for this cause
Was by his Fellow-dalesmen honoured more.
A Shepherd and a Tiller of the ground,
Studious withal, and healthy in his frame   480
Of body, and of just and placid mind,
He with his consort and his Children saw
Days that were seldom touched by petty strife,
Years safe from large misfortune, long maintained
That course which men the wisest and most pure   485
Might look on with entire complacency.
Yet in himself and near him were there faults
At work to undermine his happiness
By little and by little. Active, prompt,
And lively was the Housewife, in the Vale   490
None more industrious; but her industry
Was of that kind, 'tis said, which tended more
To splendid neatness, to a showy trim,
And overlaboured purity of house
Than to substantial thrift. He, on his part   495
Generous and easy-minded, was not free

From carelessness, and thus in course of time
These joint infirmities, combined perchance
With other cause less obvious, brought decay
Of worldly substance and distress of mind,   500
Which to a thoughtful man was hard to shun
And which he could not cure. A blooming Girl
Served them, an Inmate of the House. Alas!
Poor now in tranquil pleasure, he gave way
To thoughts of troubled pleasure; he became   505
A lawless Suitor of the Maid, and she
Yielded unworthily. Unhappy Man!
That which he had been weak enough to do
Was misery in remembrance; he was stung,
Stung by his inward thoughts, and by the smiles   510
Of Wife and children stung to agony.
His temper urged him not to seek relief
Amid the noise of revellers nor from draught
Of lonely stupefaction; he himself
A rational and suffering Man, himself   515
Was his own world, without a resting-place.
Wretched at home, he had no peace abroad,
Ranged through the mountains, slept upon the earth,
Asked comfort of the open air, and found
No quiet in the darkness of the night,   520
No pleasure in the beauty of the day.
His flock he slighted; his paternal fields
Were as a clog to him, whose Spirit wished
To fly, but whither? And yon gracious Church,
That has a look so full of peace and hope   525
And love – benignant Mother of the Vale,
How fair amid her brood of Cottages! –
She was to him a sickness and reproach.
I speak conjecturing from the little known,
The much that to the last remained unknown;   530
But this is sure: he died of his own grief,
He could not bear the weight of his own shame.

    That Ridge, which elbowing from the mountain-side
Carries into the Plain its rocks and woods,
Conceals a Cottage where a Father dwells   535
In widowhood, whose Life's Co-partner died
Long since, and left him solitary Prop
Of many helpless Children. I begin
With words which might be prelude to a Tale
Of sorrow and dejection, but I feel –   540

Though in the midst of sadness, as might seem –
No sadness, when I think of what mine eyes
Have seen in that delightful family.
Bright garland make they for their Father's brows,
Those six fair Daughters budding yet, not one,   545
Not one of all the band a full-blown flower.
Go to the Dwelling: There Thou shalt have proof
That He who takes away, yet takes not half
Of what he seems to take, or gives it back
Not to our prayer, but far beyond our prayer,   550
He gives it the boon-produce of a soil[14]
Which Hope hath never watered. Thou shalt see
A House, which at small distance will appear
In no distinction to have passed beyond
Its Fellows, will appear, like them, to have grown   555
Out of the native Rock; but nearer view
Will show it not so grave in outward mien
And soberly arrayed as for the most
Are these rude mountain-dwellings – Nature's care,
Mere friendless Nature's – but a studious work   560
Of many fancies and of many hands,
A play thing and a pride; for such the air
And aspect which the little Spot maintains
In spite of lonely Winter's nakedness.
They have their jasmine resting on the Porch,   565
Their rose-trees, strong in health, that will be soon
Roof-high; and here and there the garden wall
Is topped with single stones, a showy file
Curious for shape or hue – some round, like Balls,
Worn smooth and round by fretting of the   570
From which they have been gathered, others bright
And sparry, the rough scatterings of the Hills.
These ornaments the Cottage chiefly owes
To one, a hardy Girl, who mounts the rocks;
Such is her choice; she fears not the bleak wind;   575
Companion of her Father, does for him
Where'er he wanders in his pastoral course
The service of a Boy, and with delight
More keen and prouder daring. Yet hath She
Within the garden, like the rest, a bed   580
For her own flowers, or favorite Herbs, a space
Holden by sacred charter; and I guess
She also helped to frame that tiny Plot

---

[14] WW appears to have developed these lines in transcription from a single original line.

Of garden ground which one day 'twas my chance
To find among the woody rocks that rise   585
Above the House, a slip of smoother earth
Planted with goose-berry bushes, and in one,
Right in the centre of the prickly shrub,
A mimic Bird's-nest, fashioned by the hand,
Was stuck, a staring Thing of twisted hay,   590
And one quaint Fir-tree towered above the Whole.
But in the darkness of the night, then most
This Dwelling charms me; covered by the gloom
Then, heedless of good manners, I stop short
And (who could help it?) feed by stealth my sight   595
With prospect of the company within,
Laid open through the blazing window. There
I see the eldest Daughter at her wheel,
Spinning amain, as if to overtake
She knows not what, or teaching in her turn   600
Some little Novice of the sisterhood
That skill in this or other household work
Which from her Father's honored hands, herself,
While She was yet a Little-one, had learned.
Mild Man! He is not gay, but they are gay,   605
And the whole House is filled with gaiety.

   From yonder grey-stone that stands alone[15]
Close to the foaming Stream, look up and see,
Not less than halfway up the mountain-side,
A dusky Spot, a little grove of firs   610
And seems still smaller than it is. The Dame
Who dwells below, she told me that this grove,
Just six weeks younger than her eldest Boy,
Was planted by her Husband and herself
For a convenient shelter, which in storm   615
Their sheep might draw to. 'And they know it well,'
Said she, 'for thither do we bear them food
In time of heavy snow.' She then began
In fond obedience to her private thoughts
To speak of her dead Husband. Is there not   620
An art, a music, and a stream of words
That shall be life, the acknowledged voice of life?
Shall speak of what is done among the fields,
Done truly there, or felt, of solid good
And real evil, yet be sweet withal,   625

---

[15] The line is short metrically.

More grateful, more harmonious than the breath,
The idle breath of sweetest pipe attuned
To pastoral fancies? Is there such a stream,
Pure and unsullied, flowing from the heart
With motions of true dignity and grace,   630
Or must we seek these things where man is not?
Methinks I could repeat in tuneful verse
Delicious as the gentlest breeze that sounds
Through that aerial fir-grove, could preserve
Some portion of its human history   635
As gathered from that Matron's lips and tell
Of tears that have been shed at sight of it
And moving dialogues between this Pair,
Who in the prime of wedlock with joint hands
Did plant this grove, now flourishing while they   640
No longer flourish; he entirely gone,
She withering in her loneliness. Be this
A task above my skill; the silent mind
Has its own treasures, and I think of these,
Love what I see, and honour humankind.   645

    No, we are not alone; we do not stand,
My Emma, here misplaced and desolate,
Loving what no one cares for but ourselves.
We shall not scatter through the plains and rocks
Of this fair Vale and o'er its spacious heights   650
Unprofitable kindliness, bestowed,
On Objects unaccustomed to the gifts
Of feeling, that were cheerless and forlorn
But few weeks past, and would be so again
If we were not. We do not tend a lamp   655
Whose lustre we alone participate,
Which is dependent upon us alone,
Mortal though bright, a dying, dying flame.
Look where we will, some human heart has been
Before us with its offering; not a tree   660
Sprinkles these little pastures, but the same
Hath furnished matter for a thought, perchance
To some one is as a familiar Friend.
Joy spreads and sorrow spreads; and this whole Vale,
Home of untutored Shepherds as it is,   665
Swarms with sensation, as with gleams of sunshine,
Shadows or breezes, scents or sounds. Nor deem
These feelings – though subservient more than ours
To every day's demand for daily bread,

And borrowing more their spirit and their shape   670
From self-respecting interests – deem them not[16]
Unworthy therefore and unhallowed. No,
They lift the animal being, do themselves
By nature's kind and ever present aid
Refine the selfishness from which they spring,   675
Redeem by love the individual sense
Of anxiousness with which they are combined.
Many are pure, the best of them are pure;
The best, and these, remember, most abound,
Are fit associates of the [   ] joy,[17]   680
Joy of the highest and the purest minds;
They blend with it congenially; meanwhile,
Calmly they breathe their own undying life,
Lowly and unassuming as it is,
Through this, their mountain sanctuary (long,   685
Oh long may it remain inviolate!),
Diffusing health and sober chearfulness,
And giving to the moments as they pass
Their little boons of animating thought,
That sweeten labour, make it seem and feel   690
To be no arbitrary weight imposed,
But a glad function natural to Man.

    Fair proof of this, Newcomer though I be,
Already have I seen; the inward frame,
Though slowly opening, opens every day.   695
Nor am I less delighted with the show
As it unfolds itself, now here, now there,
Than is the passing Traveller, when his way
Lies through some region then first trod by him
(Say this fair Valley's self), when low-hung mists   700
Break up and are beginning to recede.
How pleased he is to hear the murmuring stream,
The many Voices, from he knows not where,
To have about him, which way e'er he goes,
Something on every side concealed from view,   705
In every quarter some thing visible,
Half seen or wholly, lost and found again –
Alternate progress and impediment,
And yet a growing prospect in the main.

---

[16] WW may originally have written 'these' for 'them.'
[17] In leaving this gap WW apparently rejected 'worthiest,' the reading of MS. R.

Such pleasure now is mine, and what if I – 710
Herein less happy than the Traveller –
Am sometimes forced to cast a painful look
Upon unwelcome things, which unawares
Reveal themselves? Not therefore is my mind
Depressed, nor do I fear what is to come; 715
But confident, enriched at every glance,
The more I see the more is my delight.
Truth justifies herself; and as she dwells
With Hope, who would not follow where she leads?

    Nor let me overlook those other loves 720
Where no fear is, those humbler sympathies
That have to me endeared the quietness
Of this sublime retirement. I begin
Already to inscribe upon my heart
A liking for the small grey Horse that bears 725
The paralytic Man; I know the ass
On which the Cripple in the Quarry maimed
Rides to and fro: I know them and their ways.
The famous Sheep-dog, first in all the vale,
Though yet to me a Stranger, will not be 730
A Stranger long; nor will the blind Man's Guide,
Meek and neglected thing, of no renown.
Whoever lived a Winter in one place,
Beneath the shelter of one Cottage-roof,
And has not had his Red-breast or his Wren? 735
I have them both; and I shall have my Thrush
In spring time, and a hundred warblers more;
And if the banished Eagle Pair return,
Helvellyn's Eagles, to their ancient Hold,[18]
Then shall I see, shall claim with those two Birds 740
Acquaintance, as they soar amid the Heavens.
The Owl that gives the name to Owlet-crag[19]
Have I heard shouting, and he soon will be
A chosen one of my regards. See there,
The Heifer in yon little Croft belongs 745
To one who holds it dear; with duteous care
She reared it, and in speaking of her Charge
I heard her scatter once a word or two,
[   ] domestic, yea, and Motherly,[20]

---

[18] Helvellyn is one of the highest mountains in the Lakes, and in England (3118 feet); it stands in a dominant position north of Grasmere.

[19] Owlet-crag has not been identified.

[20] In leaving this gap WW apparently rejected 'A term,' the reading of MS. R.

She being herself a Mother. Happy Beast,   750
If the caresses of a human voice
Can make it so, and care of human hands.

    And Ye as happy under Nature's care,
Strangers to me and all men, or at least
Strangers to all particular amity,   755
All intercourse of knowledge or of love
That parts the individual from the kind;
Whether in large communities ye dwell
From year to year, not shunning man's abode,
A settled residence, or be from far,   760
Wild creatures, and of many homes, that come
The gift of winds, and whom the winds again
Take from us at your pleasure – yet shall ye
Not want for this, your own subordinate place,
According to your claim, an underplace   765
In my affections. Witness the delight
With which ere while I saw that multitude
Wheel through the sky and see them now at rest,
Yet not at rest, upon the glassy lake.
They cannot rest; they gambol like young whelps,   770
Active as lambs and overcome with joy;
They try all frolic motions, flutter, plunge,
And beat the passive water with their wings.
Too distant are they for plain view, but lo!
Those little fountains, sparkling in the sun,   775
Which tell what they are doing, which rise up,
First one and then another silver spout,
As one or other takes the fit of glee –
Fountains and spouts, yet rather in the guise
Of plaything fire-works, which on festal nights   780
Hiss hiss about the feet of wanton boys.
How vast the compass of this theatre,
Yet nothing to be seen but lovely pomp
And silent majesty. The birch tree woods
Are hung with thousand thousand diamond drops   785
Of melted hoar-frost, every tiny knot
In the bare twigs, each little budding-place
Cased with its several bead; what myriads there
Upon one tree, while all the distant grove
That rises to the summit of the steep   790
Is like a mountain built of silver light!
See yonder the same pageant, and again
Behold the universal imagery

At what a depth, deep in the Lake below.
Admonished of the days of love to come,   795
The raven croaks and fills the sunny air
With a strange sound of genial harmony;
And in and all about that playful band,
Incapable although they be of rest,
And in their fashion very rioters,   800
There is a stillness, and they seem to make
Calm revelry in that their calm abode.
I leave them to their pleasure, and I pass,
Pass with a thought the life of the whole year
That is to come – the throngs of mountain flowers   805
And lilies that will dance upon the lake.

   Then boldly say that solitude is not
Where these things are: he truly is alone,
He of the multitude, whose eyes are doomed
To hold a vacant commerce day by day   810
With that which he can neither know nor love –
Dead things, to him thrice dead – or worse than this,
With swarms of life, and worse than all, of men,
His fellow men, that are to him no more
Than to the Forest Hermit are the leaves   815
That hang aloft in myriads – nay, far less,
Far less for aught that comforts or defends
Or lulls or chears. Society is here:
The true community, the noblest Frame
Of many into one incorporate;   820
That must be looked for here; paternal sway,
One Household under God for high and low,
One family and one mansion; to themselves
Appropriate and divided from the world
As if it were a cave, a multitude   825
Human and brute, possessors undisturbed
Of this recess, their legislative Hall,
Their Temple, and their glorious dwelling-place.

   Dismissing therefore all Arcadian dreams,
All golden fancies of the golden age,   830
The bright array of shadowy thoughts from times
That were before all time, or are to be
When time is not, the pageantry that stirs
And will be stirring when our eyes are fixed
On lovely objects and we wish to part   835
With all remembrance of a jarring world –
Give entrance to the sober truth; avow

That Nature to this favourite Spot of ours
Yields no exemption, but her awful rights,
Enforces to the utmost and exacts   840
Her tribute of inevitable pain,
And that the sting is added, man himself
For ever busy to afflict himself.
Yet temper this with one sufficient hope
(What need of more?): that we shall neither droop   845
Nor pine for want of pleasure in the life
Which is about us, nor through dearth of aught
That keeps in health the insatiable mind;
That we shall have for knowledge and for love
Abundance; and that, feeling as we do,   850
How goodly, how exceeding fair, how pure
From all reproach is the aetherial frame
And this deep vale, its earthly counterpart,
By which and under which we are enclosed
To breathe in peace; we shall moreover find   855
(If sound, and what we ought to be ourselves,
If rightly we observe and justly weigh)
The Inmates not unworthy of their home,
The Dwellers of the Dwelling.

                              And if this
Were not, we have enough within ourselves,   860
Enough to fill the present day with joy
And overspread the future years with hope –
Our beautiful and quiet home, enriched
Already with a Stranger whom we love[21]
Deeply, a Stranger of our Father's house,   865
A never-resting Pilgrim of the Sea,
Who finds at last an hour to his content
Beneath our roof; and others whom we love
Will seek us also, Sisters of our hearts,
And one, like them, a Brother of our hearts,[22]   870
Philosopher and Poet, in whose sight
These mountains will rejoice with open joy.
Such is our wealth: O Vale of Peace, we are
And must be, with God's will, a happy band!

   But 'tis not to enjoy, for this alone   875
That we exist; no, something must be done.

[21] The 'Stranger' is John Wordsworth, the brother who stayed with WW and DW in
Grasmere from the end of January through September, 1800.
[22] The 'Sisters of our hearts' are Mary Hutchinson, Sara Hutchinson, and Joanna
Hutchinson; the 'Brother' is STC.

I must not walk in unreproved delight
These narrow bounds and think of nothing more,
No duty that looks further and no care.
Each Being has his office, lowly some   880
And common, yet all worthy if fulfilled
With zeal, acknowledgement that with the gift
Keeps pace a harvest answering to the seed.
Of ill advised ambition and of pride
I would stand clear, yet unto me I feel[23]   885
That an internal brightness is vouchsafed
That must not die, that must not pass away.
Why does this inward lustre fondly seek
And gladly blend with outward fellowship?
Why shine they round me thus, whom thus I love?   890
Why do they teach me, whom I thus revere?
Strange question, yet it answers not itself.
That humble Roof, embowered among the trees,
That calm fire side – it is not even in them,
Blessed as they are, to furnish a reply   895
That satisfies and ends in perfect rest.
Possessions have I, wholly, solely mine,
Something within, which yet is shared by none –
Not even the nearest to me and most dear –
Something which power and effort may impart.   900
I would impart it; I would spread it wide,
Immortal in the world which is to come.
I would not wholly perish even in this,
Lie down and be forgotten in the dust,
I and the modest partners of my days,   905
Making a silent company in death.
It must not be, if I divinely taught
Am privileged to speak as I have felt
Of what in man is human or divine.

   While yet an innocent little-one, a heart   910
That doubtless wanted not its tender moods,
I breathed (for this I better recollect)
Among wild appetites and blind desires,
Motions of savage instinct, my delight
And exaltation. Nothing at that time   915
So welcome, no temptation half so dear
As that which [urged] me to a daring feat.[24]

---

[23] WW corrected 'to' to 'unto,' the reading accepted here to preserve the meter.
[24] 'urged' was supplied to fill a gap left in transcription.

Deep pools, tall trees, black chasms, and dizzy crags –
I loved to look in them, to stand and read
Their looks forbidding, read and disobey,   920
Sometimes in act, and evermore in thought.
With impulses which only were by these
Surpassed in strength, I heard of danger met
Or sought with courage, enterprize forlorn,
By one, sole keeper of his own intent,   925
Or by a resolute few, who for the sake
Of glory fronted multitudes in arms.
Yea, to this day I swell with like desire;
I cannot at this moment read a tale
Of two brave Vessels matched in deadly fight   930
And fighting to the death, but I am pleased
More than a wise Man ought to be; I wish,
I burn, I struggle, and in soul am there.
But me hath Nature tamed and bade me seek
For other agitations or be calm,   935
Hath dealt with me as with a turbulent stream –
Some Nurseling of the Mountains which she leads
Through quiet meadows after it has learned
Its strength and had its triumph and its joy,
Its desperate course of tumult and of glee.   940
That which in stealth by nature was performed
Hath Reason sanctioned. Her deliberate Voice
Hath said, 'Be mild and love all gentle things;
Thy glory and thy happiness be there.
Yet fear (though thou confide in me) no want   945
Of aspirations which have been – of foes
To wrestle with and victory to complete,
Bounds to be leapt and darkness to explore.
That which enflamed thy infant heart – the love,
The longing, the contempt, the undaunted quest –   950
These shall survive, though changed their office, these
Shall live; it is not in their power to die.'
Then farewell to the Warrior's deeds, farewell
All hope, which once and long was mine, to fill
The heroic trumpet with the muse's breath!   955
Yet in this peaceful Vale we will not spend
Unheard-of days, though loving peaceful thoughts;
A Voice shall speak, and what will be the Theme?

  On Man, on Nature, and on human Life,
Thinking in solitude, from time to time   960
I feel sweet passions traversing my Soul

Like Music; unto these, where'er I may,
I would give utterance in numerous verse.
Of truth, of grandeur, beauty, love, and hope –
Hope for this earth and hope beyond the grave –   965
Of virtue and of intellectual power,
Of blessed consolations in distress,
Of joy in widest commonalty spread,
Of the individual mind that keeps its own
Inviolate retirement, and consists   970
With being limitless the one great Life –
I sing; fit audience let me find though few!

   Fit audience find though few – thus prayed the Bard,[25]
Holiest of Men. Urania, I shall need
Thy guidance, or a greater Muse, if such   975
Descend to earth or dwell in highest heaven!
For I must tread on shadowy ground, must sink
Deep, and, aloft ascending, breathe in worlds
To which the Heaven of heavens is but a veil.
All strength, all terror, single or in bands,   980
That ever was put forth in personal forms –
Jehovah, with his thunder, and the quire
Of shouting angels and the empyreal throne –
I pass them unalarmed. The darkest Pit
Of the profoundest Hell, chaos, night,   985
Nor aught of [   ] vacancy scooped out
By help of dreams can breed such fear and awe
As fall upon us often when we look
Into our minds, into the mind of Man,
My haunt and the main region of my song.   990
Beauty, whose living home is the green earth,
Surpassing the most fair ideal Forms
The craft of delicate spirits hath composed
From earth's materials, waits upon my steps,
Pitches her tents before me when I move,   995
An hourly Neighbour. Paradise and groves
Elysian, fortunate islands, fields like those of old
In the deep ocean – wherefore should they be
A History, or but a dream, when minds
Once wedded to this outward frame of things   1000
In love, find these the growth of common day?
I, long before the blessed hour arrives,
Would sing in solitude the spousal verse

---

[25] WW quotes from Milton's invocation to his muse, Urania, in *Paradise Lost*, VII, 30–31.

Of this great consummation, would proclaim –
Speaking of nothing more than what we are –   1005
How exquisitely the individual Mind
(And the progressive powers perhaps no less
Of the whole species) to the external world
Is fitted; and how exquisitely too –
Theme this but little heard of among men –[26]   1010
The external world is fitted to the mind;
And the creation (by no lower name
Can it be called) which they with blended might
Accomplish: this is my great argument.
Such [   ] foregoing, if I oft[27]   1015
Must turn elsewhere, and travel near the tribes
And fellowships of men, and see ill sights
Of passions ravenous from each other's rage,
Must hear humanity in fields and groves
Pipe solitary anguish, or must hang   1020
Brooding above the fierce confederate storm
Of Sorrow, barricadoed evermore
Within the walls of cities – may these sounds
Have their authentic comment, that even these
Hearing, I be not heartless or forlorn!   1025
Come, thou prophetic Spirit, Soul of Man,
Thou human Soul of the wide earth that hast
Thy metropolitan Temple in the hearts
Of mighty Poets; unto me vouchsafe
Thy guidance, teach me to discern and part   1030
Inherent things from casual, what is fixed
From fleeting, that my verse may live and be
Even as a Light hung up in heaven to chear
Mankind in times to come! And if with this
I blend more lowly matter – with the thing   1035
Contemplated describe the mind and man
Contemplating, and who and what he was,
The transitory Being that beheld
This vision, when and where and how he lived,
With all his little realities of life –   1040
Be not this labour useless. If such theme
With highest things may [   ], then, Great God,[28]
Thou who art breath and being, way and guide,

---

[26] WW appears to have omitted this line accidentally, then added it in transcription.
[27] In leaving this gap, WW rejected the reading of Prospectus, MS. 1: 'pleasant haunts.'
[28] WW appears to have rejected the reading of Prospectus, MS. 2, '[?mingle],' and left a
gap for the verb; instead of supplying a word, however, he subsequently revised the line.

And power and understanding, may my life
Express the image of a better time,   1045
More wise desires and simple manners; nurse
My heart in genuine freedom; all pure thoughts
Be with me and uphold me to the end![29]

---

[29]   These lines (959–1048) were published with *The Excursion in* 1814 as a Prospectus to *The Recluse*.

Reading 1.5 William Wordsworth, from *The Prelude* (1799)

Source: Jonathan Wordsworth, M.H. Abrams and Stephen Gill (eds) (1979) *The Prelude 1799, 1805, 1850*, New York, W.W. Norton and Company, pp. 1–13. Footnotes are by the editors of this edition.

Was it for this
That one, the fairest of all rivers, loved
To blend his murmurs with my nurse's song,
And from his alder shades and rocky falls,
And from his fords and shallows, sent a voice   5
That flowed along my dreams? For this didst thou,
O Derwent, travelling over the green plains
Near my 'sweet birthplace',[1] didst thou, beauteous stream,
Make ceaseless music through the night and day,
Which with its steady cadence tempering   10
Our human waywardness, composed my thoughts
To more than infant softness, giving me
Among the fretful dwellings of mankind
A knowledge, a dim earnest, of the calm
Which Nature breathes among the fields and groves?   15
Beloved Derwent, fairest of all streams,
Was it for this[2] that I, a four years' child,
A naked boy, among thy silent pools
Made one long bathing of a summer's day,
Basked in the sun, or plunged into thy streams,   20
Alternate, all a summer's day, or coursed
Over the sandy fields, and dashed the flowers
Of yellow grunsel;[3] or, when crag and hill,

---

[1] Wordsworth's quotation marks draw attention to a borrowing from Coleridge's *Frost at Midnight*, 27–28: 'already had I dreamt / Of my sweet birth-place.' There is a special appropriateness in the reference, as 1799 was from the first written with Coleridge in mind, and at a later stage addressed to him. The river Derwent flows along the far side of the garden wall of the house where Wordsworth was born in Cockermouth.

[2] At no stage in his work on 1799 did Wordsworth provide an antecedent for the reiterated 'this' of lines 1, 6, and 17. In general terms, he is referring to failure to begin work on the main philosophical section of *The Recluse*; but correspondence in TLS in April–September 1975 showed that these opening lines reproduce an established rhetorical pattern, going back to Thomson, Pope, Milton, Ariosto, and Virgil.

[3] The plant is ragwort – i.e., ragweed – (as in the 1850 text) not the modern groundsel.

The woods, and distant Skiddaw's[4] lofty height,
Were bronzed with a deep radiance, stood alone   25
A naked savage in the thunder-shower?

   And afterwards ('twas in a later day,
Though early), when upon the mountain slope
The frost and breath of frosty wind had snapped
The last autumnal crocus, 'twas my joy   30
To wander half the night among the cliffs
And the smooth hollows where the woodcocks ran
Along the moonlight turf. In thought and wish
That time, my shoulder all with springes hung,
I was a fell destroyer. Gentle powers,   35
Who give us happiness and call it peace,
When scudding on from snare to snare I plied
My anxious visitation, hurrying on,
Still hurrying, hurrying onward, how my heart
Panted; among the scattered yew-trees and the crags   40
That looked upon me, how my bosom beat
With expectation! Sometimes strong desire
Resistless overpowered me, and the bird
Which was the captive of another's toils[5]
Became my prey; and when the deed was done   45
I heard among the solitary hills
Low breathings coming after me, and sounds
Of undistinguishable motion, steps
Almost as silent as the turf they trod.

   Nor less in springtime, when on southern banks   50
The shining sun had from his knot of leaves
Decoyed the primrose flower, and when the vales
And woods were warm, was I a rover then
In the high places, on the lonesome peaks,
Among the mountains and the winds. Though mean   55
And though inglorious were my views, the end[6]
Was not ignoble. Oh, when I have hung
Above the raven's nest, by knots of grass
Or half-inch fissures in the slipp'ry rock
But ill sustained, and almost, as it seemed,   60
Suspended by the blast which blew amain,
Shouldering the naked crag, oh, at that time,
While on the perilous ridge I hung alone,

---

[4]   Skiddaw, nine miles due east of Cockermouth, is the fourth highest peak in the Lake District (3,053 feet).
[5]   'Toils' can mean snares ('springes'), as well as labors.
[6]   Result, as opposed to aim ('views'), which was to steal ravens' eggs.

With what strange utterance did the loud dry wind
Blow through my ears; the sky seemed not a sky   65
Of earth, and with what motion moved the clouds!

    The mind of man is fashioned and built up
Even as a strain of music. I believe
That there are spirits which, when they would form
A favored being, from his very dawn   70
Of infancy do open out the clouds
As at the touch of lightning, seeking him
With gentle visitation – quiet powers,
Retired, and seldom recognized, yet kind,
And to the very meanest not unknown –   75
With me, though rarely, in my boyish days
They communed. Others too there are, who use,
Yet haply aiming at the self-same end,
Severer interventions, ministry
More palpable – and of their school was I.   80

They guided me: one evening led by them
I went alone into a shepherd's boat,
A skiff, that to a willow-tree was tied
Within a rocky cave, its usual home.
The moon was up, the lake was shining clear   85
Among the hoary mountains; from the shore
I pushed, and struck the oars, and struck again
In cadence, and my little boat moved on
Just like a man who walks with stately step
Though bent on speed.[7] It was an act of stealth   90
And troubled pleasure. Not without the voice
Of mountain echoes did my boat move on,
Leaving behind her still on either side
Small circles glittering idly in the moon,
Until they melted all into one track   95
Of sparkling light. A rocky steep uprose
Above the cavern of the willow-tree,
And now, as suited one who proudly rowed
With his best skill, I fixed a steady view
Upon the top of that same craggy ridge,   100
The bound of the horizon – for behind
Was nothing but the stars and the grey sky.
She was an elfin pinnace;[8] twenty times

---

[7] Lines 89–90 recall *Paradise Lost*, XII, 1–2: 'As one who in his journey bates at noon, / Though bent on speed.' The lake was Ullswater.
[8] An archaic word for a small boat.

I dipped my oars into the silent lake,
And as I rose upon the stroke my boat   105
Went heaving through the water like a swan –
When from behind that rocky steep, till then
The bound of the horizon, a huge cliff,
As if with voluntary power instinct
Upreared its head.[9] I struck, and struck again,   110
And, growing still in stature, the huge cliff
Rose up between me and the stars, and still,
With measured motion, like a living thing
Strode after me. With trembling hands I turned,
And through the silent water stole my way   115
Back to the cavern of the willow-tree.
There in her mooring-place I left my bark,
And through the meadows homeward went with grave
And serious thoughts; and after I had seen
That spectacle, for many days my brain   120
Worked with a dim and undetermined sense
Of unknown modes of being. In my thoughts
There was a darkness – call it solitude,
Or blank desertion – no familiar shapes
Of hourly objects, images of trees,   125
Of sea or sky, no colours of green fields,
But huge and mighty forms that do not live
Like living men moved slowly through my mind
By day, and were the trouble of my dreams.

   Ah, not in vain ye beings of the hills,   130
And ye that walk the woods and open heaths
By moon or star-light, thus, from my first dawn
Of childhood, did ye love to intertwine
The passions that build up our human soul
Not with the mean and vulgar works of man,   135
But with high objects, with eternal things,
With life and Nature, purifying thus
The elements of feeling and of thought,
And sanctifying by such discipline
Both pain and fear, until we recognise   140
A grandeur in the beatings of the heart.
Nor was this fellowship vouchsafed to me
With stinted kindness. In November days,
When vapours rolling down the valleys made

[9] The 'huge cliff' is probably Black Crag (2,232 feet, and west of Ullswater), which would
appear suddenly behind the nearer ridge, Stybarrow Crag, as the child rowed out from
the shore. 'Instinct': imbued.

A lonely scene more lonesome, among woods   145
At noon, and 'mid the calm of summer nights
When by the margin of the trembling lake
Beneath the gloomy hills I homeward went
In solitude, such intercourse was mine.

    And in the frosty season, when the sun   150
Was set, and visible for many a mile
The cottage windows through the twilight blazed,
I heeded not the summons. Clear and loud
The village clock tolled six; I wheeled about
Proud and exulting, like an untired horse   155
That cares not for its home. All shod with steel
We hissed along the polished ice in games
Confederate, imitative of the chace
And woodland pleasures, the resounding horn,
The pack loud bellowing, and the hunted hare.   160
So through the darkness and the cold we flew,
And not a voice was idle. With the din,
Meanwhile, the precipices rang aloud;
The leafless trees and every icy crag
Tinkled like iron; while the distant hills   165
Into the tumult sent an alien sound
Of melancholy, not unnoticed; while the stars,
Eastward, were sparkling clear, and in the west
The orange sky of evening died away.

    Not seldom from the uproar I retired   170
Into a silent bay, or sportively
Glanced sideway, leaving the tumultuous throng,
To cut across the shadow[10] of a star
That gleamed upon the ice. And oftentimes
When we had given our bodies to the wind,   175
And all the shadowy banks on either side
Came sweeping through the darkness, spinning still
The rapid line of motion, then at once
Have I, reclining back upon my heels
Stopped short – yet still the solitary cliffs   180
Wheeled by me, even as if the earth had rolled
With visible motion her diurnal round.
Behind me did they stretch in solemn train,[11]
Feebler and feebler, and I stood and watched
Till all was tranquil as a summer sea.   185

---

[10] Reflection, as at line 240 below.
[11] Sequence, succession.

Ye powers of earth, ye genii of the springs,
And ye that have your voices in the clouds,
And ye that are familiars of the lakes
And of the standing pools, I may not think
A vulgar hope was yours when ye employed   190
Such ministry – when ye through many a year
Thus, by the agency of boyish sports,
On caves and trees, upon the woods and hills,
Impressed upon all forms the characters[12]
Of danger or desire, and thus did make   195
The surface of the universal earth
With meanings of delight, of hope and fear,
Work[13] like a sea.

             Not uselessly employed,
I might pursue this theme through every change
Of exercise and sport to which the year   200
Did summon us in its delightful round.
We were a noisy crew; the sun in heaven
Beheld not vales more beautiful than ours,
Nor saw a race in happiness and joy
More worthy of the fields where they were sown.   205
I would record with no reluctant voice
Our home amusements by the warm peat fire
At evening, when with pencil and with slate,
In square divisions parcelled out, and all
With crosses and with cyphers scribbled o'er,[14]   210
We schemed and puzzled, head opposed to head,
In strife too humble to be named in verse;
Or round the naked table, snow-white deal,
Cherry, or maple, sate in close array,
And to the combat – lu or whist – led on   215
A thick-ribbed army, not as in the world
Discarded and ungratefully thrown by
Even for the very service they had wrought,
But husbanded through many a long campaign.[15]
Oh, with what echoes on the board they fell –   220
Ironic diamonds, hearts of sable hue,
Queens gleaming through their splendour's last decay,

[12] Marks, signs; 'impressed': stamped, imprinted, as at line 240 below.
[13] 'Work': seethe, move restlessly.
[14] Tick-tack-toe (noughts and crosses), described by a mock-heroic rendering of Milton's line, 'With centric and eccentric scribbled o'er' (*Paradise Lost*, VIII, 83).
[15] 'Lu' (line 215) is the card game, loo; 'thick-ribbed' (line 216) refers probably to the thickening of cards' edges through use.

Knaves wrapt in one assimilating gloom,
And kings indignant at the shame incurred
By royal visages. Meanwhile abroad   225
The heavy rain was falling, or the frost
Raged bitterly with keen and silent tooth,
And, interrupting the impassioned game,
Oft from the neighbouring lake the splitting ice,
While it sank down towards the water, sent   230
Among the meadows and the hills its long
And frequent yellings, imitative some
Of wolves that howl along the Bothnic main.[16]
        Nor with less willing heart would I rehearse[17]
The woods of autumn, and their hidden bowers   235
With milk-white clusters hung; the rod and line –
True symbol of the foolishness of hope –
Which with its strong enchantment led me on
By rocks and pools, where never summer star
Impressed its shadow, to forlorn cascades   240
Among the windings of the mountain-brooks;
The kite in sultry calms from some high hill
Sent up, ascending thence till it was lost
Among the fleecy clouds – in gusty days
Launched from the lower grounds, and suddenly   245
Dashed headlong and rejected by the storm.
All these, and more, with rival claims demand
Grateful acknowledgement. It were a song
Venial, and such as – if I rightly judge –
I might protract unblamed, but I perceive   250
That much is overlooked, and we should ill
Attain our object if, from delicate fears
Of breaking in upon the unity
Of this my argument,[18] I should omit
To speak of such effects as cannot here   255
Be regularly classed, yet tend no less
To the same point, the growth of mental power
And love of Nature's works.

---

[16] The northern Baltic.
[17] 'Rehearse': relate, describe; already a poeticism in Wordsworth's day.
[18] Theme, as in Paradise Lost, I, 24: 'the highth of this great argument.'

Ere I had seen
Eight summers – and 'twas in the very week
When I was first transplanted to thy vale,   260
Beloved Hawkshead;[19] when thy paths, thy shores
And brooks, were like a dream of novelty
To my half-infant mind – I chanced to cross
One of those open fields which, shaped like ears,
Make green peninsulas on Esthwaite's lake.   265
Twilight was coming on, yet through the gloom
I saw distinctly on the opposite shore,
Beneath a tree and close by the lake side,
A heap of garments, as if left by one
Who there was bathing. Half an hour I watched   270
And no one owned them; meanwhile the calm lake
Grew dark with all the shadows on its breast,
And now and then a leaping fish disturbed
The breathless stillness. The succeeding day
There came a company, and in their boat   275
Sounded with iron hooks and with long poles.
At length the dead man, 'mid that beauteous scene
Of trees and hills and water, bolt upright
Rose with his ghastly face.[20] I might advert
To numerous accidents in flood or field,[21]   280
Quarry or moor, or 'mid the winter snows,
Distresses and disasters, tragic facts
Of rural history, that impressed my mind
With images to which in following years
Far other feelings were attached – with forms   285
That yet exist with independent life,
And, like their archetypes, know no decay.[22]

[19] Wordsworth was in fact nine when he went to Hawkshead Grammar School, ca.
May 15, 1779. In an expanded form the episode of the Drowned Man (lines 258–79)
became part of Book IV of the short-lived five-Book *Prelude* of January–early
March 1804; it was then transferred to 1805, V, 450–73.

[20] James Jackson, schoolmaster at the neighboring village of Sawrey, was drowned on
June 18, 1779, while bathing in Esthwaite Water.

[21] An echo of Shakespeare's *Othello*, I, iii, 134–35: 'Wherein I spake of most disastrous
chances, / Of moving accidents by flood and field.'

[22] The link passage lines 279–87 has no counterpart in later versions of *The Prelude*, but is
of considerable importance. Visual impressions are stored in the memory, and assume
new significance with the passage of time. Theirs is an independent life of the
imagination, and within the mind they attain the permanence of the natural scenes from
which they derive (their 'archetypes').

There are in our existence spots of time
Which with distinct preeminence retain
A fructifying virtue,[23] whence, depressed   290
By trivial occupations and the round
Of ordinary intercourse, our minds –
Especially the imaginative power –
Are nourished and invisibly repaired;
Such moments chiefly seem to have their date   295
In our first childhood. I remember well
('Tis of an early season that I speak,
The twilight of rememberable life),
While I was yet an urchin, one who scarce
Could hold a bridle, with ambitious hopes   300
I mounted, and we rode towards the hills.
We were a pair of horsemen: honest James
Was with me, my encourager and guide.[24]
We had not travelled long ere some mischance
Disjoined me from my comrade, and, through fear   305
Dismounting, down the rough and stony moor
I led my horse, and stumbling on, at length
Came to a bottom[25] where in former times
A man, the murderer of his wife, was hung
In irons.[26] Mouldered was the gibbet-mast;   310
The bones were gone, the iron and the wood;
Only a long green ridge of turf remained
Whose shape was like a grave. I left the spot,
And reascending the bare slope I saw
A naked pool that lay beneath the hills,   315
The beacon on the summit,[27] and more near
A girl who bore a pitcher on her head
And seemed with difficult steps to force her way
Against the blowing wind. It was in truth
An ordinary sight, but I should need   320

---

[23] The power to make fruitful; 'renovating' (substituted in 1805 and 1850), loses the implication that the mind becomes creative.

[24] Wordsworth, probably aged five, was staying with his grandparents at Penrith. 'Honest James' was presumably their servant.

[25] Valley bottom.

[26] Wordsworth is conflating two murder stories. Thomas Nicholson had murdered a local butcher near Penrith and been hanged there in 1767, eight years before the probable date of the Prelude incident. A hundred years earlier, in 1672, Thomas Lancaster had poisoned his wife (and others) and been hung in irons on a gibbet in the water-meadows near the home of Ann Tyson, Wordsworth's landlady at Hawkshead; *Prose Works*, II, pp. 445–56.

[27] The impressive stone signal-beacon, built in 1719 on the hill (737 feet) above Penrith. Nicholson was hanged a mile or so to the east, near the Edenhall road.

Colours and words that are unknown to man
To paint the visionary dreariness
Which, while I looked all round for my lost guide,
Did at that time invest the naked pool,
The beacon on the lonely eminence,   325
The woman and her garments vexed and tossed
By the strong wind.
            Nor less I recollect –
Long after, though my childhood had not ceased –
Another scene which left a kindred power
Implanted in my mind. One Christmas-time,   330
The day before the holidays began,
Feverish, and tired, and restless, I went forth
Into the fields, impatient for the sight
Of those three horses which should bear us home,
My brothers and myself.[28] There was a crag,   335
An eminence, which from the meeting-point
Of two highways ascending overlooked
At least a long half-mile of those two roads,
By each of which the expected steeds might come –
The choice uncertain. Thither I repaired   340
Up to the highest summit.[29] 'Twas a day
Stormy, and rough, and wild, and on the grass
I sate half sheltered by a naked wall.
Upon my right hand was a single sheep,
A whistling hawthorn on my left, and there,   345
Those two companions at my side, I watched
With eyes intensely straining, as the mist
Gave intermitting prospects of the wood
And plain beneath. Ere I to school returned
That dreary time, ere I had been ten days   350
A dweller in my father's house, he died,
And I and my two brothers, orphans then,
Followed his body to the grave.[30] The event,
With all the sorrow which it brought, appeared
A chastisement; and when I called to mind   355
That day so lately passed, when from the crag
I looked in such anxiety of hope,

---

[28] The date was almost certainly December 19, 1783; Wordsworth was thirteen. Two of his three brothers, Richard (born 1768) and John (born 1772), were also at Hawkshead Grammar School at this time.

[29] Wordsworth was waiting on the ridge north of Borwick Lodge, a mile and a half from the school.

[30] John Wordsworth, Sr., died on December 30, 1783. Wordsworth's mother had died five years before.

With trite reflections of morality,
Yet with the deepest passion, I bowed low
To God who thus corrected my desires.   360
And afterwards the wind and sleety rain,
And all the business of the elements,
The single sheep, and the one blasted tree,
And the bleak music of that old stone wall,
The noise of wood and water, and the mist   365
Which on the line of each of those two roads
Advanced in such indisputable shapes[31] –
All these were spectacles and sounds to which
I often would repair, and thence would drink
As at a fountain. And I do not doubt   370
That in this later time, when storm and rain
Beat on my roof at midnight, or by day
When I am in the woods, unknown to me
The workings of my spirit thence are brought.[32]

    Nor, sedulous as I have been to trace   375
How Nature by collateral[33] interest,
And by extrinsic passion, peopled first
My mind with forms or beautiful or grand
And made me love them,[34] may I well forget
How other pleasures have been mine, and joys   380
Of subtler origin – how I have felt
Not seldom, even in that tempestuous time,
Those hallowed and pure motions of the sense
Which seem in their simplicity to own
An intellectual charm, that calm delight   385
Which, if I err not, surely must belong
To those first-born affinities[35] that fit
Our new existence to existing things,
And, in our dawn of being, constitute
The bond of union betwixt life and joy.   390

[31] Scansion: 'indíspūtáblĕ shápes.'
[32] In April 1805 an extended version of lines 288–374, the 'spots of time' sequence, became 1805, XI, 257–388. At an intervening stage in early March 1804 this extended sequence had very briefly formed the climax of a five-book *Prelude*.
[33] Indirect; 'sedulous': diligent, active.
[34] Wordsworth's stress is on the child's unconsciousness of Nature's working: her forms 'people' his memory not because he wishes them to do so, but as a result of emotions that are 'extrinsic' – not directly relevant – experienced during his 'boyish sports.' The uneasy transition in line 375 is an afterthought drawn from *Paradise Lost*, IX, 27: 'Not sedulous by nature to indite.'
[35] 'Intellectual' (line 385): in *The Prelude* consistently synonymous with 'spiritual.' 'First-born affinities' (line 387): those with which the child is born.

Yes, I remember when the changeful earth
And twice five seasons on my mind had stamped
The faces of the moving year, even then,
A child, I held unconscious intercourse
With the eternal beauty, drinking in   395
A pure organic pleasure from the lines
Of curling mist, or from the level plain
Of waters coloured by the steady clouds.
The sands of Westmoreland, the creeks and bays
Of Cumbria's[36] rocky limits, they can tell   400
How when the sea threw off his evening shade
And to the shepherd's hut beneath the crags
Did send sweet notice of the rising moon,
How I have stood, to images like these
A stranger, linking with the spectacle   405
No body of associated forms,
And bringing with me no peculiar sense
Of quietness or peace[37] – yet I have stood
Even while my eye has moved o'er three long leagues
Of shining water, gathering, as it seemed,   410
Through the wide surface of that field of light
New pleasure, like a bee among the flowers.

Thus often in those fits of vulgar joy[38]
Which through all seasons on a child's pursuits
Are prompt attendants, 'mid that giddy bliss   415
Which like a tempest works along the blood
And is forgotten, even then I felt
Gleams like the flashing of a shield. The earth
And common face of Nature spake to me
Remembrable things – sometimes, 'tis true,   420
By quaint associations, yet not vain
Nor profitless, if haply they impressed
Collateral objects and appearances,[39]

---

[36] Cumberland's.

[37] Wordsworth is looking back to a period at which the beautiful scenes of Nature could be admired in and for themselves, neither conjuring up other scenes within the mind, nor setting up a response determined by previous experience. For the educated contemporary reader, lines 406–7, 'linking * * * associated forms' would suggest David Hartley's theory of the 'association of ideas' in his *Observations on Man* (1749). According to Hartley, ideas (replicas of sense perception), which have occurred together or successively in sensation, recall one another in thought or imagination; from this basic principle of association he derives all the operations of man's mind.

[38] Ordinary pleasures (as opposed to the heightened joy of communion).

[39] Lines 420–23 are easily misread. The 'associations,' or juxtapositions, are quaint at times, but not vain or profitless if indirectly, 'collaterally,' they impress natural objects and appearances on the mind.

Albeit lifeless then, and doomed to sleep
Until maturer seasons called them forth   425
To impregnate and to elevate the mind.
And if the vulgar joy by its own weight
Wearied itself out of the memory,
The scenes which were a witness of that joy
Remained, in their substantial lineaments   430
Depicted on the brain and to the eye
Were visible, a daily sight. And thus
By the impressive agency of fear,
By pleasure and repeated happiness –
So frequently repeated – and by force   435
Of obscure feelings representative
Of joys that were forgotten, these same scenes,
So beauteous and majestic in themselves,
Though yet the day was distant, did at length
Become habitually dear, and all   440
Their hues and forms were by invisible links
Allied to the affections.[40]
            I began
My story early, feeling, as I fear,
The weakness of a human love for days
Disowned by memory – ere the birth of spring   445
Planting my snowdrops among winter snows.[41]
Nor will it seem to thee, my friend, so prompt
In sympathy, that I have lengthened out
With fond and feeble tongue a tedious tale.
Meanwhile my hope has been that I might fetch   450
Reproaches from my former years, whose power
May spur me on, in manhood now mature,
To honourable toil.[42] Yet should it be
That this is but an impotent desire –
That I by such inquiry am not taught   455
To understand myself, nor thou to know
With better knowledge how the heart was framed

---

[40] 'Affections': feelings.
[41] I.e., attributing snowdrops – a full flowering of memory – to a period when there would have been only snow.
[42] Especially writing the main philosophical section of *The Recluse*.

Of him thou lovest – need I dread from thee
Harsh judgements if I am so loth to quit
Those recollected hours that have the charm   460
Of visionary things,[43] and lovely forms
And sweet sensations, that throw back our life
And make our infancy a visible scene
On which the sun is shining?

---

[43]   Things seen in the imagination, with the inward eye.

Reading 1.6 William Wordsworth, from *The Prelude* (1805)

Source: Jonathan Wordsworth, M.H. Abrams and Stephen Gill (eds) (1979) *The Prelude 1799, 1805, 1850*, New York, W.W. Norton and Company, pp. 172–80. Footnotes are by the editors of this edition.

There was a boy – ye knew him well, ye cliffs	
And islands of Winander – many a time	390
At evening, when the stars had just begun	
To move along the edges of the hills,	
Rising or setting, would he stand alone	
Beneath the trees or by the glimmering lake,	
And there, with fingers interwoven, both hands	395
Pressed closely palm to palm, and his mouth	
Uplifted, he as through an instrument	
Blew mimic hootings to the silent owls	
That they might answer him. And they would shout	
Across the wat'ry vale, and shout again,	400
Responsive to his call, with quivering peals[1]	
And long halloos, and screams, and echoes loud,	
Redoubled and redoubled – concourse wild	
Of mirth and jocund din. And when it chanced	
That pauses of deep silence mocked his skill,	405
Then sometimes in that silence, while he hung	
Listening, a gentle shock of mild surprize	
Has carried far into his heart the voice	
Of mountain torrents;[2] or the visible scene	
Would enter unawares into his mind	410
With all its solemn imagery, its rocks,	
Its woods, and that uncertain heaven, received	
Into the bosom of the steady lake.	
This boy was taken from his mates, and died	
In childhood ere he was full ten years old.	415

[1] Used more generally than at present; 'a succession of loud sounds' (Johnson's *Dictionary*).

[2] 'This very expression, "far"', wrote Thomas De Quincey in 1839, 'by which space and its infinities are attributed to the human heart, and to its capacities of re-echoing the sublimities of nature, has always struck me as with a flash of sublime revelation' (*Recollections*, p. 161).

Fair are the woods, and beauteous is the spot,
The vale where he was born; the churchyard hangs
Upon a slope above the village school,
And there, along that bank, when I have passed
At evening, I believe that oftentimes   420
A full half-hour together I have stood
Mute, looking at the grave in which he lies.[3]
Even now methinks I have before my sight
That self-same village church: I see her sit –
The thronèd lady spoken of erewhile –   425
On her green hill, forgetful of this boy
Who slumbers at her feet, forgetful too
Of all her silent neighbourhood of graves,
And listening only to the gladsome sounds
That, from the rural school ascending, play   430
Beneath her and about her. May she long
Behold a race of young ones like to those
With whom I herded – easily, indeed,
We might have fed upon a fatter soil
Of Arts and Letters, but be that forgiven –   435
A race of real children, not too wise,
Too learned, or too good, but wanton, fresh,
And bandied up and down by love and hate;
Fierce, moody, patient, venturous, modest, shy,
Mad at their sports like withered leaves in winds;   440
Though doing wrong and suffering, and full oft
Bending beneath our life's mysterious weight
Of pain and fear,[4] yet still in happiness
Not yielding to the happiest upon earth.
Simplicity in habit, truth in speech,   445
Be these the daily strengtheners of their minds!
May books and Nature be their early joy,
And knowledge, rightly honored with that name –
Knowledge not purchased with the loss of power!

    Well do I call to mind the very week   450
When I was first entrusted to the care
Of that sweet valley – when its paths, its shores
And brooks, were like a dream of novelty
To my half-infant thoughts – that very week,
While I was roving up and down alone   455

---

[3]   There is little reason to suppose that Wordsworth had in mind the death of a particular
Hawkshead school friend.
[4]   Pain and fear are 'mysterious' – beyond normal human understanding – but may of
course be beneficial, as at *1805*, I, l. 306.

Seeking I knew not what, I chanced to cross
One of those open fields, which, shaped like ears,
Make green peninsulas on Esthwaite's Lake.
Twilight was coming on, yet through the gloom
I saw distinctly on the opposite shore   460
A heap of garments, left as I supposed
By one who there was bathing. Long I watched,
But no one owned them; meanwhile the calm lake
Grew dark, with all the shadows on its breast,
And now and then a fish up-leaping snapped   465
The breathless stillness. The succeeding day –
Those unclaimed garments telling a plain tale –
Went there a company, and in their boat
Sounded with grappling-irons and long poles:
At length, the dead man, 'mid that beauteous scene   470
Of trees and hills and water, bolt upright
Rose with his ghastly face, a spectre shape –
Of terror even.[5] And yet no vulgar fear,
Young as I was, a child not nine years old,
Possessed me, for my inner eye had seen   475
Such sights before among the shining streams
Of fairyland, the forests of romance –
Thence came a spirit hallowing what I saw
With decoration and ideal grace,
A dignity, a smoothness, like the words   480
Of Grecian art and purest poesy.

    I had a precious treasure at that time,
A little yellow canvass-covered book,
A slender abstract of the *Arabian Tales*;[6]
And when I learned, as now I first did learn   485
From my companions in this new abode,
That this dear prize of mine was but a block
Hewn from a mighty quarry – in a word,
That there were four large volumes, laden all
With kindred matter – 'twas in truth to me   490
A promise scarcely earthly. Instantly
I made a league, a covenant with a friend
Of my own age, that we should lay aside
The monies we possessed, and hoard up more,
Till our joint savings had amassed enough   495

---

[5] James Jackson, schoolmaster at the neighbouring village of Sawrey, was drowned on
June 18, 1779, while bathing in Esthwaite Water. For the original text of lines 450–73
(*1850*, 426–51), composed ca. January 1799, see *1799*, I, 258–79.
[6] *The Arabian Nights*.

To make this book our own. Through several months
Religiously did we preserve that vow,
And spite of all temptation hoarded up,
And hoarded up; but firmness failed at length,
Nor were we ever masters of our wish.   500

    And afterwards, when, to my father's house
Returning at the holidays, I found
That golden store of books which I had left
Open to my enjoyment once again,
What heart was mine! Full often through the course   505
Of those glad respites in the summertime
When armed with rod and line we went abroad
For a whole day together, I have lain
Down by the side, O Derwent, murmuring stream,
On the hot stones and in the glaring sun,   510
And there have read, devouring as I read,
Defrauding the day's glory – desperate –
Till with a sudden bound of smart reproach
Such as an idler deals with in his shame,
I to my sport betook myself again.   515

    A gracious spirit o'er this earth presides,
And o'er the heart of man: invisibly
It comes, directing those to works of love
Who care not, know not, think not, what they do.
The tales that charm away the wakeful night   520
In Araby – romances, legends penned
For solace by the light of monkish lamps;
Fictions, for ladies of their love, devised
By youthful squires; adventures endless, spun
By the dismantled warrior[7] in old age   525
Out of the bowels of those very thoughts
In which his youth did first extravagate[8] –
These spread like day, and something in the shape
Of these will live till man shall be no more.
Dumb yearnings, hidden appetites, are ours,   530
And they must have their food. Our childhood sits,
Our simple childhood, sits upon a throne
That hath more power than all the elements.[9]
I guess not what this tells of being past,
Nor what it augurs of the life to come,   535

[7] Time has dismantled the warrior and stripped him of his usefulness.
[8] Indulge; literally to wander at large, roam at will.
[9] I.e., the past state of being.

But so it is; and in that dubious hour,
That twilight when we first begin to see
This dawning earth, to recognise, expect –
And in the long probation that ensues,
The time of trial ere we learn to live   540
In reconcilement with our stinted powers,
To endure this state of meagre vassalage,
Unwilling to forego, confess, submit,
Uneasy and unsettled, yoke-fellows
To custom, mettlesome and not yet tamed   545
And humbled down – oh, then we feel, we feel,
We know, when we have friends.[10] Ye dreamers, then,
Forgers of lawless tales, we bless you then –
Imposters, drivellers, dotards, as the ape
Philosophy will call you[11] – then we feel   550
With what, and how great might ye are in league,
Who make our wish our power, out thought a deed,
An empire, a possession. Ye whom time
And seasons serve – all faculties – to whom
Earth crouches, th' elements[12] are potter's clay,   555
Space like a heaven filled up with northern lights,
Here, nowhere, there, and everywhere at once.

---

[10]   I.e., writers of imaginative literature.
[11]   Wordsworth denounces the kind of analytic and rational philosophy which condemns
works of imaginative fiction as false and trivial.
[12]   Here, 'the four elements' (earth, air, water, fire) of which the ancient world believed
matter to be composed.

Reading 2.1 Percy Bysshe Shelley, 'To a Skylark'

Source: Zachary Leader and Michael O'Neill (eds) (2003) *Percy Bysshe Shelley: The Major Works*, **Oxford, Oxford University Press, pp. 463–6. Footnotes are by the editors of this edition.**

> Hail to thee, blithe Spirit!
>   Bird thou never wert,
> That from Heaven, or near it,
>   Pourest thy full heart
> In profuse strains of unpremeditated art.   5
>
>   Higher still and higher
>   From the earth thou springest
> Like a cloud of fire;[1]
>   The blue deep thou wingest,
> And singing still dost soar, and soaring ever singest.   10
>
>   In the golden lightning
>   Of the sunken sun,
> O'er which clouds are bright'ning,
>   Thou dost float and run;
> Like an unbodied joy whose race is just begun.   15
>
>   The pale purple even
>   Melts around thy flight;
> Like a star of Heaven,
>   In the broad daylight
> Thou art unseen, – but yet I hear thy shrill delight,   20
>
>   Keen as are the arrows
>   Of that silver sphere,[2]
> Whose intense lamp narrows
>   In the white dawn clear,
> Until we hardly see – we feel that it is there.   25

This poem was composed near Leghorn in summer 1820, published with *Prometheus Unbound, with Other Poems* (1820), which supplies the copy-text, though Shelley's (S.'s) fair copy in the Larger Silsbee Notebook at Harvard (MS. Eng. 258.2; Donald H. Reiman (ed.), *Manuscripts of the Younger Romantics: Shelley* (*MYR*) 5) has also been consulted. Skylarks sing only in flight, often when too high to be seen.

[1]   A cloud illuminated by the sun, fiery.

[2]   The morning star (Venus).

All the earth and air
   With thy voice is loud,
As, when night is bare,
   From one lonely cloud
The moon rains out her beams – and Heaven is overflowed. 30

What thou art we know not;
   What is most like thee?
From rainbow clouds there flow not
   Drops so bright to see,
As from thy presence showers a rain of melody.   35

Like a poet hidden
   In the light of thought,
Singing hymns unbidden,
   Till the world is wrought
To sympathy with hopes and fears it heeded not: 40

Like a high-born maiden
   In a palace tower,
Soothing her love-laden
   Soul in secret hour
With music sweet as love, which overflows her bower: 45

Like a glow-worm golden
   In a dell of dew,
Scattering unbeholden
   Its aerial hue
Among the flowers and grass, which screen it from the view: 50

Like a rose embowered
   In its own green leaves,
By warm winds deflowered,
   Till the scent it gives
Makes faint with too much sweet those heavy-wingèd thieves: 55

Sound of vernal showers
   On the twinkling grass,
Rain-awakened flowers,
   All that ever was
Joyous, and clear, and fresh, thy music doth surpass.   60

Teach us, Sprite or Bird,
   What sweet thoughts are thine;
I have never heard
   Praise of love or wine
That panted forth a flood of rapture so divine.   65

Chorus Hymenaeal,[3]
   Or triumphal chant,
Matched with thine would be all
   But an empty vaunt,
A thing wherein we feel there is some hidden want.   70

What objects are the fountains
   Of thy happy strain?
What fields, or waves, or mountains?
   What shapes of sky or plain?
What love of thine own kind? what ignorance of pain?   75

With thy clear keen joyance
   Langour cannot be:
Shadow of annoyance
   Never came near thee:
Thou lovest – but ne'er knew love's sad satiety.   80

Waking or asleep,
   Thou of death must deem
Things more true and deep
   Than we mortals dream,
Or how could thy notes flow in such a crystal stream?   85

We look before and after,
   And pine for what is not:[4]
Our sincerest laughter
   With some pain is fraught;
Our sweetest songs are those that tell of saddest thought.   90

Yet if we could scorn
   Hate, and pride, and fear;
If we were things born
   Not to shed a tear,
I know not how thy joy we ever should come near.   95

Better than all measures
   Of delightful sound,
Better than all treasures
   That in books are found,
Thy skill to poet were, thou scorner of the ground!   100

---

[3] Pertaining to a wedding; Hymen is the Greek god of marriage.
[4] S. may be alluding to a comparable distinction between humans and animals in *Hamlet*, 4.4.23–9.

Teach me half the gladness
   That thy brain must know,
Such harmonious madness[5]
   From my lips would flow,
The world should listen then – as I am listening now.   105

Reading 2.2 Percy Bysshe Shelley, 'Ode to the West Wind'

Source: Zachary Leader and Michael O'Neill (eds) (2003) *Percy Bysshe Shelley: The Major Works*, Oxford, Oxford University Press, pp. 412–14. Footnotes are by the editors of this edition.

1

O, wild West Wind, thou breath of Autumn's being,
Thou, from whose unseen presence the leaves dead
Are driven,[1] like ghosts from an enchanter fleeing,

Yellow, and black, and pale, and hectic red,
Pestilence-stricken multitudes:[2] O, thou,   5
Who chariotest to their dark wintry bed

The wingèd seeds, where they lie cold and low,
Each like a corpse within its grave, until
Thine azure sister[3] of the Spring shall blow

Her clarion o'er the dreaming earth, and fill   10
(Driving sweet buds like flocks to feed in air)
With living hues and odours plain and hill:

Wild Spirit, which art moving everywhere;
Destroyer and Preserver;[4] hear, O, hear![5]

This poem was begun in Florence in October 1819; published in the 1820 volume, *Prometheus Unbound, with Other Poems*, which supplies the copy-text. Each of the poem's five sections is a sonnet in *terza rima*, with a concluding couplet. The Ode is concerned with rebirth and regeneration in the personal and political spheres. Throughout, the wind is addressed as though it were a god-like force, but at the close it is the poet who asserts his poetic power. S. scrawled a line in Greek from Euripides, *Heracles*, l. 342, at the end of his draft in Donald H. Reiman (ed.), *The Bodleian Shelley Manuscripts* (*BSM*) 5; translated, it reads, 'In goodness I, though mortal, surpass you, a mighty god'.

[1] Fallen autumnal leaves are a traditional image for death or defeat: see Dante, *Inferno*. 3. 112–17, and John Milton, *Paradise Lost* (*PL*) 1.302–4.

[2] Throughout, S. treats the leaves figuratively as well as literally; here, they suggest crowds of people suffering from plague.

[3] The warm west wind in spring, traditionally masculine in Greek and Latin mythology; S. makes it feminine.

[4] Titles for the Hindu gods, Shiva (the Destroyer) and Vishnu (the Preserver); S.'s poem both revises Christian imagery and draws on Indian religion.

[5] See Psalm 61:1: 'Hear my cry, O God: attend unto my prayer.'

2

Thou on whose stream, 'mid the steep sky's commotion, 15
Loose clouds[6] like earth's decaying leaves are shed,
Shook from the tangled boughs[7] of Heaven and Ocean,

Angels[8] of rain and lightning: there are spread
On the blue surface of thine airy surge,
Like the bright hair uplifted from the head   20

Of some fierce Maenad, even from the dim verge
Of the horizon to the zenith's height,
The locks of the approaching storm.[9] Thou dirge

Of the dying year, to which this closing night
Will be the dome of a vast sepulchre,   25
Vaulted with all thy congregated might

Of vapours, from whose solid atmosphere
Black rain, and fire, and hail will burst: O, hear!

3

Thou who didst waken from his summer dreams
The blue Mediterranean, where he lay,   30
Lulled by the coil of his crystalline streams,

Beside a pumice isle[10] in Baiae's bay,[11]
And saw in sleep old palaces and towers
Quivering within the wave's intenser day,[12]

All overgrown with azure moss and flowers   35
So sweet, the sense faints picturing them! Thou
For whose path the Atlantic's level powers

Cleave themselves into chasms, while far below
The sea-blooms and the oozy woods which wear
The sapless foliage of the ocean, know   40

---

[6] Wispy, cirrus clouds.
[7] S.'s metaphor is based on the exchange of water and vapour between sky and sea.
[8] Messengers.
[9] Dense clouds that run before the coming storm.
[10] Island formed from porous lava.
[11] Bay to the west of Naples, visited by the Shelleys in December 1818.
[12] When S. visited the Bay of Baiae, he was able to see 'the ruins of its ancient grandeur standing like rocks in the transparent sea under our boat' (Frederick L. Jones (ed.), *The Letters of Percy Bysshe Shelley* (L). 2. 61).

Thy voice, and suddenly grow grey with fear,
And tremble and despoil themselves: O, hear!

4

If I were a dead leaf thou mightest bear;
If I were a swift cloud to fly with thee;
A wave to pant beneath thy power, and share   45

The impulse of thy strength, only less free
Than thou, O, Uncontrollable! If even
I were as in my boyhood, and could be

The comrade of thy wanderings over Heaven,
As then, when to outstrip thy skiey speed   50
Scarce seemed a vision; I would ne'er have striven

As thus with thee in prayer in my sore need.[13]
Oh! lift me as a wave, a leaf, a cloud!
I fall upon the thorns of life![14] I bleed!

A heavy weight of hours has chained and bowed   55
One too like thee: tameless, and swift, and proud.

5

Make me thy lyre, even as the forest is:
What if my leaves are falling like its own!
The tumult of thy mighty harmonies

Will take from both a deep, autumnal tone,   60
Sweet though in sadness. Be thou, Spirit fierce,
My spirit! Be thou me, impetuous one!

Drive my dead thoughts over the universe
Like withered leaves to quicken a new birth![15]
And, by the incantation of this verse,   65

---

[13]   S. comes close to the posture and accents of biblical poetry here, a secular Psalmist or latter-day Job.
[14]   Possible sources include Keats, 'Sleep and Poetry', where he attacks poetry that merely 'feeds upon the burrs, / And thorns of life' (ll. 244–5).
[15]   The phrase has a personal resonance since Mary S. was pregnant; Percy Florence Shelley was born on 12 November 1819.

Scatter, as from an unextinguished hearth
Ashes and sparks, my words among mankind!
Be through my lips to unawakened earth

The trumpet of a prophecy! O, wind,
If Winter comes, can Spring be far behind?[16]   70

---

[16]   In a draft (*BSM* 5), S. finished with a statement: 'o Wind / When Winter comes Spring
lags not far behind.'

Reading 2.3 Percy Bysshe Shelley, 'Sonnet: England in 1819'

Source: Zachary Leader and Michael O'Neill (eds) (2003) *Percy Bysshe Shelley: The Major Works*, Oxford, Oxford University Press, p. 446. Footnotes are by the editors of this edition.

An old, mad, blind, despised, and dying King;[1]
Princes,[2] the dregs of their dull race, who flow
Through public scorn, – mud from a muddy spring;
Rulers who neither see nor feel nor know,
But leechlike to their fainting country cling   5
Till they drop, blind in blood, without a blow.
A people starved and stabbed in th'untilled field;[3]
An army whom liberticide[4] and prey
Makes as a two-edged sword to all who wield;
Golden and sanguine[5] laws which tempt and slay;   10
Religion Christless, Godless, a book sealed;
A senate, Time's worst statute, unrepealed –[6]
Are graves from which a glorious Phantom may
Burst, to illumine our tempestuous day.

This poem was composed in Florence in late 1819, sent to Leigh Hunt for publication on 23 December 1819, but only published posthumously, in Mary Wollstonecraft Shelley (ed.), *The Poetical Works of Percy Bysshe Shelley* (*MWS*) (1). The poem may have been considered for the volume of 'popular songs' S. hoped to publish in 1820. Timothy Webb (ed.), *Percy Bysshe Shelley: Poems and Prose* (*Webb*) quotes the Westminster MP and parliamentary reformer Francis Burdett (1770–1844), in an Election Address of 11 October 1812, published in Hunt's *Examiner*: 'an army of spies and informers … a Phantom for a king; a degraded aristocracy; an oppressed people … vague and sanguinary laws.' The copy-text is S.'s fair copy in the Bodleian (*BSM* 18).

[1] George III had reigned since 1760, had been insane since 1811, and was soon to die, aged 81, on 29 January 1820; his 'blindness' was metaphorical, Lear's rather than Gloucester's.

[2] George III's sons were notoriously dissolute.

[3] An allusion to the Peterloo Massacre (see first footnote for 'The Mask of Anarchy').

[4] The killing of liberty (S.'s coinage).

[5] Gold and blood ('sanguine' here means bloody rather than hopeful or confident) recurrently symbolize the twin origins and underpinnings of tyranny in S.'s poetry: money and violence.

[6] The 'senate' here is the unreformed Parliament. 'Time's worst statute, unrepealed' refers to the Test and Corporations Acts which imposed disabilities upon Dissenters and Roman Catholics (and survived several attempts at repeal and modification).

Reading 2.4 Percy Bysshe Shelley, 'To the Lord Chancellor'

Source: Zachary Leader and Michael O'Neill (eds) (2003) *Percy Bysshe Shelley: The Major Works*, **Oxford, Oxford University Press, pp. 448–50. Footnotes are by the editors of this edition.**

> Thy country's curse is on thee, darkest Crest
>   Of that foul, knotted, many-headed worm
> Which rends our mother's bosom! – Priestly Pest!
>   Masked Resurrection of a buried form![1]
>
> Thy country's curse is on thee – Justice sold,   5
>   Truth trampled, Nature's landmarks overthrown,
> And heaps of fraud-accumulated gold
>   Plead, loud as thunder, at destruction's throne.
>
> And whilst that sure, slow Fate which ever stands
>   Watching the beck of Mutability   10
> Delays to execute her high commands
>   And, though a nation weeps, spares thine and thee –
>
> O let a father's curse be on thy soul,
>   And let a daughter's hope be on thy tomb;
> Be both, on thy grey head, a leaden cowl   15
>   To weigh thee down to thine approaching doom.
>
> I curse thee! By a parent's outraged love, –
>   By hopes long cherished and too lately lost, –
> By gentle feelings thou couldst never prove,
>   By griefs which thy stern nature never crossed;   20
>
> By those infantine smiles of happy light,
>   Which were a fire within a stranger's hearth,

Dated 1819 by Mary S. but probably composed in 1820 (see *BSM* 14, pp. xviii–xix), 'To the Lord Chancellor' was published in part in Mary S.'s first 1839 edition and was published in full in her second 1839 edition. There is a draft in the Bodleian (*BSM* 14) and a later draft in Harvard MS Eng. 258.2 (*MYR* 5). A subsequent transcription by Mary S., with corrections by S., in Harvard fMS. Eng 822 (*MYR* 5) provides the copy-text. For the idea of a curse and the poem's concluding twist, S. may be indebted to Byron's *Childe Harold*, 4. 132–5.
The copy-text has 'To Lxxd Exxxn', cancelled, presumably for prudential reasons, in favour of 'To —'; the intermediate Harvard draft has 'To the Lord Chancellor', with the last two words cancelled. We have adopted the title in this intermediate draft before the cancellations, as did Mary S. and subsequent editors.
[1] 'The Star-chamber' (Mary S. in her second 1839 edition).

Quenched even when kindled, in untimely night,
    Hiding the promise of a lovely birth –[2]

By those unpractised accents of young speech   25
    Which he who is a father thought to frame
To gentlest lore, such as the wisest teach –
    Thou strike the lyre of mind! – oh, grief and shame!

By all the happy see in children's growth,
    That undeveloped flower of budding years –   30
Sweetness and sadness interwoven both,
    Source of the sweetest hopes, the saddest fears.

By all the days under a hireling's care
    Of dull constraint and bitter heaviness –
Oh, wretched ye, if any ever were –   35
    Sadder than orphans – why not fatherless?[3]

By the false cant which on their innocent lips
    Must hang like poison on an opening bloom,
By the dark creeds which cover with eclipse
    Their pathway from the cradle to the tomb –[4]   40

By thy complicity with lust and hate:
    Thy thirst for tears – thy hunger after gold –
The ready frauds which ever on thee wait –
    The servile arts in which thou hast grown old. –

By thy most killing sneer, and by thy smile –   45
    By all the snares and nets of thy black den;
And – (for thou canst outweep the crocodile) –
    By thy false tears – those millstones braining men –[5]

By all the hate which checks a father's love,
    By all the scorn which kills a father's care,   50
By those most impious hands, which dared remove
    Nature's high bounds – by thee – and by despair –

---

[2] Cancelled in copy-text; S. then wrote in the right-hand margin 'Insert this'.

[3] S. altered Mary S.'s transcription from 'yet not fatherless'.

[4] After this stanza, the copy-text has the following stanza cancelled with the instruction 'dele' (delete): 'By thy most impious Hell, and all its terror, / By all the grief, the madness, and the guilt / Which [*for* Of] thine impostures, which must be their error, / That sand on which thy crumbling Power is built'. The stanza is usually printed by editors (though not [Kelvin Everest and G.N. Matthews (eds), *The Poems of Shelley, 1806–1819*]) as part of the poem.

[5] For Eldon's notorious weeping in court, see Shelley's *Mask of Anarchy*, ll. 16–17.

Yes – the despair which bids a father groan
   And cry – 'My children are no longer mine –
The blood within those veins may be mine own,   55
   But, Tyrant, their polluted souls are thine; –'
I curse thee, though I hate thee not. – O, slave!
   If thou couldst quench that earth-consuming Hell
Of which thou art a daemon, on thy grave
   This curse should be a blessing – Fare thee well!   60

Reading 2.5 Percy Bysshe Shelley, 'Ozymandias'

Source: Zachary Leader and Michael O'Neill (eds) (2003) *Percy Bysshe Shelley: The Major Works*, **Oxford, Oxford University Press, p. 198. Footnotes are by the editors of this edition.**

I met a traveller from an antique land
Who said – 'Two vast and trunkless legs of stone
Stand in the desert. Near them, on the sand,
Half sunk, a shattered visage lies, whose frown,
And wrinkled lip, and sneer of cold command,   5
Tell that its sculptor well those passions read
Which yet survive, stamped on these lifeless things,
The hand[1] that mocked[2] them and the heart[3] that fed;
And on the pedestal these words appear:
"My name is Ozymandias, King of Kings: 10
Look on my Works, ye Mighty, and despair!"
Nothing beside remains. Round the decay
Of that colossal Wreck, boundless and bare
The lone and level sands stretch far away.'

Composed late 1817, as S.'s contribution to a competition with Horace Smith. Smith visited S. in Marlow for two nights after Christmas 1817. First published in the *Examiner*, 11 January 1818, under the pseudonymn 'Glirastes', a jokey Latin and Greek compound meaning 'Dormouse lover' ('Dormouse' being one of S.'s pet names for Mary S.). 'Ozymandias' is the Greek name for Pharaoh Ramses II (reigned 1279–1213 BC), renowned as a model ruler, and for erecting many buildings and statues during his reign. No single source inspires the poem, though behind a range of possible sources lies the description of a monument to 'Osymandias' (the conventional spelling) quoted in the *Library of History* (*c.*60 BC to 30 BC), a forty-volume world history by the Greek Sicilian historian Diodorus Siculus. The text is from *Rosalind and Helen* (1819), supplemented in places by S.'s pointing and capitalization in a careful fair copy in the Bodleian (*BSM* 3).

[1] The sculptor's.
[2] Imitated, perhaps also derided.
[3] Ozymandias'.

Reading 2.6 Percy Bysshe Shelley, 'Written on Hearing the News of the Death of Napoleon'

Source: Zachary Leader and Michael O'Neill (eds) (2003) *Percy Bysshe Shelley: The Major Works*, **Oxford, Oxford University Press, pp. 588–9. Footnotes are by the editors of this edition.**

1

What! alive and so bold, oh Earth?
   Art thou not overbold?
   What! leapest thou forth as of old
In the light of thy morning mirth,
The last of the flock of the starry fold?   5
Ha! leapest thou forth as of old?
Are not the limbs still when the ghost is fled,
And canst thou move, Napoleon being dead?

2

How! is not thy quick heart cold?
   What spark is alive on thy hearth?[1]   10
How! is not *his* death-knell knolled?
   And livest *thou* still, Mother Earth?
Thou wert warming thy fingers old
O'er the embers covered and cold
Of that most fiery spirit, when it fled –   15
What, Mother, do you laugh now he is dead?

3

'Who has known me of old,' replied Earth,
   'Or who has my story told?
   It is thou who art overbold.'

This poem was composed sometime between the death of Napoleon, on 5 May 1821 (though news of the death would not have reached S. for several weeks), and 11 November 1821, the date he sent it, along with the manuscript of *Hellas*, to his publisher, Charles Ollier, with instructions to print it 'at the end' of the *Hellas* volume (1822). This provides the copy-text. For S. on Napoleon see also 'Ode to Liberty', *The Triumph of Life*, and 'Feelings of a Republican on the Fall of Buonaparte' (not reproduced here).

[1] One of the names the Romans worshipped the earth under was Vesta: she was also the goddess of the hearth.

And the lightning of scorn laughed forth   20
As she sung, 'To my bosom I fold
All my sons when their knell is knolled,
And so with living motion all are fed
And the quick spring like weeds out of the dead.

4

'Still alive and still bold,' shouted Earth,   25
   'I grow bolder and still more bold.
   The dead fill me ten thousand fold
Fuller of speed and splendour and mirth.
I was cloudy, and sullen, and cold,
Like a frozen chaos uprolled,   30
Till by the spirit of the mighty dead
My heart grew warm. I feed on whom I fed.

5

'Aye, alive and still bold,' muttered Earth,
   'Napoleon's fierce spirit rolled,
   In terror and blood and gold,   35
A torrent of ruin to death from his birth.
Leave the millions who follow to mould
The metal before it be cold,
And weave into his shame, which like the dead
Shrouds me, the hopes that from his glory fled.'   40

Reading 2.7 Percy Bysshe Shelley, 'Mont Blanc: Lines Written in the Vale of Chamouni'

Source Zachary Leader and Michael O'Neill (eds) (2003) *Percy Bysshe Shelley: The Major Works*, **Oxford, Oxford University Press, pp. 120–4. Footnotes are by the editors of this edition.**

1

The everlasting universe of things
Flows through the mind,[1] and rolls its rapid waves,[2]
Now dark – now glittering – now reflecting gloom –
Now lending splendour, where from secret springs
The source of human thought its tribute brings   5
Of waters, – with a sound but half its own,[3]
Such as a feeble brook will oft assume

This poem was composed in July 1816 after S., Mary, and Claire Clairmont visted Chamonix and its Alpine environs (see S.'s account in *Letters* 1. 495–502). The text in *History of a Six Weeks' Tour* by Mary and P. B. Shelley (1817) provides the copy-text for version A. There is a draft in the Bodleian (*BSM* 11). In the Preface to *History* we are told that 'Mont Blanc' 'was composed under the immediate impression of the deep and powerful feelings excited by the objects which it attempts to describe' and that it is 'an undisciplined overflowing of the soul' which 'rests its claim to approbation on an attempt to imitate the untameable wildness and inaccessible solemnity from which those feelings sprang'. The poem's irregular rhyme-scheme, modelled on that of Milton's *Lycidas*, mimics the effort to give verbal form to these feelings. 'Mont Blanc' reads the Alpine landscape as sublime, but the sublimity it finds does not prove the existence of God, as it does in Coleridge's 'Hymn before Sun-Rise, in the Vale of Chamouni'. When Coleridge's poem was first printed (1802), it was accompanied by a note which included the exclamation, 'Who *would* be, who *could* be an Atheist in this valley of wonders!' In 'Mont Blanc' S., who had described himself (in Greek) in a number of Swiss hotel registers as a lover of mankind, democrat, and atheist, appears to respond to Coleridge's challenge, yet he is prepared (as in the 'Hymn') to invoke a heterodox 'power' (l. 127) or 'secret strength of things' (l. 139), possibly identifiable with the idea of Necessity. The poem begins with an emphasis on the power of the 'universe of things' (l. 1); it ends by pointing up (albeit in a question) the significance of 'the human mind's imaginings' (l. 143).

[1] Has been read as the 'Universal Mind as distinct from the individual mind' (*Longman* 1), but S. is less explicit here than he is in 'The Daemon of the World' (a reworking, published in the *Alastor* volume, of parts of *Queen Mab*), 2. 248–51: 'For birth but wakes the universal Mind / Whose mighty streams might else in silence flow / Through the vast world, to individual sense / Of outward shows'.

[2] See Wordsworth, 'Tintern Abbey', l. 103: 'And rolls through all things'.

[3] See Wordsworth, 'Tintern Abbey', ll. 106–8: 'the mighty world / Of eye and ear, both what they half-create, / And what perceive'; the referent of 'its' is more likely to be 'The source of human thought' (l. 5) than the 'universe of things' (l. 1).

In the wild woods, among the mountains lone,
Where waterfalls around it leap for ever,
Where woods and winds contend, and a vast river   10
Over its rocks ceaselessly bursts and raves.[4]

2

Thus thou, Ravine of Arve[5] – dark, deep Ravine –
Thou many-coloured, many-voicèd vale,
Over whose pines, and crags, and caverns sail
Fast cloud shadows and sunbeams: awful scene,   15
Where Power in likeness of the Arve comes down
From the ice gulfs that gird his secret throne,
Bursting through these dark mountains like the flame
Of lightning through the tempest; – thou dost lie,
Thy giant brood of pines around thee clinging,   20
Children of elder time, in whose devotion
The chainless winds still come and ever came
To drink their odours, and their mighty swinging
To hear – an old and solemn harmony;
Thine earthly rainbows stretched across the sweep   25
Of the ethereal waterfall, whose veil
Robes some unsculptured[6] image; the strange sleep
Which when the voices of the desert fail
Wraps all in its own deep eternity; –
Thy caverns echoing to the Arve's commotion,   30
A loud, lone sound no other sound can tame;
Thou art pervaded with that ceaseless motion,
Thou art the path of that unresting sound –
Dizzy Ravine! and when I gaze on thee
I seem as in a trance sublime and strange   35
To muse on my own separate fantasy,
My own, my human mind, which passively
Now renders and receives fast influencings,
Holding an unremitting interchange
With the clear universe of things around;   40
One legion of wild thoughts, whose wandering wings

[4]   The poem begins with a meditation on 'things' and 'thought' before it moves, in the second section, to the Alpine scene, read as illustrative ('Thus', l. 12) of the opening propositions.

[5]   The Arve flows through Chamouni into Lake Geneva.

[6]   Both not sculptured (because natural) and still to be sculptured (awaiting the human mind's imaginings).

Now float above thy darkness, and now rest
Where that or thou[7] art no unbidden guest,
In the still cave of the witch Poesy,
Seeking[8] among the shadows that pass by,   45
Ghosts of all things that are, some shade of thee,
Some phantom, some faint image; till the breast[9]
From which they fled recalls them, thou art there!

3

Some say that gleams of a remoter world
Visit the soul in sleep, – that death is slumber,   50
And that its shapes the busy thoughts outnumber
Of those who wake and live. – I look on high;
Has some unknown omnipotence unfurled[10]
The veil of life and death? or do I lie
In dream, and does the mightier world of sleep   55
Spread far around and inaccessibly
Its circles? For the very spirit fails,
Driven like a homeless cloud from steep to steep
That vanishes among the viewless gales!
Far, far above, piercing the infinite sky,   60
Mont Blanc appears, – still, snowy, and serene –
Its subject mountains their unearthly forms
Pile around it, ice and rock; broad vales between
Of frozen floods, unfathomable deeps,
Blue as the overhanging heaven, that spread   65
And wind among the accumulated steeps:
A desert peopled by the storms alone,
Save when the eagle brings some hunter's bone,
And the wolf tracks her there[11] – how hideously
Its shapes are heaped around! rude, bare, and high,   70
Ghastly, and scarred, and riven. – Is this the scene
Where the old Earthquake-daemon taught her young
Ruin? Were these their toys? or did a sea
Of fire envelop once this silent snow?[12]

---

[7]   Throughout this part of section 2, the referents of S.'s pronouns are elusive as he
       struggles to render 'an unremitting interchange' (l. 39). Here, 'that' may refer back to
       'My own, my human mind' (l. 37); 'thou' refers to the Ravine.
[8]   The likely subject is 'One legion of wild thoughts' (l. 41) or 'my human mind' (l. 37).
[9]   Either the poet's or some supra-human source, such as the 'Power' (l. 16).
[10] The usual sense of the word is 'unrolled', but some commentators agree with C.D.
       Locock (ed.), *The Poems of Percy Bysshe Shelley* that the intended meaning is 'drawn aside'.
[11] Version B has the more likely 'watches her'.
[12] Possible geological explanations for the Alpine scenery; ll. 73–4 refer to the theory
       proposed by the Comte de Buffon (1707–88) that the earth had begun as fluid heat and
       subsequently cooled. For S.'s awareness at this time of Buffon's ideas, see *L* 1. 499.

None can reply – all seems eternal now.   75
The wilderness has a mysterious tongue
Which teaches awful doubt, or faith so mild,[13]
So solemn, so serene, that man may be
But for such faith[14] with nature reconciled;
Thou hast a voice, great Mountain, to repeal   80
Large codes of fraud and woe; not understood
By all, but which the wise, and great, and good
Interpret, or make felt, or deeply feel.

4

The fields, the lakes, the forests, and the streams,
Ocean, and all the living things that dwell   85
Within the daedal[15] earth; lightning, and rain,
Earthquake, and fiery flood, and hurricane,
The torpor of the year when feeble dreams
Visit the hidden buds, or dreamless sleep
Holds every future leaf and flower; – the bound   90
With which from that detested trance they leap;
The works and ways of man, their death and birth,
And that of him, and all that his may be;
All things that move and breathe with toil and sound
Are born and die; revolve, subside and swell.   95
Power dwells apart in its tranquillity
Remote, serene, and inaccessible:[16]
And *this*, the naked countenance of earth,
On which I gaze, even these primeval mountains
Teach the adverting[17] mind. The glaciers creep   100
Like snakes that watch their prey, from their far fountains,
Slow rolling on; there, many a precipice,
Frost and the Sun in scorn of mortal power
Have piled: dome, pyramid, and pinnacle,

---

[13] Awe-inducing scepticism about the existence of a benevolent creative deity, or trust in
the existence of a 'Power' that differs from the Christian God by being indifferent to
human existence and thus not exploitable by those who wish to find a divine sanction
for oppressive forms of human authority ('Large codes of fraud and woe', l. 81).
[14] In version B, S. writes 'In such a faith', which makes more obvious sense. 'But for' may
mean 'Only through'.
[15] Intricately wrought, after Daedalus, mythical inventor who built the Cretan labyrinth.
[16] See the Note to *Queen Mab* (not reproduced here), 7. 13, where S. rejects the idea of 'a
creative Deity' but not of 'a pervading Spirit coeternal with the universe' (p. 79). S.'s
sense of 'Power' dwelling apart owes something to the Lucretian stricture against the
belief 'that any holy abode of the gods exists in any part of the world' (*De Rerum
Natura*, 5. 146–7).
[17] Attentive.

A city of death, distinct[18] with many a tower   105
And wall impregnable of beaming ice.
Yet not a city, but a flood of ruin
Is there, that from the boundaries of the sky
Rolls its perpetual stream; vast pines are strewing
Its destined path, or in the mangled soil   110
Branchless and shattered stand; the rocks, drawn down
From yon remotest waste, have overthrown
The limits of the dead and living world,
Never to be reclaimed. The dwelling-place
Of insects, beasts, and birds, becomes its spoil;   115
Their food and their retreat for ever gone,
So much of life and joy is lost. The race
Of man flies far in dread; his work and dwelling
Vanish, like smoke before the tempest's stream,
And their place is not known.[19] Below, vast caves   120
Shine in the rushing torrents' restless gleam,
Which from those secret chasms in tumult welling[20]
Meet in the vale, and one majestic River,[21]
The breath and blood of distant lands, for ever
Rolls its loud waters to the ocean waves,   125
Breathes its swift vapours to the circling air.

5

Mont Blanc yet gleams on high: – the power is there,
The still and solemn power of many sights,
And many sounds, and much of life and death.
In the calm darkness of the moonless nights,   130
In the lone glare of day, the snows descend
Upon that Mountain; none beholds them there,
Nor when the flakes burn in the sinking sun,
Or the star-beams dart through them: – Winds contend
Silently[22] there, and heap the snow with breath   135
Rapid and strong, but silently! Its home
The voiceless lightning in these solitudes

18 Decorated (*OED* 4).
19 See Job 7: 10: 'He shall return no more to his house, neither shall his place know him
    any more.'
20 There are echoes of Coleridge's 'Kubla Khan' here (see that poem's 'caverns
    measureless to man' (l. 4), 'deep romantic chasm' (l. 12), and river that 'sank in tumult
    to a lifeless ocean' (l. 28)): although S. did not receive his copy of Coleridge's *Christabel*
    volume (containing 'Kubla Khan') until late August 1816, he evidently knew 'Kubla
    Khan', possibly via Southey or Byron.
21 The Rhône, fed by Lake Geneva into which the Arve flows.
22 See Coleridge, 'Hymn before Sun-rise', ll. 6–7, describing how Mont Blanc 'Risest from
    forth thy silent sea of pines, / How silently!'

Keeps innocently, and like vapour broods
Over the snow. The secret strength of things
Which governs thought, and to the infinite dome   140
Of heaven is as a law, inhabits thee!
And what were thou, and earth, and stars, and sea,
If to the human mind's imaginings
Silence and solitude were vacancy?[23]

---

[23]   See S.'s comment in his journal-letter (22 June 1816) about visiting the Alps: 'All was as much our own as if we had been the creators of such impressions in the minds of others, as now occupied our own' (*L* l. 497).

Reading 2.8 Percy Bysshe Shelley, 'The Mask of Anarchy: Written on the Occasion of the Massacre at Manchester'

Source: Zachary Leader and Michael O'Neill (eds) (2003) *Percy Bysshe Shelley: The Major Works*, **Oxford, Oxford University Press, pp. 399–411. Footnotes are by the editors of this edition.**

As I lay asleep in Italy[1]
There came a voice from over the Sea,
And with great power it forth led me
To walk in the vision of Poesy.

I met Murder on the way –   5
He had a mask like Castlereagh –[2]

This poem was composed at Leghorn (Livorno) in September 1819 and sent on the 23rd to Leigh Hunt for publication in the *Examiner*, though it never appeared there (partly out of Hunt's fear of prosecution); published posthumously in an edition by Leigh Hunt (1832) and in *MWS (1)*. The poem is S.'s response, intended for a wide public audience, to the 'Peterloo Massacre' of 16 August 1819. Public revulsion at the unprovoked violence of the authorities provided opponents of the government with a powerful image of the cruelty of state repression. That this image also frightened the forces of established order, would lead, ironically, to increased repression: the 'Six Acts' of December 1819, limiting the right of assembly, reinforcing laws against 'Blasphemous and Seditious Libels', tightening the Press laws. The excuse for this new stringency was the threat of anarchy, which S.'s poem turns on its head. 'Mask' in the title means both masquerade, or allegorical pageant, and disguise or covering. The most important of the poem's political sources were Leigh Hunt's editorials about Peterloo in the issues of the *Examiner* for 22 and 29 August, the first of which pours scorn on 'these Men in the Brazen Masks of power'. Its literary models derive from poetical dream vision, a tradition stretching back to Chaucer, and popular ballad. The copy-text is Mary S.'s press copy, with S.'s additions and corrections, in the Library of Congress (MMC 1399; *MYR* 2), though we have also consulted S.'s intermediate fair copy in the British Library (Ashley MS 4086; also in *MYR* 2).

[1] Perhaps figurative and self-critical, implying S.'s lack of awareness of the political situation in England.

[2] Robert Stewart, Viscount Castlereagh (1769–1822), Foreign Secretary (since 1812) and leader of the Tories in the House of Commons. Associated with suppression in Ireland and at home; also with support of the Napoleonic wars and the reactionary Holy Alliance.

Very smooth he looked, yet grim;
Seven bloodhounds[3] followed him:

All were fat; and well they might
Be in admirable plight,   10
For one by one, and two by two,
He tossed them human hearts to chew
Which from his wide cloak he drew.

Next came Fraud, and he had on,
Like Eldon,[4] an erminèd gown;   15
His big tears, for he wept well,
Turned to mill-stones as they fell.

And the little children, who
Round his feet played to and fro,
Thinking every tear a gem,   20
Had their brains knocked out by them.[5]

Clothed with the Bible, as with light,
And the shadows of the night,
Like Sidmouth,[6] next, Hypocrisy
On a crocodile[7] rode by.   25

And many more Destructions played
In this ghastly masquerade,
All disguised, even to the eyes,
Like Bishops, lawyers, peers or spies.

---

[3]   Donald H. Reiman and Sharon B. Powers (eds), *Shelley's Poetry and Prose* (Norton) think this refers to the seven other nations (Austria, France, Russia, Prussia, Portugal, Spain, and Sweden) Britain allied itself with in 1815 when it agreed 'to postpone final abolition of the slave trade', and also points out that politicians who supported the war were frequently called 'bloodhounds' by its opponents.

[4]   John Scott, Baron Eldon (1751–1838), Lord Chancellor; in 1817 he had refused S. custody of his children by Harriet. His 'erminèd gown' marks his legal authority (and supposed 'purity', ermine being a symbol of purity). Though famous for public tears he also often separated parents from children in his Chancery judgements.

[5]   See Luke 17: 2: 'It were better for him that a millstone were hanged about his neck, and he cast into the sea, than that he should offend one of these little ones.' Among the dead and wounded at Peterloo were several children.

[6]   Henry Addington, Viscount Sidmouth (1757–1844), Home Secretary (since 1812), and thus in charge of internal spying (a realm of 'shadows' and 'disguise'). In 1818 Sidmouth lobbied for a million pounds to be spent on churches for the poor in the new industrial towns, in hopes of quieting disorder among the labouring classes.

[7]   Suggestive of hypocrisy.

Last came Anarchy:[8] he rode   30
On a white horse, splashed with blood;
He was pale even to the lips,
Like Death in the Apocalypse.

And he wore a kingly crown,
And in his grasp a sceptre shone;   35
On his brow this mark I saw –
'I AM GOD, AND KING, AND LAW.'

With a pace stately and fast,
Over English land he passed,
Trampling to a mire of blood   40
The adoring multitude.

And a mighty troop around,
With their trampling shook the ground,
Waving each a bloody sword,
For the service of their Lord.   45

And with glorious triumph they
Rode through England proud and gay,
Drunk as with intoxication
Of the wine of desolation.

O'er fields and towns, from sea to sea,   50
Passed the Pageant swift and free,
Tearing up, and trampling down,
Till they came to London town:

And each dweller, panic-stricken,
Felt his heart with terror sicken   55
Hearing the tempestuous cry
Of the triumph of Anarchy.

For with pomp to meet him came
Clothed in arms like bloody and flame,
The hired murderers, who did sing   60
'Thou art God, and Law, and King.

'We have waited, weak and lone
For thy coming, Mighty One!

---

[8] S.'s use of anarchy as a symbol of ultimate evil may derive from *PL* 2. 988, where Satan encounters Chaos, the 'anarch old,' ruler of the abyss. For details of Anarchy's personification see Revelation 6: 8: 'And I looked, and behold a pale horse; and his name that sat on him was Death, and Hell followed with him. And power was given unto them over the fourth part of the earth, to kill with sword, and with hunger, and with death, and with the beasts of the earth.' See also Benjamin West's painting *Death on the Pale Horse* (1783), in which Death, wearing a crown, and surrounded by sword-bearing followers, tramples a crowd.

Our purses are empty, our swords are cold,
Give us glory, and blood, and gold.'   65

Lawyers and priests, a motley crowd,
To the earth their pale brows bowed;
Like a bad prayer not overloud,
Whispering – 'Thou art Law and God.' –

Then all cried with one accord   70
'Thou art King, and God, and Lord;
Anarchy, to thee we bow,
Be thy name made holy now!'

And Anarchy, the Skeleton,
Bowed and grinned to every one,   75
As well as if his education
Had cost ten millions to the nation.

For he knew the Palaces
Of our Kings were rightly his;
His the sceptre, crown, and globe,[9]   80
And the gold-inwoven robe.

So he sent his slaves before
To seize upon the Bank and Tower,[10]
And was proceeding with intent
To meet his pensioned[11] Parliament   85

When one fled past, a maniac maid,
And her name was Hope, she said:
But she looked more like Despair,
And she cried out in the air:

'My father Time is weak and grey   90
With waiting for a better day;
See how idiot-like he stands,
Fumbling with his palsied hands!

'He has had child after child
And the dust of death is piled   95
Over every one but me –
Misery, oh, Misery!'[12]

Then she lay down in the street,
Right before the horses' feet,

---

[9] The orb, along with sceptre and crown, a symbol of sovereignty.
[10] In addition to being a place of imprisonment, the Tower of London is the repository of the crown jewels; hence its coupling with the Bank of England.
[11] Bribed or corrupted (as in the awarding of state pensions).
[12] *Webb* cites Wordsworth's 'The Thorn' (1798): 'And to herself she cries, / "Oh misery! oh misery! / Oh woe is me! oh misery!"' (ll. 64–6).

Expecting, with a patient eye,   100
Murder, Fraud and Anarchy,

When between her and her foes
A mist, a light, an image rose,
Small at first, and weak, and frail,
Like the vapour of a vale: 105

Till as clouds grow on the blast,
Like tower-crowned giants striding fast,
And glare with lightnings as they fly,
And speak in thunder to the sky,

It grew – a Shape[13] arrayed in mail   110
Brighter than the viper's scale,
And upborne on wings whose grain
Was as the light of sunny rain.

On its helm, seen far away,
A planet, like the Morning's,[14] lay;   115
And those plumes its light rained through
Like a shower of crimson dew.

With step as soft as wind it passed
O'er the heads of men – so fast
That they knew the presence there,   120
And looked – but all was empty air.

As flowers beneath May's footstep waken,
As stars from Night's loose hair are shaken,
As waves arise when loud winds call,
Thoughts sprung where'er that step did fall.   125

And the prostrate multitude
Looked – and ankle-deep in blood,
Hope, that maiden most serene,
Was walking with a quiet mien:

And Anarchy, the ghastly birth,   130
Lay dead earth upon the earth –
The Horse of Death tameless as wind
Fled, and with his hoofs did grind
To dust the murderers thronged behind.

A rushing light of clouds and splendour,   135
A sense awakening and yet tender
Was heard and felt – and at its close
These words of joy and fear arose

---

[13] The Shape's sudden materialization anticipates that of the 'glorious Phantom' in
'England in 1819'. Its association with a snake anticipates the imagery of ll. 227–9.
[14] The planet Venus, as the morning star.

222

As if their own indignant Earth
Which gave the sons of England birth   140
Had felt their blood upon her brow,
And shuddering with a mother's throe

Had turnèd every drop of blood
By which her face had been bedewed
To an accent[15] unwithstood –   145
As if her heart cried out aloud:

'Men of England, heirs of Glory,
Heroes of unwritten story,
Nurslings of one mighty Mother,
Hopes of her, and one another,   150

'Rise like Lions after slumber
In unvanquishable number,
Shake your chains to Earth like dew
Which in sleep had fallen on you –
Ye[16] are many – they are few.   155

'What is Freedom? – ye can tell
That which slavery is, too well –
For its very name has grown
To an echo of your own.

''Tis to work and have such pay   160
As just keeps life from day to day
In your limbs, as in a cell
For the tyrants' use to dwell,

'So that ye for them are made
Loom, and plough, and sword, and spade,   165
With or without your own will bent
To their defence and nourishment.

''Tis to see your children weak
With their mothers pine and peak,[17]
When the winter winds are bleak –   170
They are dying whilst I speak.

''Tis to hunger for such diet
As the rich man in his riot

---

[15] Utterance.
[16] Here, as in the poem's final line, S. implies a gap, at once social and geographical,
    between himself and the audience he is addressing.
[17] Droop, waste away, look sickly.

Casts to the fat dogs that lie
Surfeiting beneath his eye;   175
''Tis to let the Ghost of Gold[18]
Take from Toil a thousandfold
More than e'er its substance could
In the tyrannies of old.

'Paper coin – that forgery   180
Of the title deeds, which ye
Hold to something of the worth
Of the inheritance of Earth.

''Tis to be a slave in soul
And to hold no strong control   185
Over your own wills, but be
All that others make of ye.

'And at length when ye complain
With a murmur weak and vain
'Tis to see the Tyrant's crew   190
Ride over your wives and you –
Blood is on the grass like dew.

'Then it is to feel revenge
Fiercely thirsting to exchange
Blood for blood – and wrong for wrong –   195
Do not thus when ye are strong.

'Birds find rest, in narrow nest
When weary of their wingèd quest;
Beasts find fare, in woody lair
When storm and snow are in the air.[19]   200

'Asses, swine, have litter spread
And with fitting food are fed;
All things have a home but one –
Thou, oh, Englishman, hast none![20]

'This is slavery – savage men   205
Or wild beasts within a den

---

[18] Paper money, seen by S. as an imposture, a way of tricking the poor out of proper recompense for their labour. S. was influenced in this regard by the radical journalist William Cobbett (1763–1835), in *Paper Against Gold* (1815) and elsewhere.

[19] After this line, the following stanza is found in S.'s intermediate fair copy of the poem (and in Leigh Hunt's posthumous publication of it in 1832) but not in Mary S.'s press copy (which S. himself corrected): 'Horses, oxen, have a home, / When from daily toil they come; / Household dogs, when the wind roars, / Find a home within warm doors.' Either Mary S. forgot to transcribe the stanza or she convinced S. (or S. convinced her, on second thoughts) to omit it.

[20] See Matthew 8: 20: 'The foxes have holes, and the birds of the air have nests; but the Son of man hath not where to lay his head.'

Would endure not as ye do —
But such ills they never knew.

'What art thou, Freedom? O! could slaves
Answer from their living graves   210
This demand — tyrants would flee
Like a dream's dim imagery.

'Thou art not, as imposters say,
A shadow soon to pass away,
A superstition, and a name   215
Echoing from the cave of Fame.[21]

'For the labourer thou art bread,
And a comely table spread,
From his daily labour come
To a neat and happy home.   220

'Thou art clothes, and fire, and food
For the trampled multitude —
No — in countries that are free
Such starvation cannot be
As in England now we see.   225

'To the rich thou art a check,
When his foot is on the neck
Of his victim, thou dost make
That he treads upon a snake.[22]

'Thou art Justice — ne'er for gold   230
May thy righteous laws be sold
As laws are in England — thou
Shield'st alike both high and low.

'Thou art Wisdom — Freemen never
Dream that God will damn forever   235
All who think those things untrue
Of which Priests make such ado.

'Thou art Peace — never by thee
Would blood and treasure wasted be
As tyrants wasted them, when all   240
Leagued to quench thy flame in Gaul.[23]

'What if English toil and blood
Was poured forth, even as a flood?

---

[21] Rumour.

[22] 'This image had been used by the American Revolutionists in their "Don't Tread on Me" flag picturing a coiled rattlesnake' (*Norton*).

[23] France, leagued against in 1793 by Britain, Austria, Prussia, Holland, Spain, and Sardinia.

It availed, Oh, Liberty!
To dim, but not extinguish thee.   245

'Thou art Love – the rich have kissed
Thy feet, and like him following Christ
Give their substance to the free[24]
And through the rough world follow thee

'Or turn their wealth to arms, and make   250
War for thy beloved sake
On wealth, and war, and fraud – whence they
Drew the power which is their prey.

'Science, Poetry and Thought
Are thy lamps; they make the lot   255
Of the dwellers in a cot
So serence, they curse it not.[25]

'Spirit, Patience, Gentleness,
All that can adorn and bless
Art thou – let deeds not words express   260
Thine exceeding loveliness.

'Let a great Assembly be
Of the fearless and the free
On some spot of English ground
Where the plains stretch wide around.   265

'Let the blue sky overhead,
The green earth on which ye tread,
All that must eternal be
Witness the solemnity.

'From the corners uttermost   270
Of the bounds of English coast,
From every hut, village and town
Where those who live and suffer moan
For others' misery or their own,

'From the workhouse and the prison   275
Where pale as corpses newly risen,
Women, children, young and old
Groan for pain, and weep for cold –

---

[24] Perhaps alluding to Mary Magdalen ('him' notwithstanding), whose kiss signalled
       repentance and submission (Luke 7: 45).
[25] S.'s intermediate holograph revised this line to read 'Such, they curse their Maker not.'
       What is not clear is whether this revision occurred after Mary S. had completed the
       press copy (which would make it the preferred reading), or whether Mary S. persuaded
       him against preferring the revision while she was making the press copy.

'From the haunts of daily life
Where is waged the daily strife   280
With common wants and common cares
Which sows the human heart with tares —[26]

'Lastly from the palaces
Where the murmur of distress
Echoes, like the distant sound   285
Of a wind alive around

'Those prison-halls of wealth and fashion
Where some few feel such compassion
For those who groan, and toil, and wail
As must make their brethren pale —   290

'Ye who suffer woes untold,
Or to feel, or to behold
Your lost country bought and sold
With a price of blood and gold —

'Let a vast Assembly be,   295
And with great solemnity
Declare with measured words that ye
Are, as God has made ye, free —

'Be your strong and simple words
Keen to wound as sharpened swords,   300
And wide as targes[27] let them be
With their shade to cover ye.

'Let the tyrants pour around
With a quick and startling sound,
Like the loosening of a sea   305
Troop of armed emblazonry.

'Let the charged artillery drive
Till the dead air seems alive
With the clash of clanging wheels,
And the tramp of horses' heels.   310

'Let the fixèd bayonet
Gleam with sharp desire to wet
Its bright point in English blood,
Looking keen as one for food.

[26]   Weeds.
[27]   Shields.

'Let the horsemen's scimitars[28]   315
Wheel and flash, like sphereless stars[29]
Thirsting to eclipse their burning
In a sea of death and mourning.

'Stand ye calm and resolute,
Like a forest close and mute,   320
With folded arms and looks which are
Weapons of unvanquished war,

'And let Panic, who outspeeds
The career of armèd steeds,
Pass, a disregarded shade,   325
Through your phalanx undismayed.

'Let the laws of your own land,
Good or ill, between ye stand
Hand to hand and foot to foot,
Arbiters of the dispute,   330

'The old laws of England – they
Whose reverend heads with age are grey,
Children of a wiser day;
And whose solemn voice must be
Thine own echo – Liberty!   335

'On those who first should violate
Such sacred heralds in their state
Rest the blood that must ensue,
And it will not rest on you.

'And if then the tyrants dare   340
Let them ride among you there,
Slash, and stab, and maim, and hew –
What they like, that let them do.

'With folded arms and steady eyes,
And little fear, and less surprise,   345
Look upon them as they slay
Till their rage has died away.[30]

'Then they will return with shame
To the place from which they came,
And the blood thus shed will speak
In hot blushes on their cheek.   350

---

[28] Curved swords, especially associated with tyrannical 'Oriental' peoples (especially Turks and Persians).

[29] That is, meteors, stars shooting from their fixed spheres in the heavens.

[30] That S.'s advocacy of passive resistance could succeed as a political strategy is attested to by the examples of Gandhi, who was directly influenced by S.'s writings, and Martin Luther King.

'Every woman in the land
Will point at them as they stand –
They will hardly dare to greet
Their acquaintance in the street.

'And the bold, true warriors 355
Who have hugged Danger in wars
Will turn to those who would be free,
Ashamed of such base company.

'And that slaughter to the Nation
Shall steam up like inspiration, 360
Eloquent, oracular;
A volcano heard afar.[31]

'And these words shall then become
Like oppression's thundered doom
Ringing through each heart and brain, 365
Heard again – again – again –

'"Rise like lions after slumber
In unvanquishable number –
Shake your chains to earth like dew
Which in sleep had fallen on you – 370
Ye are many – they are few"'".

---

[31] Volcanoes as images of rebellion against tyranny frequently occur in S.'s poetry.

Reading 3.1 Thomas De Quincey, *Confessions of an English Opium-Eater: Being an Extract From the Life of a Scholar*

Source: Thomas De Quincey (1998 [1821]) *Confessions of an English Opium-Eater and Other Writings* **(ed. G. Lindop), Oxford, Oxford University Press. Footnotes in black are by the editor of this edition; footnotes in blue are by Thomas De Quincey.**

Part 1

To the Reader – I here present you, courteous reader, with the record of a remarkable period in my life: according to my application of it, I trust that it will prove, not merely an interesting record, but, in a considerable degree, useful and instructive. In *that* hope it is, that I have drawn it up: and *that* must be my apology for breaking through that delicate and honourable reserve, which, for the most part, restrains us from the public exposure of our own errors and infirmities. Nothing, indeed, is more revolting to English feelings, than the spectacle of a human being obtruding on our notice his moral ulcers or scars, and tearing away that 'decent drapery', which time, or indulgence to human frailty, may have drawn over them: accordingly, the greater part of *our* confessions (that is, spontaneous and extra-judicial confessions) proceed from demireps,[1] adventurers, or swindlers: and for any such acts of gratuitous self-humiliation from those who can be supposed in sympathy with the decent and self-respecting part of society, we must look to French literature,[2] or to that part of the German, which is tainted with the spurious and defective sensibility of the French. All this I feel so forcibly, and so nervously am I alive to reproach of this tendency, that I have for many months hesitated about the propriety of allowing this, or any part of my narrative, to come before the public eye, until after my death (when, for many reasons, the whole will be published): and it is not without an anxious review of the reasons, for and against this step, that I have, at last, concluded on taking it.

Guilt and misery shrink, by a natural instinct, from public notice: they court privacy and solitude: and, even in their choice of a grave, will

---

[1] Women of doubtful reputation; courtesans.
[2] Probably an allusion to the *Confessions* (1782) of Jean-Jacques Rousseau.

sometimes sequester themselves from the general population of the churchyard, as if declining to claim fellowship with the great family of man, and wishing (in the affecting language of Mr Wordsworth)

> – Humbly to express
> A penitential loneliness.[3]

It is well, upon the whole, and for the interest of us all, that it should be so: nor would I willingly, in my own person, manifest a disregard of such salutary feelings; nor in act or word do anything to weaken them. But, on the one hand, as my self-accusation does not amount to a confession of guilt, so, on the other, it is possible that, if it *did*, the benefit resulting to others, from the record of an experience purchased at so heavy a price, might compensate, by a vast overbalance, for any violence done to the feelings I have noticed, and justify a breach of the general rule. Infirmity and misery do not, of necessity, imply guilt. They approach, or recede from, the shades of that dark alliance, in proportion to the probable motives and prospects of the offender, and the palliations, known or secret, of the offence: in proportion as the temptations to it were potent from the first, and the resistance to it, in act or in effort, was earnest to the last. For my own part, without breach of truth or modesty, I may affirm, that my life has been, on the whole, the life of a philosopher: from my birth I was made an intellectual creature: and intellectual in the highest sense my pursuits and pleasures have been, even from my school-boy days. If opium-eating be a sensual pleasure, and if I am bound to confess that I have indulged in it to an excess, not yet *recorded*[4] of any other man, it is no less true, that I have struggled against this fascinating enthralment with a religious zeal, and have, at length, accomplished what I never yet heard attributed to any other man – have untwisted, almost to its final links, the accursed chain which fettered me. Such a self-conquest may reasonably be set off in counterbalance to any kind or degree of self-indulgence. Not to insist, that in my case, the self-conquest was unquestionable, the self-indulgence open to doubts of casuistry, according as that name shall be extended to acts aiming at the bare relief of pain, or shall be restricted to such as aim at the excitement of positive pleasure.

Guilt, therefore, I do not acknowledge: and, if I did, it is possible that I might still resolve on the present act of confession, in consideration of the service which I may thereby render to the whole

---

[3] From Wordsworth, 'The White Doe of Rylstone', 176–7.

[4] 'Not yet *recorded*,' I say: for there is one celebrated man [Samuel Taylor Coleridge] of the present day, who, if all be true which is reported of him, has greatly exceeded me in quantity.

class of opium-eaters. But who are they? Reader, I am sorry to say, a very numerous class indeed. Of this I became convinced some years ago, by computing, at that time, the number of those in one small class of English society (the class of men distinguished for talents, or of eminent station), who were known to me, directly or indirectly, as opium-eaters; such for instance, as the eloquent and benevolent __, the late dean of __; Lord __; Mr __, the philosopher; a late under-secretary of state (who described to me the sensation which first drove him to the use of opium, in the very same words as the dean of __, viz. 'that he felt as though rats were gnawing and abrading the coats of his stomach'); Mr __; and many others,[5] hardly less known, whom it would be tedious to mention. Now, if one class, comparatively so limited, could furnish so many scores of cases (and *that* within the knowledge of one single inquirer), it was a natural inference, that the entire population of England would furnish a proportionable number. The soundness of this inference, however, I doubted, until some facts became known to me, which satisfied me, that it was not incorrect. I will mention two: 1. Three respectable London druggists, in widely remote quarters of London, from whom I happened lately to be purchasing small quantities of opium, assured me, that the number of *amateur* opium-eaters (as I may term them) was, at this time, immense; and that the difficulty of distinguishing these persons, to whom habit had rendered opium necessary, from such as were purchasing it with a view to suicide, occasioned them daily trouble and disputes. This evidence respected London only. But, 2. (which will possibly surprise the reader more,) some years ago, on passing through Manchester, I was informed by several cotton-manufacturers, that their work-people were rapidly getting into the practice of opium-eating; so much so, that on a Saturday afternoon the counters of the druggists were strewed with pills of one, two, or three grains, in preparation for the known demand of the evening. The immediate occasion of this practice was the lowness of wages, which, at that time, would not allow them to indulge in ale or spirits: and, wages rising, it may be thought that this practice would cease: but, as I do not readily believe that any man, having once tasted the divine luxuries of opium, will afterwards descend to the gross and mortal enjoyments of alcohol, I take it for granted,

[5]   In the 1856 revision De Quincey complained that the names had been suppressed without his permission. He identified the people as, respectively, William Wilberforce (1759–1833), politician and philanthropist; Dr Isaac Milner (1750–1820), Dean of Carlisle; Thomas, first Lord Erskine (1750–1823), Lord Chancellor; and Coleridge. He had, however, forgotten the identity of 'Mr. Dash, the Philosopher'.

> That those eat now, who never ate before;
>
> And those who always ate, now eat the more.[6]

Indeed the fascinating powers of opium are admitted, even by medical writers, who are its greatest enemies: thus, for instance, Awsiter, apothecary to Greenwich-hospital, in his 'Essay on the Effects of Opium' (published in the year 1763), when attempting to explain, why Mead[7] had not been sufficiently explicit on the properties, counteragents, &c. of this drug, expresses himself in the following mysterious terms (φωναντα συνετοισι[8]): 'perhaps he thought the subject of too delicate a nature to be made common; and as many people might then indiscriminately use it, it would take from that necessary fear and caution, which should prevent their experiencing the extensive power of this drug: *for there are many properties in it, if universally known, that would habituate the use, and make it more in request with us than the Turks themselves*: the result of which knowledge,' he adds, 'must prove a general misfortune.' In the necessity of this conclusion I do not altogether concur: but upon that point I shall have occasion to speak at the close of my confessions, where I shall present the reader with the *moral* of my narrative.

Preliminary confessions

These preliminary confessions, or introductory narrative of the youthful adventures which laid the foundation of the writer's habit of opium-eating in after-life, it has been judged proper to premise, for three several reasons:

1   As forestalling that question, and giving it a satisfactory answer, which else would painfully obtrude itself in the course of the Opium-Confessions – 'How came any reasonable being to subject himself to such a yoke of misery, voluntarily to incur a captivity so servile, and knowingly to fetter himself with such a seven-fold chain?' – a question which, if not somewhere plausibly resolved, could hardly fail, by the indignation which it would be apt to raise as against an act of wanton folly, to interfere with that degree of sympathy which is necessary in any case to an author's purposes.

2   As furnishing a key to some parts of that tremendous scenery which afterwards peopled the dreams of the Opium-eater.

---

[6]   Parody of Thomas Parnell, 'The Vigil of Venus', 1–2.

[7]   Richard Mead (1673–1754), a well-known and controversial physician and author of numerous medical treatises.

[8]   'Speaking to the wise'.

3   As creating some previous interest of a personal sort in the confessing subject, apart from the matter of the confessions, which cannot fail to render the confessions themselves more interesting. If a man 'whose talk is of oxen,'[9] should become an Opium-eater, the probability is, that (if he is not too dull to dream at all) – he will dream about oxen: whereas, in the case before him, the reader will find that the Opium-eater boasteth himself to be a philosopher; and accordingly, that the phantasmagoria of *his* dreams (waking or sleeping, day-dreams or night-dreams) is suitable to one who in that character,

Humani nihil a se alienum putat.[10]

For amongst the conditions which he deems indispensable to the sustaining of any claim to the title of philosopher, is not merely the possession of a superb intellect in its *analytic* functions (in which part of the pretension, however, England can for some generations show but few claimants; at least, he is not aware of any known candidate for this honour who can be styled emphatically *a subtle thinker*, with the exception of *Samuel Taylor Coleridge*, and in a narrower department of thought, with the recent illustrious exception[11] of *David Ricardo*[12]) – but also on such a constitution of the *moral* faculties, as shall give him an inner eye and power of intuition for the vision and the mysteries of our human nature: *that* constitution of faculties, in short, which (amongst all the generations of men that from the beginning of time have deployed into life, as it were, upon this planet) our English poets

---

[9]   Misquoted from Ecclesiasticus 38.5.

[10]   'He deems nothing human alien to him'; from Terence, *Heauton Timoroumenos*, 77.

[11]   A third exception [the critic and essayist William Hazlitt (1778–1830), who in 1805 had published an *Essay on the Principles of Human Action*, a philosophical work] might perhaps have been added: and my reason for not adding that exception is chiefly because it was only in his juvenile efforts that the writer whom I allude to, expressly addressed himself to philosophical themes; his riper powers having been all dedicated (on very excusable and very intelligent grounds, under the present direction of the popular mind in England) to criticism and the Fine Arts. This reason apart, however, I doubt whether he is not rather to be considered an acute thinker than a subtle one. It is, besides, a great drawback on his mastery over philosophical subjects, that he has obviously not had the advantage of a regular scholastic education: he has not read Plato in his youth (which most likely was only his misfortune); but neither has he read Kant in his manhood (which is his fault).

[12]   Pioneer of political economy (1772–1823); author of *Principles of Political Economy and Taxation*, 1817.

have possessed in the highest degree – and Scottish[13] Professors[14] in the lowest.

I have often been asked, how I first came to be a regular opium-eater; and have suffered, very unjustly, in the opinion of my acquaintance, from being reputed to have brought upon myself all the sufferings which I shall have to record, by a long course of indulgence in this practice purely for the sake of creating an artificial state of pleasurable excitement. This, however, is a misrepresentation of my case. True it is, that for nearly ten years I did occasionally take opium, for the sake of the exquisite pleasure it gave me: but, so long as I took it with this view, I was effectually protected from all material bad consequences, by the necessity of interposing long intervals between the several acts of indulgence, in order to renew the pleasurable sensations. It was not for the purpose of creating pleasure, but of mitigating pain in the severest degree, that I first began to use opium as an article of daily diet. In the twenty-eighth year of my age, a most painful affection of the stomach, which I had first experienced about ten years before, attacked me in great strength. This affection had originally been caused by extremities of hunger, suffered in my boyish days. During the season of hope and redundant happiness which succeeded (that is, from eighteen to twenty-four) it had slumbered: for the three following years it had revived at intervals: and now, under unfavourable circumstances, from depression of spirits, it attacked me with a violence that yielded to no remedies but opium. As the youthful sufferings, which first produced this derangement of the stomach, were interesting in themselves, and in the circumstances that attended them, I shall here briefly retrace them.

My father died, when I was about seven years old, and left me to the care of four guardians. I was sent to various schools, great and small; and was very early distinguished for my classical attainments, especially for my knowledge of Greek. At thirteen, I wrote Greek with ease; and at fifteen my command of that language was so great, that I not only composed Greek verses in lyric metres, but could converse in Greek fluently, and without embarrassment – an accomplishment which I have not since met with in any scholar of my times, and which, in my case, was owing to the practice of daily reading off the newspapers into

---

[13] I disclaim any allusion to *existing* professors, of whom indeed I know only one.

[14] British Philosophy in the late eighteenth and early nineteenth centuries was dominated by a series of distinguished philosophers who taught at the Universities of Edinburgh and Glasgow. The professor whom De Quincey knew was John Wilson (1785–1854), Professor of Moral Philosophy at Edinburgh University; under the pseudonym 'Christopher North' Wilson edited *Blackwood's Magazine*.

the best Greek I could furnish *extempore*: for the necessity of ransacking my memory and invention, for all sorts and combinations of periphrastic expressions, as equivalents for modern ideas, images, relations of things, &c. gave me a compass of diction which would never have been called out by a dull translation of moral essays, &c. 'That boy,' said one of my masters,[15] pointing the attention of a stranger to me, 'that boy could harangue an Athenian mob, better than you or I could address an English one.' He who honoured me with this eulogy, was a scholar, 'and a ripe and good one:' and of all my tutors, was the only one whom I loved or reverenced. Unfortunately for me (and, as I afterwards learned, to this worthy man's great indignation), I was transferred to the care, first of a blockhead,[16] who was in a perpetual panic, lest I should expose his ignorance; and finally, to that of a respectable scholar, at the head of a great school on an ancient foundation. This man had been appointed to his situation by __ College, Oxford;[17] and was a sound, well-built scholar, but (like most men, whom I have known from that college) coarse, clumsy, and inelegant. A miserable contrast he presented, in my eyes, to the Etonian brilliancy of my favourite master: and besides, he could not disguise from my hourly notice, the poverty and meagreness of his understanding. It is a bad thing for a boy to be, and to know himself, far beyond his tutors, whether in knowledge or in power of mind. This was the case, so far as regarded knowledge at least, not with myself only: for the two boys, who jointly with myself composed the first form, were better Grecians than the head-master, though not more elegant scholars, nor at all more accustomed to sacrifice to the graces. When I first entered, I remember that we read Sophocles; and it was a constant matter of triumph to us, the learned triumvirate of the first form, to see our 'Archididascalus'[18] (as he loved to be called) conning our lesson before we went up, and laying a regular train, with lexicon and grammar, for blowing up and blasting (as it were) any difficulties he found in the choruses; whilst *we* never condescended to open our books, until the moment of going up, and were generally employed in writing epigrams upon his wig, or some such important matter. My two class-fellows were poor, and dependant for their future prospects at the university, on the recommendation of the head-master: but I, who had a small patrimonial property, the income of which was sufficient to

[15]   Mr Morgan, headmaster of Bath Grammar School.
[16]   The Revd Edward Spencer, headmaster of Winkfield School, Wiltshire.
[17]   Dr Charles Lawson, High Master of Manchester Grammar School, appointed by Brasenose College, Oxford.
[18]   Headmaster.

support me at college, wished to be sent thither immediately. I made earnest representations on the subject to my guardians, but all to no purpose. One, who was more reasonable, and had more knowledge of the world than the rest, lived at a distance: two of the other three resigned all their authority into the hands of the fourth; and this fourth with whom I had to negotiate, was a worthy man, in his way, but haughty, obstinate, and intolerant of all opposition to his will. After a certain number of letters and personal interviews, I found that I had nothing to hope for, not even a compromise of the matter, from my guardian: unconditional submission was what he demanded: and I prepared myself, therefore, for other measures. Summer was now coming on with hasty steps, and my seventeenth birth-day was fast approaching; after which day I had sworn within myself, that I would no longer be numbered amongst school-boys. Money being what I chiefly wanted, I wrote to a woman of high rank, who, though young herself, had known me from a child, and had latterly treated me with great distinction, requesting that she would 'lend' me five guineas. For upwards of a week no answer came; and I was beginning to despond, when, at length, a servant put into my hands a double letter, with a coronet on the seal. The letter was kind and obliging: the fair writer was on the sea-coast, and in that way the delay had arisen: she inclosed double of what I had asked, and good-naturedly hinted, that if I should *never* repay her, it would not absolutely ruin her. Now then, I was prepared for my scheme: ten guineas, added to about two which I had remaining from my pocket money, seemed to me sufficient for an indefinite length of time: and at that happy age, if no *definite* boundary can be assigned to one's power, the spirit of hope and pleasure makes it virtually infinite.

It is a just remark of Dr Johnson's[19] (and what cannot often be said of his remarks, it is a very feeling one), that we never do any thing consciously for the last time (of things, that is, which we have long been in the habit of doing) without sadness of heart. This truth I felt deeply, when I came to leave __, a place which I did not love, and where I had not been happy. On the evening before I left __ for ever, I grieved when the ancient and lofty school-room resounded with the evening service, performed for the last time in my hearing; and at night, when the muster-roll of names was called over, and mine (as usual) was called

---

[19] See *The Idler*, No. 103, 5 April 1760: 'There are few things not purely evil, of which we can say, without some emotion of uneasiness, "this is the last." ... of a place which has been frequently visited, tho' without pleasure, the last look is taken with heaviness of heart'.

first, I stepped forward, and, passing the head-master, who was standing by, I bowed to him, and looked earnestly in his face, thinking to myself, 'He is old and infirm, and in this world I shall not see him again.' I was right: I never *did* see him again, nor ever shall. He looked at me complacently, smiled goodnaturedly, returned my salutation (or rather, my valediction), and we parted (though he knew it not) for ever. I could not reverence him intellectually: but he had been uniformly kind to me, and had allowed me many indulgencies: and I grieved at the thought of the mortification I should inflict upon him.

The morning came, which was to launch me into the world, and from which my whole succeeding life has, in many important points, taken its colouring. I lodged in the head-master's house, and had been allowed, from my first entrance, the indulgence of a private room, which I used both as a sleeping room and as a study. At half after three I rose, and gazed with deep emotion at the ancient towers of __,[20] 'drest in earliest light,'[21] and beginning to crimson with the radiant lustre of a cloudless July morning. I was firm and immoveable in my purpose: but yet agitated by anticipation of uncertain danger and troubles; and, if I could have foreseen the hurricane, and perfect hail-storm of affliction which soon fell upon me, well might I have been agitated. To this agitation the deep peace of the morning presented an affecting contrast, and in some degree a medicine. The silence was more profound than that of midnight: and to me the silence of a summer morning is more touching than all other silence, because, the light being broad and strong, as that of noon-day at other seasons of the year, it seems to differ from perfect day, chiefly because man is not yet abroad; and thus, the peace of nature, and of the innocent creatures of God, seems to be secure and deep, only so long as the presence of man, and his restless and unquiet spirit, are not there to trouble its sanctity. I dressed myself, took my hat and gloves, and lingered a little in the room. For the last year and a half this room had been my 'pensive citadel:'[22] here I had read and studied through all the hours of night: and, though true it was, that for the latter part of this time I, who was framed for love and gentle affections, had lost my gaiety and happiness, during the strife and fever of contention with my guardian; yet, on the other hand, as a boy, so passionately fond of books, and dedicated to intellectual pursuits, I could not fail to have enjoyed many happy hours in the midst of general dejection. I wept as I looked round on the chair,

---

[20] The Collegiate Church of St Mary, now Manchester Cathedral.
[21] Untraced.
[22] From Wordsworth, 'Nuns fret not at their convent's narrow room', 3.

hearth, writing-table, and other familiar objects, knowing too certainly, that I looked upon them for the last time. Whilst I write this, it is eighteen years ago: and yet, at this moment, I see distinctly as if it were yesterday, the lineaments and expression of the object on which I fixed my parting gaze: it was a picture of the lovely __,[23] which hung over the mantlepiece; the eyes and mouth of which were so beautiful, and the whole countenance so radiant with benignity, and divine tranquillity, that I had a thousand times laid down my pen, or my book, to gather consolation from it, as a devotee from his patron saint. Whilst I was yet gazing upon it, the deep tones of __ clock proclaimed that it was four o'clock. I went up to the picture, kissed it, and then gently walked out, and closed the door for ever!

So blended and intertwisted in this life are occasions of laughter and of tears, that I cannot yet recal, without smiling, an incident which occurred at that time, and which had nearly put a stop to the immediate execution of my plan. I had a trunk of immense weight; for, besides my clothes, it contained nearly all my library. The difficulty was to get this removed to a carrier's: my room was at an aërial elevation in the house, and (what was worse) the stair-case, which communicated with this angle of the building, was accessible only by a gallery, which passed the head-master's chamber-door. I was a favourite with all the servants; and, knowing that any of them would screen me, and act confidentially, I communicated my embarrassment to a groom of the head-master's. The groom swore he would do any thing I wished; and, when the time arrived, went up stairs to bring the trunk down. This I feared was beyond the strength of any one man: however, the groom was a man —

> Of Atlantean shoulders, fit to bear
> The weight of mightiest monarchies;[24]

and had a back as spacious as Salisbury plain. Accordingly he persisted in bringing down the trunk alone, whilst I stood waiting at the foot of the last flight, in anxiety for the event. For some time I heard him descending with slow and firm steps: but, unfortunately, from his trepidation, as he drew near the dangerous quarter, within a few steps of the gallery, his foot slipped; and the mighty burden falling from his shoulders, gained such increase of impetus at each step of the descent, that, on reaching the bottom, it trundled, or rather leaped, right across, with the noise of twenty devils, against the very bed-room door of the

---

[23] The portrait, said to be by Van Dyck, was of a seventeenth-century Duchess of Somerset, a benefactor of the school and of Brasenose College.

[24] From Milton, *Paradise Lost*, ii, 306–7.

archididascalus. My first thought was, that all was lost; and that my only chance for executing a retreat was to sacrifice my baggage. However, on reflection, I determined to abide the issue. The groom was in the utmost alarm, both on his own account and on mine: but, in spite of this, so irresistibly had the sense of the ludicrous, in this unhappy *contretems*,[25] taken possession of his fancy, that he sang out a long, loud, and canorous peal of laughter, that might have wakened the Seven Sleepers.[26] At the sound of this resonant merriment, within the very ears of insulted authority, I could not myself forbear joining in it: subdued to this, not so much by the unhappy *étourderie*[27] of the trunk, as by the effect it had upon the groom. We both expected, as a matter of course, that Dr __ would sally out of his room: for, in general, if but a mouse stirred, he sprang out like a mastiff from his kennel. Strange to say, however, on this occasion, when the noise of laughter had ceased, no sound, or rustling even, was to be heard in the bed-room. Dr __ had a painful complaint, which, sometimes keeping him awake, made his sleep, perhaps, when it *did* come, the deeper. Gathering courage from the silence, the groom hoisted his burden again, and accomplished the remainder of his descent without accident. I waited until I saw the trunk placed on a wheel-barrow, and on its road to the carrier's: then, 'with Providence my guide,'[28] I set off on foot, – carrying a small parcel, with some articles of dress, under my arm; a favourite English poet[29] in one pocket; and a small 12mo. volume, containing about nine plays of Euripides, in the other.

It had been my intention originally to proceed to Westmorland, both from the love I bore to that county, and on other personal accounts.[30] Accident, however, gave a different direction to my wanderings, and I bent my steps towards North Wales.

After wandering about for some time in Denbighshire, Merionethshire, and Caernarvonshire, I took lodgings in a small neat house in B__.[31] Here I might have staid with great comfort for many weeks; for, provisions were cheap at B__, from the scarcity of other markets for the surplus produce of a wide agricultural district. An

---

[25] Unexpected mishap.
[26] Christian youths of Ephesus, said to have been walled up in a cave during the persecution of AD 250. They slept for 250 years, emerging when the wall had collapsed from disrepair.
[27] Blunder.
[28] Adapted from Milton, *Paradise Lost*, xii, 647.
[29] Wordsworth.
[30] The presence of Wordsworth, who lived at Grasmere.
[31] Bangor.

accident, however, in which, perhaps, no offence was designed, drove me out to wander again. I know not whether my reader may have remarked, but *I* have often remarked, that the proudest class of people in England (or at any rate, the class whose pride is most apparent) are the families of bishops. Noblemen, and their children, carry about with them, in their very titles, a sufficient notification of their rank. Nay, their very names (and this applies also to the children of many untitled houses) are often, to the English ear, adequate exponents of high birth, or descent. Sackville, Manners, Fitzroy, Paulet, Cavendish, and scores of others, tell their own tale. Such persons, therefore, find every where a due sense of their claims already established, except among those who are ignorant of the world, by virtue of their own obscurity: 'Not to know *them*, argues one's self unknown.'[32] Their manners take a suitable tone and colouring; and, for once that they find it necessary to impress a sense of their consequence upon others, they meet with a thousand occasions for moderating and tempering this sense by acts of courteous condescension. With the families of bishops it is otherwise: with them it is all up-hill work, to make known their pretensions: for the proportion of the episcopal bench, taken from noble families, is not at any time very large; and the succession to these dignities is so rapid, that the public ear seldom has time to become familiar with them, unless where they are connected with some literary reputation. Hence it is, that the children of bishops carry about with them an austere and repulsive air, indicative of claims not generally acknowledged, a sort of *noli me tangere*[33] manner, nervously apprehensive of too familiar approach, and shrinking with the sensitiveness of a gouty man, from all contact with the οι πολλοι.[34] Doubtless, a powerful understanding, or unusual goodness of nature, will preserve a man from such weakness: but, in general, the truth of my representation will be acknowledged: pride, if not of deeper root in such families, appears, at least, more upon the surface of their manners. This spirit of manners naturally communicates itself to their domestics, and other dependants. Now, my landlady had been a lady's maid, or a nurse, in the family of the Bishop of __; and had but lately married away and 'settled' (as such people express it) for life. In a little town like B__, merely to have lived in the bishop's family, conferred some distinction: and my good landlady had rather more than her share of the pride I have noticed on that score. What 'my lord' said, and 'what my lord did', how useful he was in parliament, and how

---

[32] Adapted from Milton, *Paradise Lost*, iv, 830.
[33] 'Touch me not'; from John 20: 17.
[34] 'The many'; i.e. the common people.

indispensable at Oxford,[35] formed the daily burden of her talk. All this I bore very well: for I was too good-natured to laugh in any body's face, and I could make an ample allowance for the garrulity of an old servant. Of necessity, however, I must have appeared in her eyes very inadequately impressed with the bishop's importance: and, perhaps, to punish me for my indifference, or possibly by accident, she one day repeated to me a conversation in which I was indirectly a party concerned. She had been to the palace to pay her respects to the family; and, dinner being over, was summoned into the dining-room. In giving an account of her household economy, she happened to mention, that she had let her apartments. Thereupon the good bishop (it seemed) had taken occasion to caution her as to her selection of inmates: 'for,' said he, 'you must recollect, Betty, that this place is in the high road to the Head;[36] so that multitudes of Irish swindlers, running away from their debts into England – and of English swindlers, running away from their debts to the Isle of Man, are likely to take this place in their route.' This advice was certainly not without reasonable grounds: but rather fitted to be stored up for Mrs Betty's private meditations, than specially reported to me. What followed, however, was somewhat worse: – 'Oh, my lord,' answered my landlady (according to her own representation of the matter), 'I really don't think this young gentleman is a swindler; because __:' 'You don't *think* me a swindler?' said I, interrupting her, in a tumult of indignation: 'for the future I shall spare you the trouble of thinking about it.' And without delay I prepared for my departure. Some concessions the good woman seemed disposed to make: but a harsh and contemptuous expression, which I fear that I applied to the learned dignitary himself, roused *her* indignation in turn: reconciliation then became impossible. I was, indeed, greatly irritated at the bishop's having suggested any grounds of suspicion, however remotely, against a person whom he had never seen: and I thought of letting him know my mind in Greek: which, at the same time that it would furnish some presumption that I was no swindler, would also (I hoped) compel the bishop to reply in the same language; in which case, I doubted not to make it appear, that if I was not so rich as his lordship, I was a far better Grecian. Calmer thoughts, however, drove this boyish design out of my mind: for I considered, that the bishop was in the right to counsel an old servant; that he could not have designed that his advice should be reported to me; and that the same coarseness of mind, which

---

[35]   Dr William Cleaver (1742–1815), Bishop of Bangor, who was also Master of Brasenose College, Oxford.

[36]   Holyhead.

had led Mrs Betty to repeat the advice at all, might have coloured it in a way more agreeable to her own style of thinking, than to the actual expressions of the worthy bishop.

I left the lodgings the very same hour; and this turned out a very unfortunate occurrence for me: because, living henceforward at inns, I was drained of my money very rapidly. In a fortnight I was reduced to short allowance; that is, I could allow myself only one meal a-day. From the keen appetite produced by constant exercise, and mountain air, acting on a youthful stomach, I soon began to suffer greatly on this slender regimen; for the single meal, which I could venture to order, was coffee or tea. Even this, however, was at length withdrawn: and afterwards, so long as I remained in Wales, I subsisted either on blackberries, hips, haws, &c. or on the casual hospitalities which I now and then received, in return for such little services as I had an opportunity of rendering. Sometimes I wrote letters of business for cottagers, who happened to have relatives in Liverpool, or in London: more often I wrote love-letters to their sweethearts for young women who had lived as servants in Shrewsbury, or other towns on the English border. On all such occasions I gave great satisfaction to my humble friends, and was generally treated with hospitality: and once, in particular, near the village of Llan-y-styndw[37] (or some such name), in a sequestered part of Merionethshire, I was entertained for upwards of three days by a family of young people, with an affectionate and fraternal kindness that left an impression upon my heart not yet impaired. The family consisted, at that time, of four sisters, and three brothers, all grown up, and all remarkable for elegance and delicacy of manners. So much beauty, and so much native good-breeding and refinement, I do not remember to have seen before or since in any cottage, except once or twice in Westmorland and Devonshire. They spoke English: an accomplishment not often met with in so many members of one family, especially in villages remote from the high-road. Here I wrote, on my first introduction, a letter about prize-money, for one of the brothers, who had served on board an English man of war; and more privately, two love-letters for two of the sisters. They were both interesting looking girls, and one of uncommon loveliness. In the midst of their confusion and blushes, whilst dictating, or rather giving me general instructions, it did not require any great penetration to discover that what they wished was, that their letters should be as kind as was consistent with proper maidenly pride. I contrived so to temper

---

[37] Properly Llanstumdwy, near Criccieth.

my expressions, as to reconcile the gratification of both feelings: and they were as much pleased with the way in which I had expressed their thoughts, as (in their simplicity) they were astonished at my having so readily discovered them. The reception one meets with from the women of a family, generally determines the tenor of one's whole entertainment. In this case, I had discharged my confidential duties as secretary, so much to the general satisfaction, perhaps also amusing them with my conversation, that I was pressed to stay with a cordiality which I had little inclination to resist. I slept with the brothers, the only unoccupied bed standing in the apartment of the young women: but in all other points, they treated me with a respect not usually paid to purses as light as mine; as if my scholarship were sufficient evidence, that I was of 'gentle blood.' Thus I lived with them for three days, and great part of a fourth: and, from the undiminished kindness which they continued to show me, I believe I might have staid with them up to this time, if their power had corresponded with their wishes. On the last morning, however, I perceived upon their countenances, as they sate at breakfast, the expression of some unpleasant communication which was at hand; and soon after one of the brothers explained to me, that their parents had gone, the day before my arrival, to an annual meeting of Methodists, held at Caernarvon, and were that day expected to return; 'and if they should not be so civil as they ought to be,' he begged, on the part of all the young people, that I would not take it amiss. The parents returned, with churlish faces, and '*Dym Sassenach*' (*no English*), in answer to all my addresses. I saw how matters stood; and so, taking an affectionate leave of my kind and interesting young hosts, I went my way. For, though they spoke warmly to their parents in my behalf, and often excused the manner of the old people, by saying, that it was 'only their way,' yet I easily understood that my talent for writing love-letters would do as little to recommend me, with two grave sexagenarian Welsh Methodists, as my Greek Sapphics or Alcaics:[38] and what had been hospitality, when offered to me with the gracious courtesy of my young friends, would become charity, when connected with the harsh demeanour of these old people. Certainly, Mr Shelley is right in his notions about old age:[39] unless powerfully counteracted by all sorts of opposite agencies, it is a miserable corrupter and blighter to the genial charities of the human heart.

---

[38] Metres of Greek verse.
[39] See *The Revolt of Islam*, II, xxxiii: 'old age … is … cold and cruel, and is made / The careless slave of that dark power which brings / Evil, like blight on man.'

Soon after this, I contrived, by means which I must omit for want of room, to transfer myself to London. And now began the latter and fiercer stage of my long-sufferings; without using a disproportionate expression I might say, of my agony. For I now suffered, for upwards of sixteen weeks, the physical anguish of hunger in various degrees of intensity; but as bitter, perhaps, as ever any human being can have suffered who has survived it. I would not needlessly harass my reader's feelings, by a detail of all that I endured: for extremities such as these, under any circumstances of heaviest misconduct or guilt, cannot be contemplated, even in description, without a rueful pity that is painful to the natural goodness of the human heart. Let it suffice, at least on this occasion, to say, that a few fragments of bread from the breakfast-table of one individual (who supposed me to be ill, but did not know of my being in utter want), and these at uncertain intervals, constituted my whole support. During the former part of my sufferings (that is, generally in Wales, and always for the first two months in London) I was houseless, and very seldom slept under a roof. To this constant exposure to the open air I ascribe it mainly, that I did not sink under my torments. Latterly, however, when colder and more inclement weather came on, and when, from the length of my sufferings, I had begun to sink into a more languishing condition, it was, no doubt, fortunate for me, that the same person to whose breakfast-table I had access, allowed me to sleep in a large unoccupied house, of which he was tenant. Unoccupied, I call it, for there was no household or establishment in it; nor any furniture, indeed, except a table, and a few chairs. But I found, on taking possession of my new quarters, that the house already contained one single inmate, a poor friendless child, apparently ten years old; but she seemed hunger-bitten; and sufferings of that sort often make children look older than they are. From this forlorn child I learned, that she had slept and lived there alone, for some time before I came: and great joy the poor creature expressed, when she found that I was, in future, to be her companion through the hours of darkness. The house was large; and, from the want of furniture, the noise of the rats made a prodigious echoing on the spacious stair-case and hall; and, amidst the real fleshly ills of cold, and, I fear, hunger, the forsaken child had found leisure to suffer still more (it appeared) from the self-created one of ghosts. I promised her protection against all ghosts whatsoever: but, alas! I could offer her no other assistance. We lay upon the floor, with a bundle of cursed law papers for a pillow: but with no other covering than a sort of large horseman's cloak: afterwards, however, we discovered, in a garret, an old sopha-cover, a small piece of rug, and some fragments of other articles, which added a little to our warmth. The poor child crept close to me for warmth, and for security against her ghostly enemies. When I was not more than usually ill, I took her into my arms, so that, in general, she was tolerably warm, and often slept when I could not: for, during the last two months of my sufferings, I slept much in the day-time, and was apt to fall into transient dozings at all hours. But my sleep distressed me more than my watching: for, besides the tumultuousness of my dreams (which were only not so awful as those which I shall have to describe hereafter as produced by opium), my sleep was never more than what is called *dog-sleep*; so that I could hear myself moaning, and was often, as it seemed to me, wakened suddenly by my own voice; and, about this time, a hideous sensation began to haunt me as soon as I fell into a slumber, which has since returned upon me, at different periods of my life, viz. a sort of twitching (I know not where, but apparently about the region of the stomach), which compelled me violently to throw out my feet for the sake of relieving it. This sensation coming on as soon as I began to sleep, and the effort to relieve it constantly awaking me, at length I slept only from exhaustion; and from increasing weakness (as I said before) I was constantly falling asleep, and constantly awaking. Meantime, the master of the house sometimes came in upon us suddenly, and very early, sometimes not till ten o'clock, sometimes not at all. He was in constant fear of bailiffs: improving on the plan of Cromwell,[40] every night he slept in a different quarter of London; and I observed that he never failed to examine, through a private window, the appearance of those who knocked at the door, before he would allow it to be opened. He breakfasted alone: indeed, his tea equipage would hardly have admitted of his hazarding an invitation to a second person – any more than the quantity of esculent *matériel*, which, for the most part, was little more than a roll, or a few biscuits, which he had bought on his road from the place where he had slept. Or, if he *had* asked a party, as I once learnedly and facetiously observed to him – the several members of it must have *stood* in the relation to each other (not *sate* in any relation whatever) of succession, as the metaphysicians have it, and not of co-existence; in the relation of the parts of time, and not of the parts of space. During his breakfast, I generally contrived a reason for lounging in; and, with an air of as much indifference as I could assume, took up such fragments as he had left – sometimes, indeed, there were none at all. In doing this, I

---

[40] According to Clarendon's *History of the Rebellion*, XV, 143, Cromwell 'rarely lodged two nights together in one chamber' for fear of assassination.

committed no robbery except upon the man himself, who was thus obliged (I believe) now and then to send out at noon for an extra biscuit; for, as to the poor child, *she* was never admitted into his study (if I may give that name to his chief depository of parchments, law writings, &c.); that room was to her the Blue-beard room of the house, being regularly locked on his departure to dinner, about six o'clock, which usually was his final departure for the night. Whether this child were an illegitimate daughter of Mr __,[41] or only a servant, I could not ascertain; she did not herself know; but certainly she was treated altogether as a menial servant. No sooner did Mr __ make his appearance, than she went below stairs, brushed his shoes, coat, &c.; and, except when she was summoned to run an errand, she never emerged from the dismal Tartarus[42] of the kitchens, &c. to the upper air, until my welcome knock at night called up her little trembling footsteps to the front door. Of her life during the day-time, however, I knew little but what I gathered from her own account at night; for, as soon as the hours of business commenced, I saw that my absence would be acceptable; and, in general, therefore, I went off and sate in the parks, or elsewhere, until night-fall.

But who, and what, meantime, was the master of the house himself? Reader, he was one of those anomalous practitioners in lower departments of the law, who – what shall I say? – who, on prudential reasons, or from necessity, deny themselves all indulgence in the luxury of too delicate a conscience: (a periphrasis which might be abridged considerably, but *that* I leave to the reader's taste:) in many walks of life, a conscience is a more expensive incumbrance, than a wife or a carriage; and just as people talk of 'laying down' their carriages, so I suppose my friend, Mr __ had 'laid down' his conscience for a time; meaning, doubtless, to resume it as soon as he could afford it. The inner economy of such a man's daily life would present a most strange picture, if I could allow myself to amuse the reader at his expense. Even with my limited opportunities for observing what went on, I saw many scenes of London intrigues, and complex chicanery, 'cycle and epicycle, orb in orb,'[43] at which I sometimes smile to this day – and at which I smiled then, in spite of my misery. My situation, however, at that time, gave me little experience, in my own person, of any qualities in Mr __'s character but such as did him honour; and of his whole

[41] In 1856 De Quincey explained that the lawyer called himself sometimes Brown, sometimes Brunell.
[42] The infernal regions in Greek and Roman mythology.
[43] From Milton, *Paradise Lost*, viii, 84.

strange composition, I must forget every thing but that towards me he was obliging, and, to the extent of his power, generous.

That power was not, indeed, very extensive; however, in common with the rats, I sate rent free; and, as Dr Johnson has recorded,[44] that he never but once in his life had as much wall-fruit as he could eat, so let me be grateful, that on that single occasion I had as large a choice of apartments in a London mansion as I could possibly desire. Except the Blue-beard room, which the poor child believed to be haunted, all others, from the attics to the cellars, were at our service; 'the world was all before us;'[45] and we pitched our tent for the night in any spot we chose. This house I have already described as a large one; it stands in a conspicuous situation, and in a well-known part of London.[46] Many of my readers will have passed it, I doubt not, within a few hours of reading this. For myself, I never fail to visit it when business draws me to London; about ten o'clock, this very night, August 15, 1821, being my birth-day – I turned aside from my evening walk, down Oxford-street, purposely to take a glance at it: it is now occupied by a respectable family; and, by the lights in the front drawing-room, I observed a domestic party, assembled perhaps at tea, and apparently cheerful and gay. Marvellous contrast in my eyes to the darkness – cold –silence – and desolation of that same house eighteen years ago, when its nightly occupants were one famishing scholar, and a neglected child. – Her, by the bye, in after years, I vainly endeavoured to trace. Apart from her situation, she was not what would be called an interesting child: she was neither pretty, nor quick in understanding, nor remarkably pleasing in manners. But, thank God! even in those years I needed not the embellishments of novel-accessaries to conciliate my affections; plain human nature, in its humblest and most homely apparel, was enough for me: and I loved the child because she was my partner in wretchedness. If she is now living, she is probably a mother, with children of her own; but, as I have said, I could never trace her.

This I regret, but another person there was at that time, whom I have since sought to trace with far deeper earnestness, and with far deeper sorrow at my failure. This person was a young woman, and one of that unhappy class who subsist upon the wages of prostitution. I feel no shame, nor have any reason to feel it, in avowing, that I was then on familiar and friendly terms with many women in that unfortunate

[44] See Hester Lynch Piozzi, *Anecdotes of the Late Samuel Johnson*, Ll.D. (1786), p. 13.
[45] Adapted from Milton, *Paradise Lost*, xii, 646.
[46] In 1856 De Quincey gave the address as 38 Greek Street, Soho. The house no longer exists.

condition. The reader needs neither smile at this avowal, nor frown. For, not to remind my classical readers of the old Latin proverb – '*Sine Cerere*,' &c.,[47] it may well be supposed that in the existing state of my purse, my connexion with such women could not have been an impure one. But the truth is, that at no time of my life have I been a person to hold myself polluted by the touch or approach of any creature that wore a human shape: on the contrary, from my very earliest youth it has been my pride to converse familiarly, *more Socratico*,[48] with all human beings, man, woman, and child, that chance might fling in my way: a practice which is friendly to the knowledge of human nature, to good feelings, and to that frankness of address which becomes a man who would be thought a philosopher. For a philosopher should not see with the eyes of the poor limitary creature calling himself a man of the world, and filled with narrow and self-regarding prejudices of birth and education, but should look upon himself as a Catholic creature, and as standing in an equal relation to high and low – to educated and uneducated, to the guilty and the innocent. Being myself at that time of necessity a peripatetic, or a walker of the streets, I naturally fell in more frequently with those female peripatetics who are technically called Street-walkers. Many of these women had occasionally taken my part against watchmen who wished to drive me off the steps of houses where I was sitting. But one amongst them, the one on whose account I have at all introduced this subject – yet no! let me not class thee, Oh noble minded Ann __, with that order of women; let me find, if it be possible, some gentler name to designate the condition of her to whose bounty and compassion, ministering to my necessities when all the world had forsaken me, I owe it that I am at this time alive. – For many weeks I had walked at nights with this poor friendless girl up and down Oxford Street, or had rested with her on steps and under the shelter of porticos. She could not be so old as myself: she told me, indeed, that she had not completed her sixteenth year. By such questions as my interest about her prompted, I had gradually drawn forth her simple history. Her's was a case of ordinary occurrence (as I have since had reason to think), and one in which, if London beneficence had better adapted its arrangements to meet it, the power of the law might oftener be interposed to protect, and to avenge. But the stream of London charity flows in a channel which, though deep and mighty, is yet noiseless and underground; not obvious or readily accessible to poor

[47] *Sine Cerere et Libero friget Venus* – 'Without bread and wine love freezes'; a common Latin proverb.

[48] 'In the Socratic manner'.

houseless wanderers: and it cannot be denied that the outside air and frame-work of London society is harsh, cruel, and repulsive. In any case, however, I saw that part of her injuries might easily have been redressed: and I urged her often and earnestly to lay her complaint before a magistrate: friendless as she was, I assured her that she would meet with immediate attention; and that English justice, which was no respecter of persons, would speedily and amply avenge her on the brutal ruffian who had plundered her little property. She promised me often that she would; but she delayed taking the steps I pointed out from time to time: for she was timid and dejected to a degree which showed how deeply sorrow had taken hold of her young heart: and perhaps she thought justly that the most upright judge, and the most righteous tribunals, could do nothing to repair her heaviest wrongs. Something, however, would perhaps have been done: for it had been settled between us at length, but unhappily on the very last time but one that I was ever to see her, that in a day or two we should go together before a magistrate, and that I should speak on her behalf. This little service it was destined, however, that I should never realise. Meantime, that which she rendered to me, and which was greater than I could ever have repaid her, was this: – One night, when we were pacing slowly along Oxford Street, and after a day when I had felt more than usually ill and faint, I requested her to turn off with me into Soho Square: thither we went; and we sate down on the steps of a house, which, to this hour, I never pass without a pang of grief, and an inner act of homage to the spirit of that unhappy girl, in memory of the noble action which she there performed. Suddenly, as we sate, I grew much worse: I had been leaning my head against her bosom; and all at once I sank from her arms and fell backwards on the steps. From the sensations I then had, I felt an inner conviction of the liveliest kind that without some powerful and reviving stimulus, I should either have died on the spot – or should at least have sunk to a point of exhaustion from which all reäscent under my friendless circumstances would soon have become hopeless. Then it was, at this crisis of my fate, that my poor orphan companion – who had herself met with little but injuries in this world – stretched out a saving hand to me. Uttering a cry of terror, but without a moment's delay, she ran off into Oxford Street, and in less time than could be imagined, returned to me with a glass of port wine and spices, that acted upon my empty stomach (which at that time would have rejected all solid food) with an instantaneous power of restoration: and for this glass the generous girl without a murmur paid out of her own humble purse at a time – be it remembered! – when she had scarcely wherewithal to purchase the bare necessaries of life, and when she could have no reason to expect that I should ever be able to reimburse her. – Oh! youthful benefactress! how often in succeeding years, standing in solitary places, and thinking of thee with grief of heart and perfect love, how often have I wished that, as in ancient times the curse of a father was believed to have a supernatural power, and to pursue its object with a fatal necessity of self-fulfilment, – even so the benediction of a heart oppressed with gratitude, might have a like prerogative; might have power given to it from above to chace – to haunt – to way-lay – to overtake – to pursue thee into the central darkness of a London brothel, or (if it were possible) into the darkness of the grave – there to awaken thee with an authentic message of peace and forgiveness, and of final reconciliation!

I do not often weep: for not only do my thoughts on subjects connected with the chief interests of man daily, nay hourly, descend a thousand fathoms 'too deep for tears;'[49] not only does the sternness of my habits of thought present an antagonism to the feelings which prompt tears – wanting of necessity to those who, being protected usually by their levity from any tendency to meditative sorrow, would by that same levity be made incapable of resisting it on any casual access of such feelings: – but also, I believe that all minds which have contemplated such objects as deeply as I have done, must, for their own protection from utter despondency, have early encouraged and cherished some tranquilizing belief as to the future balances and the hieroglyphic meanings of human sufferings. On these accounts, I am cheerful to this hour: and, as I have said, I do not often weep. Yet some feelings, though not deeper or more passionate, are more tender than others: and often, when I walk at this time in Oxford Street by dreamy lamplight, and hear those airs played on a barrel-organ which years ago solaced me and my dear companion (as I must always call her) I shed tears, and muse with myself at the mysterious dispensation which so suddenly and so critically separated us for ever. How it happened, the reader will understand from what remains of this introductory narration.

Soon after the period of the last incident I have recorded, I met, in Albemarle Street, a gentleman of his late Majesty's household. This gentleman had received hospitalities, on different occasions, from my family: and he challenged me upon the strength of my family likeness. I did not attempt any disguise: I answered his questions ingenuously,

---

[49] From Wordsworth, 'Ode: Intimations of Immortality', 207.

– and, on his pledging his word of honour that he would not betray me to my guardians, I gave him an address to my friend the Attorney's. The next day I received from him a 10*l*. Bank-note. The letter inclosing it was delivered with other letters of business to the Attorney: but, though his look and manner informed me that he suspected its contents, he gave it up to me honorably and without demur.

This present, from the particular service to which it was applied, leads me naturally to speak of the purpose which had allured me up to London, and which I had been (to use a forensic word) *soliciting* from the first day of my arrival in London, to that of my final departure.

In so mighty a world as London, it will surprise my readers that should I not have found some means of staving off the last extremities of penury: and it will strike them that two resources at least must have been open to me, – viz. either to seek assistance from the friends of my family, or to turn my youthful talents and attainments into some channel of pecuniary emolument. As to the first course, I may observe, generally, that what I dreaded beyond all other evils was the chance of being reclaimed by my guardians; not doubting that whatever power the law gave them would have been enforced against me to the utmost; that is, to the extremity of forcibly restoring me to the school which I had quitted: a restoration which as it would in my eyes have been a dishonor, even if submitted to voluntarily, could not fail, when extorted from me in contempt and defiance of my known wishes and efforts, to have been a humiliation worse to me than death, and which would indeed have terminated in death. I was, therefore, shy enough of applying for assistance even in those quarters where I was sure of receiving it – at the risk of furnishing my guardians with any clue for recovering me. But, as to London in particular, though, doubtless, my father had in his life-time had many friends there, yet (as ten years had passed since his death) I remembered few of them even by name: and never having seen London before, except once for a few hours, I knew not the address of even those few. To this mode of gaining help, therefore, in part the difficulty, but much more the paramount fear which I have mentioned, habitually indisposed me. In regard to the other mode, I now feel half inclined to join my reader in wondering that I should have overlooked it. As a corrector of Greek proofs (if in no other way), I might doubtless have gained enough for my slender wants. Such an office as this I could have discharged with an exemplary and punctual accuracy that would soon have gained me the confidence of my employers. But it must not be forgotten that, even for such an office as this, it was necessary that I should first of all have an introduction to some respectable publisher: and this I had no means of obtaining. To say the truth, however, it had never once occurred to me to think of literary labours as a source of profit. No mode sufficiently speedy of obtaining money had ever occurred to me, but that of borrowing it on the strength of my future claims and expectations. This mode I sought by every avenue to compass: and amongst other persons I applied to a Jew named D__.[50,51]

To this Jew, and to other advertising money-lenders (some of whom were, I believe, also Jews), I had introduced myself with an account of my expectations; which account, on examining my father's will at Doctor's Commons,[52] they had ascertained to be correct. The person there mentioned as the second son of __, was found to have all the claims (or more than all) that I had stated: but one question still remained, which the faces of the Jews pretty significantly suggested, – was *I* that person? This doubt had never occurred to me as a possible one: I had rather feared, whenever my Jewish friends scrutinized me keenly, that I might be too well known to be that person – and that some scheme might be passing in their minds for entrapping me and selling me to my guardians. It was strange to me to find my own self, *materialiter* considered (so I expressed it, for I doated on logical accuracy of distinctions), accused, or at least suspected, of counterfeiting my own self, *formaliter* considered.[53] However, to satisfy their scruples, I took the

---

[50] To this same Jew, by the way, some eighteen months afterwards, I applied again on the same business; and, dating at that time from a respectable college, I was fortunate enough to gain his serious attention to my proposals. My necessities had not arisen from any extravagance, or youthful levities (these my habits and the nature of my pleasures raised me far above), but simply from the vindictive malice of my guardian, who, when he found himself no longer able to prevent me from going to the university, had, as a parting token of his good nature, refused to sign an order for granting me a shilling beyond the allowance made to me at school – viz. 100*l*. per ann. Upon this sum it was, in my time, barely possible to have lived in college; and not possible to a man who, though above the paltry affectation of ostentatious disregard for money, and without any expensive tastes, confided nevertheless rather too much in servants, and did not delight in the petty details of minute economy. I soon, therefore, became embarrassed: and at length, after a most voluminous negotiation with the Jew, (some parts of which, if I had leisure to rehearse them, would greatly amuse my readers), I was put in possession of the sum I asked for – on the 'regular' terms of paying the Jew seventeen and a half per cent. by way of annuity on all the money furnished; Israel, on his part, graciously resuming no more than about ninety guineas of the said money, on account of an Attorney's bill, (for what services, to whom rendered, and when, whether at the siege of Jerusalem – at the building of the Second Temple – or on some earlier occasion, I have not yet been able to discover). How many perches this bill measured I really forget: but I still keep it in a cabinet of natural curiosities; and sometime or other I believe I shall present it to the British Museum.

[51] In 1856 De Quincey gave his name as Dell.

[52] The college of doctors of civil law in London where until 1857 the 'doctors and proctors' (analogous to modern barristers and solicitors) practised.

[53] Materially ... formally.

only course in my power. Whilst I was in Wales, I had received various letters from young friends: these I produced: for I carried them constantly in my pocket – being, indeed, by this time, almost the only relics of my personal incumbrances (excepting the clothes I wore) which I had not in one way or other disposed of. Most of these letters were from the Earl of __, who was at that time my chief (or rather only) confidential friend. These letters were dated from Eton. I had also some from the Marquis of __,[54] his father, who, though absorbed in agricultural pursuits, yet having been an Etonian himself, and as good a scholar as a nobleman needs to be – still retained an affection for classical studies, and for youthful scholars. He had, accordingly, from the time that I was fifteen, corresponded with me; sometimes upon the great improvements which he had made, or was meditating, in the counties of M__ and Sl__[55] since I had been there; sometimes upon the merits of a Latin poet; at other times, suggesting subjects to me on which he wished me to write verses.

On reading the letters, one of my Jewish friends agreed to furnish two or three hundred pounds on my personal security – provided I could persuade the young Earl, who was, by the way, not older than myself, to guarantee the payment on our coming of age: the Jew's final object being, as I now suppose, not the trifling profit he could expect to make by me, but the prospect of establishing a connection with my noble friend, whose immense expectations were well known to him. In pursuance of this proposal on the part of the Jew, about eight or nine days after I had received the 10*l*., I prepared to go down to Eton. Nearly 3*l*. of the money I had given to my money-lending friend, on his alleging that the stamps must be bought, in order that the writings might be preparing whilst I was away from London. I thought in my heart that he was lying; but I did not wish to give him any excuse for charging his own delays upon me. A smaller sum I had given to my friend the attorney (who was connected with the money-lenders as their lawyer), to which, indeed, he was entitled for his unfurnished lodgings. About fifteen shillings I had employed in re-establishing (though in a very humble way) my dress. Of the remainder I gave one quarter to Ann, meaning on my return to have divided with her whatever might remain. These arrangements made, – soon after six o'clock, on a dark winter evening, I set off, accompanied by Ann, towards Piccadilly; for it was my intention to go down as far as Salt-hill on the Bath or Bristol Mail. Our course lay through a part of the

---

[54]   The Earl of Altamont and his father, the Marquis of Sligo. De Quincey had visited them in the summer of 1800.

[55]   Mayo and Sligo.

town which has now all disappeared, so that I can no longer retrace its ancient boundaries: Swallow-street, I think it was called. Having time enough before us, however, we bore away to the left until we came into Golden-square: there, near the corner of Sherrard-street,[56] we sat down; not wishing to part in the tumult and blaze of Piccadilly. I had told her of my plans some time before: and I now assured her again that she should share in my good fortune, if I met with any; and that I would never forsake her, as soon as I had power to protect her. This I fully intended, as much from inclination as from a sense of duty: for, setting aside gratitude, which in any case must have made me her debtor for life, I loved her as affectionately as if she had been my sister: and at this moment, with seven-fold tenderness, from pity at witnessing her extreme dejection. I had, apparently, most reason for dejection, because I was leaving the saviour of my life: yet I, considering the shock my health had received, was cheerful and full of hope. She, on the contrary, who was parting with one who had had little means of serving her, except by kindness and brotherly treatment, was overcome by sorrow; so that, when I kissed her at our final farewell, she put her arms about my neck, and wept without speaking a word. I hoped to return in a week at farthest, and I agreed with her that on the fifth night from that, and every night afterwards, she should wait for me at six o'clock, near the bottom of Great Tichfield-street, which had been our customary haven, as it were, of rendezvous, to prevent our missing each other in the great Mediterranean of Oxford-street. This, and other measures of precaution I took: one only I forgot. She had either never told me, or (as a matter of no great interest) I had forgotten, her surname. It is a general practice, indeed, with girls of humble rank in her unhappy condition, not (as novel-reading women of higher pretensions) to style themselves – *Miss Douglass, Miss Montague*, &c. but simply by their Christian names, *Mary, Jane, Frances*, &c. Her surname, as the surest means of tracing her hereafter, I ought now to have inquired: but the truth is, having no reason to think that our meeting could, in consequence of a short interruption, be more difficult or uncertain than it had been for so many weeks, I had scarcely for a moment adverted to it as necessary, or placed it amongst my memoranda against this parting interview: and, my final anxieties being spent in comforting her with hopes, and in pressing upon her the necessity of getting some medicines for a violent cough and hoarseness with which she was troubled, I wholly forgot it until it was too late to recal her.

---

[56]   Now Gerrard Street, Soho.

It was past eight o'clock when I reached the Gloucester Coffee-house: and, the Bristol Mail being on the point of going off, I mounted on the outside. The fine fluent motion[57] of this Mail soon laid me asleep: it is somewhat remarkable, that the first easy or refreshing sleep which I had enjoyed for some months, was on the outside of a Mail-coach – a bed which, at this day, I find rather an uneasy one. Connected with this sleep was a little incident, which served, as hundreds of others did at that time, to convince me how easily a man who has never been in any great distress, may pass through life without knowing, in his own person at least, anything of the possible goodness of the human heart – or, as I must add with a sigh, of its possible vileness. So thick a curtain of *manners* is drawn over the features and expression of men's *natures*, that to the ordinary observer, the two extremities, and the infinite field of varieties which lie between them, are all confounded – the vast and multitudinous compass of their several harmonies reduced to the meagre outline of differences expressed in the gamut or alphabet of elementary sounds. The case was this: for the first four or five miles from London, I annoyed my fellow passenger on the roof by occasionally falling against him when the coach gave a lurch to his side; and indeed, if the road had been less smooth and level than it is, I should have fallen off from weakness. Of this annoyance he complained heavily, as perhaps, in the same circumstances most people would; he expressed his complaint, however, more morosely than the occasion seemed to warrant; and, if I had parted with him at that moment, I should have thought of him (if I had considered it worth while to think of him at all) as a surly and almost brutal fellow. However, I was conscious that I had given him some cause for complaint: and, therefore, I apologized to him, and assured him I would do what I could to avoid falling asleep for the future; and, at the same time, in as few words as possible, I explained to him that I was ill and in a weak state from long suffering; and that I could not afford at that time to take an inside place. The man's manner changed, upon hearing this explanation, in an instant: and when I next woke for a minute from the noise and lights of Hounslow (for in spite of my wishes and efforts I had fallen asleep again within two minutes from the time I had spoken to him) I found that he had put his arm round me to protect me from falling off: and for the rest of my journey he behaved to me with the gentleness of a woman, so that, at length, I almost lay in his

[57]   The Bristol Mail is the best appointed in the kingdom – owing to the double advantage of an unusually good road, and of an extra sum for expences subscribed by the Bristol merchants.

arms: and this was the more kind, as he could not have known that I was not going the whole way to Bath or Bristol. Unfortunately, indeed, I *did* go rather farther than I intended: for so genial and refreshing was my sleep, that the next time, after leaving Hounslow that I fully awoke, was upon the sudden pulling up of the Mail (possibly at a Post-office); and, on inquiry, I found that we had reached Maidenhead – six or seven miles, I think, a-head of Salt-hill. Here I alighted: and for the half minute that the Mail stopped, I was entreated by my friendly companion (who, from the transient glimpse I had had of him in Piccadilly, seemed to me to be a gentleman's butler – or person of that rank) to go to bed without delay. This I promised, though with no intention of doing so: and in fact, I immediately set forward, or rather backward, on foot. It must then have been nearly midnight: but so slowly did I creep along, that I heard a clock in a cottage strike four before I turned down the lane from Slough to Eton. The air and the sleep had both refreshed me; but I was weary nevertheless. I remember a thought (obvious enough, and which has been prettily expressed by a Roman poet[58]) which gave me some consolation at that moment under my poverty. There had been some time before a murder committed on or near Hounslow-heath. I think I cannot be mistaken when I say that the name of the murdered person was *Steele*, and that he was the owner of a lavender plantation in that neighbourhood. Every step of my progress was bringing me nearer to the Heath: and it naturally occurred to me that I and the accursed murderer, if he were that night abroad, might at every instant be unconsciously approaching each other through the darkness: in which case, said I, – supposing I, instead of being (as indeed I am) little better than an outcast, –

Lord of my learning and no land beside,[59]

were, like my friend, Lord __,[60] heir by general repute to 70,000*l.* per. ann., what a panic should I be under at this moment about my throat! – indeed, it was not likely that Lord __ should ever be in my situation. But nevertheless, the spirit of the remark remains true – that vast power and possessions make a man shamefully afraid of dying: and I am convinced that many of the most intrepid adventurers, who, by fortunately being poor, enjoy the full use of their natural courage,

[58] Juvenal. See *Satires*, X, 15 ff: 'The empty-handed traveller will whistle in the robber's face.'

[59] Untraced.

[60] Lord Altamont.

would, if at the very instant of going into action news were brought to them that they had unexpectedly succeeded to an estate in England of 50,000*l.* a year, feel their dislike to bullets considerably sharpened[61] – and their efforts at perfect equanimity and self-possession proportionably difficult. So true it is, in the language of a wise man whose own experience had made him acquainted with both fortunes, that riches are better fitted –

> To slacken virtue, and abate her edge,
> Than tempt her to do aught may merit praise.[62]

Parad. Regained.

I dally with my subject because, to myself, the remembrance of these times is profoundly interesting. But my reader shall not have any further cause to complain: for I now hasten to its close. – In the road between Slough and Eton, I fell asleep: and, just as the morning began to dawn, I was awakened by the voice of a man standing over me and surveying me. I know not what he was: he was an ill-looking fellow – but not therefore of necessity an ill-meaning fellow: or, if he were, I suppose he thought that no person sleeping out-of-doors in winter could be worth robbing. In which conclusion, however, as it regarded myself, I beg to assure him, if he should be among my readers, that he was mistaken. After a slight remark he passed on: and I was not sorry at his disturbance, as it enabled me to pass through Eton before people were generally up. The night had been heavy and lowering: but towards the morning it had changed to a slight frost: and the ground and the trees were now covered with rime. I slipped through Eton unobserved; washed myself, and, as far as possible, adjusted my dress at a little public-house in Windsor; and about eight o'clock went down towards Pote's.[63] On my road I met some junior boys of whom I made inquiries: an Etonian is always a gentleman; and, in spite of my shabby habiliments, they answered me civilly. My friend, Lord __, was gone to the University of __.[64] 'Ibi omnis effusus labor!'[65] I had, however, other friends at Eton: but it is not to all who wear that name in prosperity that a man is willing to present himself in distress. On recollecting

---

[61] It will be objected that many men, of the highest rank and wealth, have in our own day, as well as throughout our history, been amongst the foremost in courting danger in battle. True: but this is not the case supposed: long familiarity with power has to them deadened its effect and its attractions.

[62] Milton, *Paradise Regained*, ii, 455–6.

[63] Formerly a well-known bookshop in High Street, Eton.

[64] Cambridge.

[65] 'At that moment all the labour was poured away.' From Virgil, *Georgics*, iv, 491–2.

myself, however, I asked for the Earl of D__,[66] to whom, (though my acquaintance with him was not so intimate as with some others) I should not have shrunk from presenting myself under any circumstances. He was still at Eton, though I believe on the wing for Cambridge. I called, was received kindly, and asked to breakfast.

Here let me stop for a moment to check my reader from any erroneous conclusions: because I have had occasion incidentally to speak of various patrician friends, it must not be supposed that I have myself any pretensions to rank or high blood. I thank God that I have not: – I am the son of a plain English merchant, esteemed during his life for his great integrity, and strongly attached to literary pursuits (indeed, he was himself, anonymously, an author[67]): if he had lived, it was expected that he would have been very rich; but, dying prematurely, he left no more than about 30,000*l.* amongst seven different claimants. My mother I may mention with honour, as still more highly gifted. For, though unpretending to the name and honours of a *literary* woman, I shall presume to call her (what many literary women are not) an *intellectual* woman: and I believe that if ever her letters should be collected and published, they would be thought generally to exhibit as much strong and masculine sense, delivered in as pure 'mother English,'[68] racy and fresh with idiomatic graces, as any in our language – hardly excepting those of lady M. W. Montague.[69] – These are my honours of descent: I have no others: and I have thanked God sincerely that I have not, because, in my judgment, a station which raises a man too eminently above the level of his fellow-creatures is not the most favourable to moral, or to intellectual qualities.

Lord D__ placed before me a most magnificent breakfast. It was really so; but in my eyes it seemed trebly magnificent – from being the first regular meal, the first 'good man's table,'[70] that I had sate down to for months. Strange to say, however, I could scarcely eat any thing. On the day when I first received my 10*l.* Bank-note, I had gone to a baker's shop and bought a couple of rolls: this very shop I had two months or six weeks before surveyed with an eagerness of desire which it was almost humiliating to me to recollect. I remembered the story about Otway;[71]

---

[66]   The Earl of Desart.
[67]   Thomas Quincey published in 1744–5 *A Short Tour in the Midland Counties of England*.
[68]   Untraced.
[69]   The letters of Lady Mary Wortley Montagu (1689–1762) were published, to great acclaim, in 1763.
[70]   Misquoted from 'good man's feast', Shakespeare, *As You Like It*, II. vii. 115 and 122.
[71]   Thomas Otway (1651–85), dramatist. In *Lives of the Poets* Johnson reports a story that when destitute and starving, Otway was given money, bought a roll and choked to death on the first mouthful.

and feared that there might be danger in eating too rapidly. But I had no need for alarm, my appetite was quite sunk, and I became sick before I had eaten half of what I had bought. This effect from eating what approached to a meal, I continued to feel for weeks: or, when I did not experience any nausea, part of what I ate was rejected, sometimes with acidity, sometimes immediately, and without any acidity. On the present occasion, at lord D__'s table, I found myself not at all better than usual: and, in the midst of luxuries, I had no appetite. I had, however, unfortunately at all times a craving for wine: I explained my situation, therefore, to lord D__, and gave him a short account of my late sufferings, at which he expressed great compassion, and called for wine. This gave me a momentary relief and pleasure; and on all occasions when I had an opportunity, I never failed to drink wine – which I worshipped then as I have since worshipped opium. I am convinced, however, that this indulgence in wine contributed to strengthen my malady; for the tone of my stomach was apparently quite sunk; but by a better regimen it might sooner, and perhaps effectually, have been revived. I hope that it was not from this love of wine that I lingered in the neighbourhood of my Eton friends: I persuaded myself *then* that it was from reluctance to ask of Lord D__, on whom I was conscious I had not sufficient claims, the particular service in quest of which I had come down to Eton. I was, however, unwilling to lose my journey, and – I asked it. Lord D__, whose good nature was unbounded, and which, in regard to myself, had been measured rather by his compassion perhaps for my condition, and his knowledge of my intimacy with some of his relatives, than by an over-rigorous inquiry into the extent of my own direct claims, faultered, nevertheless, at this request. He acknowledged that he did not like to have any dealings with money-lenders, and feared lest such a transaction might come to the ears of his connexions. Moreover, he doubted whether *his* signature, whose expectations were so much more bounded than those of __, would avail with my unchristian friends. However, he did not wish, as it seemed, to mortify me by an absolute refusal: for after a little consideration, he promised, under certain conditions which he pointed out, to give his security. Lord D__ was at this time not eighteen years of age: but I have often doubted, on recollecting since the good sense and prudence which on this occasion he mingled with so much urbanity of manner (an urbanity which in him wore the grace of youthful sincerity), whether any statesman – the oldest and the most accomplished in diplomacy – could have acquitted himself better under the same circumstances. Most people, indeed, cannot be addressed on such a business, without surveying you with looks as austere and unpropitious as those of a Saracen's head.

Recomforted by this promise, which was not quite equal to the best, but far above the worst that I had pictured to myself as possible, I returned in a Windsor coach to London three days after I had quitted it. And now I come to the end of my story: – the Jews did not approve of Lord D__'s terms; whether they would in the end have acceded to them, and were only seeking time for making due inquiries, I know not; but many delays were made – time passed on – the small fragment of my bank note had just melted away; and before any conclusion could have been put to the business, I must have relapsed into my former state of wretchedness. Suddenly, however, at this crisis, an opening was made, almost by accident, for reconciliation with my friends. I quitted London, in haste, for a remote part of England: after some time, I proceeded to the university; and it was not until many months had passed away, that I had it in my power again to re-visit the ground which had become so interesting to me, and to this day remains so, as the chief scene of my youthful sufferings.

Meantime, what had become of poor Anne? For her I have reserved my concluding words: according to our agreement, I sought her daily, and waited for her every night, so long as I staid in London, at the corner of Titchfield-street. I inquired for her of every one who was likely to know her; and, during the last hours of my stay in London, I put into activity every means of tracing her that my knowledge of London suggested, and the limited extent of my power made possible. The street where she had lodged I knew, but not the house; and I remembered at last some account which she had given me of ill treatment from her landlord, which made it probable that she had quitted those lodgings before we parted. She had few acquaintance; most people, besides, thought that the earnestness of my inquiries arose from motives which moved their laughter, or their slight regard; and others, thinking I was in chase of a girl who had robbed me of some trifles, were naturally and excusably indisposed to give me any clue to her, if, indeed, they had any to give. Finally, as my despairing resource, on the day I left London I put into the hands of the only person who (I was sure) must know Anne by sight, from having been in company with us once or twice, an address to __ in __shire,[72] at that time the residence of my family. But, to this hour, I have never heard a syllable about her. This, amongst such troubles as most men meet with in this

---

[72] St John's Priory, Cheshire.

life, has been my heaviest affliction. – If she lived, doubtless we must have been sometimes in search of each other at the very same moment, through the mighty labyrinths of London; perhaps, even within a few feet of each other – a barrier no wider in a London street, often amounting in the end to a separation for eternity! During some years, I hoped that she *did* live; and I suppose that, in the literal and unrhetorical use of the word *myriad*, I may say that on my different visits to London, I have looked into many, many myriads of female faces, in the hope of meeting her. I should know her again amongst a thousand, if I saw her for a moment; for, though not handsome, she had a sweet expression of countenance, and a peculiar and graceful carriage of the head. – I sought her, I have said, in hope. So it was for years; but now I should fear to see her; and her cough, which grieved me when I parted with her, is now my consolation. I now wish to see her no longer; but think of her, more gladly, as one long since laid in the grave; in the grave, I would hope, of a Magdalen;[73] taken away, before injuries and cruelty had blotted out and transfigured her ingenuous nature or the brutalities of ruffians had completed the ruin they had begun.

Part 2

So then, Oxford-street, stony-hearted step-mother! thou that listenest to the sighs of orphans, and drinkest the tears of children, at length I was dismissed from thee: the time was come at last that I no more should pace in anguish thy never-ending terraces; no more should dream, and wake in captivity to the pangs of hunger. Successors, too many, to myself and Ann, have, doubtless, since then trodden in our footsteps – inheritors of our calamities: other orphans than Ann have sighed: tears have been shed by other children: and thou, Oxford-street, hast since, doubtless, echoed to the groans of innumerable hearts. For myself, however, the storm which I had outlived seemed to have been the pledge of a long fair-weather; the premature sufferings which I had paid down, to have been accepted as a ransom for many years to come, as a price of long immunity from sorrow: and if again I walked in London, a solitary and contemplative man (as oftentimes I did), I walked for the most part in serenity and peace of mind. And, although it is true that the calamities of my noviciate in London had struck root so deeply in my bodily constitution that afterwards they shot up and flourished

---

[73] Mary Magdalen is traditionally identified with the 'woman in the city, which was a sinner' of Luke 7: 37, and thought of as a repentant prostitute.

afresh, and grew into a noxious umbrage that has overshadowed and darkened my latter years, yet these second assaults of suffering were met with a fortitude more confirmed, with the resources of a maturer intellect, and with alleviations from sympathising affection – how deep and tender!

Thus, however, with whatsoever alleviations, years that were far asunder were bound together by subtle links of suffering derived from a common root. And herein I notice an instance of the short-sightedness of human desires, that oftentimes on moonlight nights, during my first mournful abode in London, my consolation was (if such it could be thought) to gaze from Oxford-street up every avenue in succession which pierces through the heart of Marylebone to the fields and the woods; for *that*, said I, travelling with my eyes up the long vistas which lay part in light and part in shade, '*that* is the road to the North, and therefore to __,[74] and if I had the wings of a dove,[75] *that* way I would fly for comfort.' Thus I said, and thus I wished, in my blindness; yet, even in that very northern region it was, even in that very valley, nay, in that very house to which my erroneous wishes pointed, that this second birth of my sufferings began; and that they again threatened to besiege the citadel of life and hope. There it was, that for years I was persecuted by visions as ugly, and as ghastly phantoms as ever haunted the couch of an Orestes: and in this unhappier than he, that sleep, which comes to all as a respite and a restoration, and to him especially, as a blessed[76] balm for his wounded heart and his haunted brain, visited me as my bitterest scourge. Thus blind was I in my desires; yet, if a veil interposes between the dim-sightedness of man and his future calamities, the same veil hides from him their alleviations; and a grief which had not been feared is met by consolations which had not been hoped. I, therefore, who participated, as it were, in the troubles of Orestes[77] (excepting only in his agitated conscience), participated no less in all his supports: my Eumenides, like his, were at my bed-feet, and stared in upon me through the curtains: but, watching by my pillow, or defrauding herself of sleep to bear me company through the heavy watches of the night, sate my Electra: for thou, beloved M.,[78] dear

---

[74] To Wordsworth who lived at Grasmere.
[75] From Psalm 55: 6.
[76] φιλον υπνου θελγητρον επικουρον νοσου. ['Dear spell of sleep, assuager of disease'; Euripides, *Orestes*, 211.]
[77] Orestes' father was murdered by his mother, Clytemnestra. Orestes avenged the murder, by killing his mother, and as a result was haunted by the Eumenides, punishing spirits. He was helped and comforted by his sister Electra.
[78] De Quincey's wife, Margaret.

companion of my later years, thou wast my Electra! and neither in nobility of mind nor in long-suffering affection, wouldst permit that a Grecian sister should excel an English wife. For thou thoughtst not much to stoop to humble offices of kindness and to servile[79] ministrations of tenderest affection; – to wipe away for years the unwholesome dews upon the forehead, or to refresh the lips when parched and baked with fever; nor, even when thy own peaceful slumbers had by long sympathy become infected with the spectacle of my dread contest with phantoms and shadowy enemies that oftentimes bade me 'sleep no more!'[80] – not even then, didst thou utter a complaint or any murmur, nor withdraw thy angelic smiles, nor shrink from thy service of love more than Electra did of old. For she too, though she was a Grecian woman, and the daughter of the king[81] of men, yet wept sometimes, and hid her face[82] in her robe.

But these troubles are past: and thou wilt read these records of a period so dolorous to us both as the legend of some hideous dream that can return no more. Meantime, I am again in London: and again I pace the terraces of Oxford-street by night: and oftentimes, when I am oppressed by anxieties that demand all my philosophy and the comfort of thy presence to support, and yet remember that I am separated from thee by three hundred miles, and the length of three dreary months, – I look up the streets that run northwards from Oxford-street, upon moonlight nights, and recollect my youthful ejaculation of anguish; – and remembering that thou art sitting alone in that same valley, and mistress of that very house to which my heart turned in its blindness nineteen years ago, I think that, though blind indeed, and scattered to the winds of late, the promptings of my heart may yet have had reference to a remoter time, and may be justified if read in another meaning: – and, if I could allow myself to descend again to the impotent wishes of childhood, I should again say to myself, as I look to the north, 'Oh, that I had the wings of a dove –' and with how just a

---

[79] ηδυ δουλευμα. ['sweet slavery'; adapted from *Orestes*, 211]. Eurip. Orest.

[80] From Shakespeare, *Macbeth*, II, ii. 36.

[81] αναξανδρων Αγαμεμνων ['Agamemnon, King of Men'. The phrase does not occur in the Euripides but is frequent in Homer].

[82] ομμα θεις' εισω πεπλον ['covering her face with her robe' – misquoted from Euripides, *Orestes*, 280]. [The scholar will know that throughout this passage I refer to the early scenes of the Orestes; one of the most beautiful exhibitions of the domestic affections which even the dramas of Euripides can furnish. To the English reader, it may be necessary to say, that the situation at the opening of the drama is that of a brother attended only by his sister during the demoniacal possession of a suffering conscience (or, in the mythology of the play, haunted by the furies), and in circumstances of immediate danger from enemies, and of desertion or cold regard from nominal friends.

confidence in thy good and gracious nature might I add the other half of my early ejaculation – 'And *that* way I would fly for comfort.'

The pleasures of opium

It is so long since I first took opium, that if it had been a trifling incident in my life, I might have forgotten its date: but cardinal events are not to be forgotten; and from circumstances connected with it, I remember that it must be referred to the autumn of 1804. During that season I was in London, having come thither for the first time since my entrance at college. And my introduction to opium arose in the following way. From an early age I had been accustomed to wash my head in cold water at least once a day: being suddenly seized with tooth-ache, I attributed it to some relaxation caused by an accidental intermission of that practice; jumped out of bed; plunged my head into a bason of cold water; and with hair thus wetted went to sleep. The next morning, as I need hardly say, I awoke with excruciating rheumatic pains of the head and face, from which I had hardly any respite for about twenty days. On the twenty-first day, I think it was, and on a Sunday, that I went out into the streets; rather to run away, if possible, from my torments, than with any distinct purpose. By accident I met a college acquaintance who recommended opium. Opium! dread agent of unimaginable pleasure and pain! I had heard of it as I had of manna or of Ambrosia,[83] but no further: how unmeaning a sound was it at that time! what solemn chords does it now strike upon my heart! what heart-quaking vibrations of sad and happy remembrances! Reverting for a moment to these, I feel a mystic importance attached to the minutest circumstances connected with the place and the time, and the man (if man he was) that first laid open to me the Paradise of Opium-eaters. It was a Sunday afternoon, wet and cheerless: and a duller spectacle this earth of ours has not to show[84] than a rainy Sunday in London. My road homewards lay through Oxford-street; and near 'the *stately* Pantheon,' (as Mr Wordsworth has obligingly called it)[85] I saw a druggist's shop. The druggist – unconscious minister of celestial pleasures! – as if in sympathy with the rainy Sunday, looked dull and stupid, just as any mortal druggist might be expected to look on a Sunday: and, when I asked for the tincture of opium,[86] he gave it to me as any other man might do: and furthermore, out of my shilling, returned

---

[83] Manna was the food miraculously provided for the Israelites in the wilderness (Exodus 16: 4, 14–16); ambrosia was the food of the Greek gods.

[84] De Quincey parodies Wordsworth, 'Composed Upon Westminster Bridge', I: 'Earth has not anything to show more fair'.

[85] A large building containing public assembly-rooms; De Quincey quotes Wordsworth, 'Power of Music', 3.

[86] Laudanum, a solution of opium in alcohol.

me what seemed to be real copper halfpence, taken out of a real wooden drawer. Nevertheless, in spite of such indications of humanity, he has ever since existed in my mind as the beatific vision of an immortal druggist, sent down to earth on a special mission to myself. And it confirms me in this way of considering him, that, when I next came up to London, I sought him near the stately Pantheon, and found him not: and thus to me, who knew not his name (if indeed he had one) he seemed rather to have vanished from Oxford-street than to have removed in any bodily fashion. The reader may choose to think of him as, possibly, no more than a sublunary druggist: it may be so: but my faith is better: I believe him to have evanesced,[87] or evaporated. So unwillingly would I connect any mortal remembrances with that hour, and place, and creature, that first brought me acquainted with the celestial drug.

Arrived at my lodgings, it may be supposed that I lost not a moment in taking the quantity prescribed. I was necessarily ignorant of the whole art and mystery of opium-taking: and, what I took, I took under every disadvantage. But I took it: – and in an hour, oh! Heavens! what a revulsion![88] what an upheaving, from its lowest depths, of the inner spirit! what an apocalypse of the world within me! That my pains had vanished was now a trifle in my eyes: – this negative effect was swallowed up in the immensity of those positive effects which had opened before me – in the abyss of divine enjoyment thus suddenly revealed. Here was a panacea – a φαρμακον νηπενθες[89] for all human woes: here was the secret of happiness, about which philosophers had disputed for so many ages, at once discovered: happiness might now be bought for a penny, and carried in the waistcoat pocket: portable ecstacies might be had corked up in a pint bottle: and peace of mind could be sent down in gallons by the mail coach. But, if I talk in this way, the reader will think I am laughing: and I can assure him, that nobody will laugh long who deals much with opium: its pleasures even

---

[87] *Evanesced*: – this way of going off the stage of life appears to have been well known in the 17th century, but at that time to have been considered a peculiar privilege of blood-royal, and by no means to be allowed to druggists. For about the year 1686, a poet of rather ominous name (and who, by the bye, did ample justice to his name), viz. Mr *Flatman*, in speaking of the death of Charles II. expresses his surprise that any prince should commit so absurd an act as dying because, says he, Kings should disdain to die, and only disappear. [This is misquoted from Thomas Flatman (1637–88), 'On the Death of King Charles II, a Pindarique Ode': 'Princes (like the wondrous *Enoch*) should be free / From Death's Unbounded Tyranny, / And when their Godlike Race is run, / And nothing glorious left undone, / Never submit to Fate, but only disappear.'] They should *abscond*, that is, into the other world.

[88] A recovery or restoration; a sudden violent change of feeling.

[89] 'A medicine to banish grief'; from Homer, *Odyssey*, iv, 221.

are of a grave and solemn complexion; and in his happiest state, the opium-eater cannot present himself in the character of *l'Allegro*: even then, he speaks and thinks as becomes *Il Penseroso*.[90] Nevertheless, I have a very reprehensible way of jesting at times in the midst of my own misery: and, unless when I am checked by some more powerful feelings, I am afraid I shall be guilty of this indecent practice even in these annals of suffering or enjoyment. The reader must allow a little to my infirm nature in this respect: and with a few indulgences of that sort, I shall endeavour to be as grave, if not drowsy, as fits a theme like opium, so anti-mercurial as it really is, and so drowsy as it is falsely reputed.

And, first, one word with respect to its bodily effects: for upon all that has been hitherto written on the subject of opium, whether by travellers in Turkey (who may plead their privilege of lying as an old immemorial right), or by professors of medicine, writing *ex cathedra*,[91] – I have but one emphatic criticism to pronounce – Lies! lies! lies! I remember once, in passing a book-stall, to have caught these words from a page of some satiric author:[92] – 'By this time I became convinced that the London newspapers spoke truth at least twice a week, viz. on Tuesday and Saturday, and might safely be depended upon for – the list of bankrupts.' In like manner, I do by no means deny that some truths have been delivered to the world in regard to opium: thus it has been repeatedly affirmed by the learned, that opium is a dusky brown in colour; and this, take notice, I grant: secondly, that it is rather dear; which also I grant: for in my time, East-India opium has been three guineas a pound, and Turkey eight: and, thirdly, that if you eat a good deal of it, most probably you must – do what is particularly disagreeable to any man of regular habits, viz. die.[93] These weighty propositions are, all and singular, true: I cannot gainsay them: and truth ever was, and will be, commendable. But in these three theorems, I believe we have exhausted the stock of knowledge as yet accumulated by man on the subject of opium. And therefore, worthy doctors, as there seems to be room for further discoveries, stand aside, and allow me to come forward and lecture on this matter.

---

[90] 'The cheerful man'; 'the pensive man'. See Milton's poems of these titles.

[91] 'From the chair' – i.e. speaking with the authority of their office.

[92] The joke is probably De Quincey's own.

[93] Of this, however, the learned appear latterly to have doubted: for in a pirated edition of Buchan's *Domestic Medicine* [first published in 1769, it remained a standard household book for some sixty years], which I once saw in the hands of a farmer's wife who was studying it for the benefit of her health, the Doctor was made to say – 'Be particularly careful never to take above five-and-twenty *ounces* of laudanum at once:' the true reading being probably five and twenty *drops*, which are held equal to about one grain of crude opium.

First, then, it is not so much affirmed as taken for granted, by all who ever mention opium, formally or incidentally, that it does, or can, produce intoxication. Now, reader, assure yourself, *meo periculo*,[94] that no quantity of opium ever did, or could intoxicate. As to the tincture of opium (commonly called laudanum) *that* might certainly intoxicate if a man could bear to take enough of it; but why? because it contains so much proof spirit, and not because it contains so much opium. But crude opium, I affirm peremptorily, is incapable of producing any state of body at all resembling that which is produced by alcohol; and not in *degree* only incapable, but even in *kind*: it is not in the quantity of its effects merely, but in the quality, that it differs altogether. The pleasure given by wine is always mounting, and tending to a crisis, after which it declines: that from opium, when once generated, is stationary for eight or ten hours: the first, to borrow a technical distinction from medicine, is a case of acute – the second, of chronic pleasure: the one is a flame, the other a steady and equable glow. But the main distinction lies in this, that whereas wine disorders the mental faculties, opium, on the contrary (if taken in a proper manner), introduces amongst them the most exquisite order, legislation, and harmony. Wine robs a man of his self-possession: opium greatly invigorates it. Wine unsettles and clouds the judgment, and gives a preternatural brightness, and a vivid exaltation to the contempts and the admirations, the loves and the hatreds, of the drinker: opium, on the contrary, communicates serenity and equipoise to all the faculties, active or passive: and with respect to the temper and moral feelings in general, it gives simply that sort of vital warmth which is approved by the judgment, and which would probably always accompany a bodily constitution of primeval or antediluvian health. Thus, for instance, opium, like wine, gives an expansion to the heart and the benevolent affections: but then, with this remarkable difference, that in the sudden development of kind-heartedness which accompanies inebriation, there is always more or less of a maudlin character, which exposes it to the contempt of the by-stander. Men shake hands, swear eternal friendship, and shed tears – no mortal knows why: and the sensual creature is clearly uppermost. But the expansion of the benigner feelings, incident to opium, is no febrile access, but a healthy restoration to that state which the mind would naturally recover upon the removal of any deep-seated irritation of pain that had disturbed and quarrelled with the impulses of a heart originally just and good. True it is, that even wine, up to a certain point, and with certain men, rather tends to exalt and to steady the intellect: I myself, who have never been a great wine-drinker,

---

[94] 'At my peril'; i.e. on my authority.

used to find that half a dozen glasses of wine advantageously affected the faculties – brightened and intensified the consciousness – and gave to the mind a feeling of being 'ponderibus librata suis:'[95] and certainly it is most absurdly said, in popular language, of any man, that he is *disguised* in liquor: for, on the contrary, most men are disguised by sobriety; and it is when they are drinking (as some old gentleman says in Athenaeus[96]), that men εαντου εμφανιϛουσιν οιτινες εισιν – display themselves in their true complexion of character; which surely is not disguising themselves. But still, wine constantly leads a man to the brink of absurdity and extravagance; and, beyond a certain point, it is sure to volatilize and to disperse the intellectual energies: whereas opium always seems to compose what had been agitated, and to concentrate what had been distracted. In short, to sum up all in one word, a man who is inebriated, or tending to inebriation, is, and feels that he is, in a condition which calls up into supremacy the merely human, too often the brutal, part of his nature: but the opium-eater (I speak of him who is not suffering from any disease, or other remote effects of opium) feels that the diviner part of his nature is paramount; that is, the moral affections are in a state of cloudless serenity; and over all is the great light of the majestic intellect.

This is the doctrine of the true church on the subject of opium: of which church I acknowledge myself to be the only member – the alpha and the omega: but then it is to be recollected, that I speak from the ground of a large and profound personal experience: whereas most of the unscientific[97] authors who have at all treated of opium, and even of

---

[95] Poised by its own weight'; see Ovid, *Metamorphoses*, I, 13.

[96] The author (*c.*AD 200) of *The Deipnosophists*, a rambling Greek dialogue on various subjects.

[97] Amongst the great herd of travellers, &c. who show sufficiently by their stupidity that they never held any intercourse with opium, I must caution my reader specially against the brilliant author of '*Anastasius*' [*Anastasius, or, Memoirs of a Greek*, a novel by Thomas Hope (1819). See vol. I, 231–2, where the old man, 'half plunged in stupor', warns the hero that opium-taking leads to madness]. This gentleman, whose wit would lead one to presume him an opium-eater, has made it impossible to consider him in that character from the grievous misrepresentation which he gives of its effects, at p. 215–17, of vol. I. – Upon consideration, it must appear such to the author himself: for, waiving the errors I have insisted on in the text, which (and others) are adopted in the fullest manner, he will himself admit, that an old gentleman 'with a snow-white beard,' who eats 'ample doses of opium,' and is yet able to deliver what is meant and received as very weighty counsel on the bad effects of that practice, is but an indifferent evidence that opium either kills people prematurely, or sends them into a madhouse. But, for my part, I see into this old gentleman and his motives: the fact is, he was enamoured of 'the little golden receptacle of the pernicious drug' which Anastasius carried about him; and no way of obtaining it so safe and so feasible occurred, as that of frightening its owner out of his wits (which, by the bye, are none of the strongest). This commentary throws a new light upon the case, and greatly improves it as a story: for the old gentleman's speech, considered as a lecture on pharmacy, is highly absurd: but, considered as a hoax on Anastasius, it reads excellently.

those who have written expressly on the materia medica, make it evident, from the horror they express of it, that their experimental knowledge of its action is none at all. I will, however, candidly acknowledge that I have met with one person[98] who bore evidence to its intoxicating power, such as staggered my own incredulity: for he was a surgeon, and had himself taken opium largely. I happened to say to him, that his enemies (as I had heard) charged him with talking nonsense on politics, and that his friends apologized for him, by suggesting that he was constantly in a state of intoxication from opium. Now the accusation, said I, is not *prima facie*,[99] and of necessity, an absurd one: but the defence *is*. To my surprise, however, he insisted that both his enemies and his friends were in the right: 'I will maintain,' said he, 'that I *do* talk nonsense; and secondly, I will maintain that I do not talk nonsense upon principle, or with any view to profit, but solely and simply, said he, solely and simply, – solely and simply (repeating it three times over), because I am drunk with opium; and *that* daily.' I replied that, as to the allegation of his enemies, as it seemed to be established upon such respectable testimony, seeing that the three parties concerned all agreed in it, it did not become me to question it; but the defence set up I must demur to. He proceeded to discuss the matter, and to lay down his reasons: but it seemed to me so impolite to pursue an argument which must have presumed a man mistaken in a point belonging to his own profession, that I did not press him even when his course of argument seemed open to objection: not to mention that a man who talks nonsense, even though 'with no view to profit,' is not altogether the most agreeable partner in a dispute, whether as opponent or respondent. I confess, however, that the authority of a surgeon, and one who was reputed a good one, may seem a weighty one to my prejudice: but still I must plead my experience, which was greater than his greatest by 7000 drops a day; and, though it was not possible to suppose a medical man unacquainted with the characteristic symptoms of vinous intoxication, it yet struck me that he might proceed on a logical error of using the word intoxication with too great latitude, and extending it generically to all modes of nervous excitement, instead of restricting it as the expression for a specific sort of excitement, connected with certain diagnostics. Some people have maintained, in my hearing, that they had been drunk upon green tea: and a medical student in London, for whose knowledge in his profession I have

---

[98] Probably John Abernethy (1764–1831), an eccentric and argumentative surgeon and opium-addict.

[99] 'At first sight'.

reason to feel great respect, assured me, the other day, that a patient, in recovering from an illness, had got drunk on a beef-steak.

Having dwelt so much on this first and leading error, in respect to opium, I shall notice very briefly a second and a third; which are, that the elevation of spirits produced by opium is necessarily followed by a proportionate depression, and that the natural and even immediate consequence of opium is torpor and stagnation, animal and mental. The first of these errors I shall content myself with simply denying; assuring my reader, that for ten years, during which I took opium at intervals, the day succeeding to that on which I allowed myself this luxury was always a day of unusually good spirits.

With respect to the torpor supposed to follow, or rather (if we were to credit the numerous pictures of Turkish opium-eaters) to accompany the practice of opium-eating, I deny that also. Certainly, opium is classed under the head of narcotics; and some such effect it may produce in the end: but the primary effects of opium are always, and in the highest degree, to excite and stimulate the system: this first stage of its action always lasted with me, during my noviciate, for upwards of eight hours; so that it must be the fault of the opium-eater himself if he does not so time his exhibition of the dose (to speak medically) as that the whole weight of its narcotic influence may descend upon his sleep. Turkish opium-eaters, it seems, are absurd enough to sit, like so many equestrian statues, on logs of wood as stupid as themselves. But that the reader may judge of the degree in which opium is likely to stupify the faculties of an Englishman, I shall (by way of treating the question illustratively, rather than argumentatively) describe the way in which I myself often passed an opium evening in London, during the period between 1804–1812. It will be seen, that at least opium did not move me to seek solitude, and much less to seek inactivity, or the torpid state of self-involution ascribed to the Turks. I give this account at the risk of being pronounced a crazy enthusiast or visionary: but I regard *that* little: I must desire my reader to bear in mind, that I was a hard student, and at severe studies for all the rest of my time: and certainly I had a right occasionally to relaxations as well as other people: these, however, I allowed myself but seldom.

The late Duke of __[100] used to say, 'Next Friday, by the blessing of Heaven, I purpose to be drunk:' and in like manner I used to fix beforehand how often, within a given time, and when, I would commit a debauch of opium. This was seldom more than once in three weeks: for at that time I could not have ventured to call every day (as I did

---

[100]   Charles Howard, Eleventh Duke of Norfolk (1746–1815).

afterwards) for '*a glass of laudanum negus,*[101] *warm, and without sugar.*'
No: as I have said, I seldom drank laudanum, at that time, more than
once in three weeks: this was usually on a Tuesday or a Saturday night;
my reason for which was this. In those days Grassini[102] sang at the
Opera: and her voice was delightful to me beyond all that I had ever
heard. I know not what may be the state of the Opera-house now,
having never been within its walls for seven or eight years, but at that
time it was by much the most pleasant place of public resort in London
for passing an evening. Five shillings admitted one to the gallery, which
was subject to far less annoyance than the pit of the theatres: the
orchestra was distinguished by its sweet and melodious grandeur from
all English orchestras, the composition of which, I confess, is not
acceptable to my ear, from the predominance of the clangorous
instruments, and the absolute tyranny of the violin. The choruses were
divine to hear: and when Grassini appeared in some interlude, as she
often did, and poured forth her passionate soul as Andromache, at the
tomb of Hector, &c. I question whether any Turk, of all that ever
entered the Paradise of opium-eaters, can have had half the pleasure
I had. But, indeed, I honour the Barbarians too much by supposing
them capable of any pleasures approaching to the intellectual ones of an
Englishman. For music is an intellectual or a sensual pleasure, according
to the temperament of him who hears it. And, by the bye, with the
exception of the fine extravaganza on that subject in Twelfth Night,[103]
I do not recollect more than one thing said adequately on the subject
of music in all literature: it is a passage in the *Religio Medici*[104] of Sir
T. Brown;[105] and, though chiefly remarkable for its sublimity, has also a
philosophic value, inasmuch as it points to the true theory of musical
effects. The mistake of most people is to suppose that it is by the ear
they communicate with music, and, therefore, that they are purely
passive to its effects. But this is not so: it is by the re-action of the
mind upon the notices of the ear, (the *matter* coming by the senses, the
form from the mind) that the pleasure is constructed: and therefore it is
that people of equally good ear differ so much in this point from one
another. Now opium, by greatly increasing the activity of the mind

---

[101]   Negus usually consisted of port or sherry mixed with hot water, sugar and spices.
[102]   Josephina Grassini (1773–1850), a contralto popular in London about 1804–6. She was
noted for her beauty and acting ability as well as for her voice.
[103]   Presumably I. i. 1–8.
[104]   I have not the book at this moment to consult: but I think the passage begins – 'And
even that tavern music, which makes one man merry, another mad, in me strikes a deep
fit of devotion,' &c.
[105]   The passage quoted is from Sir Thomas Browne's *Religio Medici*, II, ix.

generally, increases, of necessity, that particular mode of its activity by which we are able to construct out of the raw material of organic sound an elaborate intellectual pleasure. But, says a friend, a succession of musical sounds is to me like a collection of Arabic characters: I can attach no ideas to them. Ideas! my good sir? there is no occasion for them: all that class of ideas, which can be available in such a case, has a language of representative feelings. But this is a subject foreign to my present purposes: it is sufficient to say, that a chorus, &c. of elaborate harmony, displayed before me, as in a piece of arras work, the whole of my past life – not, as if recalled by an act of memory, but as if present and incarnated in the music: no longer painful to dwell upon: but the detail of its incidents removed, or blended in some hazy abstraction; and its passions exalted, spiritualized, and sublimed. All this was to be had for five shillings. And over and above the music of the stage and the orchestra, I had all around me, in the intervals of the performance, the music of the Italian language talked by Italian women: for the gallery was usually crowded with Italians: and I listened with a pleasure such as that with which Weld the traveller[106] lay and listened, in Canada, to the sweet laughter of Indian women; for the less you understand of a language, the more sensible you are to the melody or harshness of its sounds: for such a purpose, therefore, it was an advantage to me that I was a poor Italian scholar, reading it but little, and not speaking it at all, nor understanding a tenth part of what I heard spoken.

These were my Opera pleasures: but another pleasure I had which, as it could be had only on a Saturday night, occasionally struggled with my love of the Opera; for, at that time, Tuesday and Saturday were the regular Opera nights. On this subject I am afraid I shall be rather obscure, but, I can assure the reader, not at all more so than Marinus in his life of Proclus,[107] or many other biographers and auto-biographers of fair reputation. This pleasure, I have said, was to be had only on a Saturday night. What then was Saturday night to me more than any other night? I had no labours that I rested from; no wages to receive: what needed I to care for Saturday night, more than as it was a summons to hear Grassini? True, most logical reader: what you say is

---

[106] Isaac Weld, author of *Travels Through the States of North America* (1799). American Indian women, he says, 'speak with the utmost of ease, and the language, as pronounced by them, appears as soft as the Italian. They have ... the most delicate harmonious voices I ever heard ... I have oftentimes sat amongst a group of them for an hour or two together, merely for the pleasure of listening to their conversation, on account of its wonderful softness and delicacy.' (pp. 411–12)

[107] Proclus was a Greek Neoplatonist philosopher of the fifth century AD. His life was written by his disciple Marinus.

unanswerable. And yet so it was and is, that, whereas different men throw their feelings into different channels, and most are apt to show their interest in the concerns of the poor, chiefly by sympathy, expressed in some shape or other, with their distresses and sorrows, I, at that time, was disposed to express my interest by sympathising with their pleasures. The pains of poverty I had lately seen too much of; more than I wished to remember: but the pleasures of the poor, their consolations of spirit, and their reposes from bodily toil, can never become oppressive to contemplate. Now Saturday night is the season for the chief, regular, and periodic return of rest to the poor: in this point the most hostile sects unite, and acknowledge a common link of brotherhood: almost all Christendom rests from its labours. It is a rest introductory to another rest: and divided by a whole day and two nights from the renewal of toil. On this account I feel always, on a Saturday night, as though I also were released from some yoke of labour, had some wages to receive, and some luxury of repose to enjoy. For the sake, therefore, of witnessing, upon as large a scale as possible, a spectacle with which my sympathy was so entire, I used often, on Saturday nights, after I had taken opium, to wander forth, without much regarding the direction or the distance, to all the markets, and other parts of London, to which the poor resort on a Saturday night, for laying out their wages. Many a family party, consisting of a man, his wife, and sometimes one or two of his children, have I listened to, as they stood consulting on their ways and means, or the strength of their exchequer, or the price of household articles. Gradually I became familiar with their wishes, their difficulties, and their opinions. Sometimes there might be heard murmurs of discontent: but far oftener expressions on the countenance, or uttered in words, of patience, hope, and tranquillity. And taken generally, I must say, that, in this point at least, the poor are far more philosophic than the rich – that they show a more ready and cheerful submission to what they consider as irremediable evils, or irreparable losses. Whenever I saw occasion, or could do it without appearing to be intrusive, I joined their parties; and gave my opinion upon the matter in discussion, which, if not always judicious, was always received indulgently. If wages were a little higher, or expected to be so, or the quartern loaf[108] a little lower, or it was reported that onions and butter were expected to fall, I was glad: yet, if the contrary were true, I drew from opium some means of consoling myself. For opium (like the bee, that extracts its materials

---

[108] A loaf weighing a quarter of a stone (three and a half pounds).

indiscriminately from roses and from the soot of chimneys[109]) can overrule all feelings into a compliance with the master key. Some of these rambles led me to great distances: for an opium-eater is too happy to observe the motion of time. And sometimes in my attempts to steer homewards, upon nautical principles, by fixing my eye on the pole-star, and seeking ambitiously for a north-west passage, instead of circumnavigating all the capes and head-lands I had doubled in my outward voyage, I came suddenly upon such knotty problems of alleys, such enigmatical entries, and such sphynx's riddles of streets without thoroughfares, as must, I conceive, baffle the audacity of porters, and confound the intellects of hackney-coachmen. I could almost have believed, at times, that I must be the first discoverer of some of these *terrae incognitae*,[110] and doubted, whether they had yet been laid down in the modern charts of London. For all this, however, I paid a heavy price in distant years, when the human face tyrannized over my dreams, and the perplexities of my steps in London came back and haunted my sleep, with the feeling of perplexities moral or intellectual, that brought confusion to the reason, or anguish and remorse to the conscience.

Thus I have shown that opium does not, of necessity, produce inactivity or torpor; but that, on the contrary, it often led me into markets and theatres. Yet, in candour, I will admit that markets and theatres are not the appropriate haunts of the opium-eater, when in the divinest state incident to his enjoyment. In that state, crowds become an oppression to him; music even, too sensual and gross. He naturally seeks solitude and silence, as indispensable conditions of those trances, or profoundest reveries, which are the crown and consummation of what opium can do for human nature. I, whose disease it was to meditate too much, and to observe too little, and who, upon my first entrance at college, was nearly falling into a deep melancholy, from brooding too much on the sufferings which I had witnessed in London, was sufficiently aware of the tendencies of my own thoughts to do all I could to counteract them. – I was, indeed, like a person who, according to the old legend, had entered the cave of Trophonius:[111] and the remedies I sought were to force myself into society, and to keep my understanding in continual activity upon matters of science. But for these remedies, I should certainly have become hypochondriacally melancholy. In after years, however, when my cheerfulness was more

---

[109]   In 1856 De Quincey added a note explaining that bees often entered Lakeland chimneys to take the soot left by wood or peat fires.

[110]   Unknown lands.

[111]   Trophonius was a minor Roman god whose cave people entered to hear oracles about the future.

fully re-established, I yielded to my natural inclination for a solitary life. And, at that time, I often fell into these reveries upon taking opium; and more than once it has happened to me, on a summer-night, when I have been at an open window, in a room from which I could overlook the sea at a mile below me, and could command a view of the great town of L__,[112] at about the same distance, that I have sate, from sun-set to sun-rise, motionless, and without wishing to move.

I shall be charged with mysticism, Behmenism, quietism, &c.[113] but *that* shall not alarm me. Sir H. Vane, the younger,[114] was one of our wisest men: and let my readers see if he, in his philosophical works, be half as unmystical as I am. – I say, then, that it has often struck me that the scene itself was somewhat typical of what took place in such a reverie. The town of L__ represented the earth, with its sorrows and its graves left behind, yet not out of sight, nor wholly forgotten. The ocean, in everlasting but gentle agitation, and brooded over by a dove-like calm, might not unfitly typify the mind and the mood which then swayed it. For it seemed to me as if then first I stood at a distance, and aloof from the uproar of life; as if the tumult, the fever, and the strife, were suspended; a respite granted from the secret burthens of the heart; a sabbath of repose; a resting from human labours. Here were the hopes which blossom in the paths of life, reconciled with the peace which is in the grave; motions of the intellect as unwearied as the heavens, yet for all anxieties a halcyon calm: a tranquillity that seemed no product of inertia, but as if resulting from mighty and equal antagonisms; infinite activities, infinite repose.

Oh! just, subtle, and mighty opium![115] that to the hearts of poor and rich alike, for the wounds that will never heal, and for 'the pangs that tempt the spirit to rebel,'[116] bringest an assuaging balm; eloquent opium! that with thy potent rhetoric stealest away the purposes of wrath; and to the guilty man, for one night givest back the hopes of his youth, and hands washed pure from blood; and to the proud man, a brief oblivion for

Wrongs unredress'd, and insults unavenged;[117]

---

[112] Liverpool.

[113] Behmenists followed the thought of Jakob Boehme (1575–1624), German mystic who perceived the divine within nature (De Quincey gave a copy of his works to Coleridge). Quietism is passive contemplative mysticism.

[114] Sir Henry Vane (1613–62), Puritan and Parliamentary leader in the Civil War, author of several mystical works.

[115] An echo of the conclusion of Sir Walter Raleigh's *History of the World* – 'O eloquent, just and mighty Death!'

[116] Wordsworth, 'The White Doe of Rylstone', Dedication, 36.

[117] Wordsworth, *The Excursion*, iii, 374.

that summonest to the chancery of dreams, for the triumphs of suffering innocence, false witnesses; and confoundest perjury; and dost reverse the sentences of unrighteous judges: – thou buildest upon the bosom of darkness, out of the fantastic imagery of the brain, cities and temples, beyond the art of Phidias and Praxiteles[118] – beyond the splendour of Babylon and Hekatómpylos:[119] and 'from the anarchy of dreaming sleep,'[120] callest into sunny light the faces of long-buried beauties, and the blessed household countenances, cleansed from the 'dishonours of the grave.'[121] Thou only givest these gifts to man; and thou hast the keys of Paradise, oh, just, subtle, and mighty opium!

Introduction to the pains of opium

Courteous, and, I hope, indulgent reader (for all *my* readers must be indulgent ones, or else, I fear, I shall shock them too much to count on their courtesy), having accompanied me thus far, now let me request you to move onwards, for about eight years; that is to say, from 1804 (when I have said that my acquaintance with opium first began) to 1812. The years of academic life are now over and gone – almost forgotten: – the student's cap no longer presses my temples; if my cap exist at all, it presses those of some youthful scholar, I trust, as happy as myself, and as passionate a lover of knowledge. My gown is, by this time, I dare to say, in the same condition with many thousands of excellent books in the Bodleian,[122] viz. diligently perused by certain studious moths and worms: or departed, however (which is all that I know of its fate), to that great reservoir of *somewhere*, to which all the tea-cups, tea-caddies, tea-pots, tea-kettles, &c. have departed (not to speak of still frailer vessels, such as glasses, decanters, bed-makers,[123] &c.) which occasional resemblances in the present generation of tea-cups, &c. remind me of having once possessed, but of whose departure and final fate I, in common with most gownsmen of either university, could give, I suspect, but an obscure and conjectural history. The persecutions of the chapel-bell, sounding its unwelcome summons to six

---

[118]   Greek sculptors of the fifth and fourth centuries BC. Phidias was said to have designed the Parthenon frieze.

[119]   Babylon's architecture, particularly the famous Hanging Gardens, was legendary; Hekatompylos ('hundred-gated') is the ancient Egyptian city of Thebes, so called to distinguish it from Thebes in Greece.

[120]   From Wordsworth, *The Excursion*, iv, 87.

[121]   Perhaps a reminiscence of I Corinthians 15: 43 – 'it is sown in dishonour, it is raised in glory'.

[122]   The library of the University of Oxford.

[123]   De Quincey is being subtly bawdy. Bed-makers were college servants, often female; according to I Peter 3: 7, 'the wife' (and hence, proverbially, woman) is 'the weaker vessel'.

o'clock matins, interrupts my slumbers no longer: the porter who rang it, upon whose beautiful nose (bronze, inlaid with copper) I wrote, in retaliation, so many Greek epigrams, whilst I was dressing, is dead, and has ceased to disturb any body: and I, and many others, who suffered much from his tintinnabulous[124] propensities, have now agreed to overlook his errors, and have forgiven him. Even with the bell I am now in charity: it rings, I suppose, as formerly, thrice a-day: and cruelly annoys, I doubt not, many worthy gentlemen, and disturbs their peace of mind: but as to me, in this year 1812, I regard its treacherous voice no longer (treacherous, I call it, for, by some refinement of malice, it spoke in as sweet and silvery tones as if it had been inviting one to a party): its tones have no longer, indeed, power to reach me, let the wind sit as favourable as the malice of the bell itself could wish: for I am 250 miles away from it, and buried in the depth of mountains. And what am I doing amongst the mountains? Taking opium. Yes, but what else? Why, reader, in 1812, the year we are now arrived at, as well as for some years previous, I have been chiefly studying German metaphysics, in the writings of Kant, Fichte, Schelling, &c.[125] And how, and in what manner, do I live? in short, what class or description of men do I belong to? I am at this period, viz. in 1812, living in a cottage; and with a single female servant (honi soit qui mal y pense[126]), who, amongst my neighbours, passes by the name of my 'housekeeper.' And, as a scholar and a man of learned education, and in that sense a gentleman, I may presume to class myself as an unworthy member of that indefinite body called *gentlemen*. Partly on the ground I have assigned, perhaps; partly because, from my having no visible calling or business, it is rightly judged that I must be living on my private fortune; I am so classed by my neighbours: and, by the courtesy of modern England, I am usually addressed on letters, &c. *esquire*,[127] though having, I fear, in the rigorous construction of heralds, but slender pretensions to that distinguished honour: yes, in popular estimation, I am X.Y.Z., esquire, but not Justice of the Peace, nor Custos Rotulorum.[128] Am I married? Not yet. And I still take opium? On Saturday nights. And, perhaps, have taken it unblushingly ever since 'the rainy Sunday,' and 'the stately Pantheon,' and 'the beatific druggist' of 1804? – Even so. And how do I find my health after all this opium-eating? in short, how do I do? Why, pretty

---

[124]   Connected with bell-ringing.
[125]   German philosophers of the later eighteenth and early nineteenth centuries. The two latter were disciples of Kant, whose works De Quincey had studied closely.
[126]   'Evil be to him who thinks evil'.
[127]   The signature over which De Quincey's work appeared in the *London Magazine*.
[128]   'Keeper of the rolls' – the chief Justice of the Peace in a county.

well, I thank you, reader: in the phrase of ladies in the straw,[129] 'as well as can be expected.' In fact, if I dared to say the real and simple truth, though, to satisfy the theories of medical men, I *ought* to be ill, I never was better in my life than in the spring of 1812; and I hope sincerely, that the quantity of claret, port, or 'particular Madeira,' which, in all probability, you, good reader, have taken, and design to take, for every term of eight years, during your natural life, may as little disorder your health as mine was disordered by the opium I had taken for the eight years, between 1804 and 1812. Hence you may see again the danger of taking any medical advice from *Anastasius*; in divinity, for aught I know, or law, he may be a safe counsellor; but not in medicine. No: it is far better to consult Dr Buchan; as I did: for I never forgot that worthy man's excellent suggestion: and I was 'particularly careful not to take above five-and-twenty ounces of laudanum.' To this moderation and temperate use of the article, I may ascribe it, I suppose, that as yet, at least, (*i.e.* in 1812,) I am ignorant and unsuspicious of the avenging terrors which opium has in store for those who abuse its lenity. At the same time, it must not be forgotten, that hitherto I have been only a dilettante eater of opium: eight years' practice even, with the single precaution of allowing sufficient intervals between every indulgence, has not been sufficient to make opium necessary to me as an article of daily diet. But now comes a different era. Move on, if you please, reader, to 1813. In the summer of the year we have just quitted, I had suffered much in bodily health from distress of mind connected with a very melancholy event. This event, being no ways related to the subject now before me, further than through the bodily illness which it produced, I need not more particularly notice. Whether this illness of 1812 had any share in that of 1813, I know not: but so it was, that in the latter year, I was attacked by a most appalling irritation of the stomach, in all respects the same as that which had caused me so much suffering in youth, and accompanied by a revival of all the old dreams. This is the point of my narrative on which, as respects my own self-justification, the whole of what follows may be said to hinge. And here I find myself in a perplexing dilemma: – Either, on the one hand, I must exhaust the reader's patience, by such a detail of my malady, and of my struggles with it, as might suffice to establish the fact of my inability to wrestle any longer with irritation and constant suffering: or, on the other hand, by passing lightly over this critical part of my story, I must forego the benefit of a stronger impression left on the mind of the reader, and

[129] In childbed.

must lay myself open to the misconstruction of having slipped by the easy and gradual steps of self-indulging persons, from the first to the final stage of opium-eating (a misconstruction to which there will be a lurking predisposition in most readers, from my previous acknowledgments.) This is the dilemma: the first horn of which would be sufficient to toss and gore any column of patient readers, though drawn up sixteen deep and constantly relieved by fresh men: consequently *that* is not to be thought of. It remains then, that I *postulate* so much as is necessary for my purpose. And let me take as full credit for what I postulate as if I had demonstrated it, good reader, at the expense of your patience and my own. Be not so ungenerous as to let me suffer in your good opinion through my own forbearance and regard for your comfort. No: believe all that I ask of you, viz. that I could resist no longer, believe it liberally, and as an act of grace: or else in mere prudence: for, if not, then in the next edition of my Opium Confessions revised and enlarged, I will make you believe and tremble: and *à force d'ennuyer*,[130] by mere dint of pandiculation[131] I will terrify all readers of mine from ever again questioning any postulate that I shall think fit to make.

This then, let me repeat, I postulate – that, at the time I began to take opium daily, I could not have done otherwise. Whether, indeed, afterwards I might not have succeeded in breaking off the habit, even when it seemed to me that all efforts would be unavailing, and whether many of the innumerable efforts which I *did* make, might not have been carried much further, and my gradual reconquests of ground lost might not have been followed up much more energetically – these are questions which I must decline. Perhaps I might make out a case of palliation; but, shall I speak ingenuously? I confess it, as a besetting infirmity of mine, that I am too much of an Eudaemonist:[132] I hanker too much after a state of happiness, both for myself and others: I cannot face misery, whether my own or not, with an eye of sufficient firmness: and am little capable of encountering present pain for the sake of any reversionary benefit. On some other matters, I can agree with the gentlemen in the cotton-trade[133] at Manchester in affecting the Stoic philosophy:[134] but

---

[130] By sheer tedium.

[131] Stretching and yawning.

[132] An Eudaemonist believes in the pursuit of happiness as the highest good.

[133] A handsome news-room, of which I was very politely made free in passing through Manchester by several gentlemen of that place, is called, I think, *The Porch*: whence I, who am a stranger in Manchester, inferred that the subscribers meant to profess themselves followers of Zeno [the Portico Library still exists in Mosley Street, Manchester. Zeno, third century BC. Stoic philosopher, lectured in the Stoa or collonnade at Athens]. But I have been since assured that this is a mistake.

[134] The ancient Stoic school of philosophy stressed abstemious living and control of the passions.

not in this. Here I take the liberty of an Eclectic philosopher, and I look out for some courteous and considerate sect that will condescend more to the infirm condition of an opium-eater; that are 'sweet men,' as Chaucer says, 'to give absolution,'[135] and will show some conscience in the penances they inflict, and the efforts of abstinence they exact, from poor sinners like myself. An inhuman moralist I can no more endure in my nervous state than opium that has not been boiled. At any rate, he, who summons me to send out a large freight of self-denial and mortification upon any cruising voyage of moral improvement, must make it clear to my understanding that the concern is a hopeful one. At my time of life (six and thirty years of age) it cannot be supposed that I have much energy to spare: in fact, I find it all little enough for the intellectual labours I have on my hands: and, therefore, let no man expect to frighten me by a few hard words into embarking any part of it upon desperate adventures of morality.

Whether desperate or not, however, the issue of the struggle in 1813 was what I have mentioned; and from this date, the reader is to consider me as a regular and confirmed opium-eater, of whom to ask whether on any particular day he had or had not taken opium, would be to ask whether his lungs had performed respiration, or the heart fulfilled its functions. – You understand now, reader, what I am: and you are by this time aware, that no old gentleman, 'with a snow-white beard,' will have any chance of persuading me to surrender 'the little golden receptacle of the pernicious drug.' No: I give notice to all, whether moralists or surgeons, that, whatever be their pretensions and skill in their respective lines of practice, they must not hope for any countenance from me, if they think to begin by any savage proposition for a Lent or Ramadan[136] of abstinence from opium. This then being all fully understood between us, we shall in future sail before the wind. Now then, reader, from 1813, where all this time we have been sitting down and loitering – rise up, if you please, and walk forward about three years more. Now draw up the curtain, and you shall see me in a new character.

If any man, poor or rich, were to say that he would tell us what had been the happiest day in his life, and the why, and the wherefore, I suppose that we should all cry out – Hear him! Hear him! – As to the happiest *day*, that must be very difficult for any wise man to name: because any event, that could occupy so distinguished a place in a man's retrospect of his life, or be entitled to have shed a special felicity on any one day, ought to be of such an enduring character, as that (accidents

[135] Adapted from *Canterbury Tales*, Prologue, 221–2.
[136] Christian and Moslem fasts. Lent lasts for forty days, Ramadan for twenty-eight.

apart) it should have continued to shed the same felicity, or one not distinguishably less, on many years together. To the happiest *lustrum*,[137] however, or even to the happiest *year*, it may be allowed to any man to point without discountenance from wisdom. This year, in my case, reader, was the one which we have now reached; though it stood, I confess, as a parenthesis between years of a gloomier character. It was a year of brilliant water[138] (to speak after the manner of jewellers), set as it were, and insulated, in the gloom and cloudy melancholy of opium. Strange as it may sound, I had a little before this time descended suddenly, and without any considerable effort, from 320 grains of opium (i.e. eight[139] thousand drops of laudanum) per day, to forty grains, or one eighth part. Instantaneously, and as if by magic, the cloud of profoundest melancholy which rested upon my brain, like some black vapours that I have seen roll away from the summits of mountains, drew off in one day (νυχθημερον[140]); passed off with its murky banners as simultaneously as a ship that has been stranded, and is floated off by a spring tide –

That moveth altogether, if it move at all.[141]

Now, then, I was again happy: I now took only 1000 drops of laudanum per day: and what was that? A latter spring had come to close up the season of youth: my brain performed its functions as healthily as ever before: I read Kant again; and again I understood him, or fancied that I did. Again my feelings of pleasure expanded themselves to all around me: and if any man from Oxford or Cambridge, or from neither had been announced to me in my unpretending cottage, I should have welcomed him with as sumptuous a reception as so poor a man could offer. Whatever else was wanting to a wise man's happiness, – of laudanum I would have given him as much as he wished, and in a golden cup. And, by the way, now that I speak of giving laudanum away, I remember, about this time, a little incident,

---

[137]   A period of five years.

[138]   The transparency and lustre of a gem. Precious stones were graded as of the first, second and third waters.

[139]   I here reckon twenty-five drops of laudanum as equivalent to one grain of opium, which, I believe, is the common estimate. However, as both may be considered variable quantities (the crude opium varying much in strength, and the tincture still more), I suppose that no infinitesimal accuracy can be had in such a calculation. Tea-spoons vary as much in size as opium in strength. Small ones hold about 100 drops: so that 8000 drops are about eighty times a tea-spoonful. The reader sees how much I kept within Dr Buchan's indulgent allowance.

[140]   A period of twenty-four hours.

[141]   From Wordsworth, 'Resolution and Independence', 77.

which I mention, because, trifling as it was, the reader will soon meet it again in my dreams, which it influenced more fearfully than could be imagined. One day a Malay knocked at my door. What business a Malay could have to transact amongst English mountains, I cannot conjecture: but possibly he was on his road to a sea-port about forty miles distant.

The servant who opened the door to him was a young girl born and bred amongst the mountains, who had never seen an Asiatic dress of any sort: his turban, therefore, confounded her not a little: and, as it turned out, that his attainments in English were exactly of the same extent as hers in the Malay, there seemed to be an impassable gulph fixed between all communication of ideas, if either party had happened to possess any. In this dilemma, the girl, recollecting the reputed learning of her master (and, doubtless, giving me credit for a knowledge of all the languages of the earth, besides, perhaps, a few of the lunar ones), came and gave me to understand that there was a sort of demon below, whom she clearly imagined that my art could exorcise from the house. I did not immediately go down: but, when I did, the group which presented itself, arranged as it was by accident, though not very elaborate, took hold of my fancy and my eye in a way that none of the statuesque attitudes exhibited in the ballets at the Opera House, though so ostentatiously complex, had ever done. In a cottage kitchen, but panelled on the wall with dark wood that from age and rubbing resembled oak, and looking more like a rustic hall of entrance than a kitchen, stood the Malay – his turban and loose trowsers of dingy white relieved upon the dark panelling: he had placed himself nearer to the girl than she seemed to relish; though her native spirit of mountain intrepidity contended with the feeling of simple awe which her countenance expressed as she gazed upon the tiger-cat before her. And a more striking picture there could not be imagined, than the beautiful English face of the girl, and its exquisite fairness, together with her erect and independent attitude, contrasted with the sallow and bilious skin of the Malay, enamelled or veneered with mahogany, by marine air, his small, fierce, restless eyes, thin lips, slavish gestures and adorations. Half-hidden by the ferocious looking Malay, was a little child from a neighbouring cottage who had crept in after him, and was now in the act of reverting its head, and gazing upwards at the turban and the fiery eyes beneath it, whilst with one hand he caught at the dress of the young woman for protection. My knowledge of the Oriental tongues is not remarkably extensive, being indeed confined to two words – the Arabic word for barley, and the Turkish for opium (madjoon), which I have learnt from Anastasius. And, as I had neither a Malay dictionary, nor even Adelung's *Mithridates*,[142] which might have helped me to a few words, I addressed him in some lines from the Iliad; considering that, of such languages as I possessed, Greek, in point of longitude, came geographically nearest to an Oriental one. He worshipped me in a most devout manner, and replied in what I suppose was Malay. In this way I saved my reputation with my neighbours: for the Malay had no means of betraying the secret. He lay down upon the floor for about an hour, and then pursued his journey. On his departure, I presented him with a piece of opium. To him, as an Orientalist, I concluded that opium must be familiar: and the expression of his face convinced me that it was. Nevertheless, I was struck with some little consternation when I saw him suddenly raise his hand to his mouth, and (in the school-boy phrase) bolt the whole, divided into three pieces, at one mouthful. The quantity was enough to kill three dragoons and their horses: and I felt some alarm for the poor creature: but what could be done? I had given him the opium in compassion for his solitary life, on recollecting that if he had travelled on foot from London, it must be nearly three weeks since he could have exchanged a thought with any human being. I could not think of violating the laws of hospitality, by having him seized and drenched with an emetic, and thus frightening him into a notion that we were going to sacrifice him to some English idol. No: there was clearly no help for it: – he took his leave: and for some days I felt anxious: but as I never heard of any Malay being found dead, I became convinced that he was used[143] to opium: and that I must have done him the service I designed, by giving him one night of respite from the pains of wandering.

This incident I have digressed to mention, because this Malay (partly from the picturesque exhibition he assisted to frame, partly from the anxiety I connected with his image for some days) fastened afterwards upon my dreams, and brought other Malays with him worse than himself, that ran 'a-muck'[144] at me, and led me into a world of troubles. – But to

[142]   A polygot grammar and dictionary.
[143]   This, however, is not a necessary conclusion: the varieties of effect produced by opium on different constitutions are infinite. A London Magistrate (Harriott's *Struggles through Life*, vol. iii. p.391, Third Edition), has recorded that, on the first occasion of his trying laudanum for the gout, he took *forty* drops, the next night *sixty*, and on the fifth night *eighty*, without any effect whatever: and this at an advanced age. I have an anecdote from a country surgeon, however, which sinks Mr Harriott's case into a trifle; and in my projected medical treatise on opium, which I will publish, provided the College of Surgeons will pay me for enlightening their benighted understandings upon this subject, I will relate it: but it is far too good a story to be published gratis.
[144]   See the common accounts in any Eastern traveller or voyager of the frantic excesses committed by Malays who have taken opium, or are reduced to desperation by ill luck at gambling.

quit this episode, and to return to my intercalary year of happiness. I have said already, that on a subject so important to us all as happiness, we should listen with pleasure to any man's experience or experiments, even though he were but a plough-boy, who cannot be supposed to have ploughed very deep into such an intractable soil as that of human pains and pleasures, or to have conducted his researches upon any very enlightened principles. But I, who have taken happiness, both in a solid and a liquid shape, both boiled and unboiled, both East India and Turkey – who have conducted my experiments upon this interesting subject with a sort of galvanic battery – and have, for the general benefit of the world, inoculated myself, as it were, with the poison of 8000 drops of laudanum per day (just, for the same reason, as a French surgeon inoculated himself lately with cancer – an English one, twenty years ago, with plague – and a third, I know not of what nation, with hydrophobia),[145] – I (it will be admitted) must surely know what happiness is, if any body does. And, therefore, I will here lay down an analysis of happiness; and as the most interesting mode of communicating it, I will give it, not didactically, but wrapt up and involved in a picture of one evening, as I spent every evening during the intercalary year when laudanum, though taken daily, was to me no more than the elixir of pleasure. This done, I shall quit the subject of happiness altogether, and pass to a very different one – the *pains of opium.*

Let there be a cottage,[146] standing in a valley, 18 miles from any town – no spacious valley, but about two miles long, by three quarters of a mile in average width; the benefit of which provision is, that all the families resident within its circuit will compose, as it were, one larger household personally familiar to your eye, and more or less interesting to your affections. Let the mountains be real mountains, between 3 and 4000 feet high; and the cottage, a real cottage; not (as a witty author[147] has it) 'a cottage with a double coach-house:' let it be, in fact (for I must abide by the actual scene), a white cottage, embowered with flowering shrubs, so chosen as to unfold a succession of flowers upon the walls, and clustering round the windows through all the months of spring, summer, and autumn – beginning, in fact, with May roses, and ending with jasmine. Let it, however, *not* be spring, nor summer, nor autumn – but winter, in his sternest shape. This is a most important point in the science of happiness. And I am surprised to see people overlook it, and think it matter of

[145]   The English surgeon is probably a Dr A. White, who inoculated himself with plague in Alexandria in 1798. In 1856 De Quincey added that the third surgeon lived in Brighton; nothing more is known of him, or of the 'French surgeon'.
[146]   The description that follows is of Dove Cottage, Grasmere.
[147]   Coleridge, 'The Devil's Thoughts', 21.

congratulation that winter is going; or, if coming, is not likely to be a severe one. On the contrary, I put up a petition annually, for as much snow, hail, frost, or storm, of one kind or other, as the skies can possibly afford us. Surely every body is aware of the divine pleasures which attend a winter fire-side: candles at four o'clock, warm hearth-rugs, tea, a fair tea-maker, shutters closed, curtains flowing in ample draperies on the floor, whilst the wind and rain are raging audibly without,

> And at the doors and windows seem to call,
> As heav'n and earth they would together mell;
> Yet the least entrance find they none at all;
> Whence sweeter grows our rest secure in massy hall.[148]

– Castle of Indolence.

All these are items in the description of a winter evening, which must surely be familiar to every body born in a high latitude. And it is evident, that most of these delicacies, like ice-cream, require a very low temperature of the atmosphere to produce them: they are fruits which cannot be ripened without weather stormy or inclement, in some way or other. I am not '*particular*,' as people say, whether it be snow, or black frost, or wind so strong, that (as Mr __ says) 'you may lean your back against it like a post.' I can put up even with rain, provided it rains cats and dogs: but something of the sort I must have: and, if I have it not, I think myself in a manner ill-used: for why am I called on to pay so heavily for winter, in coals, and candles, and various privations that will occur even to gentlemen, if I am not to have the article good of its kind? No: a Canadian winter for my money: or a Russian one, where every man is but a co-proprietor with the north wind in the fee-simple[149] of his own ears. Indeed, so great an epicure am I in this matter, that I cannot relish a winter night fully if it be much past St Thomas's day,[150] and have degenerated into disgusting tendencies to vernal appearances: no: it must be divided by a thick wall of dark nights from all return of light and sunshine. – From the latter weeks of October to Christmas-eve, therefore, is the period during which happiness is in season, which, in my judgment, enters the room with the tea-tray: for tea, though ridiculed by those who are naturally of coarse nerves, or are become so from wine-drinking, and are not susceptible of influence from so refined a stimulant, will always be the favourite beverage of the intellectual: and, for my part,

---

[148] From James Thomson, *The Castle of Indolence*, I, xliii, 6–9.
[149] Absolute possession.
[150] 21 December.

I would have joined Dr Johnson in a *bellum internecinum* against Jonas Hanway,[151] or any other impious person, who should presume to disparage it. – But here, to save myself the trouble of too much verbal description, I will introduce a painter; and give him directions for the rest of the picture. Painters do not like white cottages, unless a good deal weather-stained: but as the reader now understands that it is a winter night, his services will not be required, except for the inside of the house.

Paint me, then, a room seventeen feet by twelve, and not more than seven and a half feet high. This, reader, is somewhat ambitiously styled, in my family, the drawing-room: but, being contrived 'a double debt to pay,'[152] it is also, and more justly, termed the library; for it happens that books are the only article of property in which I am richer than my neighbours. Of these, I have about five thousand, collected gradually since my eighteenth year. Therefore, painter, put as many as you can into this room. Make it populous with books: and, furthermore, paint me a good fire; and furniture, plain and modest, befitting the unpretending cottage of a scholar. And, near the fire, paint me a tea-table; and (as it is clear that no creature can come to see one such a stormy night,) place only two cups and saucers on the tea-tray: and, if you know how to paint such a thing symbolically, or otherwise, paint me an eternal tea-pot – eternal *à parte ante*, and *à parte post*;[153] for I usually drink tea from eight o'clock at night to four o'clock in the morning. And, as it is very unpleasant to make tea, or to pour it out for oneself, paint me a lovely young woman, sitting at the table. Paint her arms like Aurora's, and her smiles like Hebe's:[154] – But no, dear M., not even in jest let me insinuate that thy power to illuminate my cottage rests upon a tenure so perishable as mere personal beauty; or that the witchcraft of angelic smiles lies within the empire of any earthly pencil. Pass, then, my good painter, to something more within its power: and the next article brought forward should naturally be myself – a picture of the Opium-eater, with his 'little golden receptacle of the pernicious drug,' lying beside him on the table. As to the opium, I have no objection to see a picture of *that*, though I would rather see the original: you may paint it, if you choose; but I apprize you, that no 'little' receptacle would, even in 1816, answer *my* purpose, who was at a

---

[151] Johnson, 'a hardened and shameless tea-drinker', criticized Jonas Hanway's *Essay on Tea*; see *The Literary Magazine* II (1757), xiii. Hanway had attacked tea for its dire effects on health. *Bellum internecinum*: 'civil war'.
[152] From Goldsmith, *The Deserted Village*, 229.
[153] 'Beforehand ... afterwards'.
[154] Classical goddesses. Aurora was the Roman goddess of dawn; Hebe was cupbearer to the Greek gods.

distance from the 'stately Pantheon,' and all druggists (mortal or otherwise). No: you may as well paint the real receptacle, which was not of gold, but of glass, and as much like a wine-decanter as possible. Into this you may put a quart of ruby-coloured laudanum: that, and a book of German metaphysics placed by its side, will sufficiently attest my being in the neighbourhood; but, as to myself, – there I demur. I admit that, naturally, I ought to occupy the foreground of the picture; that being the hero of the piece, or (if you choose) the criminal at the bar, my body should be had into court. This seems reasonable: but why should I confess, on this point, to a painter? or why confess at all? If the public (into whose private ear I am confidentially whispering my confessions, and not into any painter's) should chance to have framed some agreeable picture for itself, of the Opium-eater's exterior, – should have ascribed to him, romantically, an elegant person, or a handsome face, why should I barbarously tear from it so pleasing a delusion – pleasing both to the public and to me? No: paint me, if at all, according to your own fancy: and, as a painter's fancy should teem with beautiful creations, I cannot fail, in that way, to be a gainer. And now, reader, we have run through all the ten categories of my condition, as it stood about 1816–17: up to the middle of which latter year I judge myself to have been a happy man: and the elements of that happiness I have endeavoured to place before you, in the above sketch of the interior of a scholar's library, in a cottage among the mountains, on a stormy winter evening.

But now farewell – a long farewell to happiness – winter or summer! farewell to smiles and laughter! farewell to peace of mind! farewell to hope and to tranquil dreams, and to the blessed consolations of sleep! for more than three years and a half I am summoned away from these: I am now arrived at an Iliad of woes: for I have now to record

The pains of opium

> – as when some great painter dips
> His pencil in the gloom of earthquake and eclipse.[155]

Shelley's Revolt of Islam.

Reader, who have thus far accompanied me, I must request your attention to a brief explanatory note on three points:

---

[155] From Shelley, *The Revolt of Islam*, V, xxiii, 8–9.

1   For several reasons, I have not been able to compose the notes for this part of my narrative into any regular and connected shape. I give the notes disjointed as I find them, or have now drawn them up from memory. Some of them point to their own date; some I have dated; and some are undated. Whenever it could answer my purpose to transplant them from the natural or chronological order, I have not scrupled to do so. Sometimes I speak in the present, sometimes in the past tense. Few of the notes, perhaps, were written exactly at the period of time to which they relate; but this can little affect their accuracy; as the impressions were such that they can never fade from my mind. Much has been omitted. I could not, without effort, constrain myself to the task of either recalling, or constructing into a regular narrative, the whole burthen of horrors which lies upon my brain. This feeling partly I plead in excuse, and partly that I am now in London, and am a helpless sort of person, who cannot even arrange his own papers without assistance; and I am separated from the hands which are wont to perform for me the offices of an amanuensis.

2   You will think, perhaps, that I am too confidential and communicative of my own private history. It may be so. But my way of writing is rather to think aloud, and follow my own humours, than much to consider who is listening to me; and, if I stop to consider what is proper to be said to this or that person, I shall soon come to doubt whether any part at all is proper. The fact is, I place myself at a distance of fifteen or twenty years ahead of this time, and suppose myself writing to those who will be interested about me hereafter; and wishing to have some record of a time, the entire history of which no one can know but myself, I do it as fully as I am able with the efforts I am now capable of making, because I know not whether I can ever find time to do it again.

3   It will occur to you often to ask, why did I not release myself from the horrors of opium, by leaving it off, or diminishing it? To this I must answer briefly: it might be supposed that I yielded to the fascinations of opium too easily; it cannot be supposed that any man can be charmed by its terrors. The reader may be sure, therefore, that I made attempts innumerable to reduce the quantity. I add, that those who witnessed the agonies of those attempts, and not myself, were the first to beg me to desist. But could not I have reduced it a drop a day, or by adding water, have bisected or trisected a drop? A thousand drops bisected would thus have taken nearly six years to reduce; and that way would certainly not have answered. But this is

a common mistake of those who know nothing of opium experimentally; I appeal to those who do, whether it is not always found that down to a certain point it can be reduced with ease and even pleasure, but that, after that point, further reduction causes intense suffering. Yes, say many thoughtless persons, who know not what they are talking of, you will suffer a little low spirits and dejection for a few days. I answer, no; there is nothing like low spirits; on the contrary, the mere animal spirits are uncommonly raised: the pulse is improved: the health is better. It is not there that the suffering lies. It has no resemblance to the sufferings caused by renouncing wine. It is a state of unutterable irritation of stomach (which surely is not much like dejection), accompanied by intense perspirations, and feelings such as I shall not attempt to describe without more space at my command.

I shall now enter '*in medias res*,'[156] and shall anticipate, from a time when my opium pains might be said to be at their *acmé*,[157] an account of their palsying effects on the intellectual faculties.

My studies have now been long interrupted. I cannot read to myself with any pleasure, hardly with a moment's endurance. Yet I read aloud sometimes for the pleasure of others; because, reading is an accomplishment of mine; and, in the slang use of the word *accomplishment* as a superficial and ornamental attainment, almost the only one I possess: and formerly, if I had any vanity at all connected with any endowment or attainment of mine, it was with this; for I had observed that no accomplishment was so rare. Players are the worst readers of all: __ reads vilely: and Mrs __, who is so celebrated,[158] can read nothing well but dramatic compositions: Milton she cannot read sufferably. People in general either read poetry without any passion at all, or else overstep the modesty of nature, and read not like scholars. Of late, if I have felt moved by any thing in books, it has been by the grand lamentations of Sampson Agonistes, or the great harmonies of the Satanic speeches in Paradise Regained, when read aloud by myself. A young lady sometimes comes and drinks tea with us: at her request and M.'s I now and then read W__'s poems[159] to them. (W. by the bye, is the only poet I ever met who could read his own verses: often indeed he reads admirably.)

---

156   'Into the midst of the story' – from Horace, *Ars Poetica*, 148.
157   Highest point, culmination.
158   In 1856 De Quincey identified these as the actor John Kemble (1757–1823) and his sister, the actress Sarah Siddons (1755–1831).
159   Wordsworth's.

For nearly two years I believe that I read no book but one: and I owe it to the author, in discharge of a great debt of gratitude, to mention what that was. The sublimer and more passionate poets I still read, as I have said, by snatches, and occasionally. But my proper vocation, as I well knew, was the exercise of the analytic understanding. Now, for the most part, analytic studies are continuous, and not to be pursued by fits and starts, or fragmentary efforts. Mathematics, for instance, intellectual philosophy, &c. were all become insupportable to me; I shrunk from them with a sense of powerless and infantine feebleness that gave me an anguish the greater from remembering the time when I grappled with them to my own hourly delight; and for this further reason, because I had devoted the labour of my whole life, and had dedicated my intellect, blossoms and fruits, to the slow and elaborate toil of constructing one single work, to which I had presumed to give the title of an unfinished work of Spinosa's; viz. *De emendatione humani intellectûs.*[160] This was now lying locked up, as by frost, like any Spanish bridge or aqueduct, begun upon too great a scale for the resources of the architect; and, instead of surviving me as a monument of wishes at least, and aspirations, and a life of labour dedicated to the exaltation of human nature in that way in which God had best fitted me to promote so great an object, it was likely to stand a memorial to my children of hopes defeated, of baffled efforts, of materials uselessly accumulated, of foundations laid that were never to support a superstructure, – of the grief and the ruin of the architect. In this state of imbecility, I had, for amusement, turned my attention to political economy; my understanding, which formerly had been as active and restless as a hyena, could not, I suppose (so long as I lived at all) sink into utter lethargy; and political economy offers this advantage to a person in my state, that though it is eminently an organic science (no part, that is to say, but what acts on the whole, as the whole again re-acts on each part), yet the several parts may be detached and contemplated singly. Great as was the prostration of my powers at this time, yet I could not forget my knowledge; and my understanding had been for too many years intimate with severe thinkers, with logic, and the great masters of knowledge, not to be aware of the utter feebleness of the main herd of modern economists. I had been led in 1811 to look into loads of books and pamphlets on many branches of economy; and, at my desire, M. sometimes read to me chapters from more recent works, or parts of parliamentary debates. I saw that these were generally

---

[160]   Baruch Spinoza (1632–1677) failed to complete his *Tractatus de Intellectus Emendatione* ('Treatise on the Correction of Understanding', 1662).

the very dregs and rinsings of the human intellect; and that any man of sound head, and practised in wielding logic with a scholastic adroitness, might take up the whole academy of modern economists, and throttle them between heaven and earth with his finger and thumb, or bray their fungus heads to powder with a lady's fan. At length, in 1819, a friend in Edinburgh sent me down Mr Ricardo's book: and recurring to my own prophetic anticipation of the advent of some legislator for this science, I said, before I had finished the first chapter, 'Thou art the man!'[161] Wonder and curiosity were emotions that had long been dead in me. Yet I wondered once more: I wondered at myself that I could once again be stimulated to the effort of reading: and much more I wondered at the book. Had this profound work been really written in England during the nineteenth century? Was it possible? I supposed thinking[162] had been extinct in England. Could it be that an Englishman, and he not in academic bowers, but oppressed by mercantile and senatorial cares, had accomplished what all the universities of Europe, and a century of thought, had failed even to advance by one hair's breadth? All other writers had been crushed and overlaid by the enormous weight of facts and documents; Mr Ricardo had deduced, *à priori*,[163] from the understanding itself, laws which first gave a ray of light into the unwieldy chaos of materials, and had constructed what had been but a collection of tentative discussions into a science of regular proportions, now first standing on an eternal basis.

Thus did one single work of a profound understanding avail to give me a pleasure and an activity which I had not known for years: – it roused me even to write, or, at least, to dictate, what M. wrote for me. It seemed to me, that some important truths had escaped even 'the inevitable eye'[164] of Mr Ricardo: and, as these were, for the most part, of such a nature that I could express or illustrate them more briefly and elegantly by algebraic symbols than in the usual clumsy and loitering diction of economists, the whole would not have filled a pocket-book; and being so brief, with M. for my amanuensis, even at this time, incapable as I was of all general exertion, I drew up my *Prolegomena to all*

---

[161]   From 2 Samuel 12: 7.

[162]   The reader must remember what I here mean by *thinking*: because, else this would be a very presumptuous expression. England, of late, has been rich to excess in fine thinkers, in the departments of creative and combining thought; but there is a sad dearth of masculine thinkers in any analytic path. A Scotchman of eminent name [unidentified] has lately told us, that he is obliged to quit even mathematics, for want of encouragement.

[163]   'From first principles'.

[164]   Adapted from Wordsworth, 'When to the attractions of the busy world', 82 – 'an inevitable ear'.

future Systems of Political Economy. I hope it will not be found redolent of opium; though, indeed, to most people, the subject itself is a sufficient opiate.

This exertion, however, was but a temporary flash; as the sequel showed – for I designed to publish my work: arrangements were made at a provincial press, about eighteen miles distant, for printing it. An additional compositor was retained, for some days, on this account. The work was even twice advertised: and I was, in a manner, pledged to the fulfilment of my intention. But I had a preface to write; and a dedication, which I wished to make a splendid one, to Mr Ricardo. I found myself quite unable to accomplish all this. The arrangements were countermanded: the compositor dismissed: and my 'Prolegomena' rested peacefully by the side of its elder and more dignified brother.

I have thus described and illustrated my intellectual torpor, in terms that apply, more or less, to every part of the four years during which I was under the Circean spells of opium. But for misery and suffering, I might, indeed, be said to have existed in a dormant state. I seldom could prevail on myself to write a letter; an answer of a few words, to any that I received, was the utmost that I could accomplish; and often *that* not until the letter had lain weeks, or even months, on my writing table. Without the aid of M. all records of bills paid, or *to be* paid, must have perished: and my whole domestic economy, whatever became of Political Economy, must have gone into irretrievable confusion. – I shall not afterwards allude to this part of the case: it is one, however, which the opium-eater will find, in the end, as oppressive and tormenting as any other, from the sense of incapacity and feebleness, from the direct embarrassments incident to the neglect or procrastination of each day's appropriate duties, and from the remorse which must often exasperate the stings of these evils to a reflective and conscientious mind. The opium-eater loses none of his moral sensibilities, or aspirations: he wishes and longs, as earnestly as ever, to realize what he believes possible, and feels to be exacted by duty; but his intellectual apprehension of what is possible infinitely outruns his power, not of execution only, but even of power to attempt. He lies under the weight of incubus and night-mare: he lies in sight of all that he would fain perform, just as a man forcibly confined to his bed by the mortal languor of a relaxing disease, who is compelled to witness injury or outrage offered to some object of his tenderest love: – he curses the spells which chain him down from motion: – he would lay down his life if he might but get up and walk; but he is powerless as an infant, and cannot even attempt to rise.

I now pass to what is the main subject of these latter confessions, to the history and journal of what took place in my dreams; for these were the immediate and proximate cause of my acutest suffering.

The first notice I had of any important change going on in this part of my physical economy, was from the re-awakening of a state of eye generally incident to childhood, or exalted states of irritability. I know not whether my reader is aware that many children, perhaps most, have a power of painting, as it were, upon the darkness, all sorts of phantoms; in some, that power is simply a mechanic affection of the eye; others have a voluntary, or a semi-voluntary power to dismiss or to summon them; or, as a child once said to me when I questioned him on this matter, 'I can tell them to go, and they go; but sometimes they come, when I don't tell them to come.' Whereupon I told him that he had almost as unlimited a command over apparitions, as a Roman centurion[165] over his soldiers. – In the middle of 1817, I think it was, that this faculty became positively distressing to me: at night, when I lay awake in bed, vast processions passed along in mournful pomp; friezes of never-ending stories, that to my feelings were as sad and solemn as if they were stories drawn from times before Oedipus or Priam – before Tyre – before Memphis.[166] And, at the same time, a corresponding change took place in my dreams; a theatre seemed suddenly opened and lighted up within my brain, which presented nightly spectacles of more than earthly splendour. And the four following facts may be mentioned, as noticeable at this time:

1   That, as the creative state of the eye increased, a sympathy seemed to arise between the waking and the dreaming states of the brain in one point – that whatsoever I happened to call up and to trace by a voluntary act upon the darkness was very apt to transfer itself to my dreams; so that I feared to exercise this faculty; for, as Midas turned all things to gold, that yet baffled his hopes and defrauded his human desires, so whatsoever things capable of being visually represented I did but think of in the darkness, immediately shaped themselves into phantoms of the eye; and, by a process apparently no less inevitable, when thus once traced in faint and visionary colours, like writings in sympathetic ink, they were drawn out by the fierce chemistry of my dreams, into insufferable splendour that fretted my heart.

---

[165]   See Matthew 8: 9.
[166]   The first two were legendary kings, Oedipus of Grecian Thebes, Priam of Troy, in whose fall he died. Tyre was a Phoenician seaport founded c.1400 BC; the Egyptian city of Memphis dates from c.3000 BC.

2   For this, and all other changes in my dreams, were accompanied by deep-seated anxiety and gloomy melancholy, such as are wholly incommunicable by words. I seemed every night to descend, not metaphorically, but literally to descend, into chasms and sunless abysses, depths below depths, from which it seemed hopeless that I could ever re-ascend. Nor did I, by waking, feel that I *had* re-ascended. This I do not dwell upon; because the state of gloom which attended these gorgeous spectacles, amounting at last to utter darkness, as of some suicidal despondency, cannot be approached by words.

3   The sense of space, and in the end, the sense of time, were both powerfully affected. Buildings, landscapes, &c. were exhibited in proportions so vast as the bodily eye is not fitted to receive. Space swelled, and was amplified to an extent of unutterable infinity. This, however, did not disturb me so much as the vast expansion of time; I sometimes seemed to have lived for 70 or 100 years in one night; nay, sometimes had feelings representative of a millennium passed in that time, or, however, of a duration far beyond the limits of any human experience.

4   The minutest incidents of childhood, or forgotten scenes of later years, were often revived: I could not be said to recollect them; for if I had been told of them when waking, I should not have been able to acknowledge them as parts of my past experience. But placed as they were before me, in dreams like intuitions, and clothed in all their evanescent circumstances and accompanying feelings, I *recognised* them instantaneously. I was once told by a near relative of mine,[167] that having in her childhood fallen into a river, and being on the very verge of death but for the critical assistance which reached her, she saw in a moment her whole life, in its minutest incidents, arrayed before her simultaneously as in a mirror; and she had a faculty developed as suddenly for comprehending the whole and every part. This, from some opium experiences of mine, I can believe; I have, indeed, seen the same thing asserted twice in modern books,[168] and accompanied by a remark which I am convinced is true; viz. that the dread book of account, which the Scriptures speak of, is, in fact, the mind itself of each individual. Of this at least, I feel assured, that there is no such thing as *forgetting* possible to the

---

[167]   Apparently De Quincey's mother.
[168]   Probably in Swedenborg's *Arcana Coelestia* and Coleridge's *Biographia Literaria* (see Georges Poulet, 'Timelessness and Romanticism', *Journal of the History of Ideas*, XV, 1954, 3–22).

mind; a thousand accidents may, and will interpose a veil between our present consciousness and the secret inscriptions on the mind; accidents of the same sort will also rend away this veil; but alike, whether veiled or unveiled, the inscription remains for ever; just as the stars seem to withdraw before the common light of day, whereas, in fact, we all know that it is the light which is drawn over them as a veil – and that they are waiting to be revealed when the obscuring daylight shall have withdrawn.'

Having noticed these four facts as memorably distinguishing my dreams from those of health, I shall now cite a case illustrative of the first fact; and shall then cite any others that I remember, either in their chronological order, or any other that may give them more effect as pictures to the reader.

I had been in youth, and even since, for occasional amusement, a great reader of Livy, whom, I confess, that I prefer, both for style and matter, to any other of the Roman historians: and I had often felt as most solemn and appalling sounds, and most emphatically representative of the majesty of the Roman people, the two words so often occurring in Livy – *Consul Romanus*; especially when the consul is introduced in his military character. I mean to say, that the words king – sultan – regent, &c. or any other titles of those who embody in their own persons the collective majesty of a great people, had less power over my reverential feelings. I had also, though no great reader of history, made myself minutely and critically familiar with one period of English history, viz. the period of the Parliamentary War, having been attracted by the moral grandeur of some who figured in that day, and by the many interesting memoirs which survive those unquiet times. Both these parts of my lighter reading, having furnished me often with matter of reflection, now furnished me with matter for my dreams. Often I used to see, after painting upon the blank darkness a sort of rehearsal whilst waking, a crowd of ladies, and perhaps a festival, and dances. And I heard it said, or I said to myself, 'these are English ladies from the unhappy times of Charles I. These are the wives and the daughters of those who met in peace, and sate at the same tables, and were allied by marriage or by blood; and yet, after a certain day in August, 1642, never smiled upon each other again, nor met but in the field of battle; and at Marston Moor, at Newbury, or at Naseby, cut asunder all ties of love by the cruel sabre, and washed away in blood the memory of ancient friendship.' – The ladies danced, and looked as lovely as the court of George IV. Yet I knew, even in my dream, that they had been in the grave for nearly two centuries. – This pageant would suddenly dissolve: and, at a clapping of hands, would be heard the heart-quaking sound of *Consul Romanus*: and immediately came 'sweeping by,'[169] in gorgeous paludaments,[170] Paulus or Marius, girt round by a company of centurions, with the crimson tunic hoisted on a spear, and followed by the *alalagmos*[171] of the Roman legions.

Many years ago, when I was looking over Piranesi's Antiquities of Rome, Mr Coleridge, who was standing by, described to me a set of plates by that artist, called his *Dreams*,[172] and which record the scenery of his own visions during the delirium of a fever. Some of them (I describe only from memory of Mr Coleridge's account) represented vast Gothic halls: on the floor of which stood all sorts of engines and machinery, wheels, cables, pulleys, levers, catapults, &c. &c. expressive of enormous power put forth, and resistance overcome. Creeping along the sides of the walls, you perceived a staircase; and upon it, groping his way upwards, was Piranesi himself: follow the stairs a little further, and you perceive it come to a sudden abrupt termination, without any balustrade, and allowing no step onwards to him who had reached the extremity, except into the depths below. Whatever is to become of poor Piranesi, you suppose, at least, that his labours must in some way terminate here. But raise your eyes, and behold a second flight of stairs still higher: on which again Piranesi is perceived, but this time standing on the very brink of the abyss. Again elevate your eye, and a still more aerial flight of stairs is beheld: and again is poor Piranesi busy on his aspiring labours: and so on, until the unfinished stairs and Piranesi both are lost in the upper gloom of the hall. – With the same power of endless growth and self-reproduction did my architecture proceed in dreams. In the early stage of my malady, the splendours of my dreams were indeed chiefly architectural: and I beheld such pomp of cities and palaces as was never yet beheld by the waking eye, unless in the clouds. From a great modern poet I cite part of a passage which describes, as an appearance actually beheld in the clouds, what in many of its circumstances I saw frequently in sleep:

> The appearance, instantaneously disclosed,
> Was of a mighty city – boldly say
> A wilderness of building, sinking far
> And self-withdrawn into a wondrous depth,

[169]   From Milton, *Il Penseroso*, 98.
[170]   Roman military cloaks.
[171]   Shout of acclaim.
[172]   Giambattista Piranesi (1720–78), architectural engraver. His '*Dreams*' are properly the *Carceri d'invenzione* (*Imaginary Prisons*, 1745).

Far sinking into splendour – without end!
Fabric it seem'd of diamond, and of gold,
With alabaster domes, and silver spires,
And blazing terrace upon terrace, high
Uplifted; here, serene pavilions bright
In avenues disposed; there towers begirt
With battlements that on their restless fronts
Bore stars – illumination of all gems!
By earthly nature had the effect been wrought
Upon the dark materials of the storm
Now pacified; on them, and on the coves,
And mountain-steeps and summits, whereunto
The vapours had receded, – taking there
Their station under a cerulean sky. &c. &c.[173]

The sublime circumstance – 'battlements that on their *restless* fronts bore stars,' – might have been copied from my architectural dreams, for it often occurred. – We hear it reported of Dryden, and of Fuseli in modern times, that they thought proper to eat raw meat for the sake of obtaining splendid dreams: how much better for such a purpose to have eaten opium, which yet I do not remember that any poet is recorded to have done, except the dramatist Shadwell: and in ancient days, Homer[174] is, I think, rightly reputed to have known the virtues of opium.

To my architecture succeeded dreams of lakes – and silvery expanses of water: – these haunted me so much, that I feared (though possibly it will appear ludicrous to a medical man) that some dropsical state or tendency of the brain might thus be making itself (to use a metaphysical word) *objective*; and the sentient organ *project* itself as its own object. – For two months I suffered greatly in my head, – a part of my bodily structure which had hitherto been so clear from all touch or taint of weakness (physically, I mean), that I used to say of it, as the last Lord Orford[175] said of his stomach, that it seemed likely to survive the rest of my person. – Till now I had never felt a head-ache even, or any the slightest pain, except rheumatic pains caused by my own folly.

---

[173] From Wordsworth, *The Excursion*, ii, 834–51.

[174] Dryden is not said to have eaten raw meat, but he did believe that diet affected his work and ate accordingly. The painter Henry Fuseli (1741–1825), according to Allan Cunningham's *Lives of the … British Painters*, 'supped on raw pork chops that he might dream his picture of the nightmare'. Thomas Shadwell (1642–92), poet and dramatist, was an opium addict. *Odyssey* iv, 221 (quoted by De Quincey on above) has been taken as proof that Homer knew of opium.

[175] Horace Walpole, Fourth Earl of Orford (1717–97), author of *The Castle of Otranto*.

However, I got over this attack, though it must have been verging on something very dangerous.

The waters now changed their character, – from translucent lakes, shining like mirrors, they now became seas and oceans. And now came a tremendous change, which, unfolding itself slowly like a scroll, through many months, promised an abiding torment; and, in fact, it never left me until the winding up of my case. Hitherto the human face had mixed often in my dreams, but not despotically, nor with any special power of tormenting. But now that which I have called the tyranny of the human face began to unfold itself. Perhaps some part of my London life might be answerable for this. Be that as it may, now it was that upon the rocking waters of the ocean the human face began to appear: the sea appeared paved with innumerable faces, upturned to the heavens: faces, imploring, wrathful, despairing, surged upwards by thousands, by myriads, by generations, by centuries: – my agitation was infinite, – my mind tossed – and surged with the ocean.

May, 1818. The Malay has been a fearful enemy for months. I have been every night, through his means, transported into Asiatic scenes. I know not whether others share in my feelings on this point; but I have often thought that if I were compelled to forego England, and to live in China, and among Chinese manners and modes of life and scenery, I should go mad. The causes of my horror lie deep; and some of them must be common to others. Southern Asia, in general, is the seat of awful images and associations. As the cradle of the human race, it would alone have a dim and reverential feeling connected with it. But there are other reasons. No man can pretend that the wild, barbarous, and capricious superstitions of Africa, or of savage tribes elsewhere, affect him in the way that he is affected by the ancient, monumental, cruel, and elaborate religions of Indostan, &c. The mere antiquity of Asiatic things, of their institutions, histories, modes of faith, &c. is so impressive, that to me the vast age of the race and name overpowers the sense of youth in the individual. A young Chinese seems to me an antediluvian man renewed. Even Englishmen, though not bred in any knowledge of such institutions, cannot but shudder at the mystic sublimity of *castes* that have flowed apart, and refused to mix, through such immemorial tracts of time; nor can any man fail to be awed by the names of the Ganges, or the Euphrates. It contributes much to these feelings, that southern Asia is, and has been for thousands of years, the part of the earth most swarming with human life; the great *officina gentium*.[176] Man is a weed in

---

[176] Workshop of peoples.

those regions. The vast empires also, into which the enormous population of Asia has always been cast, give a further sublimity to the feelings associated with all oriental names or images. In China, over and above what it has in common with the rest of southern Asia, I am terrified by the modes of life, by the manners, and the barrier of utter abhorrence, and want of sympathy, placed between us by feelings deeper than I can analyze. I could sooner live with lunatics, or brute animals. All this, and much more than I can say, or have time to say, the reader must enter into before he can comprehend the unimaginable horror which these dreams of oriental imagery, and mythological tortures, impressed upon me. Under the connecting feeling of tropical heat and vertical sunlights, I brought together all creatures, birds, beasts, reptiles, all trees and plants, usages and appearances, that are found in all tropical regions, and assembled them together in China or Indostan. From kindred feelings, I soon brought Egypt and all her gods under the same law. I was stared at, hooted at, grinned at, chattered at, by monkeys, by paroquets, by cockatoos. I ran into pagodas: and was fixed, for centuries, at the summit, or in secret rooms; I was the idol; I was the priest; I was worshipped; I was sacrificed. I fled from the wrath of Brama through all the forests of Asia: Vishnu hated me: Seeva laid wait for me. I came suddenly upon Isis and Osiris:[177] I had done a deed, they said, which the ibis and the crocodile trembled at. I was buried, for a thousand years, in stone coffins, with mummies and sphynxes, in narrow chambers at the heart of eternal pyramids. I was kissed, with cancerous kisses, by crocodiles; and laid, confounded with all unutterable slimy things, amongst reeds and Nilotic mud.

I thus give the reader some slight abstraction of my oriental dreams, which always filled me with such amazement at the monstrous scenery, that horror seemed absorbed, for a while, in sheer astonishment. Sooner or later, came a reflux of feeling that swallowed up the astonishment, and left me, not so much in terror, as in hatred and abomination of what I saw. Over every form, and threat, and punishment, and dim sightless incarceration, brooded a sense of eternity and infinity that drove me into an oppression as of madness. Into these dreams only, it was, with one or two slight exceptions, that any circumstances of physical horror entered. All before had been moral and spiritual terrors. But here the main agents were ugly birds, or snakes, or crocodiles; especially the last. The cursed crocodile became to me the object of more horror than almost all the rest. I was compelled to live with him;

---

[177] Respectively, three Hindu and two ancient Egyptian deities; their various attributes seem to have no special relevance here.

and (as was always the case almost in my dreams) for centuries. I escaped sometimes, and found myself in Chinese houses, with cane tables, &c. All the feet of the tables, sophas, &c. soon became instinct with life: the abominable head of the crocodile, and his leering eyes, looked out at me, multiplied into a thousand repetitions: and I stood loathing and fascinated. And so often did this hideous reptile haunt my dreams, that many times the very same dream was broken up in the very same way: I heard gentle voices speaking to me (I hear every thing when I am sleeping); and instantly I awoke: it was broad noon; and my children were standing, hand in hand, at my bed-side; come to show me their coloured shoes, or new frocks, or to let me see them dressed for going out. I protest that so awful was the transition from the damned crocodile, and the other unutterable monsters and abortions of my dreams, to the sight of innocent *human* natures and of infancy, that, in the mighty and sudden revulsion of mind, I wept, and could not forbear it, as I kissed their faces.

June, 1819. I have had occasion to remark, at various periods of my life, that the deaths of those whom we love, and indeed the contemplation of death generally, is (*caeteris paribus*[178]) more affecting in summer than in any other season of the year. And the reasons are these three, I think: first, that the visible heavens in summer appear far higher, more distant, and (if such a solecism may be excused) more infinite; the clouds, by which chiefly the eye expounds the distance of the blue pavilion stretched over our heads, are in summer more voluminous, massed, and accumulated in far grander and more towering piles: secondly, the light and the appearances of the declining and the setting sun are much more fitted to be types and characters of the Infinite: and, thirdly, (which is the main reason) the exuberant and riotous prodigality of life naturally forces the mind more powerfully upon the antagonist thought of death, and the wintry sterility of the grave. For it may be observed, generally, that wherever two thoughts stand related to each other by a law of antagonism, and exist, as it were, by mutual repulsion, they are apt to suggest each other. On these accounts it is that I find it impossible to banish the thought of death when I am walking alone in the endless days of summer; and any particular death, if not more affecting, at least haunts my mind more obstinately and besiegingly in that season. Perhaps this cause, and a slight incident which I omit, might have been the immediate occasions of the following dream; to which, however, a predisposition must have

---

[178] 'Other things being equal'.

always have existed in my mind; but having been once roused, it never left me, and split into a thousand fantastic varieties, which often suddenly re-united, and composed again the original dream.

I thought that it was a Sunday morning in May, that it was Easter Sunday, and as yet very early in the morning. I was standing, as it seemed to me, at the door of my own cottage. Right before me lay the very scene which could really be commanded from that situation, but exalted, as was usual, and solemnized by the power of dreams. There were the same mountains, and the same lovely valley at their feet; but the mountains were raised to more than Alpine height, and there was interspace far larger between them of meadows and forest lawns; the hedges were rich with white roses; and no living creature was to be seen, excepting that in the green church-yard there were cattle tranquilly reposing upon the verdant graves, and particularly round about the grave of a child[179] whom I had tenderly loved, just as I had really beheld them, a little before sun-rise in the same summer, when that child died. I gazed upon the well-known scene, and I said aloud (as I thought) to myself, 'it yet wants much of sun-rise; and it is Easter Sunday; and that is the day on which they celebrate the first fruits of resurrection. I will walk abroad; old griefs shall be forgotten to-day; for the air is cool and still, and the hills are high, and stretch away to Heaven; and the forest-glades are as quiet as the church-yard; and, with the dew, I can wash the fever from my forehead, and then I shall be unhappy no longer.' And I turned, as if to open my garden gate; and immediately I saw upon the left a scene far different; but which yet the power of dreams had reconciled into harmony with the other. The scene was an oriental one; and there also it was Easter Sunday, and very early in the morning. And at a vast distance were visible, as a stain upon the horizon, the domes and cupolas of a great city – an image or faint abstraction, caught perhaps in childhood from some picture of Jerusalem. And not a bow-shot from me, upon a stone, and shaded by Judean palms, there sat a woman; and I looked; and it was – Ann! She fixed her eyes upon me earnestly; and I said to her at length: 'So then I have found you at last.' I waited: but she answered me not a word. Her face was the same as when I saw it last, and yet again how different! Seventeen years ago, when the lamp-light fell upon her face, as for the last time I kissed her lips (lips, Ann, that to me were not polluted), her eyes were streaming with tears: the tears were now wiped away; she seemed more beautiful than she was at that time, but in all

---

[179]   The grave, in Grasmere churchyard, of Catherine Wordsworth (1808–12), the poet's daughter and a favourite of De Quincey.

other points the same, and not older. Her looks were tranquil, but with unusual solemnity of expression; and I now gazed upon her with some awe, but suddenly her countenance grew dim, and, turning to the mountains, I perceived vapours rolling between us; in a moment, all had vanished; thick darkness came on; and, in the twinkling of an eye, I was far away from mountains, and by lamp-light in Oxford-street, walking again with Ann – just as we walked seventeen years before, when we were both children.

As a final specimen, I cite one of a different character, from 1820.

The dream commenced with a music which now I often heard in dreams – a music of preparation and of awakening suspense; a music like the opening of the Coronation Anthem,[180] and which, like *that*, gave the feeling of a vast march – of infinite cavalcades filing off – and the tread of innumerable armies. The morning was come of a mighty day – a day of crisis and of final hope for human nature, then suffering some mysterious eclipse, and labouring in some dread extremity. Somewhere, I knew not where – somehow, I knew not how – by some beings, I knew not whom – a battle, a strife, an agony, was conducting, – was evolving like a great drama, or piece of music; with which my sympathy was the more insupportable from my confusion as to its place, its cause, its nature, and its possible issue. I, as is usual in dreams (where, of necessity, we make ourselves central to every movement), had the power, and yet had not the power, to decide it. I had the power, if I could raise myself, to will it; and yet again had not the power, for the weight of twenty Atlantics was upon me, or the oppression of inexpiable guilt. 'Deeper than ever plummet sounded,'[181] I lay inactive. Then, like a chorus, the passion deepened. Some greater interest was at stake; some mightier cause than ever yet the sword had pleaded, or trumpet had proclaimed. Then came sudden alarms: hurryings to and fro: trepidations of innumerable fugitives, I knew not whether from the good cause or the bad: darkness and lights: tempest and human faces; and at last, with the sense that all was lost, female forms, and the features that were worth all the world to me, and but a moment allowed, – and clasped hands, and heart-breaking partings, and then – everlasting farewells! and with a sigh, such as the caves of hell sighed when the incestuous mother[182] uttered the abhorred name of death, the

---

180   The anthem 'Zadok the Priest', composed by Handel for George II's coronation in 1727 and used repeatedly since.
181   From Shakespeare, *The Tempest*, III. iii. 101.
182   From Milton, *Paradise Lost*, x, 602.

sound was reverberated — everlasting farewells! and again, and yet again reverberated — everlasting farewells!

And I awoke in struggles, and cried aloud – 'I will sleep no more!'

But I am now called upon to wind up a narrative which has already extended to an unreasonable length. Within more spacious limits, the materials which I have used might have been better unfolded; and much which I have not used might have been added with effect. Perhaps, however, enough has been given. It now remains that I should say something of the way in which this conflict of horrors was finally brought to its crisis. The reader is already aware (from a passage near the beginning of the introduction to the first part) that the opium-eater has, in some way or other, 'unwound, almost to its final links, the accursed chain which bound him.' By what means? To have narrated this, according to the original intention, would have far exceeded the space which can now be allowed. It is fortunate, as such a cogent reason exists for abridging it, that I should, on a maturer view of the case, have been exceedingly unwilling to injure, by any such unaffecting details, the impression of the history itself, as an appeal to the prudence and the conscience of the yet unconfirmed opium-eater – or even (though a very inferior consideration) to injure its effect as a composition. The interest of the judicious reader will not attach itself chiefly to the subject of the fascinating spells, but to the fascinating power. Not the opium-eater, but the opium, is the true hero of the tale; and the legitimate centre on which the interest revolves. The object was to display the marvellous agency of opium, whether for pleasure or for pain: if that is done, the action of the piece has closed.

However, as some people, in spite of all laws to the contrary, will persist in asking what became of the opium-eater, and in what state he now is, I answer for him thus: The reader is aware that opium had long ceased to found its empire on spells of pleasure; it was solely by the tortures connected with the attempt to abjure it, that it kept its hold. Yet, as other tortures, no less it may be thought, attended the non-abjuration of such a tyrant, a choice only of evils was left; and *that* might as well have been adopted, which, however terrific in itself, held out a prospect of final restoration to happiness. This appears true; but good logic gave the author no strength to act upon it. However, a crisis arrived for the author's life, and a crisis for other objects still dearer to him – and which will always be far dearer to him than his life, even now that it is again a happy one. – I saw that I must die if I continued the opium: I determined, therefore, if that should be required, to die in throwing it off. How much I was at that time taking I cannot say; for the opium which I used had been purchased for me by a friend who afterwards refused to let me pay him; so that I could not ascertain even what quantity I had used within the year. I apprehend, however, that I took it very irregularly: and that I varied from about fifty or sixty grains, to 150 a-day. My first task was to reduce it to forty, to thirty, and, as fast as I could, to twelve grains.

I triumphed: but think not, reader, that therefore my sufferings were ended; nor think of me as of one sitting in a *dejected* state. Think of me as of one, even when four months had passed, still agitated, writhing, throbbing, palpitating, shattered; and much, perhaps, in the situation of him who has been racked, as I collect the torments of that state from the affecting account of them left by a most innocent sufferer[183] (of the times of James I.). Meantime, I derived no benefit from any medicine, except one prescribed to me by an Edinburgh surgeon of great eminence, viz. ammoniated tincture of Valerian. Medical account, therefore, of my emancipation I have not much to give: and even that little, as managed by a man so ignorant of medicine as myself, would probably tend only to mislead. At all events, it would be misplaced in this situation. The moral of the narrative is addressed to the opium-eater; and therefore, of necessity, limited in its application. If he is taught to fear and tremble, enough has been effected. But he may say, that the issue of my case is at least a proof that opium, after a seventeen years' use, and an eight years' abuse of its powers, may still be renounced: and that *he* may chance to bring to the task greater energy than I did, or that with a stronger constitution than mine he may obtain the same results with less. This may be true: I would not presume to measure the efforts of other men by my own: I heartily wish him more energy: I wish him the same success. Nevertheless, I had motives external to myself which he may unfortunately want: and these supplied me with conscientious supports which mere personal interests might fail to supply to a mind debilitated by opium.

Jeremy Taylor conjectures[184] that it may be as painful to be born as to die: I think it probable: and, during the whole period of diminishing the opium, I had the torments of a man passing out of one mode of existence into another. The issue was not death, but a sort of physical regeneration: and I may add, that ever since, at intervals, I have had a restoration of more than youthful spirits, though under the pressure of

---

[183] William Lithgow [poet and traveller (1582–1645?). His book is *Discourse of a Peregrination in Europe, Asia and Affricke* (1614)]: his book (Travels, &c.) is ill and pedantically written: but the account of his own sufferings on the rack at Malaga is overpoweringly affecting.

[184] Not Jeremy Taylor but, as De Quincey realized in 1856, Sir Francis Bacon, in his essay 'Of Death'.

difficulties, which, in a less happy state of mind, I should have called misfortunes.

One memorial of my former condition still remains: my dreams are not yet perfectly calm: the dread swell and agitation of the storm have not wholly subsided: the legions that encamped in them are drawing off, but not all departed: my sleep is still tumultuous, and, like the gates of Paradise to our first parents when looking back from afar, it is still (in the tremendous line of Milton) –

With dreadful faces throng'd and fiery arms.[185]

---

[185] Milton, *Paradise Lost*, xii, 644.

Reading 4.1 E.T.A. Hoffmann, 'The Sandman'

Source: Ritchie Robertson (trans.) (2008) *E.T.A. Hoffman: The Golden Pot and Other Tales*, Oxford, Oxford University Press, pp. 85–118 and 403. Footnotes are by the editor of this edition.

Nathanael to Lothar

You must all be very worried by my not having written for so long. Mother is probably angry, and Clara, I dare say, thinks that I am living in the lap of luxury and have completely forgotten the lovely, angelic image which is so deeply imprinted on my heart and mind. That is not so, however; I think of you all, daily and hourly, and in my sweet dreams the amiable figure of my lovely Clara passes, smiling at me with her bright eyes as charmingly as she used to whenever I called on you. Oh, how could I possibly have written to you in the tormented state of mind which has distracted all my thoughts until now! Something appalling has entered my life! Dark forebodings of a hideous, menacing fate are looming over me like the shadows of black clouds, impervious to any kindly ray of sunlight. It is time for me to tell you what has befallen me. I realize that I must, but at the very thought mad laughter bursts from within me. Oh, my dear Lothar, how am I ever to convey to you that what happened to me a few days ago has indeed managed to devastate my life so cruelly! If only you were here, you could see for yourself; but now you must undoubtedly consider me a crack-brained, superstitious fool. To cut a long story short, the appalling event that befell me, the fatal memory of which I am vainly struggling to escape, was simply this: a few days ago, at twelve noon on 30 October to be precise, a barometer-seller entered my room and offered me his wares. Instead of buying anything, I threatened to throw him downstairs, whereupon he departed of his own accord.

You will apprehend that this incident must gain its significance from associations peculiar to myself, reaching far back into my own life, and that it must have been the personality of this unfortunate tradesman that had such a repulsive effect on me. That is indeed the case. I am using all my strength to compose myself so that I may calmly and patiently tell you enough about my early youth for your lively imagination to visualize everything in distinct and luminous images. As I prepare to begin, I hear you laugh, while Clara says: 'What childish nonsense!' Laugh, I beg you, laugh and mock me as much as you please! But, God in heaven! the hair is rising on my scalp, and I feel as though I were begging you to mock me in mad despair, as Franz Moor begged Daniel.[1] Now, let me get on with the story!

During the day, except at lunch, my brothers and sisters and I saw little of our father. He was no doubt heavily occupied with his duties. After dinner, which was served at seven in accordance with the old custom, all of us, including our mother, would go into our father's study and sit at a round table. Our father would smoke tobacco and drink a big glass of beer with it. He would tell us many wondrous tales, and would become so excited over them that his pipe always went out; I would then have to light it again by holding out burning paper, which I greatly enjoyed. Often, however, he would give us picture-books and sit silent and motionless in his armchair, blowing such clouds of smoke that we all seemed to be swathed in mist. On such evenings our mother would be very melancholy, and hardly had the clock struck nine than she would say: 'Now, children, time for bed! The Sandman is coming, I can tell.'

Whenever she said this, I would indeed hear something coming noisily upstairs with rather heavy, slow steps; it must be the Sandman. On one occasion I found this hollow trampling particularly alarming, and asked my mother as she was shepherding us away: 'Mother! who is the wicked Sandman who always chases us away from Papa? What does he look like?'

'There is no such person as the Sandman, dear child,' replied my mother; 'when I say the Sandman is coming, that just means that you are sleepy, and can't keep your eyes open, as though someone had thrown sand in them.'

My mother's answer did not satisfy me; indeed my childish mind formed the conviction that our mother was only denying the Sandman's existence so that we should not be afraid of him; after all, I could always hear him coming upstairs. Filled with curiosity about this Sandman and his relation to us children, I finally asked my youngest sister's old nurse what kind of man the Sandman was.

'Why, Natty,' replied the old woman, 'don't you know that yet? He's a wicked man who comes to children when they don't want to go to bed and throws handfuls of sand into their eyes; that makes their eyes fill with blood and jump out of their heads, and throws the eyes into his bag and takes them into the crescent moon to feed his own

---

[1]   In Act 5, Scene 1 of Schiller's *Die Räuber* ('The Robbers', 1781) the villain, Franz Moor, has a terrible dream about the Last Judgement, and vainly urges his pious old servant Daniel to mock him for it.

children, who are sitting in the nest there; the Sandman's children have crooked beaks, like owls, with which to peck the eyes of naughty human children.'

I now formed a hideous mental picture of the cruel Sandman, and as soon as the heavy steps came upstairs in the evening, I would tremble with fear and horror. My mother could extract nothing from me except the stammering, tearful cry: 'The Sandman! the Sandman!' I would then run to my bedroom and be tormented all night by the frightful apparition of the Sandman.

Soon I grew old enough to realize that the nurse's tale of the Sandman and his children's nest in the crescent moon could not be exactly true; yet the Sandman remained for me a fearsome spectre, and terror, indeed horror, would seize upon me when I heard him not only coming upstairs but also pulling open the door of my father's room and entering. Sometimes he would stay away for a long period; then he would come several times in quick succession. This went on for years, during which I never became accustomed to these sinister happenings, and my image of the hideous Sandman lost nothing of its vividness. His dealings with my father began increasingly to occupy my imagination; I was prevented from asking my father about them by an unconquerable timidity, but the desire to investigate the mystery myself grew stronger as the years went by. The Sandman had aroused my interest in the marvellous and extraordinary, an interest that readily takes root in a child's mind. I liked nothing better than hearing or reading horrific stories about goblins, witches, dwarfs, and so forth; but pride of place always belonged to the Sandman, and I kept drawing him, in the strangest and most loathsome forms, with chalk or charcoal on tables, cupboards, and walls.

When I was ten, my mother made me move from my nursery to a little bedroom just along the corridor from my father's room. We were still obliged to go to bed whenever the clock struck nine and we heard the unknown being in the house. From my bedroom I could hear him entering my father's room, and soon afterwards a fine, strange-smelling vapour seemed to spread through the house. As my curiosity increased, so did my resolve to make the Sandman's acquaintance by some means or other. Often, when my mother had gone past, I would slip out of my bedroom into the corridor, but I never managed to discover anything; for the Sandman had always entered the room before I reached the spot at which he would have been visible. Finally, impelled by an irresistible urge, I decided to hide in my father's room and await the Sandman's arrival.

One evening I perceived from my father's silence and my mother's low spirits that the Sandman was coming; accordingly I pretended to be very tired, left the room before nine, and concealed myself in a recess just besides the door. The front door creaked and slow, heavy, rumbling steps approached the staircase. My mother hastened past me with my brothers and sisters. Gently, gently, I opened the door of my father's study. He was sitting, as usual, silent and motionless with his back to the door, and did not notice me; I slipped inside and hid behind the curtain which was drawn in front of an open wardrobe next to the door. The rumbling steps came closer and closer; strange sounds of coughing, scraping and muttering could be heard. My heart was quaking with fear and anticipation. Right outside the door, a firm step, a violent tug at the latch, and the door sprang open with a clatter. Bracing myself with an effort, I peeped cautiously out. The Sandman was standing in the middle of the room, facing my father, with the lights shining brightly in his face. The Sandman, the frightful Sandman, was the old advocate Coppelius,[2] who sometimes had lunch with us!

But the most hideous of shapes could not have filled me with deeper horror than this same Coppelius. Imagine a big, broad-shouldered man with a massive, misshapen head, a pair of piercing, greenish, cat-like eyes sparkling from under bushy grey eyebrows, and a large beaky nose hanging over his upper lip. His crooked mouth was often distorted in a malicious smile, and then a couple of dark red spots appeared on his cheeks, and a strange hissing sound proceeded from between his clenched teeth. Coppelius was always seen wearing an ash-grey coat of old-fashioned cut, with waistcoat and breeches to match, but with black stockings and shoes with little jewelled buckles. His small wig scarcely covered more than the crown of his head, his greasy locks stood on end above his big red ears, and a large, tightly tied pigtail stuck out from the back of his neck, disclosing the silver buckle that fastened his crimped cravat. His entire appearance was repellent and disgusting; but we children had a particular aversion to his big, gnarled, hairy hands, and anything touched by them ceased at once to be appetizing. Once he noticed this, he took delight in finding some pretext for fingering a piece of cake or fruit that our kind mother had surreptitiously put on our plates, so that our loathing and disgust prevented us, with tears in our eyes, from enjoying the titbit that was supposed to give us pleasure. He behaved in just the same way on special days, when our father would pour out a small glass of sweet

---

[2] cf. Italian *coppo* 'eye-socket'.

wine. Coppelius would then quickly pass his hand over it, or he would raise the glass to his blue lips and utter a fiendish laugh on seeing us unable to express our vexation other than by suppressed sobs. He used to refer to us only as 'the little beasts'; in his presence we were forbidden to utter a sound, and we cursed the ugly, unfriendly man, who was deliberately intent on spoiling our slightest pleasures. Our mother seemed to hate the odious Coppelius as much as we did; for as soon as he showed himself, her good spirits, her cheerful, relaxed manner, were transformed into sorrowful and gloomy gravity. Our father behaved towards him as though Coppelius were a higher being whose foibles must be endured and who had to be kept in a good mood at whatever cost. Coppelius had only to drop a hint, and his favourite dishes were cooked and rare wines opened.

On seeing Coppelius now, I realized with horror and alarm that he and none other must be the Sandman; but to me the Sandman was no longer the bogy man in the nursery store who brings children's eyes to feed his brood in their nest in the crescent moon. No! He was a hateful, spectral monster, bringing misery, hardship, and perdition, both temporal and eternal, wherever he went.

I was rooted to the spot. Despite the risk of being discovered and, as I was well aware, of being severely punished, I stayed there, listening, and poking my head between the curtains. My father welcomed Coppelius with much formality.

'Come on, let's get to work!' cried Coppelius in a hoarse, croaking voice, throwing off his coat.

My father, silent and frowning, took off his dressing-gown, and the two of them donned long black smocks. I did not notice where these came from. My father opened the folding doors of a cupboard; but I saw that what I had so long taken for a cupboard was instead a dark recess containing a small fireplace. Coppelius walked over to it, and a blue flame crackled up from the hearth. All manner of strange instruments were standing around. Merciful heavens! As my old father bent down to the fire, he looked quite different. A horrible, agonizing convulsion seemed to have contorted his gentle, honest face into the hideous, repulsive mask of a fiend. He looked like Coppelius. The latter, brandishing a pair of red-hot tongs, was lifting gleaming lumps from the thick smoke and then hammering at them industriously. It seemed to me that human faces were visible on all sides, but without eyes, and with ghastly, deep, black cavities instead.

'Bring the eyes! Bring the eyes!' cried Coppelius in a hollow rumbling voice.

Gripped by uncontrollable terror, I screamed out and dived from my hiding-place on to the floor. Coppelius seized me, gnashing his teeth and bleating, 'Little beast! Little beast!' He pulled me to my feet and hurled me on to the fireplace, where the flames began to singe my hair. 'Now we've got eyes – eyes – a fine pair of children's eyes', whispered Coppelius, thrusting his hands into the flames and pulling out fragments of red-hot coal which he was about to strew in my eyes.

My father raised his hands imploringly and cried: 'Master! Master! Let my Nathanael keep his eyes! Let him keep them!'

With a piercing laugh, Coppelius cried: 'All right, the boy may keep his eyes and snivel his way through his lessons; but let's examine the mechanism of his hands and feet.' And with these words he seized me so hard that my joints made a cracking noise, dislocated my hands and feet, and put them back in various sockets. 'They don't fit properly! It was all right as it was! The Old Man knew what he was doing!' hissed and muttered Coppelius; but everything went black and dim before my eyes, a sudden convulsion shot through my nerves and my frame, and I felt nothing more. A warm, gentle breath passed over my face, and I awoke from a death-like sleep; my mother was bending over me.

'Is the Sandman still there?' I stammered.

'No, my dear child, he's been gone for a long, long time, he'll do you no harm!' said my mother, kissing and cuddling her darling boy who was thus restored to life.

Why should I weary you, my dear Lothar? Why should I dwell on minute details, when so much remains to be told? Suffice it to say that I was caught eavesdropping and was roughly treated by Coppelius. Fear and terror brought on a violent fever, with which I was laid low for several weeks. 'Is the Sandman still there?' These were my first coherent words and the sign that I was cured, that my life had been saved. Now I need only tell you about the most terrifying moment of my early life; you will then be convinced that it is not the weakness of my eyesight that makes everything appear colourless, but that a sombre destiny has indeed veiled my life in a murky cloud, which perhaps I shall not penetrate until I die.

Coppelius did not show his face again, and was said to have left the town.

A year, perhaps, had gone by, and we were sitting one evening round the table, according to the old, unaltered custom. My father was in excellent spirits and told many delightful stories about the journeys he had made in his youth. Then, as it struck nine, we suddenly heard the front door creaking on its hinges, and slow, leaden steps came rumbling through the hall and up the stairs.

'That's Coppelius', said my mother, turning pale.

'Yes! It's Coppelius', repeated my father, in a dull, spiritless voice.

Tears burst from my mother's eyes. 'But, father, father!' she cried, 'does this have to happen?'

'This is the last time he will visit me, I promise you!' replied my father. 'Go, take the children away! Go to bed! Good night!'

I felt as though I were being crushed under a heavy, cold stone; I could hardly breathe! As I stood motionless, my mother seized me by the arm: 'Come along, Nathanael!' I allowed her to lead me away, and went into my bedroom. 'Keep quiet, and go to bed! Go to sleep!' my mother called after me; but I was so tormented by indescribable inner terror and turmoil that I could not sleep a wink. Before me stood the hateful, loathsome Coppelius, his eyes sparkling, laughing at me maliciously, and I strove in vain to rid myself of his image. It must already have been midnight when a frightful crash was heard, as though a cannon had been fired. The whole house trembled, a rattling, rustling noise passed my door, and the front door was slammed with a clatter.

'That's Coppelius!' I cried in terror, leaping out of bed. Suddenly a piercing scream of lament was heard; I raced to my father's room the door was open, a cloud of suffocating smoke billowed towards me, and the maidservant shrieked: 'Oh, the master! the master!' On the floor in front of the smoking fireplace my father was lying dead, his face burnt black and hideously contorted, while my sisters wailed and whimpered all round him and my mother lay in a dead faint.

'Coppelius, you abominable fiend, you've murdered my father!' I shouted; then I lost consciousness.

Two days later, when my father was laid in his coffin, his features were once again as mild and gentle as they had been during his life. I was comforted by the realization that his alliance with the devilish Coppelius could not have plunged him into eternal perdition.

The explosion had roused the neighbours; the incident got out and came to the attention of the authorities, who wanted to call Coppelius to account. He, however, had vanished from the town without leaving a trace.

If I now tell you, my cherished friend, that the barometer-seller who called on me was none other than the abominable Coppelius, you will not blame me for interpreting his malevolent appearance as a portent of dire misfortune. He was differently dressed, but Coppelius's figure and features are too deeply engraved on my mind for any mistake to be possible. Besides, Coppelius has not even changed his name. I am told that he claims to be a Piedmontese mechanic called Giuseppe Coppola.

I am determined to try conclusions with him and avenge my father's death, come what may.

Say nothing to my mother about the appearance of this hideous monster. Give my love to my dear Clara; I will write to her when my mind is calmer. Farewell!

Clara to Nathanael

It is true that you haven't written to me for a long time, but I am still convinced that I am in your thoughts. For you must have been preoccupied with me when, intending to send off your last letter to my brother Lothar, you addressed it to me instead of to him. I opened the letter joyfully and realized your mistake only on reading the words: 'Oh, my dear Lothar!' I should of course have read no further, but given the letter to my brother. You have sometimes teasingly accused me of such womanly calm and deliberation that if the house were about to collapse I would pause before taking flight, like the woman in the story, to smooth out a fold in the curtains; however, I need hardly tell you that I was deeply shaken by the first few sentences of your letter. I could scarcely breathe, and my head was spinning. Oh, my precious Nathanael, what terrible thing could have entered your life! The idea of parting from you, never seeing you again, pierced my heart like a red-hot dagger. I read and read! Your description of the odious Coppelius is horrible. I did not know that your good old father had met such a terrible, violent death. When I gave Lothar back his rightful property, he tried to soothe me, but without success. The frightful barometer-seller Giuseppe Coppola followed me about wherever I went, and I'm almost ashamed to confess that he disturbed even my usually sound and healthy sleep with all manner of strange dreams. But soon, on the very next day, I regained my normal state of mind. Don't be cross, dearly beloved, if Lothar happens to tell you that, despite your strange notion that Coppelius will do you an injury, I am as cheerful and relaxed as ever.

I will confess frankly that in my opinion all the terrors and horrors you describe took place only inside your head, and had very little to do with the real world outside you. Old Coppelius may have been odious enough, but it was his hatred of children that bred such a loathing of him in you children.

It was quite natural that your childish mind should connect the terrible Sandman in the nursery tale with old Coppelius, and that even when you no longer believed in the Sandman, Coppelius should seem a sinister monster, particularly hostile to children. As for his uncanny nocturnal goings-on with your father, I expect the two of them were simply conducting secret alchemical experiments, which could hardly please your mother, since a lot of money must have been squandered and moreover, as is said always to happen to such inquirers, your father became obsessed with the delusive longing for higher wisdom and was estranged from his family. Your father must have brought about his death by his own carelessness, and Coppelius cannot be to blame. Would you believe that yesterday I asked our neighbour, an experienced chemist, whether it was possible for such an explosion which killed people on the spot to occur in chemical experiments? He said, 'Why, of course', and gave me a characteristically long-winded account of how this could happen, mentioning so many strange-sounding names that I couldn't remember any of them. Now I expect you'll be angry with your Clara. You'll say: 'Her cold temperament cannot accept the mystery that often enfolds man in invisible arms; she perceives only the varied surface of the world and takes pleasure in it as a childish infant does in a glittering fruit which has deadly poison concealed within it.'

Oh, my precious Nathanael! don't you think that even a cheerful, relaxed, carefree temperament may have premonitions of a dark power that tries malevolently to attack our inmost selves? But please forgive a simple girl like me for venturing to suggest what I think about such inner conflicts. I probably shan't be able to put it into words properly, and you'll laugh at me, not because what I'm trying to say is stupid, but because I'm so clumsy at saying it.

If there is a dark power which malevolently and treacherously places a thread within us, with which to hold us and draw us down a perilous and pernicious path that we would never otherwise have set foot on – if there is such a power, then it must take the same form as we do, it must become our very self; for only in this way can we believe in it and give it the scope it requires to accomplish its secret task. If our minds, strengthened by a cheerful life, are resolute enough to recognize alien and malevolent influences for what they are and to proceed tranquilly along the path to which our inclinations and our vocation have directed us, the uncanny power must surely perish in a vain struggle to assume the form which is our own reflection. Lothar also says there is no doubt that once we have surrendered ourselves to the dark psychic power, it draws alien figures, encountered by chance in the outside world, into our inner selves, so that we ourselves give life to the spirit which our strange delusion persuades us is speaking from such figures. It is the phantom of our own self which, thanks to its intimate relationship with us and its deep influence on our minds, casts us down to hell or transports us to heaven. You see, my darling Nathanael, that Lothar and I have talked at length about dark powers and forces, and now that I have with some labour, written down the main points, it seems to me quite profound. I don't quite understand Lothar's last words, I only have a dim idea of what he means, and yet it all sounds very true. I beg you to forget all about the hateful advocate Coppelius and the barometer-man Giuseppe Coppola. Be assured that these alien figures have no power over you; only your belief in their malevolent power can make them truly malevolent to you. If every line of your letter did not reveal the deep perturbation of your spirits, if your state of mind did not cause me pain in my very soul, then, indeed, I could make jokes about the advocate Sandman and the barometer-seller Coppelius. Keep your spirits up! If the hateful Coppola should presume to annoy you in your dreams, I am determined to appear in your presence like your guardian angel and to drive him away with loud laughter. I am not the slightest bit afraid of him or his horrid hands; I wouldn't let him spoil my appetite as an advocate, nor hurt my eyes as a Sandman.

Eternally yours, my most dearly beloved Nathanael, etc.

Nathanael to Lothar

I am very annoyed that Clara should have opened and read my recent letter to you, although admittedly the mistake was due to my own absent-mindedness. She has written me a most profound philosophical letter in which she demonstrates at great length that Coppelius and Coppola exist only in my mind and are phantoms emanating from myself which will crumble to dust the moment I acknowledge them as such. Really, who would have thought that the spirit which shines from such clear, gracious, smiling, child-like eyes, like a sweet and lovely dream, could draw such intellectual distinctions, worthy of a university graduate? She appeals to your opinion. You and she have talked about me. I suppose you have given her lectures on logic to teach her how to sift and search all problems with due subtlety. Well, stop it at once!

Anyway, it seems certain that the barometer-seller Giuseppe Coppola is not the same person as the old advocate Coppelius. I am attending the lectures given by the newly arrived professor of physics, who is called Spalanzani,[3] like the famous naturalist, and is likewise of Italian descent. He has known Coppola for many years, and besides, his accent

---

[3] The name comes from the famous biologist Lazzaro Spallanzani (1729–99), who helped to explain the physiology of blood circulation in man and animals, and reproduction and respiration in animals and plants.

makes it clear that he really is a Piedmontese. Coppelius was a German, though not an honest one, in my opinion. My mind is not completely at ease. You and Clara are welcome to think me a melancholy dreamer, but I cannot shake off the impression that Coppelius's accursed face made on me. I am glad he has left the town, as Spalanzani tells me.

This professor is an odd fish. A tubby little man with projecting cheek-bones, a delicate nose, thick lips, and small piercing eyes. But you will get a better idea of him than any description can convey if you take a look at Cagliostro[4] as he is depicted by Chodowiecki[5] in some Berlin magazine. That is what Spalanzani looks like.

Not long ago, as I was going up his stairs, I noticed that a narrow strip of the glass door was left unconcealed by the curtain which is normally drawn across it. I can't tell how it was that I peeped in inquisitively. Inside the room a tall, very slim woman, beautifully proportioned and magnificently dressed, was sitting in front of a small table on which she was leaning, with her hands folded. She was facing the door, so that I had a full view of her angelic face. She seemed not to notice me, and indeed there was something lifeless about her eyes, as though they lacked the power of sight; she seemed to be asleep with her eyes open. I had a rather uncanny feeling, and crept softly into the lecture-hall next door. Afterwards I learnt that the figure I had seen was Spalanzani's daughter Olimpia, whom, strangely and reprehensibly, he keeps locked up, so that nobody at all is allowed near her. There must be something peculiar about her; perhaps she is feeble-minded, for example. But why I am writing all this to you? I could have told you all this better and more fully by word of mouth. For let me tell you that in two weeks' time I shall be with you. I must see my dear sweet angel, my Clara, again. Her presence will blow away the mood of irritation which, I must confess, almost mastered me after that damnably sensible letter. That's why I won't write to her today.

Best wishes, etc.

No invention could be stranger or more extraordinary than the events which befell my poor friend, the young student Nathanael, and which I have undertaken to recount to you, dear reader. Have you, my kind patron, ever had an experience that entirely absorbed your heart,

[4] Giuseppe Balsamo (1743–95), alias Count Alexander Cagliostro, a notorious imposter who travelled round Europe, especially Italy and France, selling the 'elixir of life' and pretending to foretell the future; he was arrested in Rome in 1789, tried for propagating Freemasonary, and sentenced to life imprisonment.
[5] Daniel Chodowiecki (1726–1801), engraver, whose works included many drawings of everyday life in Berlin; hence he is also mentioned in *My Cousin's Corner Window.*

your mind, and your thoughts, banishing all other concerns? You were seething and boiling inwardly; your fiery blood raced through your veins and gave a richer colour to your cheeks. You had a strange, fixed stare as though you were trying to make out forms, invisible to any other eyes, in empty space, and your words faded into obscure sighs. 'What's wrong, my dear fellow? Whatever's the matter, old chap?' inquired your friends. And you, anxious to convey your inner vision with all its glowing colours, its lights and shadows, laboured in vain to find words with which to begin. But you felt as though you must compress the entire wonderful, splendid, terrible, hilarious, and hideous experience into your very first word, so that it should strike your hearers like an electric shock; yet every word, all the resources of language, seemed faded, frosty, and dead. You searched and searched, and stammered and stuttered, and your friends' matter-of-fact questions were like gusts of icy air blowing on your inner glow and wellnigh extinguishing it. But if, like a bold painter, you had first sketched the outlines of your inner vision with a few careless stokes, you had little trouble in adding ever brighter colours until the swirling thong of multifarious figures seized hold of your friends' imagination, and they saw themselves, like you, in the midst of the picture that arose from your mind!

I must confess, kind reader, that nobody has actually asked me to tell the story of young Nathanael; you are aware, however, that I belong to the curious race of authors, who, if they are filled with such a vision as I have just described, feel as though everyone who approaches them, and all the world besides, were asking: 'Whatever's the matter? Tell me everything, my dear fellow!' Thus I felt powerfully impelled to tell you about Nathanael's calamitous life. Its strange and wondrous character absorbed my entire soul; but for that very reason, and because, dear reader, I have to put you in the right mood to endure an odd tale, which is no easy matter, I racked my brains to find a portentous, original, and arresting way of beginning Nathanael's story. 'Once upon a time …' – the best way to begin any story, but too down-to-earth! 'In the small provincial town of S. there lived …' – somewhat better: at least it provides some build-up to the climax. Or why not plunge *in medias res*: '"Go to the Devil!" cried the student Nathanael, wild-eyed with fury and terror, as the barometer-seller Guiseppe Coppola …'. I had in fact written this down, when I fancied there was something comical in the student Nathanael looking wild-eyed; this story, however, is no laughing matter. Unable to find words that seemed to reflect anything of the prismatic radiance of my inner vision, I decided not to begin at all. Be so good, dear reader, as to accept the three letters, kindly communicated to me by my friend Lothar, as the sketch for my portrayal; as I tell the story, I shall endeavour to add more and more colour to it. I may, like a good portraitist, succeed in depicting some figures so well that you find them good likenesses even without knowing the originals; indeed, you may feel as though you had often seen these persons with your very own eyes. Then, O my reader, you may come to believe that nothing can be stranger or weirder than real life, and that the poet can do no more than capture the strangeness of reality, like the dim reflection in a dull mirror.

In order to put you more fully in the picture, I must add that soon after the death of Nathanael's father, his mother had taken Clara and Lothar, the children of a distant relative who had likewise died and left them orphans, into the household. Clara and Nathanael became warmly attached to each other, and nobody could possibly have any objection to this; hence they were engaged by the time Nathanael left the town in order to continue his studies in G***. His last letter was written from G***, where he was attending lectures by the famous professor of physical sciences, Spalanzani.

I might now go on cheerfully with my story; but at this instant the image of Clara is so vividly present to me that I cannot look away, as always happened when she used to look at me with her lovely smile. Clara could by no means be called beautiful; that was the judgement of all professional authorities on beauty. Yet the architects praised her perfectly proportioned figure, while the painters raved about the chaste lines of her neck, her shoulders, and her breasts, fell in love with her wonderful hair, which reminded them of Battoni's Mary Magdalen,[6] and talked a lot of nonsense about Battoni's colouring techniques. One of them, however, a true fantasist, drew a very odd comparison between Clara's eyes and a lake by Ruysdael[7] which reflected the pure azure of the cloudless sky, the forests and flowery meadows, and the varied, happy life of the fertile landscape. Poets and musicians went further and said: 'Lake? Reflection? How can we look at the girl without perceiving wondrous, heavenly sounds and songs radiating from her gaze and penetrating and vivifying our very hearts? If we ourselves can't produce a decent song after that, we must be good for very little, and that indeed is the message of the sly smile that hovers around Clara's lips whenever we venture on some jingle that claims to be a song, though it consists only of a few incoherent notes.'

---

[6] Pompeo Battoni (1708–87) painted a 'Penitent Mary Magdalen' which Hoffman saw and greatly admired in the gallery at Dresden.

[7] Either Salomon van Ruysdael (1602–70) or his nephew Jacob van Ruysdael (1628–82), Dutch landscape painters.

Such was the case. Clara had the vivid imagination of a cheerful, ingenuous, child-like child, a deep heart filled with womanly tenderness, and a very acute, discriminating mind. She was no friend to muddle-headed enthusiasts; for although she uttered few words, being taciturn by nature, her clear gaze and her sly, ironic smile said: 'Dear friends, how can you expect me to treat your shifting, shadowy images as real objects full of life and motion?' Many people accordingly criticized Clara for being cold, unresponsive, and prosaic; others, however, who saw life clearly and profoundly, were very fond of the warm-hearted, sensible, child-like girl, but none so much as Nathanael, who was energetic and cheerful in his approach to art and learning. Clara was intensely devoted to him, and their parting cast the first shadow on her life. With what rapture did she fly to his arms when he entered his mother's room, having returned home as he had promised in his last letter to Lothar. Nathanael's expectations were fulfilled; for on seeing Clara he thought neither about the advocate Coppelius nor about Clara's sensible letter, and all his irritation vanished.

Nathanael, however, was quite right when he told his friend Lothar that the figure of the repulsive barometer-seller Coppola had made a malevolent intrusion into his life. Even in the first few days of his visit, it was apparent to everyone that Nathanael's character had changed entirely. He fell into gloomy reveries and took to behaving in a strange and wholly unaccustomed way. To him, all life consisted of dreams and premonitions; he kept saying that each individual, fancying himself to be free, only served as a plaything for the cruelty of dark forces; that it was in vain to resist, and one must acquiesce humbly in the decrees of destiny. He went so far as to assert that artists and scholars were under a delusion when they believed that their creative endeavours were governed by the autonomy of their will: 'for', said he, 'the inspired state which is indispensable for creation does not arise from inside ourselves; it is due to the influence of a higher principle that lies outside us'.

The sensible Clara greatly disliked these mystical flights of fancy, but there seemed no point in trying to refute them. It was only when Nathanael maintained that Coppelius was the evil principle that had seized him when he was eavesdropping behind the curtain, and that this foul demon would wreak destruction upon their happy love, that Clara would become very serious and say: 'Yes, Nathanael, you're right! Coppelius is an evil, malevolent principle; he can do terrible harm, like the visible manifestation of a devilish power; but only if you fail to dismiss him from your mind. As long as you believe in him, he is real and active; his power consists only in your belief.'

Indignant that Clara conceded the existence of the demon only in his own mind, Nathanael would try to launch into the mystical doctrine of devils and evil forces, but Clara would irritably cut the conversation short by raising some trivial subject, to Nathanael's great annoyance. He concluded that such mysteries were inaccessible to cold and insensitive temperaments, without clearly realizing that he considered Clara's temperament to be such, and accordingly persevered in his attempts to initiate her into these mysteries. Early in the morning, when Clara was helping to make the breakfast, he would stand beside her, reading aloud from all manner of mystical books, until Clara asked: 'But, Nathanael dear, what if I were to scold *you* for being the evil principle exerting a malevolent influence on my coffee? For if I drop everything, as you demand, and gaze into your eyes while you read, the coffee will run over into the fire and none of you will get any breakfast!'

Nathanael would then clap the book shut and run angrily to his room.

In the past Nathanael had shown a special gift for composing charming and vivid stories which he would write down, and which Clara would listen to with heartfelt enjoyment. Now his compositions were gloomy, unintelligible, and formless, so that, even though Clara was too kind to say so, he was aware how little they appealed to her. Nothing had a more deadly effect on Clara than tedium; her unconquerable mental drowsiness would reveal itself in her expression and her speech. Nathanael's compositions were indeed very tedious. His annoyance with Clara's cold, prosaic temperament increased, while Clara could not overcome her irritation with Nathanael's dismal, obscure, tedious mysticism, and so, without noticing it, they became increasingly estranged from one another. Nathanael himself was obliged to confess that the figure of the hateful Coppelius had begun to fade from his imagination, and he often had difficulty in imparting lively colours to Coppelius in his compositions, where the latter appeared as a dreadful bogey man and emissary of fate. Finally he conceived the plan of writing a poem about his gloomy premonition that Coppelius would destroy his happy love. He portrayed himself and Clara as joined in true love, but every so often a black hand seemed to reach into their lives and tear out some newly discovered source of pleasure. Finally, when they are standing at the altar, the fearsome Coppelius appears and touches Clara's lovely eyes, which leap into Nathanael's breast, burning and singeing him; Coppelius seizes him and hurls him into a circle of flames which is rotating with the speed of a whirlwind, dragging him along it its fury. A tumult springs up, as when the savage hurricane lashes the ocean, whose foaming waves rear up like black giants with white heads, filled with the rage of combat. But through all the tumult he hears Clara's voice saying: 'Can't you see me? Coppelius deceived you; it wasn't my eyes that burned in your breast, but red-hot drops of your own heart's blood. I have my eyes, just look at me!' 'That is Clara', thinks Nathanael, 'and I am her own eternally.' At that moment his thought seems to reach down forcibly into the circle of flames, bringing it to a halt, and the tumult fades away in a black abyss. Nathanael gazes into Clara's eyes; but what looks at him from Clara's kindly eyes is death.

While composing this, Nathanael was calm and collected; he revised and polished every line, and, having submitted to the constraints of metre, he did not rest until the entire work was pure and melodious. Yet, when he had finished and read the poem aloud to himself, he was gripped by wild horror and terror, and shrieked: 'Whose hideous voice is this?' Before long, however, he again decided that it was a highly successful poem, which could not fail to animate Clara's cold temperament, though he had no clear idea what purpose this would serve or what might result from alarming her with hideous images prophesying the destruction of their love by a terrible fate.

They were sitting, Nathanael and Clara, in her mother's little garden. Clara was in good spirits, because during the past three days, while working on his poem, Nathanael had no longer tormented her with his dreams and premonitions. Besides, Nathanael talked in a lively, cheerful manner about pleasant matters, as in the past, so that Clara said: 'Now you're completely mine again. Do you see how we've driven that hateful Coppelius away?'

Only then did Nathanael remember that he had the poem in his pocket and had been meaning to read it aloud. He promptly drew it out and began reading, while Clara, resigned to the prospect of something tedious as usual, quietly began knitting. But as the cloud of gloom swelled up in ever-deepening blackness, she let her knitting fall from her hands and gazed fixedly at Nathanael. The latter was entirely carried away by his poem: his cheeks burned with the fire within him, tears gushed from his eyes. Finished at last, he gave a sigh of exhaustion. He seized Clara's hand and moaned miserably: 'Oh! Clara! Clara!'

Clara gave him a gentle hug and said in a low voice, but slowly and seriously: 'Nathanael, my darling Nathanael! Throw the crazy, senseless, insane story into the fire.'

Nathanael sprang up indignantly and exclaimed, thrusting Clara away: 'You accursed lifeless automaton!' He rushed away, while Clara, deeply hurt, shed bitter tears.

'Oh, he never loved me, because he doesn't understand me', she wailed.

Lothar entered the bower, and Clara could not help telling him what had occurred. Since he loved his sister with all his heart, every accusing word she uttered threw sparks into his mind, so that the irritation he had long felt with the dreamy Nathanael was inflamed into furious anger. He ran to Nathanael and rebuked him harshly for his senseless behaviour towards Lothar's dearly loved sister. Nathanael flew into a passion and replied in kind. They called each other a mad, fantastical coxcomb and a wretched, vulgar philistine. A duel was inevitable. They decided to meet next morning behind the garden and fight with sharpened rapiers, as was customary among the local students. In the mean time, they crept about, silent and scowling. Clara overheard their violent quarrel and saw the fencing-master bringing the rapiers at daybreak. She guessed what was afoot. Lothar and Nathanael arrived at the scene of their duel in gloomy silence; they removed their coats and were about to assail each other, their eyes burning with the blood-thirsty fury of combat, when Clara rushed through the garden gate.

'You dreadful savages!' she cried amid her sobs, 'strike me down first before you attack each other; for how can I go on living if my lover has murdered my brother, or my brother has killed my lover!'

Lothar lowered his weapon and looked silently at the ground, but Nathanael, with a shock of heart-rending sorrow, recollected all the love he had felt for his adorable Clara in the most glorious days of his youth. The fatal implement fell from his hand and he threw himself at Clara's feet.

'Can you ever forgive me, my only, my beloved Clara! Can you forgive me, my beloved brother Lothar!'

Lothar was touched by his friend's agony; amid floods of tears, the three embraced in token of reconciliation and swore unfailing love and loyalty to one another.

Nathanael felt as though relieved of a heavy burden which had been crushing him, and as though, by resisting the dark forces which had ensnared him, he had saved his entire existence from the threat of annihilation. He spent three more blissful days among his dear ones, then returned to G***, where he intended to stay for another year before returning to his home town for good.

Everything relating to Coppelius was kept from his mother; for it was known that she could not think without horror of the man whom she, like Nathanael, held responsible for her husband's death.

On returning to his lodgings, Nathanael was astonished to discover that the whole house had been burnt to the ground. Nothing remained amid the ruins but the fire-walls separating it from the adjacent houses. Although the fire had broken out in the laboratory of the apothecary who lived on the ground floor, and the house had burnt from the bottom up, Nathanael's bold and energetic friends had managed to get into his upstairs room in time to save his books, manuscripts, and instruments. They had removed all these things, which were undamaged, to another house, and taken possession of a room there, which Nathanael immediately moved into. He paid no particular heed to the fact that he was now living opposite Professor Spalanzani; nor did he think it specially noteworthy that his window looked straight into the room where Olimpia often sat by herself, so that he could clearly make out her shape, although her features remained blurred and indistinct. He was eventually struck by the fact that Olimpia often spent hours sitting at a little table, just as he had previously glimpsed her through the glass door, without doing anything, but gazing rigidly across at him; he was also obliged to confess that he had never seen a more shapely woman, but, with Clara in his heart, he remained indifferent to the stiff and motionless Olimpia. Only occasionally did he glance up from his textbook at the beautiful statue: that was all.

Just as Nathanael was writing to Clara, there came a soft tap at the door. On his calling 'Come in!' it opened, and in peeped Coppola's repulsive face. Nathanael felt himself quaking inwardly; however, mindful of what Spalanzani had said about his fellow-countryman Coppola, and of his own sacred promise to Clara concerning the Sandman Coppelius, he felt ashamed of his childish superstition, pulled himself together with a great effort, and spoke as calmly and gently as he could: 'I don't wish to buy any barometers, my friend! Be off with you!'

Now, however, Coppola came right into the room; contorting his wide mouth into a hideous grin and giving a piercing look from under his long grey lashes, he said hoarsely: 'No barometer, no barometer! I 'ave beautiful eyes-a to sell you, beautiful eyes-a!'

'You madman,' cried Nathanael in horror, 'how can you have eyes to sell? Eyes?'

But Coppola had already put his barometers aside; he reached into the wide pockets of his coat and fetched out lorgnettes and pairs of spectacles, which he placed on the table.

'Now, now, glass-a, glass-a to wear on your nose-a, dese are my eyes-a, beautiful eyes-a!' And with these words he pulled out more and more spectacles, so that the whole table began strangely gleaming and shining. Innumerable eyes flickered and winked and goggled at Nathanael; but he could not look away from the table, and Coppola put more and more spectacles on it, and their flaming eyes sprang to and fro ever more wildly, darting their blood-red rays into Nathanael's breast. Overcome by mad terror, he shrieked: 'Stop! stop, you frightful man!' – and seized Coppola by the arm as the latter was reaching into his pocket for yet more spectacles, even though the entire table was now covered with them. Coppola freed himself gently, uttering a horrible hoarse laugh, and with the words: 'No good for you – but here, beautiful glass-a!' he swept up all the spectacles, packed them away, and produced from the side-pocket of his coat a number of large and small spyglasses. As soon as the spectacles had been removed, Nathanael became perfectly calm; thinking of Clara, he realized that the hideous apparition could only have proceeded from within himself, and that Coppola must be a thoroughly honest mechanic and optician, who could not possibly be the accursed double or ghost of Coppelius. Besides, the spyglasses that Coppola had now placed on the table had nothing remarkable about them, let alone the sinister qualities of the spectacles, and, in order to make amends for his behaviour, Nathanael decided to buy something from Coppola after all. He picked up a small, beautifully made pocket spyglass and tested it by looking out of the window. Never before in his life had he come across a spyglass that brought objects before one's eyes with such clarity, sharpness, and distinctness. He involuntarily looked into Spalanzani's room; Olimpia was sitting as usual at the little table, with her arms on it and her hands folded.

Only now did Nathanael behold Olimpia's wondrously beautiful face. It was only her eyes that seemed to him strangely fixed and dead. As he peered ever more intently through the glass, however, he thought he saw moist moonbeams shining from Olimpia's eyes. It was as though her power of vision were only now being awakened; her eyes seemed to sparkle more and more vividly. Nathanael remained at the window, as though rooted to the spot by a spell, gazing uninterruptedly at Olimpia's heavenly beauty. He was aroused, like somebody lost in a dream, by the sound of foot-scraping and throat-clearing. Coppola was standing behind him.

'Tre zecchini – three ducat!'

Nathanael, who had completely forgotten the optician, hastily paid the sum demanded.

'Beautiful glass-a, no? Beautiful glass-a?' asked Coppola in his repulsive hoarse voice, smiling maliciously.

'Yes, yes, yes!' replied Nathanael crossly. 'Good-bye, my friend!'

Coppola left the room, not without casting many strange side-glances at Nathanael, who heard him laughing loudly as he went downstairs.

'All right,' said Nathanael, 'he's laughing at me because I no doubt paid too high a price for the little spy-glass – too high a price!'

As he uttered these words in a low voice, a deep, deathly sigh seemed to send a grisly echo through the room. Nathanael caught his breath with fear. But no, it was he who had uttered the sigh, that was quite obvious.

'Clara', he said to himself, 'is probably right to think me tiresome and superstitious; but it's still a funny thing – oh, more than that, I suspect – that the silly idea that I paid too high a price for Coppola's spyglass makes me feel so oddly apprehensive; I can't think why this is.'

He then sat down in order to finish his letter to Clara, but one glance through the window convinced him that Olimpia was still sitting there, and at that instant, as though impelled by an irresistible force, he jumped up, seized Coppola's spyglass, and could not tear himself away from the alluring sight of Olimpia, until his friend and fellow-student Siegmund summoned him to Professor Spalanzani's lecture.

The curtain in front of the fateful room was drawn tight; Nathanael could neither glimpse Olimpia there nor, during the next two days, in her room, although he scarcely left his window and peered continually through Coppola's spyglass. On the third day the window was covered by drapery. In extreme despair, impelled by yearning and ardent desire, he ran out through the town gate. Olimpia's shape hovered in the air in front of him, stepped forth from the bushes, and looked at him with great radiant eyes from the clear water of the brook. The image of Clara had entirely departed from his mind; he thought only of Olimpia, and lamented out loud in a tearful voice: 'Oh, light of my life, you glorious, lofty star, did you rise upon me only to vanish again, leaving me in dark and hopeless night?'

Returning to his lodgings, he noticed a noisy upheaval going on in Spalanzani's house. The doors were open, all manner of utensils were being carried in, the first-floor windows had been taken off their hinges, busy maids were sweeping and dusting everywhere with large brooms, and inside joiners and decorators were tapping and hammering. Nathanael stood there in the street, beside himself with astonishment; Siegmund came up to him and said: 'Well, what do you think of our old Spalanzani?' Nathanael declared that he did not know what to think, since he knew nothing whatever about the Professor, but was extremely surprised to see such frantic activity going on in the quiet, gloomy house. Siegmund then informed him that Spalanzani was holding a ball and a concert the next day, and that half the university had been invited. It was rumoured abroad that Spalanzani would allow his daughter Olimpia, whom he had fearfully concealed from every human eye for so long, to make her first public appearance.

Nathanael obtained an invitation and went to the Professor's house at the appointed hour, his heart beating violently, as the carriages were rolling up and the lights were gleaming in the splendidly decorated rooms. A large and brilliant company was present. Olimpia made her appearance, sumptuously and tastefully dressed. Her beautifully moulded features and her shapely figure compelled general admiration. The slightly strange curve of her back and the wasp-like slenderness of her waist seemed to be the result of excessive tightlacing. There was something stiff and measured about her gait and posture, which many people found displeasing; it was ascribed to the constraint imposed by such a large company.

The concert began. Olimpia played the piano with great skill and likewise performed a bravura aria in a clear, almost shrill voice, like a glass bell. Nathanael was enraptured; standing in the back row, he was unable to make out Olimpia's features clearly in the dazzling light of the candles. Without anybody noticing, he therefore took out Coppola's spyglass and looked through it at the fair Olimpia. Ah! then he perceived that she was gazing at him yearningly, and that every note she uttered found its full expression in the amorous look that pierced his heart and set it afire. The artificial roulades seemed to Nathanael to be the heavenly jubilation of a heart transfigured by love, and when the cadenza was at last followed by a long trill which rang and resounded through the room, he felt as though red-hot arms had suddenly seized him; unable to restrain himself, he shrieked out in agony and rapture: 'Olimpia!'

Everyone looked round at him, and many people laughed. The cathedral organist, however, scowled yet more darkly than before and said only: 'Now, now!'

The concert was over; the ball began. 'To dance with her, with *her*!' – that was now the goal of all Nathanael's wishes and desires; but how was he to find the courage to ask her, the queen of the ball, for a dance? And yet, he himself could not tell how it came about that when the dance had already begun he found himself standing close to Olimpia, who had not yet been asked for a dance, and, scarcely able to stammer out a few words, he seized her hand. Olimpia's hand was ice-cold: a shudder went through him like a hideous, deadly frost. He stared into Olimpia's eyes, which beamed at him full of love and yearning, and at that moment a pulse seemed to begin beating in her cold hand and her life's blood to flow in a glowing stream. Love and desire flared up in Nathanael's heart; he embraced the fair Olimpia and flew with her though the ranks of the dancers.

Nathanael considered himself a good dancer, but the peculiar rhythmic regularity with which Olimpia danced often disconcerted him and made him realize how badly he kept time. However, he was reluctant to dance with any other woman, and would gladly have murdered everyone who approached Olimpia to ask her to dance. Yet this only happened on two occasions; to his astonishment, Olimpia then remained without a partner, and he did not fail to draw her on to the dance-floor again and again. If Nathanael had been capable of seeing anything other than the fair Olimpia, all manner of quarrels and disputes would have been inevitable; for the young people in various corners of the room were having difficulty in suppressing their laughter, and their tittering was evidently directed at the fair Olimpia, whom they were looking at strangely for some unaccountable reason. Excited by the dance and by generous quantities of wine, Nathanael entirely cast off his usual bashfulness. He sat beside Olimpia, clasping her hand, and spoke of his love in fiery, enthusiastic words which neither he nor Olimpia understood. But perhaps *she* did; for she gazed fixedly into his eyes and sighed repeatedly: 'Oh! oh! oh!' whereupon Nathanael said: 'O you splendid, divine woman! You ray shining from the promised afterlife of love! You profound spirit, reflecting my whole existence!' and much more along the same lines; but Olimpia only signed repeatedly: 'Oh! oh!'

Professor Spalanzani passed the happy couple once or twice and smiled upon them with an air of strange satisfaction. Although Nathanael was in the seventh heaven, he suddenly felt as though down on earth, in Professor Spalanzani's house, darkness were falling; he looked round and noticed, to his consternation, that the last two lights in the empty ballroom had burnt down to their sockets and were about to go out. The music and dancing had long since ceased. 'Parting! Parting!' he cried in frantic despair; he kissed Olimpia's hand, he bent down to her mouth, his burning lips met ice-cold ones! Just as he had done on touching Olimpia's cold hand, he felt himself gripped by inward horror, and the legend of the dead bride[8] suddenly flashed through his mind; but Olimpia was clasping him tightly, and his kiss seemed to bring warmth and life to her lips.

Professor Spalanzani walked slowly through the empty ballroom; his steps sounded hollow, and his figure, surrounded by flickering shadows, had an uncanny, ghostly appearance.

'Do you love me – do you love me, Olimpia? Just this word! Do you love me?' whispered Nathanael, but Olimpia, rising to her feet, only sighed: 'Oh! oh!'

'Yes, you lovely, magnificent light of my life,' said Nathanael, 'you will shine on me, transfiguring my heart for evermore!'

'Oh, oh!' responded Olimpia, moving away. Nathanael followed her. They stood before the Professor.

You have had a remarkably animated conversation with my daughter', said he with a smile. 'Well, my dear Nathanael, if you find pleasure in talking to the silly girl, I shall always welcome your visits.'

Nathanael was walking on air as he took his leave.

Spalanzani's ball was the main topic of conversation in the next few days. Although the Professor had endeavoured to display the utmost magnificence, the wags recounted all manner of oddities and improprieties, and criticism was levelled particularly at the rigid and silent Olimpia. Despite the beauty of her appearance, it was alleged that she was a complete imbecile, and that this was the reason why Spalanzani had kept her concealed for so long. Nathanael heard this with suppressed anger, but he held his peace; 'for', thought he, 'what would be the point of proving to these fellows that it is their own imbecility which prevents them from appreciating the wonderful depths of Olimpia's heart?'

'Do me a favour, old chap,' said Siegmund one day, 'and tell me how a sensible fellow like you could be besotted with that dummy, that wax doll?'

Nathanael was about to fly into a fury, but he controlled himself and replied: 'You tell me, Siegmund, how, with your sharp perceptions and your appreciation of beauty, you could fail to notice Olimpia's heavenly charms? But I thank the fates that, for that reason, I don't have you as a rival; otherwise one of us would have to perish.'

---

[8] An allusion to Goethe's poem *Die Braut von Korinth* ('The Bride of Corinth', 1798), in which a girl returns from the grave to join her lover.

Observing his friend's state of mind, Siegmund backed down and remarked that in love there was no disputing about tastes. 'It's odd, though', he added, 'that many of us share the same opinion of Olimpia. We thought her – don't take this amiss, old chap! – strangely stiff and lacking in animation. Her figure is regular, certainly, and so is her face. She would be beautiful, but that her eyes seem to have no ray of life; they almost seem to lack the power of sight. Her gait is curiously measured, as though her every movement were produced by some mechanism like clockwork. She plays and sings with the disagreeably perfect, soulless timing of a machine, and she dances similarly. Olimpia gave us a very weird feeling; we wanted nothing to do with her; we felt that she was only pretending to be a living being, and that there was something very strange about her.'

Nathanael refrained from giving way to the bitterness that Siegmund's words aroused in him. He mastered his annoyance and only said, in grave tones: 'Olimpia may well inspire a weird feeling in cold prosaic people like you. It is only to the poetic soul that a similarly organized soul reveals itself! I was the only one to arouse her loving gaze, which radiated through my heart and mind; only in Olimpia's love do I recognize myself. People like you may complain because she doesn't engage in trivial chit-chat, like other banal minds. She utters few words, certainly; but these few words are true hieroglyphs, disclosing an inner world filled with love and lofty awareness of the spiritual life led in contemplation of the everlasting Beyond. But you can't appreciate any of this, and I'm wasting my words.'

'God preserve you, my friend,' said Siegmund in very gentle, almost melancholy tones, 'but I feel you're in a bad way. Count on me if anything – no, I'd rather not say any more!' Nathanael suddenly felt that the cold, prosaic Siegmund was truly devoted to him, and when the latter extended his hand, Nathanael shook it very heartily.

Nathanael had entirely forgotten Clara's existence and his former love for her; his mother, Lothar, and everyone else had vanished from his memory; he lived only for Olimpia and spent several hours with her every day, holding forth about his love, the heartfelt rapport between them, and the elective affinities linking their souls, to all of which Olimpia listened with devout attention. From the darkest recesses of his desk Nathanael fetched everything he had ever written. Poems, fantasies, visions, novels, stories, were supplemented daily by all manner of incoherent sonnets, *ballades*, and *canzoni*, which he read to Olimpia for hours on end without ever wearying. But then, he had never had such a perfect listener. She did not sew or knit, she never looked out of the window, she did not feed a cage-bird, she did not play with a lap-dog or a favourite cat, she did not fiddle with scraps of paper or anything else, she never needed to conceal her yawns by a slight artificial cough: in a word, she stared fixedly at her lover for hours on end, without moving a muscle, and her gaze grew ever more ardent and more animated. Only when Nathanael finally rose and kissed her hand, and also her lips, did she say: 'Oh! Oh!' and then: 'Good night, my dear friend!'

'Oh, you wonderful, profound soul,' cried Nathanael, back in his room, 'no one but you, you alone, understands me perfectly.'

He trembled with heartfelt rapture when he considered how the marvellous harmony between his soul and Olimpia's was becoming more manifest by the day; for he felt as though Olimpia had voiced his own thoughts about his works and about his poetic gift in general; indeed, her voice seemed to come from within himself. This must indeed have been the case, for the only words Olimpia ever spoke were those that have just been mentioned. Although Nathanael did have moments of lucidity and common sense, for example just after waking up in the morning, when he recalled how entirely passive and taciturn Olimpia was, he nevertheless said: 'Words? What are words! The look in her heavenly eyes says more than any terrestrial language. Can a child of heaven ever adjust itself to the narrow confines drawn by miserable earthly needs?'

Professor Spalanzani seemed highly delighted at his daughter's relationship with Nathanael; he gave the latter many unmistakable signs of his goodwill, and when Nathanael finally ventured to hint that he might ask for Olimpia's hand in marriage, the Professor smiled broadly and declared that his daughter should have a free choice. Encouraged by these words, his heart burning with desire, Nathanael resolved that on the very next day he would implore Olimpia to tell him in so many words what her lovely eyes had told him long since: that she was willing to be his for evermore. He looked for the ring which his mother had given him on his departure, so that he might present it to Olimpia as a symbol of his devotion and of the newly budding and blossoming life that he owed to her. As he searched, Clara's and Lothar's letters fell into his hands; he tossed them indifferently aside, found the ring, put it in his pocket, and dashed off to find Olimpia.

As soon as he climbed the stairs and approached the landing, he heard an extraordinary hubbub which seemed to be coming from Spalanzani's study. There were sounds of feet stamping, glass tinkling, and blows falling on the door, mingled with curses and imprecations.

'Let go! Let go! Scoundrel! Villain! You staked your whole life? Ha, ha, ha! – that wasn't part of our wager – I made the eyes, I did – I made the clockwork – stupid wretch, you and your clockwork – you confounded brute of a half-witted clockmaker – get out – Satan – stop – you tinker – you devilish creature – stop – get out – let go!'

The voices howling and raving in such confusion were those of Spalanzani and the horrible Coppelius. In rushed Nathanael, gripped by nameless fear. The Professor had seized a female figure by the shoulders, while the Italian Coppola was holding it by the feet, and both were tugging at it for dear life, while quarrelling violently over it. Nathanael started back, filled with deep horror, on recognizing the figure as Olimpia; wild fury flared up in him, and he tried to tear his beloved from the hands of the enraged combatants, but at that moment Coppola turned round with gigantic strength, wrested the figure from the Professor's hands, and struck him such a terrible blow with it that he staggered and fell backwards over the table covered with phials, retorts, bottles, and glass cylinders, all of which were broken to smithereens. Coppola then threw the figure over his shoulder and rushed downstairs with a frightful yell of laughter, so that the figure's feet, which were hanging down in an unsightly way, gave a wooden rattling and rumbling as they knocked against the steps.

Nathanael stood stock still. He had perceived only too clearly that Olimpia's deathly pale wax face had no eyes, just black caverns where eyes should be; she was a lifeless doll. Spalanzani was writhing on the floor; his head, chest, and arms had been cut by broken glass, and blood was gushing out as though from a fountain. But he summoned all his strength and cried:

'After him, after him! Why are you standing there? Coppelius – he's stolen my best automaton – twenty years' work – I staked my life on it – the clockwork – language – walk – all mine – the eyes – he stole your eyes. The cursed scoundrel, the damned villain – after him – fetch Olimpia – here are her eyes!'

Thereupon Nathanael noticed a pair of bloody eyes lying on the floor and staring at him. Spalanzani picked them up with his unscathed hand and threw them at Nathanael, so that they struck him on the chest. Madness seized him with its red-hot claws and entered his heart, tearing his mind to pieces. 'Hey, hey, hey! Fiery circle, fiery circle! Spin, spin, fiery circle! Come on! Spin, wooden dolly, hey, spin, pretty wooden dolly ...' and with these words he flung himself on the Professor and clutched him by the throat. He would have throttled him, but the hubbub had attracted a large number of people who forced their way into the room and pulled the frenzied Nathanael to his feet, thus rescuing the Professor, whose wounds were promptly bandaged. Siegmund, despite his strength, was unable to restrain the lunatic, who kept bellowing in a frightful voice: 'Spin, wooden dolly', and brandishing his fists. At last the united efforts of several people managed to overcome Nathanael by throwing him to the ground and tying him up. His words were swallowed up in a horrible animal-like bellowing. Raving in a hideous frenzy, he was taken to the madhouse.

Before continuing, kind reader, with the story of the unfortunate Nathanael, let me assure you, just in case you should feel any sympathy for the skilful mechanic and automaton-maker Spalanzani, that he made a complete recovery from his wounds. He was, however, obliged to leave the University, since Nathanael's story had created a stir, and public opinion considered it monstrously deceitful to foist a wooden doll instead of a living person upon respectable tea-parties (Olimpia had attended some and made a quite a hit). Legal scholars described it as a subtle fraud which deserved a condign punishment inasmuch as it had been practised upon the public, and so adroitly conducted that nobody (except for the sharpest students) had observed it, although everyone was trying to display sagacity by referring to all kinds of suspicious-looking details. These details, however, threw virtually no light on the matter. For could anyone's suspicions have been aroused by the fact that, according to one elegant *habitué* of tea-parties, Olimpia had defied convention by sneezing more than she yawned? Her sneezing, explained this exquisite gentleman, was the sound of the concealed mechanism winding itself up, for there had been an audible creaking. The professor of poetry and eloquence took a pitch of snuff, snapped his box shut, cleared his throat, and said in solemn tones: 'My most esteemed ladies and gentleman! Don't you see what lies behind all this? The entire matter is an allegory – an extended metaphor! You take my meaning! *Sapienti sat!*[9] But many esteemed gentleman were not so easily reassured: the story of the automaton had made a deep impression on their minds, and a detestable distrust of human figures became prevalent. In order to make quite sure that they were not in love with wooden dolls, several lovers demanded that their beloved should fail to keep time in singing and dancing, and that, when being read aloud to, she should sew, knit, or play with her pug-dog; above all, the beloved was required not merely to listen, but also, from time to time, to speak in a manner that revealed genuine thought and feeling. The bonds

---

[9] 'That is enough for a wise person'.

between some lovers thus became firmer and pleasanter; others quietly dissolved. 'One really can't take the risk', said some. At tea-parties there was an incredible amount of yawning, but no sneezing, in order to avert any suspicion.

As mentioned earlier, Spalanzani was obliged to disappear in order to evade a criminal prosecution for fraudulently introducing an automaton into human society. Coppola had likewise vanished.

Nathanael awoke, as though from a terrible nightmare; he opened his eyes and felt an indescribable sense of bliss permeating his being with mild, heavenly warmth. He was lying in bed in his room in his father's house. Clara was bending over him, and his mother and Lothar were standing nearby.

'At last, at last, oh my darling Nathanael, you've recovered from your dangerous illness, now you're mine again!' said Clara, from the depths of her heart, folding Nathanael in her arms. The latter was so overcome by rapture and sorrow that bright, hot tears gushed from his eyes, and he uttered a deep sigh: 'My own, my own Clara!'

Siegmund, who had faithfully stood by his friend in time of trouble, entered the room. Nathanael held out his hand to him: 'My loyal friend, you did not abandon me.'

All traces of madness had vanished. Nathanael soon regained his health and strength, tended as he was by his mother, his sweetheart, his friends. Good fortune, meanwhile, had entered their house; for a miserly old uncle, from whom nobody had expected anything, had died and left Nathanael's mother not only a substantial fortune but also a small estate in a pleasant spot not far from the town. They all planned to remove thither: Nathanael's mother, Nathanael himself, with his bride-to-be Clara, and Lothar. Nathanael was now more gentle and childlike than ever before, and appreciated the heavenly purity of Clara's glorious soul for the first time. Nobody reminded him of the past, even by the slightest allusion. Only when Siegmund was leaving him did Nathanael say: 'By God, my friend, I was in a bad way, but at the right moment an angel guided me on to the path of light! Ah, it was Clara!' Siegmund prevented him from saying any more, fearing that painful memories might return with excessive clarity.

The four happy people were about to move to the estate. It was midday, and they were walking through the streets of the town. They had done plenty of shopping, and the lofty tower of the town hall was casting its gigantic shadow over the market-place.

'Why!' said Clara, 'let's climb up there one last time, and gaze at the distant mountains!'

No sooner said than done! Nathanael and Clara began the ascent, their mother went home with the maidservant, and Lothar, reluctant to climb the many steps, decided to remain below. Soon afterwards the two lovers were standing arm in arm on the highest gallery of the tower, gazing into the dim forests beyond which the blue mountains rose like a giant city.

'Look at that funny little grey bush, which really seems to be walking towards us,' said Clara.

Nathanael reached mechanically into his side-pocket; he found Coppola's spyglass, he looked sideways – Clara was standing before the glass! A convulsion ran through his every vein, he stared at Clara in deathly pallor, but an instant later rivers of fire were glowing and sparkling in his rolling eyes, and he uttered a horrible bellow, like a tormented animal; then he sprang aloft and cried in a piercing voice, interspersed with hideous laughter: 'Spin, wooden dolly! Spin, wooden dolly' – and with superhuman strength he seized Clara and was about to dash her to the ground below, but Clara clung firmly to the parapet in the desperation born of terror. Lothar heard the madman raving, he heard Clara's shriek of fright, a horrible suspicion shot through his mind, he rushed up the stairs, the door leading to the second flight of stairs was locked. Clara's shrieks grew louder. Beside himself with fury and fear, he hurled himself against the door, which flew open. Clara's cries were growing fainter and fainter: 'Help! Save me! save me!' she moaned, her voice dying away. 'She's dead – the madman has murdered her,' shrieked Lothar. The door leading to the gallery was locked as well. Desperation endowed him with prodigious strength; he pushed the door off its hinges. God in heaven! Clara, in the grip of the frenzied Nathanael, was suspended in the air, over the edge of the gallery – only one hand still clung to its iron railings. With lighting speed Lothar seized his sister, pulled her to safety, and dashed his fist in the madman's face, forcing the latter to reel back and relinquish his intended victim.

Lothar rushed downstairs, his sister unconscious in his arms. She was saved.

Meanwhile Nathanael was raving in the gallery, leaping into the air and shrieking 'Fiery circle, spin! Fiery circle, spin!'

People gathered below, attracted by his wild yells; in their midst loomed the gigantic figure of the advocate Coppelius, who had just arrived in the town and made directly for the market-place. As people began to climb the stairs in order to seize the lunatic, Coppelius laughed and said: 'Ha, ha – just wait, he'll soon come down by himself', and looked up, like the others. Suddenly Nathanael paused and stood stock still; he bent down, perceived Coppelius, and, with a piercing shriek of 'Beautiful eyes-a! Beautiful eyes-a!' he jumped over the parapet.

By the time Nathanael was lying on the pavement, his head shattered, Coppelius had vanished into the throng.

It is reported that several years later, in a distant part of the country, Clara was seen sitting hand in hand with an affectionate husband outside the door of a handsome country dwelling, with two merry boys playing in front of her. This would seem to suggest that Clara succeeded in finding the quiet domestic happiness which suited her cheerful, sunny disposition, and which she could never have enjoyed with the tormented, self-divided Nathanael.

Part 2
Home and abroad in the Victorian age

Aims

The second part of this book will:

- develop your close reading skills by introducing you to prose fiction from a range of genres prevalent during the Victorian period
- compare and contrast the representation of 'home' and 'abroad' in these writings
- discover the importance of readers and reading in the Victorian period.

Introduction to Part 2

Shafquat Towheed

The second part of this book will introduce you to some of the main Victorian ideas about home and abroad through the study of three fictional accounts from the period. Chapters 5 and 6 concentrate on Emily Brontë's haunting domestic novel, *Wuthering Heights* (1847), Chapter 7 focuses on Arthur Conan Doyle's detective story *The Sign of Four* (1890) and, finally, Chapter 8 considers Robert Louis Stevenson's South Pacific tale 'The Beach of Falesá' (1892–3). As you read through these works you will notice how important the idea of home is to them. In Brontë's novel, set on the Yorkshire moors, the narrative is intertwined with the histories of two houses – Thrushcross Grange and Wuthering Heights. In Doyle's *The Sign of Four*, the narrative begins and ends in that most famous (and most fictitious) of London addresses, Holmes's bachelor pad at 221B Baker Street, while the majority of crimes in the story take place inside people's homes. Further developing the idea of home, 'The Beach of Falesá' is about a British trader living abroad rather than at home, who marries and then settles in a tabooed house in the Pacific; it was written by Scotland's most celebrated emigrant writer soon after he himself had set up home in Samoa. All three works were written for a domestic readership, and yet all engage in varying ways with the wider world outside Britain. In order to find out *how* the Victorians understood home and abroad, in this part of the book we will also focus on the Victorians as readers, and examine some of the reading practices prevalent at the time. Reading was not just the most popular domestic pastime of the Victorians; it was also the means by which news about the wider world, often contained in fiction, was brought into their homes. As you will discover, for the Victorians in an age of empire and mass literacy, home and abroad were not always easily separated.

At home with the Victorians

In the works of social commentators such as John Ruskin (1819–1900), poets such as Coventry Patmore (1823–1896) and experts in domestic management such as Isabella Beeton (1836–1865), a safe, comfortable and righteous home became the most important and desirable expression of British Victorian morality and middle-class respectability. In an influential series of lectures given in Manchester, later published in the book *Sesame and Lilies* (1865), Ruskin set out his idea of the proper duties of men and women inside the home. For Ruskin, the role of women was to be homemakers and helpmates to their husbands, who would return from work to be comforted within a loving domestic environment. The 'true nature of home', Ruskin asserted, was as a 'place of Peace; the shelter, not only from all injury, but from all terror, doubt and division' (1865, p. 148). Women should devote themselves to the domestic sphere and make it their sacred duty, he declared, arguing that their social role was inseparable from their sex: 'wherever a true wife comes, this home is always around her' (p. 149). Ruskin equated a well-managed, comfortable house with moral correctness: an orderly home was the best expression of a virtuous society and, by extension, country. The poet Coventry Patmore crystallised Victorian ideas about domesticity in his long, serialised poem *The Angel in the House* (1863), in which he created a potent archetype of Victorian womanhood: pure, chaste, devoted to her husband, and sympathetic. Catering for the growing numbers of women wanting to make their own homes as comfortable as possible, and aspiring to become the 'Angel in the House', Isabella Beeton wrote one of the century's most influential books, *Mrs Beeton's Book of Household Management* (1861). It sold more than 2 million copies in the first decade after publication, and taught generations of women to run their homes efficiently: 'there is no more fruitful source of family discontent than a housewife's badly cooked dinners and untidy ways' (Beeton, 1861, p. iii). Like many Victorians, Ruskin, Patmore and Beeton celebrated the cultivation of the home as morally good, and argued for the central role of women as its custodians. Such an understanding of home was not uncontested, however. As we shall discover, the literature of the age questioned as well as reflected these Victorian domestic values.

An ideal example of a Victorian home is 18 Stafford Terrace in London's Kensington, known today as Linley Sambourne House (see Figure 1). This is a standard four-storey Victorian town house in a solidly respectable area. Edward Linley Sambourne (1844–1910) was a famous Victorian artist, illustrator and caricaturist (he was chief cartoonist for *Punch* magazine). Rooms are distributed throughout the house on different floors so that private and public spaces are kept separate.

You might notice how much bigger and more prosperous this house is compared to William Wordsworth's rural Dove Cottage. A visit to the house reveals that the drawing room, dining room and morning room

Figure 1   Sitting room in Linley Sambourne House, Kensington.
Photographed by Massimo Listri. Photo: © Massimo Listri/CORBIS.

(all public spaces used to entertain visitors) are noticeably more ornate than the bedrooms, and are used to project particular ideas central to a well-ordered, prosperous household. Servants' areas (below stairs, in the basement) are kept as far away from the bedrooms as possible, in order to preserve the privacy of the household. Obsessed with propriety and morality in the home, middle-class Victorians jealously guarded their privacy. Linley Sambourne's rather dubious private passion was nude photography, which he managed to keep a secret from his wife and servants alike.

While the Victorians conceived of home as a refuge from the rigour, uncertainty, anxiety and potential violence of the outside world, it could not be an absolutely secure environment. Despite the strong sense of social and sexual propriety, and heavy penalties for transgressing the rules of accepted behaviour, not everything was as it seemed within the Victorian home, especially in London, where high ideals about the perfect home often clashed with the new realities of urban life: violence, prostitution, drug addiction and rampant crime, to name a few. Often these threats could not be kept out of the family home; as Doyle's detective fiction demonstrates, domestic space could also double as the scene of the crime.

The Victorians and abroad

For all their love of domestic comfort, and their sentimental idealisation of the perfect home, the Victorians lived in a rapidly changing industrial world. The prosperity that paid for middle-class comfort was the result of an expanding and profitable overseas trading empire, with India at its centre. Imperial goods and products were conspicuous in Victorian homes: 'the empire was visible everywhere at home in the 19th century – in high politics and popular culture; in the Houses of Parliament and the homes of middle and working class people; in fiction and on the streets; in economic policy and the popular imagination' (Burton, 2007), while the 'business of the Empire', as the critic Patrick Brantlinger observes, 'seemed to be everyone's business … tea, sugar, spices, cotton, opium, wool, gold, rubber and many other commodities arrived at British ports on a daily basis' (2009, p. 3). The poorest communities in London's East End, such as dock workers and labourers, were often the most dependent on this burgeoning imperial commerce.

The most homely of monarchs, Queen Victoria preferred to spend her time in Osborne House with her numerous children and grandchildren. Despite this, she was publicly proclaimed 'Empress of India' at the Delhi Durbar on 1 January 1877, and she held this title until her death on 22 January 1901. While she took Hindi and Urdu lessons, and increasingly depended on her Indian *munshi* (Hindi and Urdu, 'clerk') Hafiz Abdul Karim (1863–1909) in the last decade of her life, she never set foot on Indian soil. Victoria's domestic life at Osborne House was idealised by her subjects. Images of the royal children tending the vegetable gardens, or of the family taking tea on the terrace, circulated widely in the popular press, and were often imitated by her loyal subjects. Perhaps less well known is that Victoria's final architectural improvement to Osborne House was the addition of a Durbar Room (1890–1) for state functions, complete with an Agra carpet, a model of a Mughal palace, and an Indian painting collection, or the fact that Hafiz Abdul Karim lived in a cottage on the estate until Victoria's death. Even this decidedly stay-at-home monarch was shaped in unexpected ways by her country's long involvement with India.

Figure 2   Queen Victoria at her desk, assisted by her Indian *munshi* ('clerk') Hafiz Abdul Karim, 1896. Photo: © Illustrated London News Ltd/Mary Evans.

The Victorian period was one of imperial expansion abroad and social upheaval at home. Millions left Britain's shores to trade, fight in wars, administer a new empire or settle in other countries. With industrialisation forcing down the cost of labour, many emigrated from economic necessity. While the majority of Britain's emigrants intended to return, many never did and, for them, the gap between their new location and their old emotional home became unbridgeable. Overseas commerce meant that the majority of Britons at home in this period (despite imperial expansion most Britons *did* stay at home) would have had some awareness of the relevance of British imperialism to their lives. Sometimes the effects of abroad upon home were plainly visible, for example through the presence of people from the colonies visiting or residing in Britain. As the world's largest city in the nineteenth century, and capital of the biggest overseas trading empire, London was a cosmopolitan, multiracial city. Freed African slaves, itinerant Indian peddlers, traders and students, Chinese dock workers – all could be seen on London's streets and are described in vivid detail by writers such as Doyle.

Reading about abroad at home

The Victorian age saw a great rise in reading, and Britain became a literate society by the end of the nineteenth century. Many Britons never travelled abroad, but after the Education Act of 1870 almost all could read with some proficiency. While people from the colonies of all ethnic backgrounds were present in ports like London and Liverpool, for most Britons, understanding of abroad was mediated through the printed and written word: by accounts in newspapers, magazines, fiction, essays, memoirs, sermons, and correspondence from friends and family living elsewhere. Newspapers such as the *Illustrated London News* were hugely influential in forming British public opinion about its empire. Newspaper reading was something that all literate people (and many semi-literates and illiterates) could participate in at very little cost. It became a culturally unifying activity, a way of cementing national identity across entrenched class divisions. The literary critic Matthew Rubery comments about this 'glimpse of the Queen's home life' (see Figure 3) that 'Queen Victoria is reading *about* the people but also *as one* of the people ... by participating in the same ritual performed on a daily basis by thousands of constituents across the country' (2009, p. 161).

Figure 3   Queen Victoria with Princess Henry of Battenberg, 1896. Photo: ©
Illustrated London News Ltd/Mary Evans.

Britain's most important imperial possession, India, was often
romanticised for readers at home. The historian Robert Montgomery
Martin (1800–1868), writing in the 1850s, asked what the words 'the
Anglo-Indian Empire' represented in 'the minds of the people of
Britain' and offered his own answer: 'dominion over a far-distant sunny
land, rich in barbaric gold, precious stones, and architectural beauty,

occupying upwards of a million square miles of the most varied, fertile, and interesting portion of this globe' (1858–60, p. 1). The empire was a mirror in which the British saw themselves as they wanted to be seen: powerful, resourceful, enterprising, hard-working, virtuous, Christian, bringers of progress, civilization and emancipation. This vision of the British mission abroad was often at odds with reality, as your reading of *The Sign of Four* and 'The Beach of Falesá' may well show, but the myth of Britain's imperial destiny was a pervasive one. When Arthur Conan Doyle came to write the first of the Holmes and Watson stories, *A Study in Scarlet* (1887), published in the year of Queen Victoria's Golden Jubilee, it would have been difficult for Britons at home not to have been aware of empire abroad, and the possibility of fabulous wealth and social advancement that it offered.

In the chapters that follow, we will be exploring how some of these certainties about home and abroad changed during the Victorian period by following these themes through our chosen texts, and seeing how these ideas were transmitted to their readers. As avid consumers of books, magazines and newspapers, the Victorians read widely and proficiently, obtained reading material from a range of different sources, and read in many different locations, both within and outside the home. All three books illuminate different Victorian reading practices, as well as offering important information about how these books were themselves read by Victorian readers. As will become clear in the chapters that follow, reading was the most important cultural activity for the Victorians and, more than anything else, the act of reading shaped views about home and abroad in this period.

Our focus in this part of the book rests on the view that the activity of reading is an important context for Victorian fiction. It is also based on the assumption that what a literary text 'means' is to a considerable extent a product of its readers' responses to it. It is not just authors, then, who create meaning; readers contribute to that process as well. Readers bring their own experiences, values and expectations to any literary text they encounter; it makes sense, then, that as values and assumptions change, so, too, do responses to works of literature. In the chapters on *Wuthering Heights* we will explore the critical reception of the novel both by Brontë's contemporaries and by more recent literary critics with a view to revealing the changing ways in which a literary text is interpreted over time. Throughout this part of the book our interest in the reader necessitates a comparable interest in genre. This is because particular genres generate particular expectations in readers; so, for example, when we read a tragedy we expect the hero to die at the end. In the chapters that follow, we will examine the ways in which different genres – as well as different forms of publication – of prose fiction create certain expectations in readers which are sometimes fulfilled and sometimes frustrated.

References

Beeton, I. (1861) *Mrs Beeton's Book of Household Management*, London, S.O. Beeton.

Brantlinger, P. (2009) *Victorian Literature and Postcolonial Studies*, Edinburgh, Edinburgh University Press.

Burton, A. (2007) 'The visible empire and the empire at home, 1832–1905', *Empire Online* [online], http://www.empire.amdigital.co.uk. libezproxy.open.ac.uk/essays/ content/Burton.aspx (Accessed 1 March 2010).

Martin, R.M. (1858–60) *The Indian Empire* (vol. 1), London, The London Printing and Publishing Company.

Patmore, C. (1863) *The Angel in the House*, London, Macmillan.

Rubery, M. (2009) *The Novelty of Newspapers: Victorian Fiction after the Invention of the News*, New York, Oxford University Press.

Ruskin, J. (1865) *Sesame and Lilies*, London, Smith, Elder & Co.

Chapter 5
Emily Brontë, *Wuthering Heights*: at home

Delia da Sousa Correa

Aims

This chapter will:

- explore the idea of 'home' in the text, and begin considering the idea of 'abroad'
- guide readers through *Wuthering Heights* and its critical and reception history
- introduce some of the main elements of realism and romance relevant to analysing novels
- explore different facets of the overarching concept of 'the reader'.

Introduction

In this chapter and Chapter 6, the theme of 'home and abroad' will be explored in relation to the 1847 novel *Wuthering Heights* by Emily Brontë (1818–1848). With its domestic settings and provincial location, *Wuthering Heights* is most immediately connected with 'home' and this will be the main focus of the discussion in this chapter. Beginning with examples of some of the first reviews of Brontë's work, this chapter examines the two contrasting homes presented in the novel, their inhabitants and external landscapes. The theme of abroad, as well as the structure and genre of *Wuthering Heights*, will also be examined in preparation for a more detailed discussion of the novel's generic composition in Chapter 6.

'Home and abroad' is, perhaps, not the most obvious context in which to consider *Wuthering Heights*. 'Home'? surely *Wuthering Heights* is, famously, a story of undying elemental passion, of raw untamed human nature set in wild moorland? And 'abroad': what has this to do with *Wuthering Heights*, so intensely focused in its remote rural setting as quite to exclude the rest of the world? Nevertheless I undertake to persuade you that *Wuthering Heights* is indeed a domestic novel, in which more things are abroad than you might initially suppose. Let's begin by considering some of the first reviews of Brontë's work.

You will need to have read the entire novel in advance of working through this chapter and the next. The edition referred to here is the Oxford World's Classics edition, edited by Ian Jack, with an introduction by Helen Small (2009). Many of the activities involve returning to particular passages in the novel and you should give yourself time to reread these carefully, and to refamiliarise yourself with the relevant chapters. The teaching material is structured so as to focus predominantly on the first half of the novel in this chapter and the later part of the novel in Chapter 6, while encouraging you to refer across the full span of the novel where appropriate.

Home at Wuthering Heights

Wuthering Heights begins with accounts by the southerner Lockwood of his first experiences of his new home in the north of England. His initial stance as a man appreciative of isolated and unrefined society is soon diminished by the rough reception accorded him. Lockwood's increasing perplexity and horror were shared by some of the novel's first reviewers who, like other readers of the novel, encountered these scenes while reading *Wuthering Heights* at their own domestic firesides. Their reviews, in turn, were published in periodicals and magazines which, like the novel, were largely read within the home:

> the incidents are too coarse and disagreeable to be attractive, the very best being improbable, with a moral taint about them, and the villainy not leading to results sufficient to justify the elaborate pains in depicting it.
>
> (*The Spectator*, December 1847, quoted in Allott, 1974, p. 217)

This was the assessment of *Wuthering Heights* recorded in one of the earliest reviews. It is often assumed that *Wuthering Heights* was an under-appreciated and misunderstood work at the time of its publication. There was certainly a wide range of responses, some of which were positive: the view quoted above represents only one element of contemporary critical **reception**. Other periodicals, with a different editorial stance from *The Spectator*, perhaps, were more generous in their assessments of the 'rugged power' of the unknown writer Ellis Bell (Emily Brontë's pseudonym). They frequently shared the *Spectator*'s view of the novel as too 'extreme' and marred by detailed and protracted depictions of violence, but praise of the novel's originality and imaginative power often ran alongside criticism of the writer's evident inexperience (Allott, 1974, pp. 230, 217). The reviewer for *Douglas Jerrold's Weekly Newspaper* for 15 January 1848, for example, praised the 'fresh, original and unconventional spirit' which *Wuthering Heights* shared with other works by 'the Bells' (Emily's sisters Charlotte (1816–1855) and Anne (1820–1849) published their first novels under the names of Currer and Acton Bell) and, while feeling that this power might be put to better purpose, saw the author as having the making of 'a great dramatic artist' (Allott, 1974, p. 227).

This discussion of *Wuthering Heights* has begun with some of the early responses to the novel because, in this part of the book, we are interested in looking at literary texts in relation to their readers' responses. Keep in mind some of these responses; we shall be referring back to them as we work through the novel and subsequent critical assessments. It can be tempting to dismiss early responses as narrowly moralistic 'Victorian' reactions to a challenging text – but why should we assume that Brontë's first readers were uniformly less perceptive and intelligent than readers now?

The first reviewers were working within a context where it was common to speak about the healthfulness or otherwise of reading material. John Ruskin, some of whose views are quoted in the Introduction preceding this chapter, constantly discussed reading in terms of a wholesome or unwholesome diet. Thus the consumption of print within the home was linked explicitly to the consumption of food, and unwholesome reading considered as likely to have deleterious effects on its inhabitants as a surfeit of sweetmeats. Notwithstanding the now quaint vocabulary of 'coarseness' and 'moral taint' in the *Spectator* review quoted above, early reviews offer a complex range of insights into Brontë's text and the contexts in which it was read. By the same token, the cultural incentives for how readers have subsequently interpreted *Wuthering Heights*, up to and including our own time, invite careful reflection.

Appropriately, given our own focus on 'home and abroad', the earliest reviewers of the novel tended to discuss the 'home' setting of *Wuthering Heights* more than the landscapes it evoked (or anything yet further 'abroad'). A review for the *Athenaeum* in December 1847, probably by the critic Henry Chorley, describes the home at Wuthering Heights as 'a prison which might be pictured from life ... let us hope [the author] will spare us further interiors so gloomy as the one here elaborated with such dismal minuteness' (quoted in Allott, 1974, pp. 218–19).

Activity 1

To remind yourself of the setting the reviewer has in mind, read the paragraph giving Lockwood's account of the part of the interior known as 'the house' at Wuthering Heights in the first chapter of the novel, beginning 'One step brought us into the family sitting-room ...', on p. 2, and ending '... and other dogs haunted other recesses', on p. 3. Is this the 'prison ... elaborated with such dismal minuteness' that the reviewer recalls?

Discussion

Minuteness of description there certainly is, although Lockwood's first impressions are of heat and light reflecting 'splendidly from ranks of immense pewter dishes, interspersed with silver jugs and tankards, towering row after row, in a vast oak dresser' (p. 2). These bright, un-dismal objects suggest a life of prosperity and plenty, confirmed by the 'frame of wood laden with oatcakes, and clusters of legs of beef, mutton and ham' (p. 3) hanging from the roof. Given subsequent events in the novel, the 'villainous old guns' (p. 3) hanging above the chimney and the dog lurking beneath the dresser, could be ominous, but the impression upon Lockwood is one of rustic decency; his eye is drawn to the tea canisters on the mantelpiece (tea being a relatively expensive commodity in 1801, at the time of the novel's setting, and an implicit sign, too, of connections between the domestic world of the novel and the world of imperial trade 'abroad'). The homely details that Lockwood notes include the 'smooth, white stone' (p. 3) of the floor, which suggests a clean, well-kept abode. Wuthering Heights clearly has the appearance of a well-ordered home; arguably it *is* a well-ordered home within which is revealed the full domestic chaos of a disordered family. When we read on, we find that in the next paragraph Lockwood reflects that '[t]he apartment and furniture would have been nothing extraordinary as belonging to a homely, northern farmer … But Mr. Heathcliff forms a singular contrast to his abode and style of living' (p. 3). Indeed the reviewer noted that the gloomy and prison-like atmosphere of Wuthering Heights was largely determined by the pervasive presence of 'the brutal master of the lonely house' (Allott, 1974, p. 218).

Activity 2

Finish rereading the first chapter now, and then continue rereading up to the middle of Volume I, Chapter III (as far as '… still it wailed, "Let me in!" and maintained its tenacious gripe, almost maddening me with fear' at the top of p. 21).

How are Lockwood's and the reader's expectations of 'home' played upon in these chapters?

Discussion

On Lockwood's next visit, he is pleased to find himself, after his frozen walk, once again 'in the large, warm, cheerful' sitting room at Wuthering Heights, which 'glowed delightfully in the radiance of an immense fire, compounded of coal, peat, and wood' with 'the table, laid for a plentiful evening meal' (p. 7). As previously, there is an extreme – and comic – discrepancy between the expectations inspired by this interior and his rude reception by its inhabitants and the most unconventional tea party that follows. The exchange between Lockwood and Catherine as he attempts to help her reach a tea canister during the preparations for this is worthy of *Alice in Wonderland*: '"I don't want your help," she snapped, "I can get them for myself." … "Were you asked to tea?" she demanded' (p. 8). The comedy plays over several pages where Lockwood's social platitudes come up against Catherine's overt hostility, Hareton's boorishness and Heathcliff's increasing savagery. By the time Lockwood finds himself pinned down by Heathcliff's dogs in the snow outside, comedy has transmuted into something more brutal (pp. 13–14); this physical onslaught at the conclusion of Chapter II is followed in Chapter III by Lockwood's introduction to the more truly gloomy part of the Wuthering Heights' interior where he spends the night. It is also followed by his own physical cruelty to the waif-like would-be-inhabitant of the house 'looking through the window', whose grasp he escapes only by rubbing 'its wrist' across 'the broken pane' (p. 21).

The 'extreme' events in the novel were among the features that led critics to describe *Wuthering Heights* as the setting of a 'drama': 'a rude old-fashioned house, at the top of one of the high moors or fells in the north of England' becomes the central stage-set; 'the whole drama takes place in the house' writes the reviewer for *The Examiner* in January 1848 (quoted in Allott, 1974, pp. 220–1). For this reviewer and others, the force of the drama taking place in that 'rude' (that is, rough and rustic) setting was apparently such as to erase any recollection of the moors themselves, or of the novel's other domestic location, Thrushcross Grange.

Outside the home

While the *Athenaeum* reviewer's attention was focused on the interior of the house, a few of the early reviews dwelt on the joint significance of Wuthering Heights as both a wild, abandoned landscape and a house, noting connections between events taking place inside and the exterior weather and landscape. Echoing Lockwood's definition of the term 'wuthering' (p. 2), the reviewer in the *New Monthly Magazine* for January 1848 notes that 'Wuthering Heights' is expressive 'in provincial phraseology' of 'the frequency of atmospheric tumults out of doors', tumults which are far 'surpassed in frequency and violence by the disturbances that occur in doors' (quoted in Allott, 1974, p. 229).

Activity 3

Look back to the opening of the novel where you will find Lockwood's description of the exterior setting for the house at Wuthering Heights, particularly the paragraph beginning 'Wuthering Heights is the name of Mr. Heathcliff's dwelling ...' in the first chapter (p. 2). What does Lockwood's account of the exterior of the house and the first sighting of its inhabitants lead us to anticipate?

Discussion

As one might expect, given Lockwood's definition of 'wuthering' as 'descriptive of the atmospheric tumult to which [the house's] station is exposed in stormy weather' (p. 2), the effects of the north wind are paramount in this paragraph. Our introduction to 'sinewy' old Joseph and his savage master has already prepared us to find a connection between the inhabitants of the Heights and 'the excessive slant of a few, stunted firs at the end of the house'; and the 'range of gaunt thorns all stretching their limbs one way, as if craving alms of the sun' (p. 2). On Lockwood's second visit, as the snowstorm sets in, the 'bleak hill top ... hard with a black frost' and the locked gate over which he has to climb before 'running up the flagged causeway bordered with straggling gooseberry bushes' and knocking 'vainly for admittance' (p. 6) on the farmhouse door, is very obviously a reminder of the chilly reception he previously enjoyed and a premonition of turbulence to come.

Readers of its initial chapters are left in no doubt as to the significance of the natural setting of *Wuthering Heights*. This wild external landscape has a pervasive presence in the text. However, its significance for readers nowadays tends to be overlaid by the moorland settings that dominate film adaptations. Nelly Dean subsequently tells us that Catherine and Heathcliff loved to 'run away to the moors' as children (p. 40), but there are, in fact, very few scenes in the novel featuring Catherine and Heathcliff on the moors. The now instantly recognisable image of them perched above moorland wilderness dates from the 1939 film adaptation of the novel starring Merle Oberon and Laurence Olivier; a famous advertising still, familiar to many readers who have not seen the film, shows them sitting on a rocky outcrop gazing romantically into the distance (Figure 5.1).

Figure 5.1   Film still of *Wuthering Heights*, dir. William Wyler (United Artists, 1939). Photo: © UNITED ARTISTS/Album/akg-images.

In the novel itself, exterior landscapes tend to be symbolic of events in the story rather than the immediate location for its action. The modernist writer Virginia Woolf (1882–1941) noticed how the landscapes in the Brontës' novels, their 'storms, moors, lovely spaces of summer weather … carry the emotion and light up the meaning' of their books (1994 [1925], p. 168). The landscapes in *Wuthering Heights* certainly work in this way on the reader – as a spatial expression of the themes and emotions portrayed – regardless of the fact that most of the atmospheric tumult after the opening storm takes place indoors, as the reviewer in the *New Monthly Magazine* quoted earlier observed. Charlotte Brontë emphasised a view of her sister's creativity as inherently attuned to her natural environment. In her preface to the 1850 edition of *Wuthering Heights*, published after Emily's death (reprinted in Appendix 1, pp. 307–12, of the World's Classics edition), Emily is a 'nursling of the moors' (p. 307) – much as the Romantic poet William Wordsworth portrayed his imagination as nurtured by his native Lakeland landscape. In Charlotte's view, *Wuthering Heights* is a work hewn from the moorland crag, 'terrible and goblin-like', yet planted about with 'blooming bells and balmy fragrance' (p. 310).

It is hardly surprising that a director would realise this aspect of the novel in the medium of film by resituating some of the drama outdoors.

However, Wuthering Heights is not the only house, nor the only natural setting which the novel portrays, and Woolf's 'lovely spaces of summer weather' are there aplenty as well as stormy turbulence.

Home at Thrushcross Grange

There are two houses in *Wuthering Heights*. The central importance of the house at the Heights has tended to dominate the reading experience – or at least memories – of Brontë's commentators. However, after her death, a cutting was found in her desk of a perceptive, still anonymous review, of 1847 or January 1848, which identifies the contrast between the two houses as fundamental to the novel: 'An antiquated farm-house, a neighbouring residence of somewhat more pretending description with their respective inmates', these 'constitute the materials … of one of the most interesting stories we have read for many a long day' (Allott, 1974, pp. 243–4).

Activity 4

Read the first description in the novel of Thrushcross Grange as observed by Catherine and Heathcliff in Volume I, Chapter VI. This is the paragraph beginning '"Don't you cant, Nelly," he said', on p. 41, and ending '… painting the house-front with Hindley's blood!', on p. 42. What are the immediate contrasts with Wuthering Heights?

Discussion

This first description of the Grange is Heathcliff's narration retold by Nelly. He and Catherine have run all the way 'from the top of the Heights … and planted' themselves 'under the drawing-room window' (p. 41). We get an account at this stage only of the interior of this house, intensifying the contrast between the wild, exuberant race – in Catherine's case barefoot – and the glories and constraints of its domestic space. Heathcliff's account begins with the obvious contrast with the miseries of the house at Wuthering Heights, where he and Catherine spend their Sunday evenings 'standing shivering in corners' (p. 41) while Hindley and his wife sit 'eating and drinking, and singing and laughing, and burning their eyes out before the fire' (p. 41):

> ah! it was beautiful – a splendid place carpeted with crimson, and crimson-covered chairs and tables, and a pure white ceiling bordered by gold, a shower of glass-drops hanging in silver chains from the centre, and shimmering with little soft

tapers. Old Mr. and Mrs. Linton were not there. Edgar and his sister had it entirely to themselves; shouldn't they have been happy? We should have thought ourselves in heaven!

(pp. 41–2)

'Heaven' is how Heathcliff describes it. His comment conveys his child's-eye view of the gilded and brightly lit interior. But if contemporary readers were inclined to view the Grange in terms of some of the ideals of home quoted in Shafquat Towheed's 'Introduction to Part 2', this was likely to be unsettled by the fact that the inhabitants of the Grange seem only marginally less badly behaved than those of Wuthering Heights. Having observed Edgar and Isabella shrieking and squabbling, Heathcliff himself would not swap their heaven for even the hell of his oppression by Hindley Earnshaw. Readers might reasonably wonder whether the inhabitants of this home are really more civilised than those at Wuthering Heights, since competition is clearly rife in both households and both employ brutal animalistic means to protect their interests, whether directly or indirectly: the Lintons' dogs savage Catherine just as Heathcliff's later fell Lockwood. However, the contrasts with the life at the Heights are clear. Such contrasts are fundamental to the opposing thematic and metaphorical patterns, the careful balance of locations (and characters), that help to structure the novel, even if some of these oppositions break down on closer inspection.

We know that Thrushcross Grange enjoys a lower, less exposed situation, but having rushed straight from the top of the Heights to the drawing room, we have to wait some time, until after the marriage of Catherine to Edgar Linton, before we get much detail as to its exterior and setting. Although Heathcliff and Catherine first view the house as excluded outsiders, the focus of attention on its interior means that the reader seems to learn about this house from indoors, rather than being introduced, as we are by Lockwood's narrative, to Wuthering Heights from its exterior to its internal spaces.

Activity 5

If you now turn to Volume I, Chapter X, you will find a brief account by Nelly of the situation of the Grange. Read Nelly's account from 'On a mellow evening in September …', on p. 81, to '– it rather dips down on the other side', on p. 83. Pay particular attention to this final paragraph, noting again the contrasts with Wuthering Heights.

Discussion

Nelly's account here includes one of many **lyrical** descriptions of the seasons, weather and landscape that appear throughout the novel. It is 'a mellow evening in September' (p. 81) and she is returning from the orchard at dusk with a basket of apples, having enjoyed breathing 'the soft, sweet air' (p. 82). Although Nelly's description is of the exterior landscape and the contrasting situations of Wuthering Heights and the Grange, the house is simultaneously imagined as viewed by Catherine and Edgar. They sit indoors, at an unlatticed window through which is

> displayed, beyond the garden trees and the wild green park, the valley of Gimmerton, with a long line of mist winding nearly to its top … Wuthering Heights rose above this silvery vapour; but our old house was invisible.
>
> (p. 83)

This viewpoint from the Grange is, perhaps, paralleled by the way in which readers at home viewed the world of the novel from the comfort of their own domestic interiors.

Nelly's account combines precise topographical features of the Grange's valley setting – '(for very soon after you pass the chapel, as you may have noticed, the sough that runs from the marshes joins a beck which follows the bend of the glen)' (p. 83) – with a poetic evocation of its green softness, wrapped in a protective silver mist above which Wuthering Heights stands exposed. This lyricism takes some of its poignancy from the fact that Nelly is the messenger of a paradise already disturbed by a revenant from Wuthering Heights. Just previously, a **Gothic** moment has intruded, as moonlight causes 'undefined shadows to lurk' (p. 81) in the porch from which Heathcliff's voice, both 'foreign' and 'familiar', suddenly issues (p. 82).

'Mysterious inhabitants'

The unidentified review from which I quoted earlier contrasts 'the comfortable cheerfulness of one abode, and the cheerless discomfort of the other'; however, it regards the atmosphere of Wuthering Heights as 'less the result of a cold and bleak situation ... than of the strange and mysterious character of its inhabitants' (quoted in Allott, 1974, pp. 243–4).

Activity 6

How, from your reading of the novel's opening chapters, do these inhabitants appear 'strange and mysterious'? Take a few moments to reflect on this and jot down your thoughts.

Discussion

Lockwood's narrative, as I have already mentioned, shows him as entirely disconcerted by the inhabitants of the house – a feeling shared by many readers confronted by such wild behaviour while reading in the apparent safety of their own homes. Lockwood cannot understand the behaviour of the Wuthering Heights family, or even work out what their relationships are one to the other. They are strange and mysterious enough in themselves, even before the addition of the terrifying apparition at his window. Strangest of all is Heathcliff. His origins remain unexplained, as does the source of the wealth and education he acquires when he temporarily disappears. He has a powerful effect on everybody else, and, apart from Catherine and her father, who feel affection towards him, the main emotion he inspires is fear.

Heathcliff's character preoccupied commentators on the novel for a good century after its publication, and I would like you at this point to note some of the language Brontë uses to describe him.

Activity 7

Reread the descriptions of Heathcliff's appearance, speech and behaviour in the first chapter of the novel (pp. 1–3). Make a note of the terms in which he is described.

Discussion

After the initial few pages where Lockwood has informed the reader only of the extreme terseness of Mr Heathcliff's welcome to his new tenant, he provides his first physical description of him:

> He is a dark-skinned gypsy in aspect, in dress and manners a gentleman – that is, as much a gentleman as many a country squire ... he has an erect and handsome figure – and rather

> morose – possibly some people might suspect him of a degree of under-bred pride.
>
> (p. 3)

Within the ordinary domestic setting that Lockwood has just detailed, Heathcliff's strangeness stands out, despite a degree of familiarity as to his 'dress and manners'. Lockwood has just described the figure that we might normally expect to find seated in the comfortable kitchen at Wuthering Heights, 'a homely, northern farmer, with a stubborn countenance, and stalwart limbs set out to advantage in knee-breeches and gaiters' (p. 3). Heathcliff, by contrast, with his 'gypsy'-like appearance, suggests a mysterious wealth of possible origins which, for Lockwood, would contradict a gentlemanly status.

Dark, gypsy-like Heathcliff is a foreign thing: his origin a mystery in a novel where genealogy is vital, as is signalled by the name 'Hareton Earnshaw', which has stood above the doorway to Wuthering Heights since 1500. The centrality of genealogy is reinforced by the incessant repetition and interchange of first names as well as family names: Hareton, Catherine, Linton. The elder Catherine inscribes her book with her various possible names: '*Catherine Earnshaw*', '*Catherine Heathcliff*', '*Catherine Linton*' (p. 15). Heathcliff owns but one name. 'Catherine Earnshaw' becomes 'Linton' but never 'Heathcliff', thus her passionate declaration that 'I *am* Heathcliff' (p. 73) is in defiance of the genealogy that triumphs within the novel's plot. Despite his marriage to Isabella Linton and the younger Catherine's to his son, Heathcliff is never properly knitted into the genealogical pattern. The novel's ending cements the union between the Lintons and the Earnshaws and Heathcliff's role has been predominantly as an external catalyst for relationships, both harmonious and conflicted, between others.

However, while foreign in numerous ways in this novel, in other respects Heathcliff is at home in literature – a recognisable descendant of figures that inhabit previous prose fiction and poetry. His 'erect and handsome figure', and even the fact that Heathcliff is 'morose' (p. 3), suggest that he might share the characteristics of a hero, or indeed villain, from a genre which is in contrast to the polite domestic novel of manners that Lockwood seems designed for, but would have been well known to Brontë's readers.

The 1848 reviewer of *Wuthering Heights* for *The Examiner* compared Heathcliff with the hero of *The Corsair* (1814) by the Romantic poet Lord Byron (1788–1824): 'Like the Corsair, and other such melodramatic heroes, he is "Linked to one virtue and a thousand crimes"' (quoted in Allott, 1974, p. 220). Heathcliff shares the foreignness that is highlighted in *The Corsair* (which is presented as a text taken 'from the Turkish'). The following lines from Byron's poem also contain parallels with Heathcliff's dark, obsessive mentality, his strange mixture of attractive and repulsive qualities, and his capacity to inspire fear and wreak devastation on his enemies:

> His features' deepening lines and varying hue
> At times attracted, yet perplexed the view,
> As if within that murkiness of mind
> Worked feelings fearful, and yet undefined.
>
> …
>
> There was a laughing Devil in his sneer,
> That raised emotions both of rage and fear;
> And where his frown of hatred darkly fell,
> Hope withering fled – and Mercy sighed farewell!
>
> (Byron, 1981 [1814], canto I, 9, 209–12, 223–6)

Like Heathcliff, the Corsair sets himself outside social and moral boundaries:

> He knew himself a villain – but he deemed
> The rest no better than the thing he seemed;
>
> …
>
> He knew himself detested, but he knew
> The hearts that loathed him, crouched and dreaded too.
> Lone, wild, and strange, he stood alike exempt
> From all affection and from all contempt …
>
> (Byron, 1981 [1814], canto I, 11, 265–6, 269–72)

Heathcliff might also be compared to the protagonist of Byron's verse drama *Manfred* (1816–19) who, dark, proud, tormented by secret sin and the death of his sister Astarte, defies accepted religious forms of redemption even at the point of death.

In *Wuthering Heights*, Heathcliff is portrayed as proud, courageous, brooding, defiant of laws and conventions, given to violent utterance and action, with flashing 'basilisk eyes' (pp. 158, 160). Such qualities typical of Byron's heroes also figure prominently in the hero-villains of popular Gothic romances. Malcolm, the murderous villain of *The Castles of Athlin and Dunbayne* (1789), for example, the first work of the Gothic novelist Ann Radcliffe (1764–1823), is 'proud, oppressive, revengeful' (Radcliffe, 1994 [1789], p. 1). Further characterisation is scarcely needed, the type being well established in this genre. As the title suggests, *The Castles of Athlin and Dunbayne* involves two warring households. Set in a remote northern location, the 'bleak winds' that howl 'mournfully' around its towers and the 'dreary prospect of the barren Highlands' beyond are predecessors of the blasted moorland setting of *Wuthering Heights* (Radcliffe, 1994 [1789], p. 11). Malcolm, like any number of Gothic villains, is bent on revenge, physically courageous and possessed of a 'wild and terrific' countenance; a character in whom potential virtue has been replaced by viciousness of action: like Heathcliff, he has usurped the property rights of the hereditary owners of his house (Radcliffe, 1994 [1789], pp. 72–5).

Thus, while in some respects Heathcliff is mysterious, in others he can be identified with character types familiar to Victorian readers, and from whom extreme behaviour was to be expected. In fact, it was the pervasiveness of emotional and physical violence, rather than Heathcliff's character alone, that seemed most to have disturbed early readers of the novel. '*Wuthering Heights* would have been better romance if Heathcliff alone had been a being of stormy passions, instead of all the other characters being nearly as violent and destructive as himself' remarked the *Britannia*'s reviewer in January 1848 (quoted in Allott, 1974, p. 224). Heathcliff as a recognisable Byronic or Gothic hero-villain might be manageable – but far more unsettling for this reviewer was the way in which the novel represented all the occupants of his house in their 'wild state' (quoted in Allott, 1974, p. 223). The heroines of Gothic novels are demure, accomplished, passive and so exceptionally modest as never to betray their passions except by downcast looks, blushes and the occasional overheard lyric as they console themselves at their lutes. Nothing could be further from the behaviour of the young women in *Wuthering Heights*, a work that, as the *American Review* for June 1848 saw it, immodestly 'lifts the veil and shows boldly the dark side of our depraved nature' (quoted in Allott, 1974, p. 240).

The structure of *Wuthering Heights*

Things were going on in the family at Wuthering Heights that were at odds with the domestic ideals outlined in the Introduction to Part 2 and which also contributed to the way in which the novel puts pressure on familiar literary classifications. The novel's treatment of familiar genres increases the sense of uncanny disturbance that is produced in the reader by the strange–familiar events it depicts, and this recurs throughout the novel's generic make-up. A sense of disturbed familiarity is also produced by the way in which the novel is structured. This section considers the structure of *Wuthering Heights* in relation to the idea of 'home', the narrators and narrative frames through which the novel's story is told, the patterns of repetition and variation between events and characters, and the novel's carefully presented chronology.

Home and structure

The very idea of 'home' and the house at Wuthering Heights can provide a reference-point for the formal composition of this novel. Critics have often discussed the novel form in general by analogy with the rooms of a house through which the reader progresses. The novelist Henry James (1843–1916) famously conceived of 'the house of fiction' in order to represent the formal structures that writers build to frame their characters, a house whose many windows represent the multitudinous perspectives the novelist can evoke (James, 1995 [1881], preface, p. 8). Following these chapters on *Wuthering Heights* you will be introduced to related ideas as they appear in the work of James's contemporary, Robert Louis Stevenson (1850–1894).

For readers of *Wuthering Heights*, their progression through its domestic spaces feels anything but orderly or decorous. However, the novel itself is, on examination, structured along highly organised lines with a clearly indicated span of dates both for Lockwood's narrative and for the events that Nelly Dean narrates. In addition, there is a constant symmetrical patterning of contrast and repetition between characters. Characters are related not just through naming and genealogy, but through their similar-yet-different experiences. Catherine's daughter goes to Wuthering Heights, echoing her mother's move to the Grange, Hareton's deprivations repeat those inflicted on Heathcliff, Catherine feels trapped at the Grange, and Isabella and the second Catherine are both incarcerated at Wuthering Heights. These are but a few examples and you could add more; they all contribute to a sense of a tightly organised literary structure. Nevertheless, the relentless patterns of repetition-with-variation are also disconcerting, constantly inviting and frustrating interpretation. Moreover, demands are placed on the reader by the complex set of narrative frames through which Brontë tells her story.

Narrators and narrative frames

In the memory of its readers, *Wuthering Heights* tends to survive as a direct and unmediated expression of passionate emotion and dramatic incident. However, for the reader embarking on the text, its events are mediated by the narrative structure that Brontë employs. In this section you will have the opportunity to think through how Brontë structures the story of *Wuthering Heights* and the impact this has on you as a reader.

Activity 8

You have already had an opportunity to refamiliarise yourself with the initial chapters of the novel. There are two main narrators in *Wuthering Heights*, both of whom have a role in shaping our experience of the text. Lockwood, the tenant at the Grange, introduces the novel. His narrative forms an outer frame for the whole, reporting the central narrative as related by Nelly from Volume I, Chapter IV onwards. How would you characterise Lockwood as a narrator?

Discussion

Lockwood, a cultivated southerner relating his first encounters with the inhabitants of his new northern home, is the initial filter for our own disorientating introduction to Wuthering Heights. The people whom Lockwood encounters are (to his perspective) foreign as to their mode of living, manners and speech, which in Joseph's case is a Yorkshire dialect impenetrable to outsiders. Joseph's language remains a challenge for most readers today, his constant references to the Bible, with which, in general, we are less familiar than Brontë's readership, adding to the difficulties of decoding his Yorkshire dialect. We could, perhaps, consider the sense of estrangement that this produces as a useful parallel with the unfamiliarity of so much in the novel to its readers and the frame-narrator. Lockwood, clearly, is not at home at Wuthering Heights, and in this he is representative of the geographical and class location of the majority of the novel's readership. Externally, *Wuthering Heights* was a three-volume novel like any other that

Victorians were accustomed to read in the comfort of their homes. Within its covers, however, they encountered a confusing disregard of social and literary codes.

This is something that Charlotte Brontë identifies in her 1850 preface to the novel, where she stresses the 'alien and unfamiliar' nature of the inhabitants, customs and landscape of Yorkshire to those 'unacquainted with the locality where the scenes of the story are laid' (p. 307). For such readers the 'wild moors of the north of England can ... have no interest; the language, the manners, the very dwellings and household customs of the scattered inhabitants of those districts, must be ... in great measure unintelligible, and – where intelligible – repulsive' (p. 307). These readers 'will hardly know what to make of the rough, strong utterance, the harshly manifested passions, the unbridled aversions, and headlong partialities' of people 'who have grown up untaught and unchecked, except by mentors as harsh as themselves' (p. 307). Haworth, a small, busy industrial town, in fact had a thriving cultural life. Charlotte Brontë is exaggerating somewhat here, or, rather, producing a view of Yorkshire society that coheres with stereotypes available to the novel's mainly southern, middle-class readership, stereotypes largely confirmed by the lives her sister portrayed.

In Lockwood (and, perhaps, by implication, in Charlotte, too), we find a representative of ourselves as readers who is also an example of how not to read (Hillis Miller, 1982, p. 58). His initial bewilderment is understandable, but his foppish limitations rapidly make him the subject of satire rather than sympathy, and the central narrative is carried forward instead by his housekeeper, Nelly Dean, who takes the story back twenty years. Brontë's introduction to her novel via Lockwood's encounter with Heathcliff and the second-generation characters has plunged us straight into a bewildering conjunction of everyday domesticity with ghosts and strange emotional excess. This prepares us for the more traumatic events that will take place in Nelly Dean's narrative after she has provided an account of Catherine and Heathcliff's childhood years.

'For a specimen of true benevolence and homely fidelity, look at the character of Nelly Dean', comments Charlotte Brontë in her 1850 preface (p. 309). Many others have seen Nelly as a wholesome and nurturing presence. She *is* at home at Wuthering Heights, and later also at the Grange. She can move readily between these two worlds and, as is fairly universally the case with servants, knows much more about her masters than they – or we, for that matter – can ever know of her. Yet she, naturally, has her own opinions of the tale she tells, and readers who look askance at Lockwood's inadequacies might also be prudent not to depend too securely on her as their guide through this house of fiction. Like so many first-person narrators, she is less than entirely reliable.

Nelly's sympathies are certainly not to be identified with the novel's romantic protagonists, Catherine and Heathcliff. She tells Lockwood that she was always predisposed to take Linton's side in any dispute, and does not readily accept Catherine's account of the severity of her collapse following the physical conflict between Heathcliff and Linton (pp. 104–5). Critics have often read Nelly as the voice of convention and narrow-minded prejudice. However, to some extent she speaks on behalf of our own scepticism as readers as we consider how to interpret Catherine and Heathcliff's exorbitant declarations of romantic union and Heathcliff's repellent behaviour. There is an improbable romanticism in Catherine's declarations that she will die, as Nelly suggests (pp. 106–5). But die she does, and the reader can hardly trust the reliability of Nelly's account, let alone her 'true benevolence and homely fidelity'. Nelly represents the domestic, 'home', but home in *Wuthering Heights* is something other than merely benevolent, as readers know.

Moreover, by the time we have completed the fourth chapter, we have heard the voices of multiple narrators, and might hesitate to depend upon any one of them.

Activity 9

Return now to the third and fourth chapters of *Wuthering Heights* and remind yourself of how the narratives are brought together (pp. 15–34). How many narrators are you aware of in these chapters?

Discussion

Indisputably, there are two chief narrators of the novel. But before we even begin on Nelly's story, another voice has intervened when, in Chapter III, Lockwood reads Catherine's diaries in the form of her annotations in the books in the chamber where he spends the night (p. 18). We gain the impression, albeit framed by Lockwood's reported reading of her account, of Catherine's as yet mysteriously disembodied voice in direct communication with us. Lockwood's reading of her diary provokes the apparition of the waif-like child Catherine trying to get back into the house. In the reader this raises expectations that she will find a way in as the teller of her own tale. However, for the rest of the novel, Catherine's voice is heard only in Nelly's reported dialogue, although we tend to forget this under the spell of her most compelling speeches.

Catherine's diaries give us (and Lockwood) some of the backstory needed to make sense of the novel's present. Elsewhere in the novel, events are briefly related in other voices, such as via Isabella's letter in Volume I, Chapter XIII. Here, the novel calls to mind the form of earlier **epistolary novels** (novels told in the form of letters). In particular, its narrative structure is reminiscent of Mary Shelley's *Frankenstein or, The Modern Prometheus* (1818), narrated by a frame-narrator, to whom Frankenstein relates his history. This narrator thus becomes the 'editor' of Frankenstein's tale, much as Lockwood does of Nelly's (and indeed Charlotte, posthumously, of Emily's). Similarities of narrative structure are underpinned by the ways in which the snowstorm at the beginning of *Wuthering Heights* echoes the frozen wastes on which Frankenstein is discovered. Brontë's novel shares a number of thematic affinities with *Frankenstein*; these will be touched on in the next chapter.

The multiple narrative viewpoints in *Wuthering Heights* mean that readers tend to experience a lack of authoritative stance – about the events and, most notably, the violence depicted in the novel. What are we to make of Isabella's account (reported by Nelly) of Hindley's drunken attempt on Heathcliff's life, of the savage physical injuries that Heathcliff inflicts in retaliation, or her apparently casual mention of Hareton hanging a litter of puppies from a chair as she passes him when making good her escape from the Heights (pp. 155–61)? We are given only Isabella's account without authorial comment: 'The burden of interpretation lies firmly with the reader' (Fegan, 2008, p. 35). Perhaps this sense of narrative uncertainty explains why the novel has frequently been considered confused, despite its highly symmetrical structure and chronological scheme.

Chronology

With Lockwood's initial narrative dated 1801 and his closing section 1802, the time span of the novel is explicitly defined. Within this frame, the events narrated retrospectively by Nelly cover a much longer period, the first twenty years of which is occupied by the story of Catherine and Heathcliff. The second half of the novel is given to the second-generation plot, although this tends to occupy a shorter space in the memories of readers (and is entirely erased from most film versions). The more exciting events portrayed in the first-generation story are one reason for this disparity, as is the way in which this half of the novel seems to have a formal coherence independent of the remaining narrative. Indeed, as Helen Small explains in her introduction to the World's Classics edition, *Wuthering Heights* was possibly composed initially as a single-volume novella and later expanded to fit the three-volume format conventional for novels at the time (p. xvi). However, whether originally envisaged as a full-length novel or not, *Wuthering Heights* in the form we have it has a highly organised coherence. Alongside its tight chronological organisation, the opposing locations and voices in the novel help to structure the narrative, as do the genealogical ties that are of such thematic importance to the story.

The formal unity of *Wuthering Heights* has long been admired by critics. Terry Eagleton described it as offering 'a unified vision of brilliant clarity' (1988 [1975], pp. 97–8). Yet readers are often confused with good reason and are surprised to realise that this is not the result of a lack of formal organisation, but *despite* the novel's structural coherence. Eagleton draws attention to the decentring effects created as much by the different narrative voices in this 'elusive, enigmatic text' as by the bizarre events it narrates:

> With its 'Chinese boxes' effect of narratives within narratives, its constant regressions of perspectives and instabilities of viewpoint, it is a strangely 'decentred' fiction which subverts the dominance of the conventional authorial 'voice' as markedly as aspects of its subject-matter threaten to undermine the received forms of bourgeois society.
>
> (Eagleton, 1988 [1975], pp. xviii–xix)

Brontë's incorporation of the features of a variety of literary genres into her novel also contributes to the oppositional formal unity of the work, while simultaneously having decidedly disorientating effects on the reader. The next section examines the contrasting realist and romance modes of fiction at work within *Wuthering Heights*.

Romance and realism

'*Wuthering Heights* would have been better *romance* if Heathcliff alone had been a being of stormy passions' (quoted in Allott, 1974, p. 224; my emphasis). This word 'romance' signalled a set of expectations about what a novel should be. The reviewer who made this comment also saw the novel's author as having the potential to be 'a great dramatic artist' (quoted in Allott, 1974, p. 227).

'Romance', 'drama': these terms that feature in the earliest reviews of the novel signal that the generic make-up of *Wuthering Heights* was at issue from the start. The novel form is often described as a **hybrid** (literally a mongrel-breed). Drawing on a multiplicity of other literary forms, each novel enjoys a complex relationship with earlier texts and traditions. Readers consciously and unconsciously navigate their way amid expectations – fulfilled and thwarted – and narrative surprises emerging from these intertextual relationships. *Wuthering Heights* draws on numerous literary genres, but the discussion below and in the chapter that follows will concentrate chiefly on the crucial interaction of **realism** and **romance** within the novel.

Wuthering Heights as romance

Activity 10

How can *Wuthering Heights* be read as a romance? Spend a few minutes jotting down the ways in which you think this term is relevant to the novel.

Discussion

You might describe *Wuthering Heights* as a romance because it is a love story; or because it is a work of imagination; or because it has an important relationship to the Romantic period in literature, which you explored in the first part of this book. All these associations are valid. Catherine and Heathcliff's declarations of romantic union have convinced generations of readers that theirs is a love story, despite the fact that the novel contains almost no scenes of physical passion between the protagonists – a 'lack' for which film adaptations have found it necessary to compensate extensively. The connotations of 'romance' with an imagined tale are also relevant to the historical origins of the novel as a genre.

Originating as a term for fictional adventures and tales of courtly love in the Middle Ages, the notion of 'romance' came, during the Romantic period, to describe works of introspection and imagination. At its most fundamental level, the term 'romance' is used as a synonym for the term 'novel' and generally denotes a mode of writing that engages with the desires and imaginative lives of its characters and readers. The reviewer quoted at the beginning of this section on 'Romance and realism' could have been thinking of numerous fictional genres in which the portrayal of the villain is typically offset by other more temperate characters: the historical romances of Sir Walter Scott (1771–1832), for example, some of which included characters whom Heathcliff strongly resembles. *Wuthering Heights* also has strong connections with Gothic romances over and beyond the Gothic characteristics of Heathcliff that I have already discussed.

Gothic novels cultivated an atmosphere of terror, using remote and rugged settings and a paraphernalia of storms, shadows, apparitions and portents. The threat of sexual violence is generally integral to the atmosphere of these novels, in which women are constantly incarcerated in castle vaults and required to escape along labyrinthine underground passages. Isabella and the young Catherine's incarceration at Wuthering Heights is reminiscent of this aspect of the Gothic, and feminist criticism has firmly established modes of reading the genre as expressive of the physical and psychological oppression of women within patriarchal society.

However, there are many contrasts as well as overlaps between Brontë's novel and the Gothic genre. Gothic heroines are usually virtuous and passive, not major characteristics of Catherine Earnshaw, who instead manifests some of the characteristics of the cruel queen Augusta, the 'Byronic heroine' of Brontë's own poetry set in the imagined realm of Gondal (Fegan, 2008, p. 10). Instead of the expected feminine contrast to Heathcliff's savagery, readers encountered a recalcitrant heroine who, like the other residents of Wuthering Heights, is no model of refined behaviour. 'Her heroines *scratch*, and *tear*, and *bite*, and *slap*', commented the reviewer for the *Christian Remembrancer* in July 1857, who drew attention to the ways in which the human inhabitants of Wuthering Heights are constantly described in the same animalistic language as Heathcliff's dogs, forever fighting and devouring food (quoted in Allott, 1974, pp. 367–8). None of the female characters meets expected standards for a romantic heroine, any more than they serve as ideal domestic role models.

Brontë is no more decorous in her use of literary genres than her heroines are in their observations of social niceties. In *Wuthering Heights* she brings together the romance elements of genres such as the Gothic with unapologetically realistic depictions of character, dialogue and behaviour. 'An interpreter ought always to have stood between her and the world' wrote Charlotte Brontë in her 1850 'Biographical Notice of Ellis and Acton Bell' (p. 306; reprinted in Appendix 1 of the World's Classics edition). But much of the force of *Wuthering Heights* seems to arise precisely because Emily Brontë did not draw on other literary genres as polite models for interpretation, but made startling transpositions of a variety of different modes of writing to represent what she saw as reality.

The critic George Henry Lewes (1817–1878) found in *Wuthering Heights* a combination of heightened description and a telling engagement with real issues and emotions, which for him was the basis for the realist novel's claim to 'truth'. ('Realism' is the name generally given to novels that aim to provide a faithful rather than idealised portrayal of life. The term can be variously defined and novels can achieve realist effects using a wide range of literary techniques.) In his 1850 review for *The Leader* magazine, Lewes develops an analogy with painting to convey Brontë's 'strange wild pictures of incult humanity', which are 'painted as if by lurid torchlight, though painted with unmistakeable power – the very power only heightening their repulsiveness'; although finding an 'excessive predominance of shadows darkening the picture', Lewes's review was a defence of the novel's realism: 'although there is a want of air and light in the picture we cannot deny its truth; sombre, rude, brutal, yet true' (quoted in Allott, 1972, pp. 291–2).

The brutal truths which *Wuthering Heights* presents include the realities of domestic life, social exclusion and economic dispossession. A combination of romance and realism is also characteristic of Charlotte Brontë's *Jane Eyre* (2000 [1847]), which also engages with domestic politics (in both the familial and the national meanings of that phrase). In this respect, *Wuthering Heights* can be linked with other novels more obviously concerned with what was termed 'the condition of England', particularly those dealing with the plight of homeless, displaced children, like the 'foundling novel' *Oliver Twist* (1837) by Charles Dickens (1812–1870).

Finally, while the lack of a conventional heroine may have altered the kind of romance that readers found in Brontë's book, romance, in the sense of romantic love, is also an important element in the novel. Lewes's appreciation of the 'truth' of Brontë's novel included the conviction with which we accept Heathcliff's 'burning and impassioned love for Catherine, and … her inextinguishable love for him' (Allott, 1974, p. 292). However, the status of *Wuthering Heights* as a romance in the sense of 'one of the greatest love stories' is most emphasised in later interpretations of the novel, such as in the 1939 film. The final scene between Catherine and Heathcliff in the novel is full of violently eroticised language. However, faced with a novel in which the only scene of physical passion occurs when the heroine is heavily pregnant and on the point of death, most film-versions eroticise the childhood love between Catherine and Heathcliff instead, supplying adolescent trysts on the moors in order to meet our own expectations of what romance should be.

Conclusion

This chapter has looked at the portrayal of the theme of home in *Wuthering Heights*. It has also considered some of the narrative and generic complexities of the novel, such as its borrowings from a range of genres and its multiple narrators, which work in opposition to the novel's structural coherence and can often create uncertainty and disorientation in the reader. Throughout the chapter, our focus has been on the reader: on the critical responses to the novel, especially contemporary ones, and on the ways in which the text's formal, narrative and generic qualities engender particular expectations and responses. In the next chapter, we will expand on our examination of the theme of 'abroad' while continuing to explore the generic richness of Brontë's novel and the diverse ways it has been read and interpreted since its publication.

References

Allott, M. (ed.) (1974) *The Brontës: The Critical Heritage*, London, Routledge.

Brontë, C. (2000 [1847]) *Jane Eyre* (ed. M. Smith; introduction and revised notes by Sally Shuttleworth), Oxford World's Classics, Oxford, Oxford University Press.

Brontë, E. (2009 [1847]) *Wuthering Heights* (ed. I. Jack; introduction and additional notes Helen Small), Oxford World's Classics, Oxford, Oxford University Press.

Byron, G.G. (1981 [1814]) *The Corsair: A Tale* in McGann, J.J. (ed.) *The Complete Poetical Works* (vol. 3), Oxford, Clarendon Press, pp. 148–213.

Eagleton, T. (1988 [1975]) *Myths of Power: A Marxist Study of the Brontës*, Basingstoke, Macmillan.

Fegan, M. (2008) *Wuthering Heights: Character Studies*, London, Continuum.

Hillis Miller, J. (1982) '*Wuthering Heights*: repetition and the uncanny' in *Fiction and Representation: Seven English Novels*, Cambridge, MA, Harvard University Press, pp. 42–72. There is an extract in Allott (ed.) (1992 [1970]) *Emily Brontë: Wuthering Heights, A Casebook* (rev. edn), Basingstoke and London, Macmillan. pp. 224–35.

James, H. (1995 [1881]) *The Portrait of a Lady* (ed. N. Bradbury), Oxford World's Classics, Oxford, Oxford University Press.

Radcliffe, A. (1994 [1789]) *The Castles of Athlin and Dunbayne*, Stroud, Sutton Publishing.

Woolf, V. (1994) [1925]) '"Jane Eyre" and "Wuthering Heights"' in McNellie, A. (ed.) *The Common Reader*, First Series, *The Essays of Virginia Woolf* (Vol. 4), London, Hogarth Press, pp. 165–9.

Further reading

Stoneman, P. (1993) *Wuthering Heights*, New Casebooks, Basingstoke, Macmillan.

Stoneman, P. (ed.) (2000) *Wuthering Heights: A Reader's Guide to Essential Criticism*, Cambridge, Icon Books.

Chapter 6
Emily Brontë, *Wuthering Heights*: abroad

Delia da Sousa Correa

Aims

This chapter will:

- explore the idea of 'abroad' in the text, while continuing to develop your understanding of the theme of home
- guide you further through *Wuthering Heights* with particular attention to issues of genre
- explore and expand on the concept of 'the reader'.

Introduction

This second chapter on *Wuthering Heights* explores ways in which the idea of 'abroad' might be relevant to the novel from a range of perspectives. It will also continue to develop the theme of home, which was the main emphasis in Chapter 5. The chapter examines a variety of nineteenth-, twentieth- and twenty-first-century responses to the novel and reflects on its continuing cultural significance.

Wuthering Heights and the world beyond

Whereas most early British critical responses to *Wuthering Heights* balanced criticism of its 'coarseness' with praise for its power and originality, some North American reviews were significantly less favourable. The *American Review* for June 1848 employed a house **metaphor** to criticise Brontë: 'we fear that the author of *Wuthering Heights* has some unsound timbers in here' (quoted in Allott, 1974, p. 244). The rotten goings-on within Wuthering Heights the house are here applied not just to the building, but to the novel's author. A quirky application of the literal and psychological ramifications of 'home' in the novel, this **metonym** (a form of metaphor where a comparison is made via a substitution of a part for the whole: in this case, the unsound timbers represent the entire house, and the house the novel) was, perhaps, considered likely to have particular resonance with the reviewer's American readers as they contemplated the literary (and domestic) structures of corrupt old Europe.

Activity 1

Thinking about American readers brings us to the idea of 'abroad' in its everyday sense: that is, in the sense of 'elsewhere' or 'other countries'. Before moving on, take a minute or two now to consider how this sense of 'abroad' features in the novel or in your reading of it.

Discussion

It is not too difficult to see how the contrasting worlds of Wuthering Heights and Thrushcross Grange might represent a conflict between northern rural values and the more urban cultures of the south of England. To Lockwood, the north is strikingly 'other', a foreign place. To the inhabitants of the north, London and the south are equally foreign. Perhaps you have Heathcliff at the top of your list, for not only is his appearance foreign and his origin unknown, but he has apparently travelled abroad to make his fortune in the time he spends away from Wuthering Heights.

The mid-twentieth-century critic Queenie Leavis saw Wuthering Heights as home to a 'wholesome', 'primitive' and 'natural' society pitted against the overdeveloped, artificial culture of the Grange; however, as we noted in the previous chapter, neither location offers a particularly wholesome version of domestic life, and Eagleton has suggested that

> One of *Wuthering Heights'* more notable achievements is ruthlessly to de-mystify the Victorian notion of the family as a pious, pacific space within social conflict.
>
> (Eagleton, 1988 [1975], pp. 105–6)

The domestic spaces in which the novel's action takes place cannot readily be viewed by readers today as divorced from the conflicts of the world beyond, and that world outside extends much further 'abroad' than the cultivated society of the south of England or the class conflicts of the nation as a whole.

Heathcliff is the most obvious representative of 'abroad' in the context of the local and domestic world of the novel. He enters the domestic scene from another world: from the streets of Liverpool, the imperial trading port where Mr Earnshaw finds him, and from elsewhere before that. Speaking some 'gibberish' foreign tongue, he is 'a gift of God, though it's as dark almost as if it came from the devil,' says Mr Earnshaw; he is a 'gypsy brat', declares his wife (p. 31). He is, perhaps, 'a little Lascar, or an American or Spanish castaway', concludes old Mr Linton (p. 44). As we saw in Chapter 5, Lockwood describes him as 'a dark-skinned gypsy in aspect' (p. 3). Lascars were ship's crew of Indian origin, often left to starve on arrival at the ship's destination; Spanish or American castaways might be runaway African slaves from South America or the United States; and gypsies were, of course, discriminated against. Taken together with his possible Irish background, the indeterminate array of possible origins for Heathcliff might make him an angel of revenge on behalf of a formidable collective of oppressed ethnic groups (Meyer, 1996, p. 102). Nelly, meanwhile, adds to the list of possible origins by recommending him to use his otherness to construct a family romance: 'You're fit for a prince in disguise. Who knows, but your father was Emperor of China, and your mother an Indian queen?' (p. 50).

In Shakespeare's *A Midsummer Night's Dream*, Titania and Oberon fight over a changeling boy 'stol'n from an Indian king' (Greenblatt et al., 2008, 2.1.22). The mysterious heroes of Gothic romances and Romantic verse dramas are also frequently foreign. In addition to these literary models, Heathcliff has predecessors in the early juvenile writings of the Brontë children, including Charlotte Brontë's 1833 tale *The Green Dwarf*, which features Quashia, a rebellious Ashantee leader adopted into the Duke of Wellington's family.

Romantic literary hero and fairy-tale changeling, Heathcliff's foreignness nevertheless also has historical origins within the contemporary context of the novel, providing another example of the interaction of romance and realism in the text which we noted in Chapter 5. Nelly may invoke a fairy-tale version of abroad, but the Brontë family was far from isolated from contemporary political and intellectual life. The Yorkshire town of Haworth had a considerable population and a cultural life that included concerts, meetings and lectures of topical interest. The occupants of the parsonage had access, from childhood, to newspapers and periodicals and to the circulation of news and gossip that has left only partial traces for us to discover, including stories of particular cuckoo-like adoptees who attempted to take over the estates of the families who had taken them in (see Ian Jack's note in Brontë, 2009 [1847], p. 325).

At a basic level, Heathcliff represents the experience of society's marginalised and dispossessed. Though not a 'regular black' (p. 50), his ethnicity is uncertain and his class to begin with that of a beggar. More specifically, Brontë's depiction of him may owe something to newspaper reports and illustrations of starving Irish peasants during the Great Famine, a period of mass starvation and emigration in British-ruled Ireland between 1845 and 1852 (see Figure 6.1). A collection on behalf of famine victims was taken at Haworth church and others arrived by ship at Liverpool, possibly witnessed by Emily's brother Branwell in 1845, shortly before she began work on her novel (Gerin, 1971, pp. 225–6).

None of this is certain. The mystery over Heathcliff's origins, over his whereabouts when he disappears from the novel, and over the source

BOY AND GIRL AT CAHERA.

Figure 6.1   Famished children at Cahera, Ireland. *Illustrated London News*, 20 February 1847. Photo: © Illustrated London News Ltd/Mary Evans.

of the wealth with which he returns connect him in a suggestive but non-specific way with the world of commercial enterprise and colonial exploitation. There is no precise location for the colonial contexts of this novel, as there is for Charlotte Brontë's *Jane Eyre*, published in the same year as *Wuthering Heights*, which specifies the West Indies as the source of Rochester's wife Bertha's origins and Jane's eventual wealth. However, this very lack of specificity opens up a wealth of possible connections that have been explored in recent postcolonial and cultural criticism, including views of Heathcliff not just as a racial 'other' but of the yet more topical category of 'terrorist'. In this analysis, terror, in literature and society, is seen to arise from a failure to pay sufficient attention to those who come from abroad, a refusal to recognise that '"elsewhere"' is 'a shadow of "home"' (Khair, 2006, p. 162).

The uncanny

Thinking about what is foreign, or 'abroad', disturbs our assumptions of what is familiar about 'home'. As I hope is becoming evident, 'home' and 'abroad' are very closely interrelated in Brontë's novel. In this section, I discuss the concept of 'the uncanny' in these terms. *Wuthering Heights* combines realistic storytelling with some of the most fantastical modes of Romantic narration, to which the concept of the uncanny is central.

Activity 2

Note down some of the features of *Wuthering Heights* that you would describe as uncanny. Your list might be quite varied! Does thinking about the uncanny offer you further, less obvious ways, of thinking about the theme of 'abroad'? You may find it helpful to look back at the discussion of the uncanny in Chapter 4 of this book to remind yourselves of how the 'uncanny' is discussed there in relation to Freud (pp. 113–7).

Discussion

The 'uncanny' is a concept that has no single definition, although as readers we frequently agree about the kinds of things that we would describe as uncanny: in the main, those that disturb our sense of the familiar. 'The familiar' suggests 'what is known', or, literally, what is 'of the family'; the word is thus close to our theme of 'home'. As you saw in Chapter 4 of this book, the uncanny has an immediate contrasting association with what is strange and unfamiliar, which relates to our other theme of 'abroad'. Ghosts 'walk abroad', after all. It can involve incongruity; inanimate objects that move are uncanny, as, for instance, statues or portraits in Gothic novels or later horror movies. The sense of an animating presence within ostensibly inanimate nature might be described as uncanny. The final paragraph of *Wuthering Heights*, as was discussed earlier, describes a wind that 'breathes' through the grasses (and will rise to a gale to ruin the kirk roof). The poeticised language of Lockwood's account effects a lyrical resolution, yet this animism troubles the perceptive reader's, if not Lockwood's, sense of the closing calm, and is allied to the possibility that the spirits of Cathy and Heathcliff might walk abroad on that 'quiet earth'.

A sense of disturbing presences in nature is every bit as typical of Romantic poetry as the more joyous pantheism (literally, 'god in everything') which we will encounter later in this chapter. The grotesque is another quality that might be associated with the uncanny. The *Britannia* reviewer, quoted in Chapter 5, who complained, in 1848, that *Wuthering Heights* unsettled his expectations of a romance described Brontë's novel as 'wildly grotesque' (quoted in Allott, 1974, p. 223). There are certainly numerous grotesque moments in *Wuthering Heights*: for example, the apparition at Lockwood's window, or the 'ghoul' or 'vampire' Heathcliff's 'frightful, life-like gaze of exultation' in death, or indeed his behaviour during his final encounter with Catherine, when he seems to Nelly a creature of another species (pp. 293, 298, 141). Reviewers and others were prompted to comparisons with German Romantic literature, in particular E.T.A. Hoffmann's literature of terror, which you encountered in Chapter 4 of this book (Allott, 1974, pp. 32, 223, 376).

There are specific possible sources for *Wuthering Heights* in Hoffmann's novel *The Devil's Elixir* (*Die Elixiere des Teufels*, 1815–16), and in his story 'The Entail' ('Das Majorat', from *Die Serapionsbrüder*, 1818–21), which shows the impact of disinheritance and fratricide over three generations. Brontë could readily have had access to these works via translations in the periodicals that she read at home in the Haworth parsonage: *Blackwood's*, for example, or *Fraser's Magazine*. A general affinity with the way in which Hoffmann's tales, such as 'The Sandman' ('Der Sandmann', from *Die Nachtstücke*, 1816–17), disclose uncanny presences within the everyday world is also apparent in *Wuthering Heights*.

Critics Andrew Bennet and Nicholas Royle provide a helpful summary of some of the common features of the uncanny, emphasising how the uncanny defamiliarises – how it turns 'home' into 'abroad':

> The uncanny has to do with a sense of strangeness, mystery or eeriness. More particularly it concerns a sense of unfamiliarity which appears at the very heart of the familiar, or else a sense of familiarity which appears at the very heart of the unfamiliar. The

uncanny is not just a matter of the weird or spooky, but has to do more specifically with a disturbance of the familiar.

(Bennet and Royle, 1995, p. 33)

Wuthering Heights could certainly be seen as the *locus suspectus* (literally 'suspect place') which Freud cited as the Latin equivalent of the uncanny in his account of Hoffmann (Freud, 1985 [1919], p. 341). As you learned in Chapter 4 of this book, Hoffmann's fellow-romantic, the philosopher Schelling, defined the uncanny as that which 'ought to have remained … secret and hidden but has come to light' (Freud, 1985 [1919], p. 34). The reviewer who complained that *Wuthering Heights* 'lifts the veil and shows boldly the dark side of our depraved nature' saw the novel as uncanny in this sense (quoted in Allott, 1974, p. 240). The German term for the uncanny is also appropriate: there is something *unheimlich* (literally 'un-homely') going on at Wuthering Heights. Or, perhaps, it is something '*heimlich*' (this word, which means 'homely' in German, carries with it a notion of the uncanny, even without the prefix '*un*', and is used to describe things usually kept private, thus strange and unattractive; indeed the use of 'homely' to mean 'unattractive' is common in American English). The way in which this adjectival form has taken on the connotations of its apparent opposite is very useful for us as we consider the strangeness that is inherent in, rather than in contrast to, the portrayal of home and family in Brontë's novel.

Home and abroad can both be mapped onto the uncanny, with Heathcliff's otherness a matter of his uncanny nature as much as his foreign origin. The atmosphere of terror reigning over the contemporary domestic sphere at Wuthering Heights is relevant, too, of course. This homely uncanny, central to the novel, clearly shapes its challenging employment of the Gothic elements that were discussed in Chapter 5. For while the hero-villains of Gothic romances preside over remote castles, Heathcliff, as we know, rules over the domestic hearth. Unaccustomed to meeting Byron's *Manfred* or *The Corsair* within doors, the reviewer who saw Heathcliff as Byronic hero remarked: 'It is with difficulty that we can prevail upon ourselves to believe in the appearance of such a phenomenon so near our own dwellings as the summit of a Lancashire or Yorkshire moor' (quoted in Allott, 1974, p. 221). Wild and remote as we may consider the Yorkshire moors to be, they are too close to home for this reviewer, who would prefer Heathcliff to terrorise a conventional Gothic novel rather than a work that makes claims to domestic realism.

Hybrid in form, the novel itself has, like Heathcliff, no single home. For readers, each set of generic expectations is constantly unsettled by others, and this sense of the uncanny as a feature of reading *Wuthering Heights* is reinforced by the unsettling repetition of names and events, each repetition containing salient differences that disturb the sense that we are already familiar with the characters and what is happening to them.

If we take the uncanny to be the disturbance of the familiar through an intermixing of strange and familiar elements, then the uncanny can be regarded as endemic to the process of reading. *Wuthering Heights* presents an extreme case of this, I would propose, not just because of its strangeness, but because of its devotion to home. The doorway of Wuthering Heights, as described by Lockwood, is historically Renaissance, but suggestive nonetheless of 'Gothic' in its embellishment with a 'quantity of grotesque carving' (p. 2). It opens, not onto the twisting staircases, subterranean passages and lofty turrets of a Gothic castle, but onto 'the house', the family sitting room, the heart of home. It allows us to consider, as the contemporary novelist Kirsty Gunn proposes, 'the idea of the gothic opening its doors to show domestic chaos and detail' (Gunn, 24 April 2010). This positive appreciation for the way in which *Wuthering Heights* focuses on the domestic is a subject to which we will return in the last sections of this chapter.

Wuthering Heights and Romantic poetry

As we have seen, genre is a central issue in thinking about the literary 'home' of *Wuthering Heights*. The uncanny returned us to thinking about the Gothic elements of the novel. From the moment of its publication, *Wuthering Heights* invited comparisons with forms outside the novel and its chief 'home' genre, the romance. In Chapter 5, we saw how the unidentified review found in Brontë's desk describes *Wuthering Heights* as a 'domestic drama' (quoted in Allott, 1974, p. 244). Emily Brontë has also been frequently described as a writer whose work has its true home not in prose fiction but in poetry. An unsigned review in the American periodical *The Galaxy* in February 1873 described the following lines of Heathcliff's as 'in themselves a dramatic poem' (quoted in Allot, 1974, pp. 393–4):

'Disturbed her? No! she has disturbed me, night and day, through eighteen years – incessantly – remorselessly – till yesternight – and yesternight, I was tranquil. I dreamt I was sleeping the last sleep, by that sleeper, with my heart stopped, and my cheek frozen against hers.

(p. 255)

Activity 3

How would you describe the poetic qualities in this passage that impressed the reviewer? And why do you think he or she describes this as a 'dramatic poem'?

Discussion

Brontë's language in this passage builds up a sequence of balancing phrases and rhythmic repetitions, just as poetry often does: 'Disturbed her'/'disturbed me', 'till yesternight – and yesternight,' 'sleeping the last sleep, by that sleeper'. These draw attention to the ways in which the effect of the passage results as much from what we could call the musicality of the language as from the actual meaning of the words used. These effects are not exclusive to poetry, of course, but prose is described as 'poetic' when these qualities are prominent in its use of language. Some of the words that Brontë chooses for this passage, its **diction**, are also reminiscent of poetry: the archaic 'till yesternight', for example.

We could describe this as a 'dramatic poem' because of the way it is delivered by Heathcliff (the term **dramatic monologue** might be applied here – meaning a poem in which an imaginary speaker addresses an imaginary audience). In fact, it has a decided air of declamation about it, as Heathcliff poses and answers the initial question, 'Disturbed her? No! she has disturbed me'. In the terse declaration that follows, 'night and day, through eighteen years – incessantly – remorselessly', the two rhyming four-syllable adverbs ('incessantly – remorselessly') create an insistent rhythmic portrayal of the mental disturbance they describe. The fraught motion of this speech comes to a pause, 'till yesternight', before continuing 'and yesternight, I was tranquil'. In a lyrical last sentence the passage closes with the 'stopped' heart of Heathcliff's dream and a final cadence, 'my cheek frozen against hers'. ('**Cadence**' comes from the Latin 'cadere' to fall. It denotes the final chord progression of a phrase of music, the music returning 'home' if you like. In literature it describes the melodic pattern of a writer's voice, or denotes the closing of a poetic line.)

The novel's relationship with poetry is certainly a crucial aspect of its composition. Both Brontë's own work as a poet and her extensive reading of poetry had a profound impact on the language and rhythms of *Wuthering Heights*. There are constant echoes of the poetic language of the Bible, of the seventeenth-century poet John Milton and above all of the Romantic poets. We saw in Chapter 5 that Heathcliff bears many similarities to the heroes of Byron's poetry. The next section discusses the relationship of the novel to Romantic poetry and to Romanticism more widely.

Wuthering Heights and Romanticism

Wuthering Heights' affinities with Romantic literature are especially strong in its portrayals of romantic union and of the natural world. Specific allusions to Romantic poetry underpin Catherine and Heathcliff's passionate declarations of a union of souls. Catherine's 'I *am* Heathcliff' (p. 73) echoes a line from Shelley's 'Epipsychidion' (1821), 'I am not thine: I am a part of *thee*' (l. 52). Heathcliff's invocations of Catherine in Volume I, Chapter III and Volume II, Chapter II, 'Come in … hear me' (p. 24), 'Be with me always – take any form – drive me mad' (p. 148), recall Manfred's speech to his dead sister Astarte in Byron's verse drama, *Manfred* (1817):

> Hear me, hear me –
> Astarte! my beloved! speak to me:
> Look on me! The grave hath not changed thee more
> Than I am changed for thee …
> …
> Speak to me! though it be in wrath …
>
> (Byron, 1986 [1817], Act 2, Scene 4, ll. 117–48)

These echoes of Romantic evocations of kindred souls help to explain the extent to which the relationship between Heathcliff and Catherine remains one of mirroring sibling love rather than adulterous romantic passion; Patsy Stoneman points out that this intense relationship with Romantic poetry means that Heathcliff, after Catherine's death, becomes a Romantic hero, with a capital 'R', rather than a romantic hero of the type represented by Rochester in Charlotte Brontë's *Jane Eyre* (see Stoneman, 2011, pp. 112–18).

A further link with Romanticism is apparent in the novel's constant evocations of the natural world, whether stormy or lyrical, and the notion of an earthly afterlife for some of the protagonists. These invite comparison with a pantheistic sense of spiritual presences within nature in the Romantic poetry that Emily Brontë knew and loved, famously exemplified in Coleridge's celebration, in his poem 'The Eolian Harp', of 'the one Life within us and abroad, /... Rhythm in all thought, and joyance everywhere' (1912 [1796], ll. 26–7).

That nature in *Wuthering Heights* is not possessed only by the brooding presences that characterise popular conceptions of the novel is illustrated by the reverberation of Coleridge's lines in the younger Catherine's joyous imagining of a perfect July day spent 'rocking in a rustling green tree':

> with a west wind blowing, and bright, white clouds flitting rapidly above; and not only larks, but throstles, and blackbirds, and linnets, and cuckoos pouring out music on every side, and the moors seen at a distance, broken into cool dusky dells; but close by, great swells of long grass undulating in waves to the breeze; and woods and sounding water, and the whole world awake and wild with joy.
>
> (p. 218)

Throughout *Wuthering Heights*, every mood and season in nature, its weather, skies, birdsong, is lovingly detailed, as in Catherine's speech above, or Nelly's description of 'a fresh watery afternoon' in autumn, 'when the turf and paths were rustling with moist, withered leaves, and the cold, blue sky was half hidden by clouds – dark grey streamers, rapidly mounting from the west, and boding abundant rain' (p. 202), or in Lockwood's final account of 'moths fluttering among the heath, and hare-bells' and the 'soft wind breathing through the grass' beside the graveyard where Catherine, Edgar and Heathcliff are buried (p. 300). Lockwood's failure to believe that ghosts could walk under 'that benign sky' might prompt ironic thoughts about the limitations of his imagination, but does not diminish the lyricism of the novel's elegiac closing lines, 'unquiet slumbers … in that quiet earth' (p. 300). Helen Small's introduction to the novel identifies this as an echo of stanza 14 of Shelley's 'Adonais' (1821), 'Pale Ocean in unquiet slumber lay' (p. xi). ('**Elegy**', a Greek term for 'lament', is used for poems of mourning.)

Romantic views of *human* nature, and the corrupting effects upon it of a lack of sympathy, have also informed some readings of *Wuthering Heights* which, like Mary Shelley's *Frankenstein*, can be interpreted as a story about the distortion of innate affections. It was interpreted in this way by George Henry Lewes in his 1850 review for *The Leader* magazine:

> The fierce ungoverned instincts of powerful organizations, bred up amidst violence, revolt, and moral apathy, are here seen in operation; such brutes we should all be, or the most of us, were our lives as insubordinate to law; were our affections and sympathies as little cultivated, our imaginations as undirected. And herein lies the moral of the book.
>
> (Lewes quoted in Allott, 1974, p. 292)

Nelly relates that 'from childhood' Heathcliff 'had a delight in dwelling on dark things', a tendency clearly encouraged by the brutal treatment he receives (p. 288). Romantic ideas of the importance of childhood experience for the formation of character are suggested here. In telling the story of Heathcliff's progress from impoverished foundling to vengeful gentleman-capitalist, *Wuthering Heights*, like *Jane Eyre*, shares aspects of the Romantic *Bildungsroman*, or 'novel of education'. This facet of the novel was important to the critical focus on Heathcliff which dominated accounts of *Wuthering Heights* from the nineteenth century through to the Marxist critic Terry Eagleton's writing in the 1970s, by which time the focus of interest was shifting to other, particularly female, characters.

Eagleton saw *Wuthering Heights* as aligned with a non-Byronic form of Romanticism, concerned less with the individual pitted against anonymous forces than with an alternative vision of society. He particularly valued the combination of Romantic individualism and social comment in Brontë's text. In Heathcliff, the qualities of a Byronic hero are transferred to a man who is emphatically not aristocratic. This, in itself, has radical implications and it is hardly surprising that Heathcliff's rise from obscurity should have a compelling significance for a critic concerned with the class implications of Marxist theory. (Eagleton was writing about Brontë's novel within a decade or two of the generation of 'Angry Young Men' like John Braine, whose *Room at the Top* (1957) asserted the claims of working-class protagonists and authors.)

Wuthering Heights and the world within

Each mode of literary criticism will claim to have changed forever the way in which readers read, and in important respects this is true. Students of nineteenth-century novels cannot now, for example, avoid taking specific account of the pervasive reach of imperialism into every aspect of life. We may feel that we have an understanding of contemporary contexts of the novel that exceeds that available to those who experienced those contexts directly – and this, of course, is not just because of what literary criticism offers us, but because of what we jointly, critics and readers, have experienced or understood in the time between then and now. However, whereas Victorian readers of *Wuthering Heights* may not have read the novel with explicit reference to the economic and political contexts foregrounded by more recent criticism, that does not mean that they lacked apprehension of the ways in which the interior worlds of the novel connected with the world beyond. Victorian readers' own encounters with the novel were inevitably conditioned by their awareness of contemporary contexts (including mercantile competition, Irish immigration and social marginalisation), even if issues of class, race and gender are more sharply emphasised in current criticism. Information about issues at home and abroad will frequently have been gathered from the same magazines and periodicals that featured reviews of novels like *Wuthering Heights*, and read in the same domestic environment in which Victorians read novels.

Moreover, the dominant models of psychology at the time presented a view of the individual interior life as driven by warring energies fighting for dominion as energetically as in the political and economic struggles of the world outside. In phrenology, the most widely accepted psychological theory at the time of *Wuthering Heights*' publication, the mind was envisaged as consisting of competing faculties. These faculties required an outlet, and while the exercise of self-control was crucial to achieving a balance between the forces within each individual, over-tyrannical suppression was likely to breed revolt. Focusing on this particular contemporary context, the critic Sally Shuttleworth sees Heathcliff as 'an imaginative projection of what may happen if the energy of the oppressed is harnessed and controlled in the service of aggressive individualism and upward mobility' (1996, p. 5). Heathcliff's psychology, in other words, might be understood as a microcosm of aggressive capitalism abroad.

Shuttleworth compares Heathcliff with Bertha, Rochester's incarcerated wife in Charlotte Brontë's *Jane Eyre*. Both figures demonstrate the consequences of suppressing the socially marginalised. Mad Bertha's suppressed energies erupt in uncontrolled revolution, Heathcliff's in controlled revenge. Unlike Bertha, Heathcliff is not mad; at least Nelly assures us that his actions are perfectly sane, apart from his 'monomania' over his attachment to Catherine Earnshaw (p. 288). Thus Heathcliff *is* mad: but only in one respect. The notion of monomania, or partial insanity, was a new idea in nineteenth-century psychology which rapidly became popular. It supports a view of the mind as a divided entity within a 'world of struggling, conflicting energies' (Shuttleworth, 1996, p. 245).

An understanding of Heathcliff as demonstrating the results of dangerous suppression and perversion of energies overlaps with the Romantic, Frankenstein-like view of him as representing the perversion of the natural affections that we considered earlier. However, in Heathcliff, Romantic individualism acquires a very Victorian form of expression: not a harmonious union of souls but 'the competitive ethos of capitalism at work in the private domain' (Shuttleworth, 1996, p. 245).

Shuttleworth's study of relationships between the novel and contemporary psychological theories complements critical work investigating the significance of imperialism and race within the novel. For Susan Meyer, *Wuthering Heights* provides 'an extended critique of imperialism ... in part by exploring what would happen if the

Figure 6.2   Peter Forster, wood engraving, from *Wuthering Heights*, 1991 (Folio Edition). Photo: © Peter Forster. The illustration shows Heathcliff, Hareton and the younger Catherine, with a portrait of the first Catherine looking on.

suppressed power of the "savage" outsiders were unleashed' (1966, pp. 100–1). Heathcliff's programme of revenge might thus speak to Victorian anxieties about the uncanny potential of both dispossessed classes and maltreated races to usurp the pre-eminence of those currently in possession of wealth and power. The way in which issues of race have become an overt concern of more recent readers is reflected in a set of illustrations produced by Peter Forster for a 1991 Folio edition of *Wuthering Heights*, which shows Heathcliff with African features (Figure 6.2).

Theology and domestic ideals

'If I were in heaven, Nelly, I should be extremely miserable. … I dreamt, once, that I was there … heaven did not seem to be my home; and I broke my heart with weeping to come back to earth; and the angels were so angry that they flung me out, into the

middle of the heath on the top of Wuthering Heights; where
I woke sobbing for joy.'

(p. 71)

'To-day I am within sight of my heaven ... hardly three feet to
sever me!'

(p. 292)

Emily Brontë locates the afterlives of her protagonists at home on
Earth rather than in Heaven, suggesting a pantheistic rather than
conventionally Christian world view and exploiting the potential of the
Romantic uncanny to reveal and revel in *Das (Un)heimliche* within the
heart of home. Her novel conflates distinctions between 'home' and
'abroad': the domestic and the Romantic transcendent cohabit; the dead
walk 'abroad' in the landscape they frequented while living, a landscape
that in Brontë's day was not just wild and solitary, but inhabited by the
historical originals of Nelly and her numerous contemporaries going
about their daily business.

The theology implied by this vision is obviously 'something heterodox',
to quote Lockwood's thoughts in response to Nelly's question on the
afterlife (p. 146). The relationship of Heaven and Hell is explicitly
brought into question from the point of Catherine's speech quoted at
the beginning of this section, and Heathcliff's 'heaven' is buried within
the Earth. However, not until the publication of Sandra Gilbert and
Susan Gubar's *The Madwoman in the Attic* in 1979 was the novel seen as
a systematic reversal of Biblical hierarchies that goes well beyond the
more obvious satire levelled against the Bible-spouting character of old
Joseph (frequently seen as a parody of the narrow Methodism of the
aunt who helped to bring the Brontë children up). Gilbert and Gubar's
objective was to provide 'models for understanding the dynamics of
female literary response to male literary assertion and coercion' (1979, p.
xii). They analysed Victorian women writers as subverting the dominant
traditions of authoritative texts: thus Charlotte Brontë's *Jane Eyre*
becomes an inversion of the well-known allegorical tale by John Bunyan
(1628–1688), *The Pilgrim's Progress* (written between 1678 and 1684). In
the chapter 'Looking Oppositely: Emily Brontë's Bible of Hell',
Wuthering Heights is read as a rebellious reversal of the Bible and John
Milton's *Paradise Lost* (1667) (Gilbert and Gubar, 1979, pp. 248–308).

Among the Miltonic elements in Brontë's novel are the links between Heathcliff and Milton's fallen angel Satan. From the start, Heathcliff is seen as a gift less of God than of the Devil (p. 31). Nelly, Isabella and Catherine herself also compare him with the Devil. To Isabella, his eyes are the 'clouded windows of hell' from which a 'fiend' looks out (p. 160). Milton's Satan thus forms one of his literary antecedents along with the Byronic hero-villains of Romantic literature.

Gilbert and Gubar's reading of Brontë's relationship with Milton contributed to a shift of focus from Heathcliff to the novel's female characters. They draw from Charlotte Brontë's 1849 novel *Shirley*, in which Shirley wants to remind Milton 'that the first men of the earth were Titans, and that Eve was their mother' (Brontë, 2007 [1849], p. 270). This heroic vision of an originating giant race suits Gilbert and Gubar, who read *Wuthering Heights* as a revised myth of the fall of woman, a 'fall from hell into heaven', a 'fall into culture'; the novel becomes 'a rebelliously topsy-turvy retelling of Milton's and Western culture's central tale of the fall of woman and her shadow self, Satan' (1979, p. 255).

Gilbert and Gubar celebrate the subversive spirit of Brontë's text, the 'fresh, original, and unconventional spirit' praised since the 1848 *Jerrold's* review of the novel which we discussed in Chapter 5 (quoted in Allott, 1974, p. 227). Previous readings tended to concentrate on the character of Heathcliff as the force of rebellion, while in the hands of Gilbert and Gubar *Wuthering Heights* becomes a powerful text of feminist revolt. Catherine becomes the protagonist of a female *Bildungsroman*, with Heathcliff now of most interest as her alter-ego, her true double.

Gilbert and Gubar view the novel as a daring inversion of the hierarchies of Heaven and Hell and a valorisation of natural passions beyond the ken of the novel's inadequate frame-narrator or of domestic beings like Nelly. Theological inversion thus works in tandem with the Gothic, which they, like many other critics, see as voicing the outrage and madness that follows from women's incarceration by Victorian domesticity. For, if Catherine's view that 'heaven did not seem to be my home' (p. 71) subverts religious hierarchies, it also seems to undermine Victorian idealisations of the domestic. Ideals such as those expressed by the popular advice author Sarah Ellis, while no guide as to the way in which the Victorian family actually behaved, are an indication of to what they were supposed to aspire.

'[V]erse has never found a more prolific theme, nor music sung a more enchanting lay' enthused Ellis on the subject of 'home' in her book *Prevention Better than Cure*, published in the same year as *Wuthering Heights*: 'If there be one thing real in this life, it is the influence which home has exercised upon the heart, the conduct, and the experience of mankind' (Ellis, 1847, p. 258).

As we saw in the Introduction to Part 2 of this book, such attitudes to home rested on particular views of women's domestic roles. These views argued not only that women should remain within the domestic sphere and behave in a genteel manner, but also that they could have a transforming effect upon the world through the domestic work best suited to their supposedly more affectionate natures. Through the nurturing of children and the domestic affections, woman's 'mission among her fellow creatures' was, for Maria Grey and Emily Shirreff, two sisters writing about female education just after the publication of *Wuthering Heights*:

> a mission of gentleness and consolation, of soothing and gladness. It is hers to make goodness beautiful, and to associate the love of virtue with man's deepest and warmest affections. It is hers to bring peace, to gather up that golden chain of sympathy, which should bind the whole human race ... Such is her appointed task, and a woman without active and tender sympathies and affections is a mere rebel against nature.
>
> (Grey and Shirreff, 1850, p. 59)

Such passages give us a useful sense of some of the dominant feminine ideals which a novel like *Wuthering Heights* both reflects and challenges. The ideas promulgated in advice books, then, were not simply accepted. As Mary Poovey has noted, 'the middle class ideology we most often associate with the Victorian period was both contested and always under construction' (1989, p. 3). There are, naturally, conflicts between different accounts of women's roles that reflect diverse religious, educational and political agendas. Above all, it is the absence of stable attitudes towards the status of women within individual texts that is most striking. Individual writers were quite capable of representing women, on the one hand, as more moral and spiritual than men and, on the other, as more likely to succumb to ungoverned emotions; they were naturally suited to the fostering of domestic harmony, yet the prevalence of advice literature on the topic indicates that they needed constant reminding of this: advice on the subject would hardly have been necessary if it was already widely followed in practice. There were deeply held differences of opinion about how women should be educated and what they should be educated for. The different voices in this contemporary debate, and the contradictions within their utterances, highlight the fact that *Wuthering Heights* was not simply a radical statement in opposition to a firmly agreed ideology, but a powerful intervention within a highly unstable ideological context; Brontë's readers would have been aware of a huge variety of issues with regard to women and the home, while holding highly ambivalent views about them.

Clearly Ellis Bell was no Sarah Ellis, and Catherine Earnshaw is in some respect Grey and Shirreff's 'rebel against [feminine] nature' (1850, p. 59). Feminism and feminist critics have made us conscious of the very considerable force of the novel as a dramatisation of female rage. However, viewing the first Catherine's story as following the myth of the fall, as Gilbert and Gubar and many other readers have done, still leaves open to interpretation the nature of that fall. For Catherine Earnshaw, the end point of rebellion is death. In Gilbert and Gubar's view, as in Eagleton's, this is because her subjugation in marriage to Edgar Linton has starved her nature of its true wild and uncivilised home. Is it possible to map our theme of home and abroad onto a conflict between nature (our true home) and civilisation (as imposed from 'abroad')? Is Linton and all he represents the real villain of this romance and the sole object of Catherine's fury? In the section that follows I will consider a variety of ways in which the novel's contrasting worlds have been read before coming back to these questions.

A 'fall into culture'?

For many readers, *Wuthering Heights* dramatises a struggle between nature and civilisation, which reflects Romantic ideas about the superiority of nature over culture that are as attractive to us today as they were to the Victorians. This is a conflict that civilisation must always, and tragically, win.

A view of the novel as dramatising a conflict between civilisation and nature is, in fact, long-standing and appears in one of the first critical responses to the novel, written by George Henry Lewes shortly after it was republished in 1850:

> It was a happy thought to make [Catherine] love the kind, weak, elegant Edgar, and yet without lessening her passion for Heathcliff. Edgar appeals to her love of refinement, and goodness and culture; Heathcliff clutches her soul in his passionate embrace.
>
> (Lewes quoted in Allott, 1974, pp. 292–3)

This assessment (from the same review quoted earlier in the chapter) identified Catherine's divided attraction to Edgar and Heathcliff as the hub of the drama played out in the two competing locations of the novel. While Edgar is an appropriate husband, she loves Heathcliff 'with a passionate abandonment which sets culture, education, the world, at defiance' (quoted in Allott, 1974, p. 293).

'It is in the treatment of this subject that Ellis Bell shows real mastery', Lewes concludes (quoted in Allott, 1974, p. 293). Lewes's reading of the novel as an elemental conflict between nature and civilisation resonates in later twentieth- and twenty-first-century interpretations of Brontë's work. David Cecil characterised *Wuthering Heights* as a universalising drama of 'children of the storm' and 'children of calm', with the children of the storm firmly aligned with the forces of nature (quoted in Allott, 1992, pp. 121–2). This is a view of the novel that still underpins the majority of film adaptations. While much recent criticism has moved away from this view, Gilbert and Gubar's assertion that Heathcliff remains as Catherine's primordial self after her marriage to Linton exemplifies the extent to which the Romantic ideal of a unity of souls has pervaded the critical history of the novel as well as its popular afterlife. These Romantic ideals are powerfully embodied in the wood engravings created by the German-American artist Fritz Eichenberg to illustrate a 1943 edition of the novel (Figures 6.3 and 6.4).

Gilbert and Gubar's sympathies were firmly on the side of nature, and they assumed that Brontë's were too. For them, *Wuthering Heights*, for all its cruelty, provided an authentic sphere for Catherine and Heathcliff's 'true' uncivilised natures, and the injury that forces Catherine's entry into the world of Thrushcross Grange symbolised the crippling repression of women within middle-class domesticity. In their version of the dramatic contest between nature and civilisation, nature's claims remain paramount, notwithstanding what they saw as the irritating final

Figure 6.3   Frtiz Eichenberg, Heathcliff standing under a leafless tree in the wind, wood engraving, from *Wuthering Heights*, 1943 (Random House).
Photo: © Fritz Eichenberg Trust/VAGA, NewYork/DACS, London 2011.

Figure 6.4   Fritz Eichenberg, Catherine's death scene, wood engraving, from *Wuthering Heights*, 1943 (Random House). Photo: © Fritz Eichenberg Trust/VAGA, New York/DACS, London 2011.

domestic scene in which Catherine and Heathcliff's descendants betray the elemental passions of their parental generation – young Catherine arranging primroses in Hareton's porridge and teaching him to read. The fact that civilisation has to write the story – and teach Hareton to read it – is a regrettable necessity in this view of the novel. But what is this 'nature' that remains so implacably apart from civilisation, even in defeat? More particularly, is there an authentic human nature that has no part in the workings of culture?

A reading of the relationship between home and abroad as a conflict between nature and culture becomes difficult to sustain along binary lines. We are aware that the conclusion of the novel's tightly structured genealogical pattern is an end to the Earnshaws at Wuthering Heights, but registering this as a loss does not automatically entail a rejection of the values of the Grange, or a polarised view of the two houses as separate representatives of nature and civilisation. Eagleton highlights the 'natural' competitive energies involved in economic activity and acquisition of culture (1988 [1975], pp. 109–10). Helen Small finds at the end of the novel an 'optimistic turn' characteristic of much of Emily Brontë's poetry and other writings, 'a move away from a brutalist model of natural law towards a view of human nature which values the desire to cultivate the mind' (p. xx).

Despite the clear patterning of characters and locations within the novel, the variety of readings that I have outlined illustrates J. Hillis Miller's view that *Wuthering Heights* never offers its readers a 'single, unified and logically coherent' meaning (1982, p. 51). We can always find something to complicate our efforts of interpretation, and this is an essential richness in the experience of reading the novel.

Domestic readings of *Wuthering Heights*

The shift of critical attention towards female characters has worked in the service of a variety of readings. Interestingly, Lewes's view of the civilisation/nature conflict has affinities with feminist readings that see the more radical aspect of the novel residing not in a championing of union with Heathcliff as a rebellious ideal, but in the sense that, as Lewes perceives, Catherine has reasons to desire both Heathcliff and Edgar and becomes equally enraged, as she herself declares, at both (pp. 104, 139). Such a reading highlights the ways in which the apparently contrasting male characters in the novel are alike in their abuse of power, and queries the 'loving equality between Catherine and Heathcliff' which critics wedded to the idea of the novel as a celebration of Romantic rebellion have assumed (Eagleton, 1988 [1975], p. 103).

Is Emily Brontë herself, so passionately attached to home and heath that she could not bear ever to be elsewhere, really such a long way away in her fiction from her sister Charlotte, whose *Jane Eyre* so palpably values home, in the unashamedly domestic sense, above all other material and spiritual goods? It is possible to see Catherine's desire for a well-ordered home as reasonable, and to argue that her destruction is brought about by the forced choice between mates rather than her 'false' choice of Edgar. Whether Brontë originally conceived the first half of the novel as a stand-alone text or not, she provided a second part which carefully balances the excesses of the first, drawing the Wuthering Heights' family into the gentler order of the Grange. Such a reading means that we can recuperate not an ideal of 'home' but the idea of the domestic – in its full horror and glory – as being of overriding importance within the novel, rather than something to be impatiently dismissed in favour of a transcendent Romantic ideal. This accommodation of the domestic alongside the Romantic elements in the novel, whatever irresolvable conflicts it engenders, also seems more akin to Brontë's aesthetic practice of mixing romance and realism. The categories of romance and realism, home and abroad, coexist as much as they compete within the novel. This coexistence, which, as I've previously observed, is crucial to the characteristic way in which Brontë can be seen to flout literary decorum in this novel, continued her earliest literary practice when, as an adolescent, she simultaneously recorded in her diary that her imaginary race of Gondals are 'discovering the interior of Gaaldine' and 'Sally Mosely is washing in the back kitchen' (quoted in Gilbert and Gubar, 1979, p. 257). While this untempered mixing of the prosaic and the fantastic is particularly a feature of Brontë's fiction, a sense that ordinary domesticity is a fit subject for the novel is something that *Wuthering Heights* shares with a great number of Victorian novels.

In terms of its genre, the novel can be seen as tracing a gradual progression away from the predominantly Gothic mode of the first-generation story towards the form of realist domestic fiction that came to dominate the Victorian novel (Pykett, 1993, p. 90). The first-generation story is characterised by domestic violence, a 'forced' marriage, and incarceration, whereas the second-generation story ends with the withdrawal of the hero and heroine into the nuclear family and the gentler home-world of Thrushcross Grange; thus, to some extent, the novel indicates 'both changing patterns of fiction and the emergence of new forms of the family' (Pykett, 1993, p. 96). Feminist readings of the second-generation plot view it as either a retelling or a revision of the first-generation story, depending on whether they read the novel as voicing protest against the triumph of patriarchal power or as depicting its reform (Pykett, 1993, pp. 93–4). Perhaps it does both. As I have emphasised, the constant overlapping of the Gothic and the domestic is one of the distinctive features of this novel. There is certainly no schematic separation of genres. The Gothic is used from the start to show the shadow side of the Victorian domestic ideal, which can leave women the unequal partners under domestic tyranny, and it persists in the power of the ghosts of Cathy and Heathcliff to disturb us until the end (Pykett, 1993, p. 93). *Wuthering Heights* never allows us to arrive at the kind of harmonious and unexamined idea of the domestic encouraged by Ruskin, Patmore and others. However, 'home', notwithstanding, remains centre stage in this novel. In *Wuthering Heights*, the coexistence of the literary and domestic is also emphasised by the numerous domestic scenes in which books and reading feature.

Domestic reading in *Wuthering Heights*

I have mentioned some of the ways in which Brontë's own reading is evident in *Wuthering Heights*. In addition to these intertexual references to other works of literature, books themselves make numerous dramatic appearances within her story, reminding us of our own situation as readers and interpreters of *Wuthering Heights*.

Activity 4

Can you recall occasions in the novel when books are read? What is read and how? How are books and reading significant to the novel in your view?

Discussion

When Lockwood reads the first Catherine's diaries in the form of annotations written in a copy of the Bible, we are exposed to the heroine's defiant attitude to the most authoritative of texts. Catherine records how she and Heathcliff damage the religious pamphlets they have been set to read by Joseph before absconding onto the moors: 'Miss Cathy's riven th' back off "Th' Helmet uh Salvation,"' bellows Joseph in one of the novel's many exuberantly comic moments, 'un'

Heathcliff's pawsed his fit intuh t' first part uh "T' Brooad Way to Destruction'" (p. 17).

However, writing in the margins of books might equally be a sign of Catherine's marginal family and gender status (as Melissa Fegan notes in an interesting discussion of the novel (2008, p. 90)). Books are not only symbols of intellectual independence and resistance to tyranny. They have a material presence and value, and are predominantly the preserve of rich men (Lockwood piles books against the window to try and keep Catherine's ghost out, and Edgar retreats to his books when in conflict with his wife). The second Catherine uses books as currency in her barter with the groom who helps her to visit Wuthering Heights (p. 217), and ultimately also with Hareton. But her books become Linton's on their marriage, and she is entirely deprived of her books by Heathcliff and has not even their margins to write on (p. 266).

Hareton's desperate desire to read suggests the recuperative as well as empowering value of culture. Under Catherine's mockery of his illiteracy, he burns with shame and burns his store of books (p. 268). But when Lockwood returns to Wuthering Heights in the following September, he finds Catherine teaching a willing and devoted Hareton to read (p. 273). For old Joseph, this is competing literary activity, a threat to the authority of his Bible reading just as much as Nelly's irreligious ballad singing (pp. 280, 274). And Heathcliff's discovery of Catherine and Hareton reading together seems a decisive point in his loss of appetite for revenge (pp. 286–7).

Thus Catherine buys her way into, and eventually out of trouble with books; as does Hareton. Nelly, moreover, is able to narrate because she reads. Her account of having sampled most of the contents of the household library might seem a device for explaining how she is equipped for her task as narrator. But regardless of how we assess the benevolence or otherwise of her character, her literacy gives her a voice not typically available to a domestic servant. Joseph's obsessive and cantankerous reading of the Bible also shapes his voice, making him, at one level, spokesman of a repressive religious authority, but at another, giving him an idiom which reflects what would have been one of the few texts available to a person of his class. We might surely be mindful that Heathcliff, in his youthful oppressed state, is not the only disenfranchised resident of domestic society that the novel represents.

The readers in *Wuthering Heights* are also interpreters, and often narrators, of their stories. Hareton's acquisition of reading skills presages the rapid increase of access to print culture within the Victorian home and suggests a corresponding increase of interpretive activity. The frequent scenes of reading in the novel continue to mirror our own constant efforts to interpret the wealth of significant detail within the text. If you find it difficult to settle on one overarching interpretation of the novel, this might be a good thing, for 'any formulation of a single ordering principle' will leave something out, even if we feel strongly invited by the generic and other devices of the narrative 'to move step by step … room by room, into the "penetralium" of Brontë's strange vision' (Hillis Miller, 1982, pp. 46, 51). 'Penetralium' (the comically inflated term that Lockwood uses on entering Wuthering Heights (p. 2)) denotes an innermost secret place, but there is no final unveiling of home in Brontë's house of fiction. The generic components, characters and events of the novel incessantly promote and undermine conflicting expectations and there is no reason why the reader, any more than the novel, should feel obliged to resolve the logical contradictions that arise, or to close down the process of interpretation that continues even after the book is closed.

A divided afterlife

Unlike Charlotte Brontë's *Jane Eyre*, *Wuthering Heights* was no immediate popular success; *Jane Eyre*'s 1847 publication inspired a rapid proliferation of stage adaptations and other retellings of the novel. The status of *Wuthering Heights* as a popular novel is a twentieth-century phenomenon, following the success of the 1939 film with Laurence Olivier and Merle Oberon. In the three weeks following the film's release, more copies of the novel were sold than in any five-year period since its publication (Stoneman, 1996, p. 155). Thus a vast number of readers of the novel have come to it with the image of Catherine and Heathcliff perched atop Penistone Crag fixed in their minds; the wild moorland landscape also features constantly in romantic publicity posters for later films (Figures 6.5 and 6.6). The idealised romantic love conveyed by Wyler's vision represents (indeed initiated) the dominant mode of popular readings of the novel over the past seventy years.

Emily Brontë's own moorland home has become an important point of reference for readers of *Wuthering Heights*. In addition to the vast numbers of visitors to the village of Haworth every year, many more can explore the Brontë Parsonage Museum website for information about the town during the time the Brontës lived there, read the Brontë

Figure 6.5   Film poster for *Wuthering Heights*, dir. William Wyler (United Artists, 1939). Photo: © UNITED ARTISTS/Album/akg-images.

Figure 6.6   Film poster for *Emily Brontë's Wuthering Heights*, dir. Peter Kosminsky (Paramount, 1992). Photo: © Paramount/The Kobal Collection.

Society blog and view images of the cobbled High Street at Haworth and the moors beyond. The website provides fascinating information about the busy, populous world the Brontës inhabited, but perhaps nothing can compete with the stone walls, wind-blasted trees and wheeling skies pictured at Top Withens, thought to be the location for the house at Wuthering Heights.

One effect of film adaptations of *Wuthering Heights* was a decisive shift of attention to the female characters of the story. In this respect there is a limited interaction with the directions taken by academic studies of the novel. However, I suggested earlier that films of *Wuthering Heights* generally tell us more about twentieth- and twenty-first-century expectations of domestic romance within the film genre than about the novel itself. In contrast, critics such as Helen Small, in her introduction to the novel, emphasise Brontë's 'acute, and at times comedic, willingness to invoke and disturb expectations of genre, above all of sentimental romance' (p. ix).

Conclusion

From the beginning of its popularity in the twentieth century, *Wuthering Heights* has enjoyed a divided afterlife. Whereas academic studies of the novel have wanted to investigate its particular historical and cultural contexts, and bring a sequence of theoretical concerns to bear on readings of it, film adaptations have consistently aimed to make *Wuthering Heights* a timeless and universal romantic myth. This profound split between critical and popular representations of the novel exemplifies how stories take on a life of their own within our culture independent of their original contexts. Readers and audiences contribute to any text's meaning, as they interpret it in terms of their own interests and concerns. Texts go abroad. We make them at home.

For critical readers of the novel, 'at home' in *Wuthering Heights* is no simple matter. At least, that is what these two chapters have aimed to bring home to you. The themes of home and abroad, and the concept of the reader, have been used to interpret the novel. We cannot expect to reach a definitive interpretation of a text that constantly disturbs our expectations as readers, but these themes have helped to frame an exploration of the novel's ideological and generic complexity from which readers can venture further abroad for themselves.

References

Allott, M. (ed.) (1974) *The Brontës: The Critical Heritage*, London, Routledge.

Allott, M. (ed.) (1992 [1970]) *Emily Brontë:* Wuthering Heights, *A Casebook* (rev. edn), Basingstoke and London, Macmillan.

Bennet, A. and Royle, N. (1995) *An Introduction to Literature, Criticism and Theory*, Hemel Hempstead, Harvester Wheatsheaf.

Brontë, C. (2000 [1847]), *Jane Eyre* (ed. M. Smith, introduction and revised notes by Sally Shuttleworth), Oxford World's Classics, Oxford, Oxford University Press.

Brontë, C. (2007 [1849]) *Shirley* (ed. H. Rosengarten and M. Smith, introduction and notes by J. Gezari), Oxford World's Classics, Oxford, Clarendon Press.

Brontë, E. (2009 [1847]) *Wuthering Heights* (ed. I. Jack; introduction and additional notes H. Small), Oxford World's Classics, Oxford, Oxford University Press.

Byron, G.G. (1986 [1817]) *Manfred: A Dramatic Poem* in McGann, J.J. (ed.) *The Complete Poetical Works* (vol. 4), Oxford, Clarendon Press, pp. 51–102.

Coleridge, S.T. (1912 [1796]) 'The Eolian Harp' in Coleridge, E.H. (ed.) *Poetical Works*, Oxford, Oxford University Press, pp. 100–2.

Eagleton, T. (1988 [1975]) *Myths of Power: A Marxist Study of the Brontës*, Basingstoke, Macmillan.

Ellis, S.S. (1847) *Prevention Better than Cure: Or, The Moral Wants of the World We Live In*, London, Fisher.

Fegan, M. (2008) *Wuthering Heights: Character Studies*, London, Continuum.

Freud, S. (1985 [1919]) 'The "uncanny"' in Dickenson, A. (ed.) *Art and Literature: Jensen's Gravida, Leonardo da Vinci and Other Works*, The Pelican Freud Library (vol. 14), Harmondsworth, Penguin.

Gerin, W. (1971) *Emily Brontë*, Oxford, Oxford University Press.

Gilbert, S. and Gubar, S. (1979) *The Madwoman in the Attic: The Woman Writer and the Nineteenth-Century Literary Imagination*, London, Routledge.

Greenblatt, S., Cohen, W., Howard, J.E. and Maus, K.E. (eds.) (2008) *The Norton Shakespeare* (2nd edn) (with an essay on the Shakespearean stage by Andrew Gurr), New York, W.W. Norton and Co.

Grey, M.G. and Shirreff, E. (1850) *Thoughts on Self Culture* (2 vols), London, Edward Moxon.

Gunn, K. (24 April 2010) 'Modernism and Music workshop', email to Delia da Sousa Correa.

Hillis Miller, J. (1982) '*Wuthering Heights*: repetition and the uncanny' in *Fiction and Representation: Seven English Novels*, Cambridge, MA, Harvard University Press, pp. 42–72. (There is an extract in Allott (ed.) (1992 [1970]), pp. 224–35.)

Hoffmann, E.T.A. (1982), *Tales of Hoffmann* (trans A.J. Hollingdale), Harmondsworth, Penguin.

Khair, T. (2006) '"LET ME IN–LET ME IN!"', *Journal of Postcolonial Writing*, vol. 42, no. 2, pp. 155–64 [online], http://dx.doi.org/10.1080/17449850600973268 (Accessed 25 May 2010).

Meyer, S. (1996) *Imperialism at Home: Race and Victorian Women's Fiction*, Ithaca and London, Cornell University Press.

Poovey, M. (1989) *Uneven Developments: The Ideological Work of Gender in Mid-Victorian Britain*, London, Virago.

Pykett, L. (1993) 'Gender and genre in *Wuthering Heights*' in Stoneman, P. (ed.) *Wuthering Heights*, New Casebooks, Basingstoke, Macmillan, pp. 86–99. (This is a reprint of chapter five of *Emily Brontë*, Basingstoke, Macmillan, 1989.)

Shuttleworth, S. (1996) *Charlotte Brontë and Victorian Psychology*, Cambridge, Cambridge University Press.

Small, H. (2009) 'Introduction' in Brontë, E. *Wuthering Heights* (ed. I. Jack; introduction and additional notes H. Small), Oxford World's Classics, Oxford, Oxford University Press, pp. viii–xxi.

Stoneman, P. (1996) *Brontë Transformations: The Cultural Dissemination of Jane Eyre and Wuthering Heights*, London, Prentice-Hall.

Stoneman, P. (2011) 'Rochester and Heathcliff as Romantic heroes', *Bronte Studies*, vol. 36, no. 1, pp. 111–18.

Further reading

Alexander, C. (ed.) (2003) *The Oxford Companion to the Brontës*, Oxford, Oxford University Press.

Gezari, J. (2007) *Last Things: Emily Brontë's Poems*, Oxford and New York, Oxford University Press.

Glen, H. (ed.) (2002) *The Cambridge Companion to the Brontës*, Cambridge, Cambridge University Press. Essays on Haworth, the Brontë juvenilia, poetry and novels; the ideological, gender and religious contexts for their writing and 'The Brontë Myth'.

Mitchie, E.B. (1993) '"The yahoo, not the demon": Heathcliff, Rochester, and the simianization of the Irish' in *Outside the Pale: Cultural Exclusion, Gender Difference, and the Victorian Woman Writer*, Ithaca and London, Cornell University Press.

Pykett, L. (1992) *The Improper Feminine: Women's Sensation Novel and the New Woman Writing*, London, Routledge.

Stoneman, P. (2003) Entries on 'Ballet adaptations', 'Exhibitions of Bronteana', 'Film adaptations and biographies', 'Illustrations of the Brontë works', 'Operatic and musical versions', 'Sculpture', 'Sequels and incremental literature', 'Television and radio adaptations' and 'Theatre adaptations and biographies' in Alexander, C. and Smith, M. (eds) *The Oxford Companion to the Brontës*, Oxford, Oxford University Press, pp. 28–9, 183, 190–5, 260, 355–8, 446–7, 448–55, 492–3, 504–6.

Chapter 7
Arthur Conan Doyle, *The Sign of Four*

Shafquat Towheed

Aims

This chapter will:

- explore the idea of 'home' and 'abroad' in *The Sign of Four*, with specific reference to the relationship between Britain and India
- provide an overview of the rise of the genre of detective fiction, and its developing readership
- examine how the Victorians read, by studying the publication, distribution and readership contexts of *The Sign of Four*.

Introduction

In this chapter, we will begin by looking at the idea of home in the domestic settings of *The Sign of Four* (1890) by Arthur Conan Doyle (1859–1930), before studying the rise of detective fiction as a form of writing for Victorian readers. We will then investigate the publishing history of Doyle's novel, and conclude by looking at how abroad, in this case India, is presented in the book. Throughout the chapter, we will consider the relationship between ideas about home and abroad in the novel, and the importance of reading for the Victorians. As this chapter discusses *The Sign of Four* in some detail, it invariably gives away major points of the plot. Therefore, in order to enjoy the story as the author intended, at this point read through the whole of *The Sign of Four*, before returning to this chapter. The text referred to here is my edition, published by Broadview Press (2010). You will be asked to return to specific sections of the book in the activities and discussions below.

At home with the Victorians: London life

You have already been introduced to some of the main ideas that shaped how the Victorians thought of home, in both the domestic and the national sense. In the works of thinkers such as John Ruskin (1819–1900), poets such as Coventry Patmore (1823–1896) and experts in domestic management such as Isabella Beeton (1836–1865), creating a safe and morally righteous home was the most important expression of Victorian social values. The family home was idealised, from Queen Victoria's own household at Osborne House, to the millions of newly built town houses in London. As well as being a detective novel, *The Sign of Four* is also a domestic novel, for we are taken on a tour of a number of London interiors as part of the story: Thaddeus Sholto's house in Brixton; Mrs Forrester's in Camberwell; Bartholomew Sholto's 'Pondicherry Lodge' in Upper Norwood; and, most prominently of all, Sherlock Holmes's and Dr Watson's bachelor home at 221B Baker Street, which is where the story starts and finishes. Part of the reason for the enduring success of *The Sign of Four* and the other Holmes and Watson stories that followed is the familiar domesticity of 221B Baker Street. The episodic structure of the novel keeps bringing us back to this address, and the narrative repeatedly introduces us to the rituals associated with comfortable bourgeois life: a convivial dinner with fine wines, reading the newspaper over breakfast, practising the violin, taking afternoon tea. Holmes's padded, book-lined and cluttered drawing room, filled with the material objects of an increasingly prosperous society, would have been instantly familiar to many readers in late Victorian Britain. At the end of the story, we feel we know 221B Baker Street well, for Doyle gives us much detail about the interior (objects, furnishings, views, and so on) and the habits of Holmes and Watson. This is something that he carried on in the fifty-six stories featuring Holmes and Watson (between 1891 and 1927) that followed *The Sign of Four*, giving readers a sense of continuity through the detective stories. You can see a very accurate modern reconstruction of Holmes's room based on the descriptions in the Holmes and Watson stories in Figure 7.1.

Figure 7.1   Reconstruction of Sherlock Holmes's room, at the Sherlock Holmes pub, London. Photo: © John Bethell/The Bridgeman Art Library.

Activity 1

This activity is a playful test of your powers of observation and detection as a reader. Look at Figure 7.1, after having read through *The Sign of Four*, and see how many of the objects in the photograph are mentioned in the novel. Don't worry if you can't identify or find references to all the objects – just pick three or four.

Discussion

This modern reconstruction draws upon references to objects in the Holmes and Watson stories. Holmes is an avid reader, as well as the author of several books, and so the stacked books on the shelf are entirely appropriate – the first time Holmes speaks in the novel, he looks up from an 'old black-letter volume' (p. 49) that he has been reading. When Holmes carefully reconstructs Watson's movements on the morning the story opens, he leans back 'luxuriously in his armchair and [smokes on] … his pipe' (p. 53) – you can see a wicker armchair in the extreme bottom right of the image, and a rocker in the extreme left, and three different pipes on the pipe rack above the mantelpiece. The boxing gloves hanging next to them, and framed boxing prints, remind us of Holmes's skill in the ring, something not forgotten by the former prize-fighter, McMurdo (p. 77). On top of the inlaid Oriental table sits a coffee pot and cups – Holmes is a coffee drinker, and pours Watson's coffee at breakfast (p. 105). The violin on the chaise longue alerts us to one of Holmes's favourite hobbies; he takes up the violin to play a 'melodious air' (p. 110) and lull Watson to sleep, but he does not read a musical score, improvising instead.

As well as describing a domestic interior familiar to many of its readers, the level of domestic detail in *The Sign of Four* is designed to 'flesh out' the character of Holmes, and make him a realistic and believable personality. The clutter of objects described in the domestic interiors in the text is typical of the Victorian period, but it also serves to train you to see and read the text in a particular way. You will almost certainly have had your own visual image of Holmes and Watson shaped by numerous television and film adaptations, but Victorian readers also had visual cues to aid their reading of the stories. One of the reasons for the great success of the Holmes and Watson stories has been their visual appeal, something that was fostered by the dozens of illustrations by Sidney Paget (1860–1908) that accompanied the stories when they were first published in *The Strand Magazine*. Paget was largely responsible for the visual image of Holmes (his aquiline features and pipe) with which we are familiar today. See, for example, the illustration of Holmes conducting a chemistry experiment that was drawn to accompany 'The Adventure of the Naval Treaty' in *The Strand Magazine* in 1893 (Figure 7.2).

Figure 7.2   Sidney Paget, Dr Watson watching Sherlock Holmes working on chemical investigation, from 'The Adventure of the Naval Treaty', Conan Doyle's *Adventures of Sherlock Holmes* in *The Strand Magazine*. Photo: © Time Life Pictures/Getty Images.

Holmes undertakes a similar chemistry experiment in *The Sign of Four* (p. 113), designed to keep his mind occupied during a hiatus in his detective work. Paget's illustration reminds us of Holmes's love of chemical experiments and the fact that he undertakes these to keep his intellect from becoming stagnant. For readers of the stories, the illustrations serve to provide a hinterland for the characterisation in the narrative – thus Holmes's features and most typical gestures and habits are illustrated, in order to make him a 'real' person in the reader's imagination.

The descriptions of 221B Baker Street are cluttered with details of a domestic interior that readers grew to think of as real, rather than imaginary. So strong has been the sense of realism conveyed through the stories, that the Sherlock Holmes museum has claimed this fictional address, even though it is not located at 221B Baker Street (there is in fact, no such actual address), and has modelled itself on the textual descriptions and illustrations that accompanied the original Holmes and Watson stories in *The Strand Magazine*. The architect Russell Stutler has even reconstructed the floor plans of the address based on the textual evidence offered by Doyle's stories.

If 'Wuthering Heights' represents a Gothic, wild, uncanny house, troubled by its past, 221B Baker Street embodies much of the cosiness that Victorian readers would have known from their own homes. As the story unfolds, 221B Baker Street serves as a marker of domestic security in an unpredictable and sometimes frightening world. High ideals about the perfect home often clashed with the violent realities of urban life, as noted in the Introduction to Part 2 of this book. Arthur Conan Doyle was keenly aware of this. Born in Edinburgh in 1859 to an Irish immigrant family that experienced some financial hardship during his childhood, he had an excellent education at private school, and later at Edinburgh University, thanks to the generosity of an uncle. As a student of medicine in Edinburgh, and later as a practising doctor, he saw both sides of the social divide, and recognised that prosperity and respectability lived cheek by jowl with poverty and crime. Doyle knew from his own experience that even the seemingly happy Victorian home could hide dark secrets; his own father was an alcoholic, and had to be institutionalised in 1885, while Doyle's own medical research examined the effects of syphilis. The threat that the outside world presented to the home is an ever-present theme in *The Sign of Four*, in which domestic space repeatedly doubles as a crime scene. Even the comforting, cluttered world of 221B Baker Street is not all that it seems. We are told at the very beginning of the novel that Holmes is a drug addict, and injects himself three times a day with a 'seven-per-cent solution' (p. 50) of cocaine in the drawing room that, for millions of readers, has become the familiar home of the most famous consulting detective in the world.

Detective fiction

Detective fiction is a predominantly modern genre, and one with which you may already be familiar. In the form of both the novel and the short story, it is very much a development of the Victorian age; typically, from its beginnings, a single criminal case (almost always a murder or theft, or both) was solved through the concerted action of a consulting detective. Based around the solution of a particular crime that is unravelled through the narrative, detective fiction from the start encouraged the reader to engage with the text in a meticulous way.

Reading detective fiction

The earliest detective fiction in the English-speaking world was 'The Murders in the Rue Morgue' (1841) written by the American Gothic short story writer and poet, Edgar Allan Poe (1809–1849). Poe's story was set in Paris, and the first detective in English language fiction, C. August Dupin, was a Frenchman. 'The Murders in the Rue Morgue' was published in April 1841 in the Philadelphia-based journal *Graham's Magazine* before being serialised in French in the pages of the Paris daily newspaper *La Quotidienne* (June 1846), where it proved immensely popular. Poe followed this up with two further August Dupin stories, 'The Mystery of Marie Rôget' (1843) and 'The Purloined Letter' (1844). However, Dupin was more a cipher to explain the plot than a distinct personality. It was in France and in the hands of Émile Gaboriau (1832–1873) that detective fiction began to assume something more like its modern form. Gaboriau's *L'Affaire Lerouge* ('The Lerouge Affair', 1866) introduced a new type of hero, the specialist police detective, in the form of Monsieur Lecoq.

The earliest use of the term 'detective' was in an article in the Edinburgh-based *Chamber's Journal* in 1843, which referred to the work of the 'detective police', although it was Charles Dickens (1812–1870) in the journal that he founded and edited, *Household Words*, who first applied the term in its current, professional sense, referring specifically to the idea of a detective investigator as different from an ordinary policeman ('The Household Narrative of Current Events' in *Household Words*, October 1850). Inspector Bucket in Dickens's novel *Bleak House* (1852–3) was the first self-declared 'police detective' in English fiction, though he was only a minor character. On the other hand, Dickens's collaborator and friend Wilkie Collins (1824–1889) produced the single most famous example of Victorian detective fiction before the Holmes and Watson stories, in his long novel about the theft and return of a holy Indian precious stone, *The Moonstone* (1868), but without the fictional depiction of a consulting detective. *The Moonstone* was serialised in thirty-two weekly parts (January to August 1868) in the journal *All the Year Round*, which Dickens edited, and which boasted a circulation of well over 100,000 copies a week. As is illustrated from this summary history, detective fiction was becoming very popular with magazine and newspaper readers by the end of the nineteenth century. Despite this, the form of the detective story and the central personality of the private consulting detective did not fully mesh together until the appearance of the first of the Holmes and Watson stories, the short novel *A Study in Scarlet* (1887), in the pages of *Beeton's Christmas Annual*.

Central to the plot development of detective fiction is the ability of the detective to amass data from the case, distinguish between relevant and irrelevant information, eliminate scenarios that are illogical or implausible, and draw the correct conclusion: there can, of course, be only one conclusion. In *The Sign of Four*, Sherlock Holmes, the 'only unofficial consulting detective' and the 'last and highest court of appeal in detection' (p. 50) tells us more than once about the scientific method of investigation that he practises – the 'science of deduction' (p. 49) – and why this is an efficient and infallible method: 'when you have eliminated the impossible, whatever remains, *however improbable*, must be the truth' (p. 84). Deduction for Holmes is an infallible methodology, and as readers of detective fiction, we are encouraged to adopt it ourselves as we work our way through the story. As the onus is on the detective to prove guilt or innocence with complete certainty, detective fiction, like the testimony and cross-examination offered in a courtroom, is evidence-based, empirical and factual. But how should the reader know which facts to consider, and which to ignore? Detective fiction abounds in **significant** and **insignificant** detail. Significant detail provides valuable information about a case, a sequence of events, or a person. It is hard, **empirical evidence** (evidence which can be measured or recorded accurately, such as distance, weight, time or frequency), and will be useful (and hopefully remembered) in every successive reading of the text. Insignificant detail fleshes out the scene, place, person or event described; it has no first-hand value as evidence, but can help to form our opinions as readers. For detective fiction to work as a satisfying read, some of the significant detail should come across as insignificant, and vice versa.

We saw in the chapters on *Wuthering Heights* that Brontë's eclectic mix of genres resulted in a highly innovative text that produced (and continues to produce) any number of diverse responses from its readers. The genre conventions of detective fiction generate equally powerful but ultimately more predictable reader responses, stimulating an attention to detail – significant or otherwise – reminiscent of the detective protagonist and drawing readers into the plot through the promise of narrative resolution and closure.

Activity 2

Turn back to *The Sign of Four* and reread the first part of Mary Morstan's statement of her case, from 'I relapsed into my chair', at the bottom of p. 57, to Holmes's remark, '"Your statement is most interesting"', on p. 59.

What does Mary tell us about her case, and what questions does Sherlock Holmes ask her? How does Doyle present significant and insignificant detail in this passage?

Discussion

Mary Morstan offers us the bare skeleton of relevant information about the case that she possesses. She confirms the dates of Captain Morstan's return, her own life and career (with rough dates), and her father's connection to Major Sholto. Holmes's three questions in this passage are entirely empirical, and designed to ascertain what additional material evidence or material witnesses need to be followed up. He has established the following through just three questions: when Captain Morstan disappeared; that the material evidence in the form of a suitcase left behind will be of no further use in the case; and that Morstan's former army colleague, Major Sholto, had returned to England before Morstan, and he was now avoiding him. While readers of other types of literary fiction are encouraged by the author to be aware of characterisation, the reader of detective fiction is forced to pay attention to small details in the text. Constantly made conscious of the fact that both significant and insignificant details abound in the story, the reader must be careful not to let anything slip by their attention, while at the same time, they must try to distinguish between these two types of detail.

Rereading a detective story, therefore, is evidently not the same experience as reading a detective story for the first time. You may want to try this experiment yourself as you reread *The Sign of Four*. Writers of detective fiction use significant and insignificant detail to develop and resolve the plot, but they also manipulate this device to maintain our interest right until the end of the narrative. This tactic relates closely to the ways in which detective fiction was both published and read.

Publishing detective fiction

The first Holmes and Watson narrative, the short novel *A Study in Scarlet*, appeared in the 1887 edition of *Beeton's Christmas Annual*. This magazine had been founded by Samuel Orchart Beeton (1831–1877), husband of Isabella Beeton; each year it brought together a selection of the best new fiction in a single volume, published just before the Christmas book-buying and gift-giving season. Because of the astonishing fame of the Holmes and Watson stories in the 125 years since the first story appeared, first editions of the 1887 *Christmas Annual* (only thirty copies are known to survive) are now the most expensive magazines in the world, fetching over £100,000 at auction. Although *A Study in Scarlet* was critically well received, it was not initially a particularly great sales success, and Doyle was still in two minds about whether to write any further Holmes and Watson stories; up to this point, he was mainly a writer of conventional historical novels still experimenting with detective fiction. The fate of the Holmes/Watson partnership was sealed by a one-off commission for Doyle's next book, *The Sign of Four*.

The first publication of *The Sign of Four* was in the February 1890 edition of the Philadelphia literary journal, *Lippincott's Monthly Magazine*, where it appeared alongside Oscar Wilde's novel of aestheticism, decadence and murder in London, *The Picture of Dorian Gray*. Both authors had been specially commissioned to write for *Lippincott's* by the magazine's agent, Joseph Stoddard, at a dinner given at the Langham Hotel on 30 August 1889 (in *The Sign of Four*, Captain Morstan stays at the Langham on his return from India). *Lippincott's* was a well-regarded literary magazine, and sold in reasonable numbers, and Doyle's commission ensured that he was able to continue with the Holmes and Watson stories. However, the turning point in Doyle's literary career was Holmes and Watson's third outing in 'A Scandal in Bohemia', which appeared in *The Strand Magazine* in July 1891. Founded by the Victorian publishing impresario George Newnes (1851–1910), *The Strand* was a lavishly illustrated, standard size monthly magazine featuring a combination of new fiction (especially short stories) and journalism. Launched just before Christmas 1890 and retailing for only sixpence, circulation in the first month was an impressive 300,000 copies; this rose to over 500,000 copies within a few years, and remained at this astonishingly high level for the next four decades.

The Strand had literally millions of readers, and many of them bought the magazine simply to enjoy the next Holmes and Watson case. The detective fiction genre, together with the short story form, the magazine's excellent illustrations provided by Sidney Paget, and the personality of Sherlock Holmes, proved to be an irresistible combination for readers, offering a comfortingly predictable and yet thrilling outcome each month. The appearance of the Holmes and Watson short stories, Mike Ashley observes, 'revolutionised English-language popular fiction – and not only in the field of the crime or detective tale … what Doyle and *The Strand* gave to the world was the linked series of short stories, centred on recurring lead characters and conceived, in effect, as "situation comedy"' (Ashley, 2006, p. 199). The unravelling of each complicated plot kept readers engaged, while they were still reassured by the certain knowledge that Holmes would solve the mystery and identify the culprit.

The success of the Holmes and Watson stories in *The Strand Magazine* meant that successive British editions of *The Sign of Four* were offered at lower prices and reached a larger readership. George Newnes's decision to include it as the ninth title of his 'Penny Library of Famous Books' in 1896 ensured sales of over 50,000 copies. As well as cheap editions for the British market, *The Sign of Four* was extensively serialised in the provincial and popular press; it was reprinted in the *Bristol Observer*, the *Hampshire Telegraph* and *Sussex Chronicle*, the *Birmingham Weekly Mercury*, the *Glasgow Weekly Citizen*, and in George Newnes's cheapest magazine, *Tit-Bits*. It featured as number 2698 on Bernhard Tauchnitz's immensely popular 'Collection of British Authors' series (Leipzig, 1891), which was mainly aimed for readers of English fiction in Continental Europe. *The Sign of Four* was pirated widely in the American market, with over two hundred different editions appearing in Doyle's lifetime. It was the success of the stories in *The Strand Magazine* that caused *The Sign of Four* to be widely reprinted, reissued and serialised after 1891.

In total, fifty-six short stories and two novels – *The Hound of the Baskervilles* (1901–2) and *The Valley of Fear* (1914–15) – featuring Holmes and Watson appeared in the pages of *The Strand Magazine* between 1891 and 1927. For the bulk of its readers, the magazine was synonymous with Sherlock Holmes: 'the success of the Sherlock Holmes stories was so stunning that, in a sense, *The Strand Magazine* never recovered from

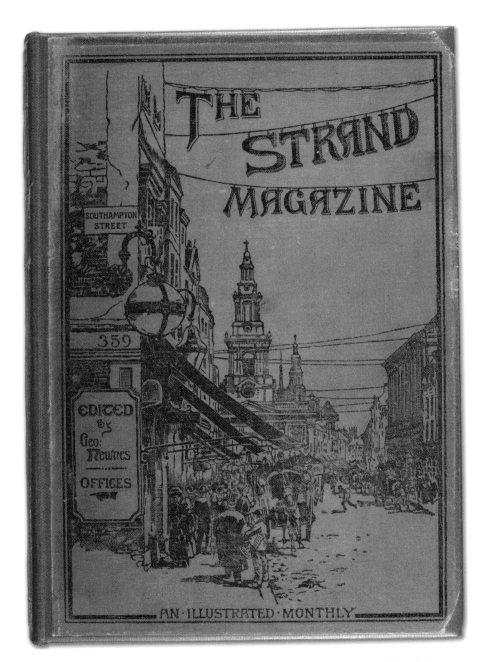

Figure 7.3   Front cover of *The Strand Magazine, an Illustrated Monthly*, London, 1891. British Library, London, p.p.6004.g.k. Photo: © The British Library Board.

it' (Ashley, 2006, p. 199). These stories made Doyle's career and kept the circulation of *The Strand Magazine* high, but they also constructed a vast reading community with shared tastes. Unlike the realist novel, detective fiction is driven by the resolution of the plot, rather than the gradual development of character. The structure is repetitive and predictable, with the narrative always offering a definitive resolution in a preordained trajectory: 'most of the stories open with Holmes and Watson in their cosy rooms in Baker Street, and most end with them back there again, with the mystery solved, the status quo restored' (Ashley, 2006, p. 199). From the beginning of the genre, detective fiction has been inseparable from the growing nineteenth-century world of popular magazines and mass circulation newspapers. Detective fiction was written for (and often described) readers who inhabited a newly industrialised urban world, stuffed with the new wealth of commerce, wracked with social inequality, and filled with anxiety about crime. Consuming detective fiction like the Holmes stories in bite-sized, regular chunks provided readers with a sense of engagement with the threat of crime, while offering them comforting reassurance that all was indeed well.

Activity 3

Look back through your copy of *The Sign of Four* and note how the text is structured. You will observe that it is divided into twelve parts and that each part is given a summary title; apart from the very last chapter (which is substantially longer), each is roughly 3,000 words in length. Why do you think the text is organised in this way? What might this indicate about the way Victorian readers read *The Sign of Four* and other detective stories?

When you've done this, think about the kinds of reading practices that are on display in the novel itself. What can we infer from them? Think carefully about the relationship between the structure of the novel, its narrative pace, and the way in which Victorian readers may have read this work.

Discussion

The Sign of Four originally appeared in a single number of *Lippincott's Monthly Magazine*, before being published in volume form as a book. However, following the success of the Holmes and Watson stories in *The Strand Magazine*, it was also extensively serialised in the regional and popular press. The short chapter structure is designed to facilitate easy serialisation in the pages of a newspaper or magazine. The episodic character of the narrative clearly indicates the type of readership and reading experience: mass market, largely mobile readers who read small chunks of fiction (in this case, detective fiction) for thirty minutes or so at a time. This is a very different way of reading from the practice of borrowing expensive three-volume novels (such as *Wuthering Heights*) from the lending libraries. Remember that almost all the Holmes and Watson stories that appeared in the 1890s in *The Strand Magazine* were also structured in this way.

Different types of reading practice are mentioned in *The Sign of Four*, but it is newspaper reading that is the most prevalent. Mary Morstan and the police place an advertisement in the newspapers to try to gather information about Captain Morstan's disappearance (p. 58), while Thaddeus Sholto, who 'read the details in the papers' (pp. 70–1) of Morstan's disappearance, places a notice in *The Times* (p. 59) to establish contact with Mary Morstan, and thereby send her individual pearls from the chaplet. The first account of Athelney Jones's botched handling of Bartholomew Sholto's murder are reported in the pages of the *Standard* (p. 106) and read gleefully by Holmes, while the following day's *Standard* carrying news of the release of Thaddeus Sholto (p. 113) is read by a relieved Watson. You will have noticed that Holmes uses the popular press – in this case 'an advertisement in the agony column' of the *Standard* (p. 114) – to flush out Jonathan Small from his hiding place. All of the action of the novel takes place over just ninety-six hours, and all the major figures in the story read newspapers regularly, strongly suggesting that Victorian readers depended heavily upon newspapers for up-to-date information.

It might be useful to think of Britain in the Victorian era as entering what is today referred to as an **'information economy'**, that is, one in which increasing numbers of people were literate, and had ready access to information, and where information itself had an intrinsic economic value. Information of all kinds, educational, vocational, and entertainment-related, was available through cheap fiction, magazines and newspapers, as well as through membership of public and lending libraries and other institutions, such as working men's clubs or guilds. W.E. Forster's Education Act (1870) had made schooling compulsory, and by the time Doyle's novel was published, the overwhelming majority (over eighty per cent) of Britain's population was at least functionally literate. Newspapers feature prominently in *The Sign of Four* as the hub of the information economy, both spreading and collecting together valuable information. All the characters in the novel, with the notable exception of the Andamanese Tonga, and Small's three Indian co-conspirators in Agra, are presented as literate and engaged in the world of print. Even Wiggins, the grubby leader of the 'Baker Street irregulars', has the ability to read Holmes's telegraph and report for duty (p. 107); he is paid to act as a lookout, again emphasising the increasing value of information in the Victorian period. This is a very different world from that presented a generation earlier, in the novels of Charles Dickens, for example, in which illiterate and semi-literate characters exist in large numbers. Although reading is an important activity in *Wuthering Heights*, the storytelling of Nelly Dean remains the chief method of conveying narrative, most of which is told (and retold) orally rather than through print. The Victorian information economy, however, was not simply restricted to Britain, as the rest of this chapter will show.

The Victorians and abroad

India in London

India, the largest, most diverse and unwieldy of Victorian Britain's imperial possessions, looms large in the narrative of *The Sign of Four*, as it did in the imagination of its Victorian readers.

Activity 4

Skim through your copy of *The Sign of Four*, noting any references to India. Now take a moment to jot down three or four of the ways in which India figures in Doyle's novel.

Discussion

References to Indian place names, events, objects and people, often in Hindi or Urdu (and all without explanatory notes in the original publication) abound throughout the text, and suggest that many of the book's intended readers would have been familiar with these terms. Mimicking Queen Victoria's Durbar Room, Thaddeus Sholto's suburban South London home is furnished with tiger-skins, hookahs and richly decorated Indian fabrics, gleaned from his family's lengthy and financially rewarding involvement with India. His brother Bartholomew has inherited their father Major Sholto's 'huge clump of a house' (p. 78), Pondicherry Lodge, in leafy Upper Norwood, named ironically after a French and not an English colonial territory in South India (Pondicherry, now Puducherry, is an Indian Union Territory). Major Sholto, Thaddeus informs us, 'had prospered in India, and brought back with him a considerable sum of money, a large collection of valuable curiosities, and a staff of native servants' (p. 70). The future Mrs Watson, Mary Morstan, was born in

India, before being sent 'home' to Edinburgh to start her schooling (probably at the age of seven). Captain Morstan spends many years serving as an officer in the British army in India, in both Agra and the Andaman Islands, before returning to England, ostensibly on leave but really to pursue his claim to a share of the Agra treasure.

Although he is not an ex-colonial, Holmes is well aware of the importance of India to British life, and, particularly, its relationship to crime committed in the metropolitan centre of London. He reads British gazetteers to find out about India, especially about the Andaman Islands (pp. 108–9), and can apparently tell the difference between Hindu and Muslim footprints (p. 108). Among his areas of specialised forensic study is the cigarette ash from various types of prepared tobacco, both British and Indian, a subject on which he has written a book, 'Upon the Distinction between the Ashes of the Various Tobaccos' (p. 52). Holmes tells us that he can distinguish between the 'black ash of a Trichinopoly' (a type of cigar made in Trichinopoly, now called Tiruchirapalli, a major city situated to the south-west of Chennai) and the 'white fluff of a bird's-eye' (a type of pre-cut pipe tobacco produced commercially in Britain). For Holmes, the ability to identify a potential culprit by whether he is smoking an Indian cigar is of vital importance: 'If you can say definitely, for example, that some murder had been done by a man who was smoking an Indian lunkah, it obviously narrows your field of search' (p. 52), he tells the incredulous Watson. As an imported and widely consumed commodity, tobacco was one of the goods central to Britain's imperial trade; India is the world's second largest producer of tobacco. Not only is the novel peopled with Britons returned from India and stuffed with Indian goods, but Indian servants are also conspicuous in the London homes depicted in *The Sign of Four*.

Activity 5

Looking through your copy of *The Sign of Four*, see if you can identify the Indian servants in the novel. How many such characters are there? What are their names? What do we know about them?

Discussion

Scrutinising the text in Holmesian fashion, you will find that there are at least three Indian servants in the employ of the Sholtos: Thaddeus

Sholto's nameless *khitmutgar* (Hindi and Urdu for 'butler'), 'clad in a yellow turban' (p. 66), who greets Holmes and Watson on their arrival in Brixton; Major Sholto's late butler, the 'faithful old Lal Chowdar' (p. 72), who helped dispose of Captain Morstan's body; and Bartholomew Sholto's butler, Lal Rao (p. 97), an accessory to his employer's murder at the hands of Jonathan Small and his unlikely Andaman Island accomplice, the blowpipe wielding Tonga. All were apparently brought back from India by Major Sholto upon his retirement soon after the disappearance of the Agra treasure. Working within the domestic sphere, the Indian butlers have information about the crimes committed inside Pondicherry Lodge – Lal Chowdar witnessed the death of Captain Morstan, for example. Athelney Jones arrests Lal Rao as an accomplice in the murder of Bartholomew Sholto (p. 106), and Holmes later indicates that Lal Rao was indeed the 'confederate in the house' (p. 156) who let Small and Tonga into Pondicherry Lodge to reclaim the treasure. Despite this, at no point in the story does Holmes interrogate Lal Rao.

Holmes's knowledge of India is a largely intellectual and theoretical one, derived from his reading, but Watson's experience is altogether more practical: he is another ex-colonial in the novel. In case we are in any doubt about the recurring cost in blood and treasure of holding on to India as the jewel in the crown of Britain's imperial possessions, Doyle reminds us at the very beginning of the narrative that Dr Watson is a veteran of a war on British India's borders. The good doctor carries a leg wound and a recurring pain from a 'Jezail bullet' (p. 51) fired during the 'Afghan campaign' (p. 50). This is a direct reference to his participation as an army doctor in the disastrous Battle of Maiwand (27 July 1880) during the Second Anglo-Afghan War (1878–80); fought on a single day on the borders of Helmand and Kandahar provinces, the battle cost an estimated 969 British and over 2,000 Afghan lives. The Second Anglo-Afghan War was fought specifically to establish Afghanistan's status as a neutral buffer state between British-controlled India, and Russia's expanding Central Asian empire. Despite the heavy casualties, public opinion at home was supportive, for the campaign seemed designed to ensure continued British rule over India.

If London in *The Sign of Four* represents, on the surface at least, the comfortable world of domestic interiors, conviviality, emotional order and the prospect of blissful marriage, India is depicted as its polar opposite: a land of extremes of wealth and poverty, danger, lawlessness and, above all, financial opportunity. Both the wealth and the danger of

India constantly threaten to destabilise London life. While bringing home the wealth of India can make life in London extremely comfortable, the prospect of retributive violence (whether by Indians or fellow Britons) being brought home at the same time is an ever-present danger. This formula was used to great effect by Wilkie Collins in the *The Moonstone* (1868), as well as by Doyle in his first detective novel, the Scottish-Indian revenge story *The Mystery of Cloomber* (1889). Central to the construction and resolution of the detective plot of *The Sign of Four* is the recovery of Mary Morstan's vast inheritance and prospective dowry: the Agra treasure was valued at 'not less than half a million sterling' (p. 76), or about £40 million in today's money. The loot of India represents the difference between Mary Morstan's genteel poverty as Mrs Forrester's governess in Camberwell, and becoming one of London's most eligible matches. As Watson ruefully notes, 'Miss Morstan, could we secure her rights, would change from a needy governess to the richest heiress in England' (p. 76).

The 'Mutiny'

One historical event that shapes the narrative of *The Sign of Four* is the outbreak on 10 May 1857 of the violent rebellion of Indian soldiers and civilians against British East India Company rule. Usually referred to as the Indian Mutiny, it lasted until 8 July 1858 and was the first serious challenge to British control in India. Because of the contested nature of the historical events of 1857–8, I have placed the word 'Mutiny' in quotation marks throughout this chapter. Simmering resentments about pay, working conditions, status, missionary attempts at conversion, and the lack of opportunities for promotion in the Bengal regiments of the East India Company's army were compounded by the issue of new paper cartridges for the army's regulation-issue Enfield rifles, which were greased with animal fat, variously described as pork lard (forbidden to Muslims) or beef tallow (forbidden to Hindus). The sepoys (from the Persian word *sipahi*, meaning foot soldier) would have to bite these paper cartridges open before loading their rifles, thereby violating their religious beliefs. Rumours about the cartridges spread across the Indian regiments like wildfire, inflaming a widely held conviction that the East India Company had a secret policy of converting its soldiers to Christianity.

The 'Mutiny' broke out in Meerut, north-east of Delhi, during the hottest month of the year, and while the British were in church. It soon spread across a wide area of northern and central India. More than two-thirds of the 200,000 Indian sepoys turned on their officers, often killing their British commanders and their families on sight. In various parts of India, the mutinous sepoys were joined by peasants, members of the former Mughal elite, and feudal landowners, all of whom had their own grievances against the British East India Company. Peasant farmers were deeply unhappy about the British policy of forced (and heavily taxed) indigo cultivation. In *The Sign of Four*, Jonathan Small, the whip-bearing overseer, is the only British survivor of the massacre at the Mathura indigo plantation; the plantation owner Abel White, the manager Dawson, and Dawson's bookkeeper wife, are all killed by the rebels (pp. 135–6).

In Agra, the city depicted by Doyle in *The Sign of Four*, the resident British population of nearly 2,000 men, women and children took refuge from the 'Mutiny' inside Agra Fort on 1 July, and stayed there until the beginning of December, secure inside the fort's impervious walls. Conditions for the British besieged in Lucknow and Cawnpore (Kanpur) were far worse. In Kanpur, the prospect of the British recapturing the city provoked the single largest atrocity against British civilians during the conflict, when on 15 July 1857, some 120 women and children were hacked to death with meat cleavers and their bodies thrown down a well in the infamous Bibighar Massacre. In Lucknow, British soldiers and civilians were besieged inside the Lucknow Residency from 30 June until 27 November 1857; it took two separate attempts (the second with the help of Nepalese Gurkha soldiers) before the British could successfully relieve the siege. By July 1858 the 'Mutiny' had been crushed and brutal British reprisals, including the mass execution of suspected rebels and ordinary civilians, took place. Looting was widespread, with many British soldiers and their Indian allies settling scores by looting the wealth of the rebel cities they recaptured. Doyle's depiction of the murder of Achmet and the theft of the Agra jewels by Small and his sworn Sikh accomplices (pp. 141–4) during the 'Mutiny' in Agra is entirely plausible, but his trial and conviction is not. Few if any looters (whether British or Indian) of Indian property in the aftermath of the 'Mutiny' were even caught, let alone punished.

The political impact of the Indian 'Mutiny' was to transform British rule in India from the indirect authority of the East India Company to the direct rule of the crown as a colony, with an appointed Governor General representing the monarch. This process was formalised by the proclamation of Queen Victoria as Empress of India in 1877.

Literary responses to the 'Mutiny'

The cultural impact of the events of 1857–8 on the British public was wide and long-lasting. In the following decades, dozens of novels were written and published on this theme, as well as scores of histories, memoirs, paintings, poetry and privately printed volumes of correspondence; 'more than any other event in the British career in India the rebellion was the single favourite subject for metropolitan and Anglo-Indian novelists' (Chakravarty, 2005, p. 3). This was especially evident in magazine and newspaper journalism during 1857–8, which fed an inexhaustible British public appetite for information about events in India. 'No episode in British imperial history', Patrick Brantlinger notes, 'raised public excitement to a higher pitch than the Indian Mutiny of 1857' (1988, p. 199). Newspapers and magazines as varied as the *Illustrated London News*, *Punch* and *Household Words* carried increasingly hysterical (sometimes wildly inaccurate) reports from India, and with it, intemperate calls for revenge.

For British readers on the home front, the 'Mutiny' was, in fact, a series of literary reinterpretations that turned historical fact into popular mythology. The 'epochal impact' of the 'Mutiny' on the Victorians, the critic Christopher Herbert comments, 'can only be meaningfully studied by considering it not as a geopolitical event, but as a literary and in effect a fictive one – as a story recounted over and over, in one stylistic register after another, in various journalistic media' (2008, p. 3). Novelists such as Charles Dickens, Wilkie Collins and Mary Elizabeth Braddon (1837–1915), and the poet Alfred Tennyson (1809–1892), contributed forcefully to the shaping of the 'Mutiny' in the British popular consciousness; the latter's 'The Defence of Lucknow' (1879) is reprinted as Reading 7.1 (you should read this now).

Even writers without family connections to India responded to these events. The poem 'In the Round Tower at Jhansi, 8 June 1857', by Christina Rossetti (1830–1894), is one of the most vivid literary responses to the newspaper reports of atrocities committed by mutinous sepoys. Rossetti was a leading nineteenth-century British poet, sister of the Pre-Raphaelite painter and poet Dante Gabriel Rossetti (1828–1882), a devout Christian, and an accomplished practitioner of the sonnet form. Her poem voices an imaginary last conversation between Captain Skene, the Political Superintendent in charge of the administration of Jhansi district, and his wife, both of whom were killed (together with their two small children) in controversial circumstances during the first weeks of the 'Mutiny' in the town of Jhansi.

Activity 6

Rossetti's poem, 'In the Round Tower at Jhansi' is reprinted as Reading 7.2 in 'Readings for Part 2' at the back of this book. Take some time to read the poem now, along with the reports in *The Times* for 2 and 11 September 1857 (Readings 7.3 and 7.4).

How would you summarise the subject of this poem? In what ways does it relate to the two newspaper articles? Are there any major differences in the events described in the two articles and the poem?

Discussion

Rossetti's poem was inspired by reading the account of the death of Captain Skene and his wife in the *Illustrated London News* on 5 September 1857, which presented a tragically heroic sequence of events; this account was reprinted from *The Times* of 2 September 1857 (see Reading 7.3). Holed up in the round tower at Jhansi, running out of ammunition, hopelessly outnumbered by the mutineers, and facing the prospect of being captured, Captain Skene shoots his wife, before committing suicide. Rossetti's poem presents their suicide as an act of patriotic love: the couple prefer death to dishonour at the hands of the mutineers. The unstated fear in Rossetti's poem is that of the possible rape of Mrs Skene by the Indian sepoys; this fear was one widely held at the time of the 'Mutiny'. Press reports repeatedly raised the spectre of the rape of British women. In fact, while civilians (including British women and children) were murdered by the mutineers, the many official histories, memoirs (including those by women who survived) and reports of the events of 1857–8 that emerged in the years following found no evidence of rape as a weapon in the conflict. Indeed, the report of the massacre of officers and their families at Jhansi in *The Times* of 11 September 1857 (see Reading 7.4) refuted the two most central aspects of Rossetti's poem: that the Skenes committed suicide (they were, in fact, captured and then killed by the rebels), and that there was any risk of Mrs Skene being raped – the British women were 'spared any violence save death' (*The Times*, 11 September 1857). In the 1875 publication of the poem in the volume *Goblin Market, The Prince's Progress and Other Poems*, Rossetti was obliged to append a note to her poem: 'I retain this little poem, not as historically accurate, but as written and published before I heard the supposed facts of its first verse contradicted' (Sisson (ed.), 1984, p. 215). Rossetti's note admits that the Skenes' suicide as originally reported had not been substantiated.

The engraving of 'The Death of Major Skene and his Wife at Jhansi' is another highly dramatised visual representation of an event that is at odds with the facts. It appeared as an illustration in Charles Ball's *The History of the Indian Mutiny* (1859) (see Figure 7.4). The text of Ball's *History* supports the second, revised account of the Skenes' death (they were captured and executed) that appeared in *The Times* of 11 September 1857 and in all subsequent accounts; however, like Rossetti's poem, the engraving perpetuates the first account, this time adding a small dead child for emotional charge. This engraving and Rossetti's poem express the emotional response of British readers, rather than representing a factually accurate event. The reinterpretation of the events of the Indian 'Mutiny' had started even before the outcome of the conflict was certain.

Figure 7.4   Holding the dead body of his wife, Major Skene shoots himself as Indian soldiers close in on him during the Indian Mutiny at Jhansi, India, 1857. Illustration from Ball, C. (1859) *The History of the Indian Mutiny*, 2 vols, London, London Printing and Publishing Company. Photo: © Getty Images.

Rossetti and the engraver of Ball's *History* mythologise an interpretation of the 'Mutiny' that was not supported by historical fact. A massacre of officers and their families did take place at Jhansi in June 1857, but the circumstances differed from the events depicted in Rossetti's poem and the engraving in Ball's *History*. Doyle, when he came to write *The Sign of Four* more than three decades after the events of the 'Mutiny', drew upon many of those very same myths, by now deeply ingrained in British popular memory, and told and retold many times through histories, memoirs, verse, fiction and the visual arts.

Activity 7

Turn back to *The Sign of Four* and reread Jonathan Small's account of the outbreak of the Indian 'Mutiny' in Mathura. This begins 'Well, I was never in luck's way long', on p. 135, and ends 'our powder gave out, and we had to fall back upon the city', on p. 137. Pay particular attention to the language and visual imagery being used and see if you can answer the following questions.

How does Small present the change in his life in India brought about by the 'Mutiny'? How does he describe the atrocities that he witnessed? And finally, what knowledge of the events of 1857 does Doyle expect from his readers?

Discussion

Remembering the information given earlier in this chapter about the publication and readership of *The Sign of Four*, we can conclude that Small's account of the 'Mutiny' is solidly aimed at British readers at home. He compares his life in India before the 'Mutiny' to the comfort of domestic life in the Home Counties of England – 'one month India lay as still and peaceful, to all appearance, as Surrey or Kent' – before describing the conflict in apocalyptic terms: 'two hundred thousand black devils let loose, and the country was a perfect hell' (p. 135). Small's account describes the rebels in demonic terms: they are 'black fiends', 'dancing and howling', and a 'swarm of bees' (p. 136). His depiction of the atrocities he sees is in graphic, even pictorial terms. Mrs Dawson is described as being 'cut into ribbons', while Dawson is 'lying on his face, quite dead, with an empty revolver in his hand' (p. 136). Small explicitly mentions that he expects the British listeners to his confession (Holmes and Watson) to 'know all about it … a deal more than I do … since reading is not in my line' (p. 135). Implicitly, Doyle is expecting the same from his British readers. This suggests that more than thirty years after the events of 1857, the large number of British readers at home who had never witnessed the 'Mutiny' (as was the case with Doyle) could still be expected to know something about it.

More books were published about the 'Mutiny' in the 1880s and 1890s than at any other time, and Doyle is clearly tapping into his readers' awareness here. Visual representations of the massacres of British civilians during the 'Mutiny' were both graphic and commonplace in the journalism of the time and the visual art that followed. These pictorial representations (paintings as well as engravings in books) shaped the British understanding of the 'Mutiny' as much as written accounts did. Christina Rossetti, the illustrator of 'The Death of Major Skene and his Wife at Jhansi', and Arthur Conan Doyle, all had one thing in common: none had been to India or were present as witnesses to the Indian 'Mutiny', and yet all engaged with it in their work. All these representations are text- or image-based, rather than witness-centred, and elicit a particular emotional response from their readers/viewers. In the Victorian imagination, the events of the Indian 'Mutiny' were fixed for generations to come by those first, often lurid accounts in newspapers and magazines, further amplified through fiction, poetry and visual representation. The Victorians at home could not have been indifferent to the perceived threat, as well as the real benefits, of empire.

Conclusion

The Victorian age was Britain's greatest period of imperial expansion abroad, and economic and social development at home. The two processes were mutually interdependent, although not always acknowledged as such. Hall and Rose observe that 'the Empire's influence on the metropole [i.e. the imperial capital, London] was undoubtedly uneven ... there were times when it was simply there, not a subject of popular critical consciousness', while 'at other times it was highly visible, and there was widespread awareness of matters imperial on the part of the public as well as those who were charged with governing it' (2006, p. 2). Doyle's novel provides us with a perfect snapshot of this uneven influence of the empire on the metropolis. The narrative assumes an unproblematic relationship between Britain and India, never, for example, questioning the legitimacy of British rule. However, the entire plot of this detective novel is dependent upon the chaos brought about by the Indian 'Mutiny' of 1857, as well as the individual greed, treachery and criminality of a range of British colonists – Jonathan Small, Captain Morstan, Major Sholto, the prison guards on the Andaman Islands and Bartholomew Sholto.

The Sign of Four is a detective story written for an increasingly urban, mass readership accessing and consuming fiction through affordable periodicals such as *Lippincott's Monthly Magazine* and *The Strand Magazine*, and reading about the world through cheap newspapers such as the *Illustrated London News* and the *Evening Standard*. The narrative is driven by the plot rather than by character development, and the texture of reality is provided by Doyle's careful assembly of significant and insignificant recognisable details throughout the text: real places, objects, times, and the geography of London are plausibly referenced. As in all detective fiction, the triumphant plot resolution, complete with the prospect of Watson's marriage to Mary Morstan and a new phase of his domestic life, vindicates the investment of the reader in the book; they read detective fiction because they know that the crime will be exposed and the culprit punished. Holmes's ability to solve each case is as predictably reliable as the London fog or Watson's bouts of obtuseness. *The Sign of Four* shows us the Victorians at home at their most comfortable and reassured: living an ordered, secure, domestic life, with threats to their material and physical well-being systematically eliminated through the logical application of Holmes's famous and infallible maxim, 'when you have eliminated the impossible, whatever remains, *however improbable*, must be the truth' (p. 84).

For all its interest in home, both literally and metaphorically, *The Sign of Four* is also a novel about the Victorian abroad. Written *by* a novelist who had never been to India and was born after the events of 1857, and *for* a domestic audience whose knowledge of the 'Mutiny' would have been shaped almost entirely by books, newspapers and visual images, this detective novel articulates the anxiety about empire felt, but not always expressed, by so many British readers in the last decade of the nineteenth century. Doyle's politics were uncomplicated; he was a committed supporter of empire, a campaigner in favour of the British effort in the Second Anglo-Boer War (1899–1902), and later a chronicler of the First World War (1914–18). Despite this, *The Sign of Four* clearly illustrates at least one potential blowback of empire – that the effect of crimes committed in India would be felt at home in Britain, even in suburban London. Many Victorians were uncomfortable with the increasingly intricate relationship between home and abroad. As Hall and Rose ask, 'Was it possible to be "at home" with an empire and with the effects of imperial power or was there something dangerous and damaging about such an entanglement? Did empires enrich but also corrupt? Were the expenses they brought worth the burdens and responsibilities?' (2006, p. 1). Dr Watson is only too pleased that the Agra treasure is at the bottom of the Thames, beyond the reach of all who seek to possess it, whether legitimately, or illegitimately. After all, by losing the treasure, he gains a wife.

References

Ashley, M. (2006) *The Age of the Storytellers: British Popular Fiction Magazines, 1880–1950*, London, Oak Knoll Press and the British Library.

Ball, C. (1859) *The History of the Indian Mutiny: A Detailed Account of the Sepoy Insurrection in India*, London, London Printing and Publishing.

Brantlinger, P. (1988) *Rule of Darkness: British Literature and Imperialism, 1830–1914*, Ithaca, Cornell University Press.

Chakravarty, G. (2005) *The Indian Mutiny and the British Imagination*, Cambridge, Cambridge University Press.

Collins, W. (1868) *The Moonstone*, London, Tinsley Brothers.

Doyle, A.C. (2010 [1890]) *The Sign of Four* (ed. S. Towheed), Peterborough, ON, Broadview Press.

Hall, C. and Rose, S.O. (eds) (2006) *At Home with the Empire: Metropolitan Culture and the Imperial World*, Cambridge, Cambridge University Press.

Herbert, C. (2008) *War of No Pity: The Indian Mutiny and Victorian Trauma*, Princeton, NJ, Princeton University Press.

Sisson, C.H. (ed.) (1984) *Christina Rossetti: Selected Poems*, Manchester, Fyfield Books.

Further reading

Brantlinger, P. (2009) *Victorian Literature and Postcolonial Studies*, Edinburgh, Edinburgh University Press.

Hall, C. (2002) *Civilising Subjects: Metropole and Colony in the English Imagination, 1830–1867*, Cambridge, Polity Press.

Martin, R.M. (1858–60) *The Indian Empire* (vol. 1), London, The London Printing and Publishing Company.

Chapter 8

Robert Louis Stevenson, 'The Beach of Falesá'

Shafquat Towheed

Aims

This chapter will:

- guide you through 'The Beach of Falesá', its composition and publication history
- explore the idea of 'home' and 'abroad' in the text
- further your understanding of Victorian readers by examining the relationship between places of writing and reading in Stevenson's life.

Introduction

This chapter introduces you to some poetry and a relatively little known story by one of the most widely read writers of the nineteenth century: Robert Louis Stevenson (1850–1894). Keeping with the theme of 'Home and abroad in the Victorian age', we begin by looking at Stevenson's childhood home in Edinburgh, examining how he then works ideas of home into two of the poems in *A Child's Garden of Verses* (1885). The main section of this chapter will encourage you to examine Stevenson's intriguingly experimental South Pacific domestic realist story, 'The Beach of Falesá' (1892–3). We will explore the complicated relationship between 'home' and 'abroad' in this story, written after the author emigrated to Samoa. Throughout the chapter, we will consider how Victorian readers, while reading at home, might have approached literature written about foreign subjects. You may have read something by Stevenson already: perhaps *Treasure Island* (1883), or *Kidnapped* (1886), or *The Strange Case of Dr Jekyll and Mr Hyde* (1885). Those of you who haven't are likely to know something about him through the enormous influence his writing has had on popular culture and cinema. There have been over fifty film adaptations of *Treasure Island* alone, and 'Jekyll and Hyde' has entered common English usage to denote a violently split personality. As an author, Stevenson's popularity has proved long-lasting, with many of his books continuously in print from the date of first publication to the present day. In the chapters on Wordsworth, De Quincey and Shelley in the first part of this book, you will have encountered the idea of the author as a person of cultural, political and economic significance, but perhaps no one in the nineteenth century better exemplifies the elevation of the author to celebrity, and the writer's life to the stuff of myth, than Robert Louis Stevenson. Stevenson's writing from and about the Pacific broadened the imaginative horizons of millions of British readers, giving them an insight into societies they could not have experienced first hand. The act of reading brought distant lands home to British readers.

At home with the Victorians: Edinburgh life

Unlike Emily Brontë, who lived and died in relatively obscurity, and whose writing only became celebrated after her death, or Arthur Conan Doyle, whose fictional detective Sherlock Holmes became more famous than his creator, Stevenson was a major literary celebrity in his own lifetime. Born in 1850 in Edinburgh, Stevenson was from a solidly respectable upper-middle-class Scottish family. His father Thomas Stevenson (1818–1887) was one of the leading lighthouse engineers in the Victorian era, while his mother's family, the Balfours, boasted many prominent lawyers and clergymen. In May 1857, when Stevenson was six and a half years old, the family moved to 17 Heriot Row, a four-storey Georgian town house in Edinburgh's New Town, and this remained his main residence in Britain until 1880. A sickly child who could rarely complete a term without being withdrawn from school, Stevenson was efficiently and rather over-solicitously cared for by his personal nurse, the devout Presbyterian Alison Cunningham (1822–1913), known affectionately as 'Cummy'. She read the Bible and works on Presbyterian morality, rather than fiction, to her young charge. Stevenson's domestic life was significantly more privileged than that of many of the authors you have already come across, such as William Wordsworth, Emily Brontë or Arthur Conan Doyle. Growing up in material security and some comfort, Stevenson did not have to contend with the lack of living space of Dove Cottage, or the cramped and draughty conditions of Haworth Parsonage. However, prosperity and social respectability in the Victorian era often brought with it a greater level of domestic scrutiny and restrictions on liberty. The main way in which Stevenson chose to allow his mind to wander was through reading, especially about faraway lands.

Activity 1

Look at Figures 8.1 and 8.2, which show a plan of 17 Heriot Row and a view from the nursery. What kind of house would you say it was? How would you describe the view? What do you think Stevenson's childhood would have been like (in the nursery on the top floor)?

Discussion

Looking at Figure 8.1, one of the first things you notice is that 17 Heriot Row is arranged over four levels, with the kitchen and storage in the basement, the reception and dining rooms on the ground floor, the drawing room and main bedrooms on the first floor and other bedrooms (including the nursery) on the top floor. This is a very similar arrangement of space to that of Linley Sambourne House, which you encountered in the introduction to this part of the book. As with all Victorian residences, the major aim of the distribution of space is clearly to separate public from private spheres, thereby maintaining the privacy and respectability of the family. Servants are kept as far from the main bedrooms as possible; they have their own entrance in the basement, separate from the main family entrance on the ground floor.

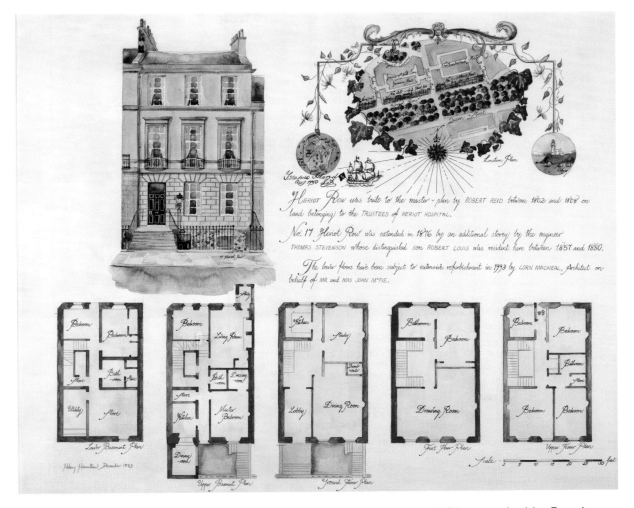

Figure 8.1   House plans of Stevenson House, 17 Heriot Row, Edinburgh. Photographed by Brendan Macneill. Photo: © Brendan Macneill Photography.

Stevenson's nursery room, and the adjacent room of his nurse, was on the very top floor of the house. The view from his nursery room has not changed substantially since the 1870s. Looking out of the window across the rooftops of Edinburgh's New Town, you can just make out a body of water, the Firth of Forth, beyond the docks at Leith. Across the water, the hills of Fife are barely discernible. The view from Stevenson's nursery (effectively his sickroom) provided tantalising glimpses of the wider world beyond, such as the sails of the schooners and the funnels of steamships plying the Firth of Forth.

Figure 8.2   View from the nursery, Stevenson House, 17 Heriot Row, Edinburgh. Photographed by Brendan Macneill. Photo: © Brendan Macneill Photography.

In such a respectable and prosperous domestic environment, the young Stevenson would have been insulated from the often grim reality of life in Victorian Edinburgh, and especially the unmodernised Old Town: poverty, pollution, overcrowding and epidemics of infectious diseases. Unlike the natural childhood environment being promoted a generation earlier by Romantic poets such as Wordsworth and Shelley, Stevenson's childhood was physically secure, but psychologically stifling. Then, as now, Edinburgh was a vibrant, outward-looking, trading port city. The wealth of its citizens, and their domestic security depended upon external trade. As the pre-eminent lighthouse engineer of the time, Stevenson's father was central to the development of safe navigation for commercial shipping, and thus, the expansion of Britain's trading empire. In the other direction, the view from the nursery room looks out onto the elegantly planned Queen Street Gardens, the enclosed, private green space exclusively for Edinburgh New Town's wealthy inhabitants. Stevenson would have been able to see other children – his neighbours – play in Queen Street Gardens, while he remained confined indoors because of his health. While 17 Heriot Row presents the security and restriction of an ideal Victorian home, it also depends for its very existence on the expansion of trade abroad.

From an early age, Stevenson suffered from the respiratory illness that would plague him for the rest of his life – it would eventually kill him – and much of his childhood was spent indoors. There are clear parallels here with Emily Brontë's life in Haworth Parsonage, where she and her siblings created the imaginary worlds of Gondal and Angria, partly as a result of not being able to experience much beyond their immediate vicinity. While the Brontë family's relatively modest means meant that sickness could not be kept at bay, Stevenson's parents went to great expense to make sure he was safeguarded from the worst of the Scottish weather (trips to the south of England and to France, under careful parental supervision, were regularly taken). From home, Stevenson instead read extensively and developed the wide-ranging imagination that would become the hallmark of his fiction.

How might Stevenson's childhood have shaped his imagination and literary ambitions? We can start to answer this question by looking closely at two of the sixty-five poems brought together in *A Child's Garden of Verses* (1885), 'Foreign Lands' and 'Travel'. This volume was, perhaps, the most widely read poetry that Stevenson ever wrote; the various richly illustrated editions that have appeared over the last 125 years have proved to be enduringly popular with children. It is worth remembering that Stevenson wrote these poems as an adult reminiscing about his childhood and adopting the poetic voice of a child, rather than as a child writing children's poems for his own pleasure.

Activity 2

Read 'Foreign Lands' and 'Travel' (reproduced as Readings 8.1 and 8.2 at the end of this part of the book). Think about how 'abroad' is represented in these poems. What images does Stevenson use? List the foreign objects or images that the speaker sees in these poems.

Discussion

The poem 'Foreign Lands' clearly indicates the child Stevenson's fascination and curiosity with the world that lay beyond 17 Heriot Row, one he could glimpse only briefly and partially. In this poem, Stevenson imagines himself as a boy climbing a cherry tree, to catch sight of what lies beyond his home. But what 'foreign' lands does the boy in the cherry tree see? His vision moves telescopically from the near, to the distant, and finally to the imaginary: next door's garden, the road outside, the river flowing into the sea, fairy land. In 'Foreign Lands', Stevenson's imaginative vision of the wider world is literalised from his own childhood experience; that is, he imagines what it would be like to have a clearer view of the Firth of Forth ('To where the grown-up river slips / Into the sea among the ships' (ll. 15–16)) rather than the partial one he has from his nursery window. Stevenson's poem draws upon two senses of the word 'foreign': foreign as in strange or unfamiliar; in this case, like the 'next door garden' (l. 5) that he has seen for the very first time; but also foreign in the sense of abroad rather than home; in this case, the ships heading out through the Firth of Forth, and the imaginary road leading to 'fairy land' (l. 18).

In the poem 'Travel', Stevenson presents a more conventional, exoticised vision of abroad; here, abroad is everything home is *not*. His starting point is one of the most famous works of English literature, a book that many children growing up in Victorian Britain would have known well: Daniel Defoe's castaway novel, *Robinson Crusoe* (1719). The young Stevenson imagines 'Lonely Crusoes' (l. 6) building boats on their desert island, 'watched by cockatoos and goats' (l. 5). This focus on Crusoe's desert island then expands outwards to encompass the wonders of the world: the Great Wall of China, crocodiles basking on the banks of the Nile, mosques, minarets, jungles and deserts. Stevenson's language in 'Travel' is insistently visual; he lists and describes all the things encountered in travelling abroad that are not to be found at home – from camel caravans to red flamingos, and from 'Man-devouring tigers' (l. 26) to 'forests, hot as fire' (l. 17). This poem captures the spirit of adventure and romance that was still associated with travel and exploration in the nineteenth century. The child's poetic voice imagines his adult self as an explorer, a commander of 'a camel caravan' (l. 40) who will find a deserted city in the sands.

As both 'Travel' and 'Foreign Lands' indicate, Stevenson's interest in the wider world outside the home started in early childhood. From this confined domestic space, he grew up to become not only one of the greatest writers of the era, but also one of its most celebrated travellers. During the period of his apprenticeship and development as a writer, 17 Heriot Row was Stevenson's main address, and although he made lengthy trips away from Edinburgh during his teens and twenties, he returned periodically to his protective parental home. His physical journeys became more adventurous and productive; trips to the near-abroad of France produced two travel books, *An Inland Voyage* (1878) and *Travels with a Donkey* (1879). While Edinburgh was Stevenson's birthplace and home for much of his life, the breadth of his reading (and the frequency of his travels) suggests that by the 1880s he was thinking of himself as a citizen of the world, rather than the inhabitant of a single city or place. Looking at the poems 'Travel' and 'Foreign Lands' should give you an understanding of how ideas of home and abroad were related to one another in Stevenson's life and writing. Despite a sheltered childhood, his imaginative compass was far-reaching, and his interest in the world beyond Edinburgh and Scotland more than merely cursory. In 1888 he left for the Pacific, never to return. The rest of this chapter examines how Stevenson's representation of home and abroad in his writing changed after he emigrated to a world as far from the Scottish capital as it was possible to be.

Reading 'The Beach of Falesá'

The rest of this chapter will guide you through a short story, 'The Beach of Falesá', that Stevenson wrote after he emigrated to Samoa in 1889. The edition of the text referred to here is that reproduced in the Oxford World Classic's edition of *South Sea Tales*, edited by Roslyn Jolly (1996; reissued 2008). As 'The Beach of Falesá' is a short piece of fiction, you are advised to read it in full now. If possible, try to read it in a single sitting. There is a specific reason why you might want to do this, as it will help you understand the context of the story's composition and publication.

Once you have read 'The Beach of Falesá', you should take some time to reflect on your reading. If you succeeded in reading it in a single sitting, did you find that an easy task? Did you stumble over any of the words or references in the story? Did you need to use the glossary or explanatory notes to make sense of non-English or unfamiliar words? And did you find the representation of dialect and accent difficult to understand? There are particular reasons and circumstances why you may have encountered such difficulties; we will explore some of these and answer some of these questions by looking at the composition, publication and reception of 'The Beach of Falesá', as well as Stevenson's ambitious intentions for the story.

A hybrid form

'The Beach of Falesá' is a longish short story, divided into five chapters. It is longer than the short stories (or 'tales') written by a number of prominent writers, including Arthur Conan Doyle, Rudyard Kipling (1865–1936), Henry James (1843–1916) and Stevenson himself, that appeared in the burgeoning literary magazines of the 1880s and 1890s;

these stories were usually fewer than 10,000 words in length, and always appeared in single instalments. It is, however, too short to be considered a novel, such as Doyle's *The Sign of Four*, which has often been published as a single volume. 'The Beach of Falesá' is best defined as a **novella** or a short novel, a work of prose fiction between 20,000 and 40,000 words in length; it is therefore a hybrid (or mixed) form – too short to be considered a novel, too long to be a short story. Why might he have produced a text of this length?

Stevenson wrote 'The Beach of Falesá' to be serialised in instalments in a newspaper, rather than in a single number of a magazine; this form of serialisation, in short weekly chunks, determined the length of the work. The first version appeared in six weekly instalments in the newspaper the *Illustrated London News* during July and August 1892 under the title 'Uma; or the Beach of Falesá (Being the Narrative of a South-Sea Trader)'. Founded in 1842, the *Illustrated London News* was the largest circulating illustrated weekly newspaper in Britain, with sales of over 300,000 copies per week; for its readers, it was both their first source for news of the world outside of Britain, and a regular source of serialised fiction. Stevenson's story was guaranteed a large readership, but the unfamiliarity of the topic and the foreign words in the title necessitated the addition of a subtitle ('Being the Narrative of a South-Sea Trader') to make the story understandable to a mass British readership.

The content matter of the story caused problems. As you will know from your reading of the text, one of the central premises of the plot is that John Wiltshire, the Scottish trader in Falesá, tricks Uma into marriage through a false contract, lasting one night. This was too much for the editor of the *Illustrated London News*, Clement Shorter, who considered the plot to be scandalously indecent. Shorter deemed Stevenson's domestic story of the Pacific inappropriate for the sitting rooms of British homes (the story was also illustrated with an image of a bare-breasted Pacific island woman). Stevenson was asked to change the bogus marriage plot before serialisation, which he refused to do. Shorter then took matters into his own hands, and when 'The Beach of Falesá' finally appeared in his newspaper, reference to the false marriage had been entirely removed from Chapter 1 of the text. Stevenson was understandably furious, and insisted that the false marriage be reinstated when the story was published in book form. This finally took place in April 1893, when the revised version of the story (containing Stevenson's own corrections) was published in the volume *Island Nights'*

Entertainment. This is the version of the text which represents the author's final intentions, as far as can be judged, and it is this version that is reproduced in Jolly's edition of *South Sea Tales*. Stevenson was not the only author subject to this kind of censorship by editors and publishers; writers such as Thomas Hardy and Oscar Wilde were also forced to make changes before publication, or had cuts imposed upon them on the grounds of decency. You can find out more about the publication history of 'The Beach of Falesá' in the section entitled 'Note on the Texts' (pp. xxxiv–xxxvii) in Jolly's edition of *South Sea Tales*.

'The Beach of Falesá' is a hybrid work not only because it is too short to be a novel and too long to be a short story, but also because of its content: it mixes realism with more romantic and poetic modes; it even gives a central place to the supernatural. In this work, as in several other tales that he wrote at the time, such as the novella *The Ebb-Tide* (1894), he experimented with different genres and styles of writing. Stevenson had made his literary reputation as a writer of adventure romances often pitched at boys, such as the extraordinarily popular *Treasure Island*, which was first serialised in the pages of the British children's magazine *Young Folks* in 1881–2. This reputation was cemented by his historical romances, such as *The Master of Ballantrae* (1889) and *Kidnapped* (1886). As an established literary critic and one of the leading champions of adventure romance in the late nineteenth century, Stevenson had criticised the nineteenth-century realist novel for what he saw as its excessive attention to detail and refusal fully to engage the imaginative potential of its readers. In his essay 'A Note on Realism' (1883), he described realism as a 'technical method' that risked being 'tedious and inexpressive' through its faithful devotion to depicting reality at the expense of entertaining readers (Stevenson, 1883, p. 26). However, by the time he had moved permanently to Samoa, and probably spurred by the very different environment that he encountered there, Stevenson was beginning to move away from adventure romance and towards realism. As Roslyn Jolly observes: 'Victorian Britain's most theoretically sophisticated critic of literary realism suddenly and unexpectedly turned towards the realistic, even naturalistic, representation of contemporary life' (2009, p. 27). You can see elements of both the realist novel and the adventure romance in 'The Beach of Falesá'; let us look at some examples of this in the narrative, such as in the opening section of the story.

Activity 3

Reread the opening of 'The Beach of Falesá', from the first sentence, 'I saw that island first ...', on p. 3, to the end of the captain's account of John Adams, ending, 'Poor John!', on p. 4.

Then think about the following questions. How does Wiltshire describe his first sight of the island? What does the captain tell us about the house? What kind of story does this first exchange between Wiltshire and the captain set up for its readers? Think carefully about how readers are expected to read this opening, what they are expected to know, and how they are guided into the island.

Discussion

The first thing you might notice in the opening paragraph is the poetic and descriptive language used by the first-person narrator, later identified as the Scottish copra trader John Wiltshire. The opening paragraph describes his first glimpse of the island, Falesá, as their boat approaches landfall. Wiltshire arrives in a time of transition, 'when it was neither night nor morning', with the moon setting, but the sun not yet having risen. His language is full of strongly visual imagery conveying the beauty of the natural world: the 'broad and bright' moon, the pink dawn, and 'the daystar [that] sparkled like a diamond'. Wiltshire engages all his senses in describing his first impressions of the island: the smell of the 'wild lime and vanilla', the cool temperature of the breeze blowing in his face, the prospect of hearing new words in a 'tongue [that] would be quite strange to me' (p. 3). Stevenson's opening paragraph sets the scene for his British readers, encountering this story about the Pacific on the other side of the world. He draws in his readers by letting them see Falesá for the first time as Wiltshire does, through the perspective of his first-person narration.

In the next three paragraphs, Stevenson moves our viewpoint from the general to the specific; he does this literally, with Wiltshire looking through the captain's telescope to get a closer look at the shoreline. What Wiltshire sees immediately takes us from the world of the imaginary paradise island to the often grubby reality of the life of a nineteenth-century foreign trader in the Pacific. Through the telescope, Wiltshire (and the reader) can make out the islanders' homes among the trees, and the solitary white coral house, used by his white predecessor, John Adams. Stevenson uses the captain's dialogue with Wiltshire to provide us with the 'back-history' of the trade settlement at Falesá, and indicate the peculiar problems of the place. The captain points out that the windward side of the island is uninhabited, and that John Adams, one of the first white traders on the island, declined into illness and insanity. Stevenson also uses the dialogue between Wiltshire (the newcomer) and the captain (a frequent visitor) to provide us with additional significant detail relevant to Wiltshire's possible future life on the island, noting, for example, that John Adams died raving about 'somebody watering his copra' (p. 4).

In his deployment of such poetic language in the opening paragraph, Stevenson is capturing as closely as possible the magical first encounter so many visitors to the South Pacific, from Captain Cook onwards, have related in fiction, travel writing, correspondence and memoirs. Stevenson recorded his own experience of landfall on his first Pacific island, Nuku-Hiva in the Marquesas group (today's French Polynesia), on 20 July 1888. This account was posthumously published in the volume *In the South Seas* (1896). Stevenson's words are almost identical to Wiltshire's in 'The Beach of Falesá': 'the first experience can never be repeated. The first love, the first sunrise, the first South Sea island, are memories apart and touched a virginity of sense ... the moon was an hour down by four in the morning. In the east a radiating centre of brightness told of the day; and beneath, on the skyline, the morning bank was already building, black as ink' (Stevenson, 1998 [1896], p. 6). In this opening paragraph, Stevenson is echoing the accounts of previous visitors to the Pacific in describing Falesá; this is something that would most likely have been familiar to his readers. This opening section of the story draws the reader in through the romance of the first encounter with a Pacific island, and then presents us with a realist account of the problems of previous foreign traders on Falesá. Stevenson draws upon the adventure romance and travel writing traditions and the expectations of his readers before showing them the reality of life on Falesá, which, despite its beauty, is far from being an exotic island paradise. In doing so, Stevenson takes his traditional readers, who might have been expecting another adventure story, into new territory: a realist account of contemporary life in the South Pacific, witnessed first hand by the author. Like Doyle, then, deftly managing his readers' responses through his construction of gripping detective narratives, Stevenson wrote with his readers very much in mind, playing on their expectations of romantic adventure in order to coax them into a quite different reading experience.

A new realism

In 'The Beach of Falesá', Stevenson was attempting something new in his literary career. The change of environment and his encounters with a new and developing Pacific society meant that, for the first time, he started writing stories that could be described as 'realist' or 'realistic'. Writing to his friend and literary advisor Sidney Colvin (1845–1927), Stevenson described his excitement at being able to write about his Pacific experiences in this way, and not just in the modes of adventure or romance. 'It is the first realistic South Sea story: I mean with real South Sea character and details of life', he declared, adding to his intended reader that 'you will know more about the South Seas after you have read my little tale than if you had read a library' (Booth and Mehew (eds), 1994–5, vol. 4, pp. 100–1). Despite the fact that the plot of 'The Beach of Falesá' deliberately uses the supernatural (the taboo around Wiltshire's house, and the islanders' belief in *Tiapolo* or the devil), Stevenson's narrative deals with these phenomena in a realist fashion. Case's cave of evil spirits is exposed as a fraud concocted with luminous paint and Aeolian harps, while Wiltshire maintains a resolute scepticism about the effectiveness of both island beliefs and Christianity. While Falesá is an imaginary island (no such place exists), Stevenson took great pains to make his representation of island life as accurate as possible, basing many of the attitudes, practices, beliefs and aspirations of the islanders on the Samoans whom he interacted with on a daily basis. There are two other aspects of realism in Stevenson's story that we will be looking at in the next section of this chapter: the use of dialect in the narrative, and the circulation of books.

New forms of English

One of the things that you might notice when reading 'The Beach of Falesá' is Stevenson's use of dialect and slang. Like Doyle, who peppers *The Sign of Four* with Hindi and Urdu words, Stevenson uses many Polynesian (mainly Samoan) ones. Moreover, parts of the novella are not written in the standard literary English that would normally have been found in the fiction serialised in the pages of the *Illustrated London News*. As a Scot, Stevenson was acutely aware of the differences of dialect, accent and usage in the British Isles. In his essay, 'The foreigner at home' (1882), Stevenson maintained that the categories of home and abroad could not be supported linguistically within the British Isles itself: 'it is not only when we cross the seas that we go abroad … Ireland, Wales and the Scottish mountains still cling, in part, to their old Gaelic speech', he reminded his readers (in Stevenson, 1990 [1887], p. 2; this essay has been reproduced as Reading 8.3). Remember that Brontë uses regional dialect (that of her native Yorkshire) to great effect in *Wuthering Heights*, while Doyle uses cockney sporadically in *The Sign of Four*. However, unlike those novels, Stevenson's story attempts realistically to represent a new, evolving, and still unstable dialect of English, broadly called Pidgin, which emerged as a new language out of the trading relationships on the beach between different communities (Europeans, Americans, Chinese, various Pacific islanders) across the Pacific.

Variously known as Bêche-de-mer, Bislama or Pidgin, this fast-changing, mixed form of English has continued to evolve in much of the Pacific and variations of it have since been adopted as the national language of Vanuatu (Bislama), Papua New Guinea (Tok Pisin) and the Solomon Islands (Pijin blong Solomon). Often, these new and existing Pacific languages were given formal recognition through the translation and publication of the Bible. Chief among the translators was one of nineteenth-century Britain's most successful enterprises, the British and Foreign Bible Society, which was founded in 1804, and continues working to this day as the Bible Society. The British and Foreign Bible Society was committed to printing cheap Bibles in English and circulating them as widely as possible; it was also responsible for commissioning translations into local languages and dialects to support missionary work. In the last two centuries, it has translated the Bible into over 2,000 languages, and has printed and distributed more than 550 million copies. In 'The Beach of Falesá', Uma's Bible is one of these translations – Wiltshire pointedly turns to the title page, which is in English – although it is still printed and shipped from England: "*'London: Printed for the British and Foreign Bible Society, Blackfriars'*" (p. 60). For millions of people in Africa, Asia, the Americas and the Pacific, their first encounter with literacy and the printed book was often such a translated Bible; in almost every Pacific language, the first printed book was a translation of the Bible. Lacking a language in common, Uma uses the English-based island Pidgin trading language to communicate with her husband, Wiltshire. Linguistically, in this depiction of the domestic life of Wiltshire and Uma, 'The Beach of Falesá' swaps the categories of home and abroad for its Victorian British readers. Stevenson's commitment to realism in the story meant that he had to depict Samoan life as he saw it, and this included an attempt to reproduce the Pidgin English that was becoming the trading language of the Pacific, and was increasingly being used by islanders in their negotiations with outsiders.

Activity 4

Now reread the first page of Chapter 5, from the beginning, 'Well, I was committed now …', to '… the last word I've got to say', on p. 60).

What does this episode tell us about Wiltshire and Uma's domestic life? How do they communicate? How does Wiltshire use the Bible in this discussion? And what does this domestic episode tell us about the circulation of books and readers?

Discussion

The opening page of Chapter 5 presents some of the complications of Wiltshire's home life, and also indicates the global circulation of books and ideas by the end of the nineteenth century. Wiltshire brings out the Bible in an attempt to placate Uma, and prove that he will be unscathed by venturing into the windward side of the island at night; however, Uma questions the efficacy of the Bible ('She swore a Bible was no use') against the island spirits. Wiltshire resorts to the Bible because he is clearly unable to persuade her otherwise, despite his apparently superior British knowledge and her alleged 'Kanaka [i.e. native] ignorance'; '[y]ou know her style of arguing', he tells us resignedly. While Wiltshire as the narrator speaks in standard colloquial English, Uma's responses (as represented by Wiltshire) show the word order and simple structure of Pidgin English. Stevenson's commitment to realism is at its clearest here in its depiction of an everyday marital argument.

Wiltshire's decision to take the Bible into his meeting with Case in this scene carefully replicates the earlier false marriage contract that was used to trick Uma into marriage. However, in this case it is Wiltshire who is tricked, and Uma who has the last word. Far from resigned passivity, and despite her own fears of the *aitus* (devils) in the windward side of the island, Uma secretly follows Wiltshire into the cave, and the inevitable final bloody confrontation with Case. This episode of swearing an oath on the Bible (and carrying it with him as a protection against evil spirits) precipitates Uma's unconditional support for Wiltshire, and demonstrates their marriage in the spirit as well as the letter of the law. For all Wiltshire's scepticism towards the missionaries and religious symbols, and in spite of Uma's superstitious regard for the spirits of the island, the couple have a common, textual point of reference: the Bible printed in Blackfriars and shipped to the other side of the world. Once again, 'The Beach of Falesá' reminds us of the increasing interconnectedness brought about by trade and empire. However, this interconnectedness, as Wiltshire and Uma's domestic life shows, brought with it problems as well as opportunities. Chief among these perceived problems was the prospect of the mixing of the races and the dilution of British values and certainties that may occur as a result.

Stevenson in the South Pacific

Stevenson's emigration to Samoa titillated and scandalised late Victorian British society. His removal to Samoa added immeasurably to his appeal as an exotic, romantic writer-traveller in the mode of Byron or Shelley earlier in the century. It generated publicity and sales; Stevenson's celebrity meant that he was pursued by journalists across the Pacific. So strong is the tradition of his readers following in his footsteps that Vailima (and Stevenson's grave on Mount Vaea) now rank among Samoa's top tourist destinations. However, Stevenson's emigration also intensified Victorian anxieties about propriety, both moral and literary. Many critics and fellow novelists, among them Oscar Wilde, Henry James and even his friend Sidney Colvin, felt that the move to Samoa had negatively affected Stevenson's writing.

While Stevenson vigorously rebutted accusations that his literary talent was ill-served by life in Samoa (about as far from the literary centre of London as it is possible to be), he was less able (and less willing) to defend himself against insinuations that he was 'going native'. Stevenson and his American wife Fanny Vandegrift Osbourne Stevenson (1840–1914) often went barefoot, and this was seen as evidence of his 'supposed decline, his exposure to a foreign land, and his repudiation of Western culture' (Colley, 2004, p. 55). Stevenson was fascinated by island life wherever he encountered it in his travels across the Pacific. He bought Hawaiian grammars, collected and transcribed local oral poetry and myths, read travel books on the region, and eventually taught himself passable Samoan. Stevenson's use of Polynesian epic verse is evident in the ballad 'Rahéro' (an extract from which is reprinted as Reading 8.4). Figure 8.3 shows the extent to which Stevenson immersed himself in all aspects of Pacific life. This picture was taken during his second voyage through the Pacific (on the schooner the *Equator*) on the island of Butaritari in present-day Kiribati (pronounced 'Kiribass') in June 1889. Stevenson is pictured relaxed on the ground, with Fanny and a prominent Butaritari couple, the bride, Nei Takauti, and her much younger husband, Nan Tok'. Fanny Stevenson and Nei Takauti sit in the centre of the picture, holding hands, but not engaging in eye contact, while their respective (and both much younger) husbands lie on the ground flanking their wives, and looking at the photographer. All are barefoot and wearing flower garlands. This seemingly innocuous image of Pacific island innocence had the power to offend Victorian sensibilities. Not only are the Stevensons no longer in a state of Western dress (thereby undermining their racial and cultural identity), but they are also apparently endorsing the relationship between the dominant, materially wealthy and sexually experienced Nei Takauti, and her much younger and submissive husband, Nan Tok'. Stevenson (1998 [1896]) described the inexperienced Nan Tok' as 'his wife's wife' and explained their relationship thus: 'they reversed the parts indeed, down to the least particular; it was the husband who showed himself the ministering angel in the hour of pain, while the wife displayed the apathy and heartlessness of the proverbial man' (pp. 203–4). This socially accepted marriage on Butaritari was violently at odds with British Victorian norms of gender roles in marriage. By seeming to endorse this behaviour as normal, Stevenson undermined one of the most central beliefs that underpinned the Victorian ideal of the home: female subservience to male power.

Figure 8.3   Stevensons in Butaritari, Kiribati, 1889, from the album of the cruise of the *Equator*. From left to right: Nan Tok', Fanny Stevenson, Nei Takauti and Robert Louis Stevenson. The Writers' Museum, Edinburgh, LSH 149/91. Photo: © RLS photograph/The Writers' Museum Collection, Edinburgh.

Stevenson's new life in the Pacific consciously engaged with the peoples, cultures and places that he encountered. The American linguist and critic Mary Louise Pratt has used the term 'contact zone' to refer to 'social spaces where cultures meet, clash, and grapple with each other, often in contexts of highly asymmetrical relations of power, such as colonialism, slavery, or their aftermaths as they are lived out in many parts of the world today' (1991, p. 33). For the vast majority of European and American traders, missionaries and settlers in the Pacific, that 'contact zone' had a very specific place: the beach, the location where trade and conversation and all other forms of exchange (financial, sexual, and so on) took place. In 'The Beach of Falesá', the entire narrative is played out on this contact zone. While Stevenson's engagement with Pacific culture and its contact zones was emotionally and creatively positive, not all encounters were quite so unproblematic. Let us examine, for example, Stevenson's depiction of Wiltshire's first encounter with his adversary Case, which takes place on the contact zone of Falesá's leeward-facing, and un-tabooed, beach.

Activity 5

Go back to the first chapter of the story and read from 'When these two traders came aboard …', at the bottom of p. 4, to '… in her own place', towards the end of p. 5. Pay careful attention to the description of Case. How is he described in terms of his physical appearance, race, nationality and behaviour?

Discussion

Wiltshire's initial response to Case is one of instinctive racial and national solidarity. Having arrived in Falesá after 'four years at the line', that is, a solitary posting on one of the equatorial islands (probably present-day Kiribati), Wiltshire is deprived of contact with his countrymen: 'I was sick for white neighbours', he tells us (p. 4). On closer inspection, he finds Case difficult to place. While the smart clothes 'would have passed muster in the city', Case's complexion is curiously yellow (jaundice? alcoholism? too much sun? – we aren't told). Stevenson's first-person narration allows us to see Case through Wiltshire's eyes. The initial excitement at meeting a fellow Briton on Falesá is replaced by a growing sense of uncertainty about Case's social, national and moral standing. 'No man knew his country, beyond he was of English speech' (p. 5), Wiltshire tells us, throwing open the question of whether he is English, Scottish, American, Australian or something else. While Wiltshire notices that Case is clearly highly educated and an 'accomplished' accordion player, he is also quick to point out Case's chameleon-like ability to adapt to circumstances and situations. 'He could speak … fit for a drawing-room; and when he chose he could blaspheme worse than a Yankee boatswain' (p. 5), Wiltshire comments. Case is evidently not what British Victorian readers would recognise as 'a gentleman', and Wiltshire is at pains to point out his essential opportunism: 'The way he thought would pay best at the moment, that was Case's way, and it always seemed to come natural' (p. 5). Wiltshire's own racial solidarity gives way to the recognition that Case does not represent the values or principles of home.

Wiltshire's engagement with Case highlights one of the central problems that European imperial expansion in the nineteenth century presented for fixed ideas about race and nationality. On the one hand, British traders, missionaries and settlers were expected to be ambassadors of British virtues, and to remain faithful to those values however long they spent 'abroad'. On the other hand, their increasing distance and dislocation from the values of 'home', and the fact that the contexts of social class and kinship meant far less, resulted in the inevitable dissipation of the racial and national attitudes that they had brought with them. For Stevenson and his wife visiting the island of Butaritari, this meant entering into Pacific life, complete with bare feet and flower garlands, and the reversal of the established Victorian roles of husband and wife, encapsulated by the relationship between Nei Takauti and Nan Tok'. In 'The Beach of Falesá', Case has spent so long in the Pacific that he no longer has a discernible nationality beyond the fact that he is English-speaking. Captain Randall has been in Falesá for such a long time that he now squats 'on the floor native fashion … naked to the waist' (p. 8). Case has a Samoan wife who 'dyed her hair red, Samoa style' (p. 5) and his first (and most enduring) act is to arrange a marriage for Wiltshire. For Wiltshire, the choice is clear: marry a Polynesian woman or remain a bachelor. Racial and national categories, as with the ideas of home and abroad, were increasingly destabilised by the realities of trade, imperial expansion, and emigration and settlement. Ironically, the further the British ventured from home, the more strictly they tried to live by the ideals and principles of the mother country; and yet, making a new home abroad invariably meant creating a new, mixed way of life. Nowhere is this clearer in 'The Beach of Falesá' than in its closing sections.

Activity 6

Now turn to the end of 'The Beach of Falesá'. Reread the last three paragraphs, from 'As for the old lady …', on p. 70, to the end of the story, on p. 71. What does Wiltshire tell us about his married life? What are his racial assumptions and prejudices?

Discussion

The last three paragraphs provide a postscript to Wiltshire's life on Falesá, and make us realise that the main action of the narrative happened some years earlier (i.e. in the 1870s or 1880s), for Wiltshire has since moved away from the island, and has had children with Uma who are nearly grown up. Despite her increased weight and tendency to give away the profits of the station, Wiltshire describes her as an 'A 1 wife' (p. 71); however, he ascribes her faults not to her character, but to her race ('that's natural in Kanakas' (pp. 70–1)). Wiltshire's own racial prejudices are clear throughout the story; he is dismissive of the islanders for their alleged lack of logic, and frequently uses racially offensive terms ('Kanaka'). In addition, he makes it clear that he does not want his daughters to marry Pacific islanders, despite their own mixed ancestry: 'I can't reconcile my mind to their taking up with Kanakas, and I'd like to know where I'm to find the whites?' (p. 71). Wiltshire is unapologetic about his prejudice, boasting that 'there's nobody thinks less of half-castes than I do' (p. 71); he accurately reflects the unthinking prejudices of many Victorian British traders, settlers and emigrants. However, he has been successful in making a home for himself and his family in the Pacific, unlike the missionary Tarleton, who has 'gone home … parsonizing down Somerset way' (p. 71). Revealingly, Wiltshire no longer refers to Britain as home, but rather as 'a white man's country' (p. 71).

If Wiltshire's family was racially and socially ambiguous and undetermined, Stevenson's Vailima household was equally miscellaneous: neither conformed in the slightest to Victorian ideals of the perfect and ordered family. Stevenson's wife was an American divorcee, with two children from her first husband, Samuel Osbourne: Lloyd Osbourne (1868–1947), who would later become a playwright, and Isobel Strong, later Field (1858–1953). Isobel's first husband was the artist Joe Strong (wearing the Samoan lava-lava or male wraparound skirt in Figure 8.4), but the marriage ended in divorce in 1892, largely due to Strong's alcoholism; their son Austin Strong spent his school holidays at Vailima. Stevenson's mother, Margaret (1829–1897), lived in Samoa with her son until his death in 1894. The Vailima household was a socially and culturally diverse reconstituted family.

Figure 8.4   The family and household staff of Robert Louis Stevenson gathered on the veranda at Vailima, Samoa, 1892. In the back row are Joe Strong with a parrot on his shoulder; Margaret Stevenson; Lloyd Osbourne; Robert Louis Stevenson; Fanny Stevenson; and Simi the butler. In front of them sit Mary; Taloja the cook; Belle and Austin Strong; Lafaele the cattleman; and (standing) Tomasi the assistant cook. At the front are Savea the plantation boy; Elena the laundress; and Arrick the pantryman. Photo: ©The Writers' Museum, Edinburgh Museums & Galleries.

Figures 8.4 and 8.5 indicate that Stevenson's domestic life in Vailima conformed to neither the exacting standards of Victorian domestic life, nor the long-standing traditions of village life in Samoa. Stevenson insisted on dressing for dinner each evening, eating at a table set in the European style, accompanied by imported wine, and continued to order his books from Britain. However, Samoan staff and members of his family (including his wife) continued to wander the house without shoes, maintain the strong clan relationships intrinsic to Samoan life, and engage in the protracted social rituals of chiefly consultation.
As Ilaria Sborgi points out, '*Home* was Stevenson's means of responding to the novel situation he encountered in his South Sea travels …
Stevenson's representation of *home* in his Pacific travel account reflects both his *sympathy* as a reader/interpreter/observer and as a writer/ ethnographer/storyteller' (2007, p. 194).

Figure 8.5　Stevenson family with Samoan domestic servants on the porch at Vailima, Samoa, 1892. Photo: Beinecke Rare Book & Manuscripts Library, Yale University.

Conclusion

Set in an exotic, fictionalised and unidentifiable location, with a plot involving an interracial romance, the supernatural and a fight to the death between good and evil, 'The Beach of Falesá' was as far from the domestic world of most late Victorian readers as can be imagined. Stevenson combines elements of the adventure story with romance and travel narrative, while Wiltshire's sometimes sardonic first-person narration helps maintain the reader's interest. However, 'The Beach of Falesá' is also a domestic story – the account of Wiltshire's establishment of a life with Uma – written in an increasingly realist style. This clearly reflected the lives and lifestyles Stevenson was witnessing in the six years he spent in the Pacific. Appearing in the *Illustrated London News*, this South Sea tale provoked some consternation among British readers and reviewers, not least because the author had used his 'exotic' setting to write a matter-of-fact domestic story. Rather like Emily Brontë's generic innovations in *Wuthering Heights*, Stevenson's experiments with genre produced some resistance among readers who felt the novella failed to fulfil their expectations of a Stevenson text.

There was intense interest – sometimes mixed with a sense of betrayal – in Stevenson's choice of Samoa as home. This was complicated by his subject matter and style of writing while living there; once the champion of the adventure romance, Stevenson had turned to realism (even *domestic* realism) in several of his Pacific tales. As Roslyn Jolly (2009) points out, 'while much of Stevenson's Pacific writing alienated his readers at home, the fact of his residence in Samoa provoked enormous public interest' (p. 159). By the time of his death, 'Tusitala' (the teller of tales) had become the most famous foreigner ever to settle in Samoa, and was an admired and loved member of his adoptive community. For all his nostalgia for Scotland (seen, for example, in the poem 'Christmas at sea'; reprinted as Reading 8.5), Stevenson had deliberately chosen to make his home in Samoa; Vailima was not simply a reconstruction of a way of living he knew from his childhood, but a new, mixed existence, combining aspects of domestic life from both British and Pacific traditions. Fittingly, Stevenson's tomb on the slopes of Mount Vaea, overlooking his last home at Vailima, featured the following lines from his poem 'Requiem' engraved upon it:

> Under the wide and starry sky,
> Dig the grave and let me die.
> Glad did I live and gladly die,
> And I laid me down with a will.
>
> This be the verse you grave for me:
> Here he lies where he longed to be;
> Home is the sailor, home from sea,
> And the hunter home from the hill.

(Stevenson, 1887, p. 43)

Conscious of his own failing health, Stevenson had written 'Requiem' as his epitaph at a time when he was already leading a peripatetic life, but before he had decided to relocate to the Pacific. By 1887, he was aware that his illness could kill him without warning, and that this might happen far from home – itself an idea that he was beginning to question. In the poem, Stevenson positions himself as a perpetual traveller, returned home to his final resting place ('home from sea', 'home from the hill'). However, what is most important here is that Stevenson does not mention any specific place for his final resting site, which can be anywhere '[u]nder the wide and starry sky'. The place is determined by the engraved verse ('the verse you grave for me'), Stevenson deliberately playing with two senses of the word 'grave' (i.e. a place of burial and 'to engrave'). Stevenson's intention is clear: as a dedicated traveller and writer, the right and appropriate resting place for him is not one determined solely by birth or nationality, but rather by his profession and affiliation.

References

Booth, B. and Mehew, E. (eds) (1994–5) *The Letters of Robert Louis Stevenson* (8 vols), New Haven, CT, Yale University Press.

Colley, A.C. (2004) *Robert Louis Stevenson and the Colonial Imagination*, Aldershot, Ashgate.

Jolly, R. (2009) *Robert Louis Stevenson in the Pacific: Travel, Empire, and the Author's Profession*, Aldershot, Ashgate.

Pratt, M.L. (1991) 'Arts of the contact zone', *Profession*, no. 91, pp. 33–40.

Sborgi, I. (2007) '"Home" in the South Seas', *Journal of Stevenson Studies*, vol. 4, pp. 185–98.

Stevenson, R.L. (2008 [1892–3]) 'The Beach of Falesá' in *South Sea Tales* (ed. R. Jolly), Oxford, Oxford University Press.

Stevenson, R.L. (1998 [1896]) *In the South Seas* (ed. N. Rennie), Harmondsworth, Penguin.

Stevenson, R.L. (1882) 'The foreigner at home' in *Memories and Portraits* (1990 [1887]), London, T. Nelson & Son.

Stevenson, R.L. (1883) 'A Note on Realism', *The Magazine of Art*, 7 November, pp. 24–8.

Stevenson, R.L. (1887) 'Requiem' in *Underwoods*, London, Chatto and Windus, p. 43.

Further reading

Harman, C. (2005) *Myself and the Other Fellow: A Life of Robert Louis Stevenson*, London, HarperCollins.

Jolly, R. (1999) 'Stevenson's "sterling domestic fiction", "The Beach of Falesá"', *Review of English Studies*, vol. 50, no. 200, pp. 463–83.

Manguel, A. (2004) *Stevenson Under the Palm Trees*, Edinburgh, Canongate Books.

Rennie, N. (1995) *Far-Fetched Facts: The Literature of Travel and the Idea of the South Seas*, Oxford, Oxford University Press.

Conclusion to Part 2

Shafquat Towheed

The expansion of the British empire, the sharp rise in emigration and immigration, the new trades in goods and commodities, industrialisation, urbanisation, and the rise in literacy – all these factors profoundly affected how the Victorians thought about home and abroad as the nineteenth century progressed. We might like to assume that the Victorians had fixed certainties about what home represented: a refuge from the world of work, a haven from the political upheaval of Continental Europe and the conflicts of empire, a fit environment for women to bring up children, a space to display the new goods and values of the middle class. However, as your study of a selection of literary texts by three important Victorian writers has shown, home (in both the domestic and the national sense) was not a fixed and unproblematic category. Drawing upon the Gothic novel and ideas of the uncanny previously explored by Hoffmann, Brontë's *Wuthering Heights* demonstrates that the family home can be a site of emotional upheaval, trauma and profound disquiet. For Brontë, home is a site of haunting and retributive violence rather than comfort and security; even Nelly Dean's sentimental telling of the story cannot hide the discord at its core. Doyle's *The Sign of Four* shows that the domestic world of Victorian London is riven with violence; with the exception of Tonga's death on the Thames, all the deaths that take place in London occur within the confines of private residences. The science of detection is used by Holmes to defend the security of Victorian families in their homes, but the unearthing of the plot displays how this very domestic security is an illusion, beset on all sides by the threats created by British imperial expansion abroad. Stevenson's 'The Beach of Falesá' shifts the focus on the idea of 'home' to the unlikely setting of a copra trader's new domestic life with his Polynesian 'wife', Uma, in a home blighted by bad luck and believed to be cursed.

Unlike Brontë and Doyle, Stevenson's engagement with the complicated relationship between home and abroad extended beyond his writing into his personal life. While *Wuthering Heights* and *The Sign of Four* discuss the fears and adventures of abroad, neither Brontë nor Doyle lived outside England for any considerable period of time. Apart from a brief (and largely unhappy) stint in Brussels, Brontë spent her entire life in her beloved Yorkshire, and this was the focal point of all her literary activity. She wrote passionately and imaginatively about the world that she knew from her home in Haworth Parsonage. While Doyle had travelled abroad as a ship's doctor to Africa, this did not become central to his practice as a writer; he never visited India, despite its centrality to *The Sign of Four*. Stevenson's case is very different. A cosmopolitan dilettante married to an expatriate American divorcee, Stevenson had cut his teeth as a writer with two books of travel writing set in France. His first popular success, *Treasure Island* (1883), deliberately engaged the curiosity of adolescent teenage British readers about the wider world abroad; where, after all, was the imaginary island that Stevenson had immortalised? Stevenson had written about his own experiences of relocating from Scotland to America in *The Silverado Squatters* (1883), *Across the Plains* (1892) and *The Amateur Emigrant* (1895); his account of three Pacific cruises before settling in Samoa was published posthumously as *In the South Seas* (1896).

As British imperial trade expanded, 'abroad' often was *home* for millions of people, many of whom, like Stevenson in Samoa, never came back. The increasing availability of cheaply printed books, magazines and newspapers meant that even readers who never ventured beyond their living rooms were still aware of the importance of the wider world. By the end of the century, Victorian readers could not have been unaware of the world beyond their shores. As the image of Queen Victoria reading the newspaper (reproduced in the Introduction to Part 2) suggests, the Victorians were living in an information economy, with the circulation of news at its core. Often this circulation of ideas took place through fiction. Readers of *The Strand Magazine* and the *Illustrated London News* were offered tales by Stevenson set in the South Pacific, or Sherlock Holmes stories whose plot resolutions depended upon colonial or foreign adventures. From the comfort of their sitting rooms, Victorian readers could vicariously experience the Yorkshire moors, the Indian Mutiny or life in the South Pacific; they could also be comforted by the description of fictional interiors (such as Thrushcross Grange or 221B Baker Street) much like their own. Reading was not only the most important cultural activity for the Victorians but also the main way in which they understood their immediate environment as well as the wider world. The boundaries between 'home' and 'abroad' in the Victorian era were not stable and, in many cases, merged into one another. As you will have experienced in your reading, these boundaries were often explored and tested in the fiction of the period. Most importantly, the very certainties that many Victorian thinkers, like Ruskin, Patmore and Beeton, had confidently espoused about the home in the middle of the century, no longer held true by the end of it. As the Victorian era drew to a close, home and abroad were no longer separate, easily distinguished categories.

Throughout this second part of the book, we have examined the chosen literary texts in the context of Victorian reading practices. We have seen not only how important an activity reading was in the Victorian age, but also how important a part readers play in the process of literary creation. The rich and complex meanings of *Wuthering Heights* are in part a product of the novel's readers, both Victorian and otherwise, who have read and interpreted the text in such diverse ways since its publication. Our focus on the reader has thus shown us the extent to which literary texts involve complex interactions between author and reader. Brontë's experiments with the novel, Doyle's with detective fiction and Stevenson's with the adventure story entailed employing and, in some cases, departing from particular generic conventions, a process which, in turn, elicited particular responses from the reading public. Literary texts, then, create a certain kind of reader – but they are also created and changed as different readers encounter them.

Readings for Part 2

Contents

Reading 7.1 Alfred Tennyson, 'The defence of Lucknow'

Source: *Littell's Living Age*, vol. 26, no. 1822, 1879, pp. 447–8.

I

Banner of England, not for a season, O banner
   of Britain, hast thou
Floated in conquering battle or flapt to the battle-cry!
Never with mightier glory than when we had
   rear'd thee on high
Flying at top of the roofs in the ghastly siege of
   Lucknow –
Shot thro' the staff or the halyard, but ever we
   raised thee anew,   5
And ever upon the topmost roof our banner
   of England blew.

II

Frail were the works that defended the hold
   that we held with our lives –
Women and children among us, God help them,
   our children and wives!
Hold it we might – and for fifteen days or
   for twenty at most.
'Never surrender, I charge you, but every man
   die at his post!'   10
Voice of the dead whom we loved, our Lawrence
   the best of the brave:
Cold were his brows when we kiss'd him – we
   laid him that night in his grave.
'Every man die at his post!' and there hail'd on
   our houses and halls
Death from their rifle-bullets, and death from
   their cannon-balls,
Death in our innermost chamber, and death at
   our slight barricade,   15
Death while we stood with the musket, and death
   while we stoopt to the spade,
Death to the dying, and wounds to the wounded,
   for often there fell

Striking the hospital wall, crashing thro' it, their
   shot and their shell,
Death, for their spies were among us, their
   marksmen were told of our best,
So that the brute bullet broke thro' the brain
   that could think for the rest;   20
Bullets would sing by our foreheads, and bullets
   would rain at our feet –
Fire from ten thousand at once of the rebels
   that girdled us round –
Death at the glimpse of a finger from over
   the breadth of a street,
Death from the heights of the mosque and
   the palace, and death in the ground!
Mine? yes, a mine! Countermine! down, down!
   and creep thro' the hole!   25
Keep the revolver in hand! You can hear
   him – the murderous mole.
Quiet, ah! Quiet – wait till the point of the
   pickaxe be thro'!
Click with the pick, coming nearer and nearer
   again than before –
Now let it speak, and you fire, and the dark
   pioneer is no more;
And ever upon the topmost roof our banner
   of England blew.   30

III

Ay, but the foe sprung his mine many times, and
   it chanced on a day
Soon as the blast of that underground thunderclap
   echo'd away,
Dark thro' the smoke and the sulphur like so
   many fiends in their hell –
Cannon-shot, musket-shot, volley on volley,
   and yell upon yell –
Fiercely on all the defences our myriad enemy fell.   35
What have they done? where is it? Out yonder.
   Guard the Redan!
Storm at the Water-gate! storm at the Bailey-gate!
   storm, and it ran
Surging and swaying all round us, as ocean on every side
Plunges and heaves at a bank that is daily
   drown'd by the tide –

So many thousands that if they be bold enough,
    who shall escape?   40
Kill or be kill'd, live or die, they shall know we
    are soldiers and men!
Ready! take aim at their leaders – their masses
    are gapp'd with our grape –
Backward they reel like the wave, like the wave
    flinging forward again,
Flying and foil'd at the last by the handful they
    could not subdue;
And ever upon the topmost roof our banner of
    England blew.   45

IV

Handful of men as we were, we were English in
    heart and in limb,
Strong with the strength of the race to command,
    to obey, to endure,
Each of us fought as if hope for the garrison
    hung but on him;
Still – could we watch at all points? we were every
    day fewer and fewer.
There was a whisper among us, but only a whisper
    that past: 50
'Children and wives – if the tigers leap into the
    fold unawares –
Every man die at his post – and the foe may
    outlive us at last –
Better to fall by the hands that they love, than to
    fall into theirs!'
Roar upon roar in a moment two mines by the
    enemy sprung
Clove into perilous chasms our walls and our
    poor palisades.   55
Rifleman, true is your heart, but be sure that your
    hand be as true!
Sharp is the fire of assault, better aim'd are your
    flank fusillades –
Twice do we hurl them to earth from the ladders
    to which they had clung,
Twice from the ditch where they shelter we drive
    them with hand-grenades;
And ever upon the topmost roof our banner of
    England blew.   60

V

Then on another wild morning another wild
    earthquake out-tore
Clean from our lines of defence ten or twelve
    good paces or more,
Rifleman, high on the roof, hidden there from
    the light of the sun –
One has leapt up on the breach, crying out:
    'Follow me, follow me!' –
Mark him – he falls! then another, and *him* too,
    and down goes he.   65
Had they been bold enough then, who can tell
    but the traitors had won?
Boardings and rafters and doors – an embrasure!
    make way for the gun!
Now double-charge it with grape! It is charged
    and we fire, and they run.
Praise to our Indian brothers, and let the dark
    face have his due!
Thanks to the kindly dark faces who fought with us,
    faithful and few,   70
Fought with the bravest among us, and drove them,
    and smote them, and slew,
That ever upon the topmost roof our banner
    in India blew.

VI

Men will forget what we suffer and not what
    we do. We can fight;
But to be soldier all day and be sentinel all thro'
    the night –
Ever the mine and assault, our sallies, their lying alarms. 75
Bugles and drums in the darkness, and shoutings
    and soundings to arms,
Ever the labor of fifty that had to be done by five,
Ever the marvel among us that one should be left alive,
Ever the day with its traitorous death from the
    loopholes around,
Ever the night with its coffinless corpse to be laid
    in the ground,   80
Heat like the mouth of a hell, or a deluge of
    cataract skies,
Stench of old offal decaying, and infinite torment of flies,

Thoughts of the breezes of May blowing over
    an English field,
Cholera, scurvy, and fever, the wound that *would*
    not be heal'd,
Lopping away of the limb by the pitiful-pitiless knife, –   85
Torture and trouble in vain, – for it never could
    save us a life,
Valor of delicate women who tended the hospital bed,
Horror of women in travail among the dying and dead,
Grief for our perishing children, and never a
    moment for grief,
Toil and ineffable weariness, faltering hopes of relief,   90
Havelock baffled, or beaten, or butcher'd for all
    that we knew –
Then day and night, day and night, coming down
    on the still-shatter'd walls
Millions of musket-bullets, and thousands of
    cannon-balls –
But ever upon the topmost roof our banner of
    England blew.

VII

Hark cannonade, fusillade! is it true what was
    told by the scout?   95
Outram and Havelock breaking their way thro' the
    fell mutineers!
Surely the pibroch of Europe is ringing again in our ears!
All on a sudden the garrison utter a jubilant shout,
Havelock's glorious Highlanders answer with
    conquering cheers,
Forth from their holes and their hidings our women
    and children come out,   100
Blessing the wholesome white faces of Havelock's
    good fusileers,
Kissing the war-harden'd hand of the Highlander
    wet with their tears!
Dance to the pibroch! – saved! we are saved! – is
    it you? is it you?
Saved by the valor of Havelock, saved by the blessing
    of Heaven!
'Hold it for fifteen days!' we have held it for
    eighty-seven!   105
And ever aloft on the palace roof the old banner
    of England blew.

Reading 7.2 Christina Rossetti, 'In the round tower at Jhansi'

Source: C.H. Sisson (ed.) (1984) *Christina Rossetti: Selected Poems*, **Manchester, Fyfield Books, p. 69. (First published in 1862 in** *Goblin Market, The Prince's Progress and Other Poems*, **London, Macmillan. The note was first published in the revised edition of 1875.)**

A hundred, a thousand to one; even so;
  Not a hope in the world remained:
The swarming, howling wretches below
  Gained and gained and gained.

Skene looked at his pale young wife: —   5
  'Is the time come?' – 'The time is come!' –
Young, strong, and so full of life:
  The agony struck them dumb.

Close his arm about her now,
  Close her cheek to his,   10
Close the pistol to her brow –
  God forgive them this!

'Will it hurt much?' – 'No, mine own:
  I wish I could bear the pang for both.'
'I wish I could bear the pang alone: 15
  Courage, dear, I am not loth.'

Kiss and kiss: 'It is not pain
  Thus to kiss and die.
One kiss more.' – 'And yet one again.' –
  'Good by. – 'Good by.'   20

NOTE. – I retain this little poem, not as historically accurate, but as written and published before I heard the supposed facts of its first verse contradicted.

Reading 7.3 'The mutiny at Jhansi'

Source: *The Times*, 2 September 1857.

The following extract from a letter, just received, giving a detailed account of the death of Captain Skene, Superintendent of the Jhansi District, and of his noble wife, also of Captain Gordon, Assistant Superintendent, will be read with thrilling interest by all to whom those officers were known: –

'It is all true about poor Frank Gordon. He, Alick Skene, his wife, and a few Peons managed to get into a small round tower when the disturbance began; the children and all the rest were in other parts of the fort – altogether 60. Gordon had a regular battery of guns, also revolvers; and he and Skene picked off the rebels as fast as they could fire, Mrs. Skene loading for them. The Peons say they never missed once, and before it was all over they killed 37, besides many wounded. The rebels, after butchering all in the fort, brought ladders against the tower, and commenced swarming up. Frank Gordon was shot through the forehead and killed at once. Skene then saw it was of no use going on any more, so he kissed his wife, shot her, and then himself.'

Reading 7.4 'Events at Jhansi'

Source: *The Times*, **11 September 1857.**

These villainous, bloodthirsty troopers had never been suspected at Jhansi. At Nowgong some of us had for many days distrusted them. The fort gates were barricaded inside with stones, and the garrison Christians only, with some native servants, awaited their enemies, who began the attack on the 6th. One man said the garrison gave in on the 8th; another says the 11th was the day. The latter authority was inside the fort during the defence. Burgess, he said, killed 14 men. Poor Powys shot a man who tried to open one of the gates, and was killed with sword cuts in return. Burgess killed his murderers. Both tales agree on this point, and also that Captain Gordon was hit in the head when looking over the wall parapet. He died of it. Some of the writers tried to escape in native clothes, letting themselves down by ropes, but they were caught and killed. At last Major Skene and the rest were deceived by assurances that their lives would be spared if they surrendered, and they opened the gate, the Hindoos and Mahomedans having both sworn to them. Two attempts to send word to Nagode and to Gwalior for help had failed, and so, taking the hand of some man or other, Major Skene marched out first; they were taken to a garden, tied to two ropes in two rows, men and women separate, – Burgess's servant says the men alone were tied, – and then every soul, whatever the age, rank, or sex, was killed by the sword. The men died first, Burgess taking the lead, his elbows tied behind his back, and a Prayerbook in his hands. What a sad end for so kind-hearted and unselfish a man! But to die confessing the faith is a noble death. The rest died in the same way.

Reading 8.1 Robert Louis Stevenson, 'Foreign Lands'

Source: Robert Louis Stevenson (1895) *A Child's Garden of Verses*, **New York, Charles Scribner's Sons/London, John Lane, pp. 13–14.**

Up into the cherry tree
Who should climb but little me?
I held the trunk with both my hands
And looked abroad on foreign lands.

I saw the next door garden lie,   5
Adorned with flowers before my eye,
And many pleasant places more
That I had never seen before.

I saw the dimpling river pass
And be the sky's blue looking-glass;   10
The dusty roads go up and down
With people tramping in to town.

If I could find a higher tree
Farther and farther I should see,
To where the grown-up river slips   15
Into the sea among the ships,

To where the roads on either hand
Lead onward into fairy land,
Where all the children dine at five,
And all the playthings come alive.   20

Reading 8.2 Robert Louis Stevenson, 'Travel'

Source: Robert Louis Stevenson (1895) *A Child's Garden of Verses*, **New York, Charles Scribner's Sons/London, John Lane, pp. 17–19.**

I should like to rise and go
Where the golden apples grow; –
Where below another sky
Parrot islands anchored lie,
And, watched by cockatoos and goats,   5
Lonely Crusoes building boats; –
Where in sunshine reaching out
Eastern cities, miles about,
Are with mosque and minaret
Among sandy gardens set,   10
And the rich goods from near and far
Hang for sale in the bazaar; –
Where the Great Wall round China goes,
And on one side the desert blows,
And with bell and voice and drum,   15
Cities on the other hum; –
Where are the forests, hot as fire,
Wide as England, tall as a spire,
Full of apes and cocoa-nuts
And the negro hunters' huts; –   20
Where the knotty crocodile
Lies and blinks in the Nile,
And the red flamingo flies
Hunting fish before his eyes; –
Where in jungles near and far,   25
Man-devouring tigers are,
Lying close and giving ear
Lest the hunt be drawing near,
Or a comer-by be seen
Swinging in a palanquin: –   30
Where among the desert sands
Some deserted city stands,
All its children, sweep and prince,
Grown to manhood ages since,
Not a foot in street or house,   35

Not a stir of child or mouse,
And when kindly falls the night,
In all the town no spark of light.
There I'll come when I'm a man
With a camel caravan;   40
Light a fire in the gloom
Of some dusty dining-room;
See the pictures on the walls,
Heroes, fights and festivals;
And in a corner find the toys   45
Of the old Egyptian boys.

Reading 8.3 Robert Louis Stevenson, 'The foreigner at home'

Source: Robert Louis Stevenson (1990 [1887]) *Memories and Portraits*, **Glasgow, Richard Drew, pp. 1–16.**

'This is no' my ain house;
I ken by the biggin' o't.'

Two recent books,[1] one by Mr. Grant White on England, one on France by the diabolically clever Mr. Hillebrand, may well have set people thinking on the divisions of races and nations. Such thoughts should arise with particular congruity and force to inhabitants of that United Kingdom, peopled from so many different stocks, babbling so many different dialects, and offering in its extent such singular contrasts, from the busiest over-population to the unkindliest desert, from the Black Country to the Moor of Rannoch. It is not only when we cross the seas that we go abroad; there are foreign parts of England; and the race that has conquered so wide an empire has not yet managed to assimilate the islands whence she sprang. Ireland, Wales, and the Scottish mountains still cling, in part, to their old Gaelic speech. It was but the other day that English triumphed in Cornwall, and they still show in Mousehole, on St. Michael's Bay, the house of the last Cornish-speaking woman. English itself, which will now frank the traveller through the most of North America, through the greater South Sea Islands, in India, along much of the coast of Africa, and in the ports of China and Japan, is still to be heard, in its home country, in half a hundred varying stages of transition. You may go all over the States, and – setting aside the actual intrusion and influence of foreigners, negro, French, or Chinese – you shall scarce meet with so marked a difference of accent as in the forty miles between Edinburgh and Glasgow, or of dialect as in the hundred miles between Edinburgh and Aberdeen. Book English has gone round the world, but at home we still preserve the racy idioms of our fathers, and every county, in some parts every dale, has its own quality of speech, vocal or verbal. In like manner, local custom and prejudice, even local religion and local law, linger on into the latter end of the nineteenth century – *imperia in imperio*, foreign things at home.

---

[1] 1881.

In spite of these promptings to reflection, ignorance of his neighbours is the character of the typical John Bull. His is a domineering nature, steady in fight, imperious to command, but neither curious nor quick about the life of others. In French colonies, and still more in the Dutch, I have read that there is an immediate and lively contact between the dominant and the dominated race, that a certain sympathy is begotten, or at least a transfusion of prejudices, making life easier for both. But the Englishman sits apart, bursting with pride and ignorance. He figures among his vassals in the hour of peace with the same disdainful air that led him on to victory. A passing enthusiasm for some foreign art or fashion may deceive the world, it cannot impose upon his intimates. He may be amused by a foreigner as by a monkey, but he will never condescend to study him with any patience. Miss Bird, an authoress with whom I profess myself in love, declares all the viands of Japan to be uneatable – a staggering pretension. So, when the Prince of Wales's marriage was celebrated at Mentone by a dinner to the Mentonese, it was proposed to give them solid English fare – roast beef and plum pudding, and no tomfoolery. Here we have either pole of the Britannic folly. We will not eat the food of any foreigner; nor, when we have the chance, will we suffer him to eat of it himself. The same spirit inspired Miss Bird's American missionaries, who had come thousands of miles to change the faith of Japan, and openly professed their ignorance of the religions they were trying to supplant.

I quote an American in this connection without scruple. Uncle Sam is better than John Bull, but he is tarred with the English stick. For Mr. Grant White the States are the New England States and nothing more. He wonders at the amount of drinking in London; let him try San Francisco. He wittily reproves English ignorance as to the status of women in America; but has he not himself forgotten Wyoming? The name Yankee, of which he is so tenacious, is used over the most of the great Union as a term of reproach. The Yankee States, of which he is so staunch a subject, are but a drop in the bucket. And we find in his book a vast virgin ignorance of the life and prospects of America; every view partial, parochial, not raised to the horizon; the moral feeling proper, at the largest, to a clique of States; and the whole scope and atmosphere not American but merely Yankee. I will go far beyond him in reprobating the assumption and the incivility of my country-folk to their cousins from beyond the sea; I grill in my blood over the silly rudeness of our newspaper articles; and I do not know where to look when I find myself in company with an American and see my countrymen unbending to him as to a performing dog. But in the case of Mr. Grant White example were better than precept. Wyoming is, after all, more readily accessible to Mr. White than Boston to the English, and the New England self-sufficiency no better justified than the Britannic.

It is so, perhaps, in all countries; perhaps in all, men are most ignorant of the foreigners at home. John Bull is ignorant of the States; he is probably ignorant of India; but considering his opportunities, he is far more ignorant of countries nearer his own door. There is one country, for instance – its frontier not so far from London, its people closely akin, its language the same in all essentials with the English – of which I will go bail he knows nothing. His ignorance of the sister kingdom cannot be described; it can only be illustrated by anecdote. I once travelled with a man of plausible manners and good intelligence – a University man, as the phrase goes – a man, besides, who had taken his degree in life and knew a thing or two about the age we live in. We were deep in talk, whirling between Peterborough and London; among other things, he began to describe some piece of legal injustice he had recently encountered, and I observed in my innocence that things were not so in Scotland. 'I beg your pardon,' said he, 'this is a matter of law.' He had never heard of the Scots law; nor did he choose to be informed. The law was the same for the whole country, he told me roundly; every child knew that. At last, to settle matters, I explained to him that I was a member of a Scottish legal body, and had stood the brunt of an examination in the very law in question. Thereupon he looked me for a moment full in the face and dropped the conversation. This is a monstrous instance, if you like, but it does not stand alone in the experience of Scots.

England and Scotland differ, indeed, in law, in history, in religion, in education, and in the very look of nature and men's faces, not always widely, but always trenchantly. Many particulars that struck Mr. Grant White, a Yankee, struck me, a Scot, no less forcibly; he and I felt ourselves foreigners on many common provocations. A Scotchman may tramp the better part of Europe and the United States, and never again receive so vivid an impression of foreign travel and strange lands and manners as on his first excursion into England. The change from a hilly to a level country strikes him with delighted wonder. Along the flat horizon there arise the frequent venerable towers of churches. He sees at the end of airy vistas the revolution of the windmill sails. He may go where he pleases in the future; he may also see Alps, and Pyramids, and lions; but it will be hard to beat the pleasure of that moment. There are, indeed, few merrier spectacles than that of many windmills bickering together in a fresh breeze over a woody country; their halting alacrity of movement, their pleasant business, making bread all day with uncouth gesticulations, their air, gigantically human, as of a creature half alive, put a spirit of romance into the tamest landscape. When the Scotch child sees them first he falls immediately in love; and from that time forward windmills keep turning in his dreams. And so, in their degree, with every feature of the life and landscape. The warm, habitable age of towns and hamlets, the green, settled, ancient look of the country; the lush hedgerows, stiles, and privy pathways in the fields; the sluggish, brimming rivers; chalk and smock-frocks; chimes of bells and the rapid, pertly-sounding English speech – they are all new to the curiosity; they are all set to English airs in the child's story that he tells himself at night. The sharp edge of novelty wears off; the feeling is scotched, but I doubt whether it is ever killed. Rather it keeps returning, ever the more rarely and strangely, and even in scenes to which you have been long accustomed suddenly awakes and gives a relish to enjoyment or heightens the sense of isolation.

One thing especially continues unfamiliar to the Scotchman's eye – the domestic architecture, the look of streets and buildings; the quaint, venerable age of many, and the thin walls and warm colouring of all. We have, in Scotland, far fewer ancient buildings, above all in country places; and those that we have are all of hewn or harled masonry. Wood has been sparingly used in their construction; the window-frames are sunken in the wall, not flat to the front, as in England; the roofs are steeper-pitched; even a hill farm will have a massy, square, cold and permanent appearance. English houses, in comparison, have the look of cardboard toys, such as a puff might shatter. And to this the Scotchman never becomes used. His eye can never rest consciously on one of these brick houses – rickles of brick, as he might call them – or on one of these flat-chested streets, but he is instantly reminded where he is, and instantly travels back in fancy to his home. 'This is no' my ain house; I ken by the biggin' o't.' And yet perhaps it is his own, bought with his own money, the key of it long polished in his pocket; but it has not yet, and never will be, thoroughly adopted by his imagination; nor does he cease to remember that, in the whole length and breadth of his native country, there was no building even distantly resembling it.

But it is not alone in scenery and architecture that we count England foreign. The constitution of society, the very pillars of the empire, surprise and even pain us. The dull, neglected peasant, sunk in matter, insolent, gross and servile, makes a startling contrast with our own long-legged, long-headed, thoughtful, Bible-quoting ploughman.

A week or two in such a place as Suffolk leaves the Scotchman gasping. It seems incredible that within the boundaries of his own island a class should have been thus forgotten. Even the educated and intelligent, who hold our own opinions and speak in our words, yet seem to hold them with a difference or from another reason, and to speak on all things with less interest and conviction. The first shock of English society is like a cold plunge. It is possible that the Scot comes looking for too much, and to be sure his first experiment will be in the wrong direction. Yet surely his complaint is grounded; surely the speech of Englishmen is too often lacking in generous ardour, the better part of the man too often withheld from the social commerce, and the contact of mind with mind evaded as with terror. A Scotch peasant will talk more liberally out of his own experience. He will not put you by with conversational counters and small jests; he will give you the best of himself, like one interested in life and man's chief end. A Scotchman is vain, interested in himself and others, eager for sympathy, setting forth his thoughts and experience in the best light. The egoism of the Englishman is self-contained. He does not seek to proselytise. He takes no interest in Scotland or the Scotch, and, what is the unkindest cut of all, he does not care to justify his indifference. Give him the wages of going on and being an Englishman, that is all he asks; and in the meantime, while you continue to associate, he would rather not be reminded of your baser origin. Compared with the grand, tree-like self-sufficiency of his demeanour, the vanity and curiosity of the Scot seem uneasy, vulgar, and immodest. That you should continually try to establish human and serious relations, that you should actually feel an interest in John Bull, and desire and invite a return of interest from him, may argue something more awake and lively in your mind, but it still puts you in the attitude of a suitor and a poor relation. Thus even the lowest class of the educated English towers over a Scotchman by the head and shoulders.

Different indeed is the atmosphere in which Scotch and English youth begin to look about them, come to themselves in life, and gather up those first apprehensions which are the material of future thought and, to a great extent, the rule of future conduct. I have been to school in both countries, and I found, in the boys of the North, something at once rougher and more tender, at once more reserve and more expansion, a greater habitual distance chequered by glimpses of a nearer intimacy, and on the whole wider extremes of temperament and sensibility. The boy of the South seems more wholesome, but less thoughtful; he gives himself to games as to a business, striving to excel, but is not readily transported by imagination; the type remains with me as cleaner in mind and body, more active, fonder of eating, endowed with a lesser and a less romantic sense of life and of the future, and more immersed in present circumstances. And certainly, for one thing, English boys are younger for their age. Sabbath observance makes a series of grim, and perhaps serviceable, pauses in the tenor of Scotch boyhood – days of great stillness and solitude for the rebellious mind, when in the dearth of books and play, and in the intervals of studying the Shorter Catechism, the intellect and senses prey upon and test each other. The typical English Sunday, with the huge midday dinner and the plethoric afternoon, leads perhaps to different results. About the very cradle of the Scot there goes a hum of metaphysical divinity; and the whole of two divergent systems is summed up, not merely speciously, in the two first questions of the rival catechisms, the English tritely inquiring, 'What is your name?' the Scottish striking at the very roots of life with, 'What is the chief end of man?' and answering nobly, if obscurely, 'To glorify God and to enjoy Him for ever.' I do not wish to make an idol of the Shorter Catechism; but the fact of such a question being asked opens to us Scotch a great field of speculation; and the fact that it is asked of all of us, from the peer to the ploughboy, binds us more nearly together. No Englishman of Byron's age, character and history, would have had patience for long theological discussions on the way to fight for Greece; but the daft Gordon blood and the Aberdonian schooldays kept their influence to the end. We have spoken of the material conditions; nor need much more be said of these: of the land lying everywhere more exposed, of the wind always louder and bleaker, of the black, roaring winters, of the gloom of high-lying, old stone cities, imminent on the windy seaboard; compared with the level streets, the warm colouring of the brick, the domestic quaintness of the architecture, among which English children begin to grow up and come to themselves in life. As the stage of the University approaches, the contrast becomes more express. The English lad goes to Oxford or Cambridge; there, in an ideal world of gardens, to lead a semi-scenic life, costumed, disciplined and drilled by proctors. Nor is this to be regarded merely as a stage of education; it is a piece of privilege besides, and a step that separates him further from the bulk of his compatriots. At an earlier age the Scottish lad begins his greatly different experience of crowded class-rooms, of a gaunt quadrangle, of a bell hourly booming over the traffic of the city to recall him from the public-house where he has been lunching, or the streets where he has been wandering fancy-free. His college life has little of restraint, and nothing of necessary gentility. He will find no quiet clique of the exclusive, studious and cultured; no rotten borough of the arts. All classes rub shoulders on the greasy benches. The raffish young gentlemen in gloves must measure his scholarship with the plain, clownish laddie from the parish school. They separate, at the session's end, one to smoke cigars about a watering-place, the other to resume the labours of the field beside his peasant family. The first muster of a college class in Scotland is a scene of curious and painful interest; so many lads, fresh from the heather, hang round the stove in cloddish embarrassment, ruffled by the presence of their smarter comrades, and afraid of the sound of their own rustic voices. It was in these early days, I think, that Professor Blackie won the affection of his pupils, putting these uncouth, umbrageous students at their ease with ready human geniality. Thus, at least, we have a healthy democratic atmosphere to breathe in while at work; even when there is no cordiality there is always a juxtaposition of the different classes, and in the competition of study the intellectual power of each is plainly demonstrated to the other. Our tasks ended, we of the North go forth as freeman into the humming, lamplit city. At five o'clock you may see the last of us hiving from the college gates, in the glare of the shop windows, under the green glimmer of the winter sunset. The frost tingles in our blood; no proctor lies in wait to intercept us; till the bell sounds again, we are the masters of the world; and some portion of our lives is always Saturday, *la trève de Dieu*.

Nor must we omit the sense of the nature of his country and his country's history gradually growing in the child's mind from story and from observation. A Scottish child hears much of shipwreck, outlying iron skerries, pitiless breakers, and great sea-lights; much of heathery mountains, wild clans, and hunted Covenanters. Breaths come to him in song of the distant Cheviots and the ring of foraying hoofs. He glories in his hard-fisted forefathers, of the iron girdle and the handful of oatmeal, who rode so swiftly and lived so sparely on their raids. Poverty, ill-luck, enterprise, and constant resolution are the fibres of the legend of his country's history. The heroes and kings of Scotland have been tragically fated; the most marking incidents in Scottish history – Flodden, Darien, or the Forty-five – were still either failures or defeats; and the fall of Wallace and the repeated reverses of the Bruce combine with the very smallness of the country to teach rather a moral than a material criterion for life. Britain is altogether small, the mere taproot of her extended empire: Scotland, again, which alone the Scottish boy adopts in his imagination, is but a little part of that, and avowedly cold, sterile and unpopulous. It is not so for nothing. I once seemed to have perceived in an American boy a greater readiness of sympathy for lands that are great, and rich, and growing, like his own. It proved to be quite otherwise: a mere dumb piece of boyish romance, that I had lacked penetration to divine. But the error serves the purpose of my argument; for I am sure, at least, that the heart of young Scotland will be always touched more nearly by paucity of number and Spartan poverty of life.

So we may argue, and yet the difference is not explained. That Shorter Catechism which I took as being so typical of Scotland, was yet composed in the city of Westminster. The division of races is more sharply marked within the borders of Scotland itself than between the countries. Galloway and Buchan, Lothian and Lochaber, are like foreign parts; yet you may choose a man from any of them, and, ten to one, he shall prove to have the headmark of a Scot. A century and a half ago the Highlander wore a different costume, spoke a different language, worshipped in another church, held different morals, and obeyed a different social constitution from his fellow-countrymen either of the south or north. Even the English, it is recorded, did not loathe the Highlander and the Highland costume as they were loathed by the remainder of the Scotch. Yet the Highlander felt himself a Scot. He would willingly raid into the Scotch lowlands; but his courage failed him at the border, and he regarded England as a perilous, unhomely land. When the Black Watch, after years of foreign service, returned to Scotland, veterans leaped out and kissed the earth at Port Patrick. They had been in Ireland, stationed among men of their own race and language, where they were well liked and treated with affection; but it was the soil of Galloway that they kissed at the extreme end of the hostile lowlands, among a people who did not understand their speech, and who hated, harried, and hanged them since the dawn of history. Last, and perhaps most curious, the sons of chieftains were often educated on the continent of Europe. They went abroad speaking Gaelic; they returned speaking, not English, but the broad dialect of Scotland. Now, what idea had they in their minds when they thus, in thought, identified themselves with their ancestral enemies? What was the sense in which they were Scotch and not English, or Scotch and not Irish? Can a bare name be thus influential on the minds and affections of men, and a political aggregation blind them to the nature of facts? The story of the Austrian Empire would seem to answer, No; the far more galling business of Ireland clenches the negative from nearer home. Is it common education, common morals, a common language or a common faith, that join men into nations? There were practically none of these in the case we are considering

The fact remains: in spite of the difference of blood and language, the Lowlander feels himself the sentimental countryman of the Highlander. When they meet abroad, they fall upon each other's necks in spirit; even at home there is a kind of clannish intimacy in their talk. But from his compatriot in the south the Lowlander stands consciously apart. He has had a different training; he obeys different laws; he makes his will in other terms, is otherwise divorced and married; his eyes are not at home in an English landscape or with English houses; his ear continues to remark the English speech; and even though his tongue acquire the Southern knack, he will have a strong Scotch accent of the mind.

Reading 8.4 Robert Louis Stevenson, 'Rahéro'

Source: Robert Louis Stevenson (1890) *Ballads*, London, Chatto and Windus, Piccadilly, pp. 40–54.

Rahéro was there in the hall asleep: beside him
　　his wife,
Comely, a mirthful woman, one that delighted
　　in life;
And a girl that was ripe for marriage, shy and
　　sly as a mouse;
And a boy, a climber of trees: all the hopes of
　　his house.
Unwary, with open hands, he slept in the midst
　　of his folk,　　　　　　　　　　　　　　　　　　5
And dreamed that he heard a voice crying without,
　　and awoke,
Leaping blindly afoot like one from a dream
　　that he fears.
A hellish glow and clouds were about him;
　　– it roared in his ears
Like the sound of the cataract fall that plunges
　　sudden and steep;
And Rahéro swayed as he stood, and his reason
　　was still asleep.　　　　　　　　　　　　　　　10
Now the flame struck hard on the house, wind-wielded,
　　a fracturing blow,
And the end of the roof was burst and fell on
　　the sleepers below;
And the lofty hall, and the feast, and the prostrate
　　bodies of folk,
Shone red in his eyes a moment, and then were
　　swallowed of smoke,
In the mind of Rahéro clearness came; and he
　　opened his throat;　　　　　　　　　　　　　　15
And as when a squall comes sudden, the straining
　　sail of a boat
Thunders aloud and bursts, so thundered the voice
　　of the man.
– 'The wind and the rain!' he shouted, the mustering
　　word of the clan,

And 'up!' and 'to arms, men of Vaiau!' But
  silence replied,
Or only the voice of the gusts of the fire, and
  nothing beside.   20
Rahéro stooped and groped. He handled his
  womankind,
But the fumes of the fire and the kava had
  quenched the life of their mind,
And they lay like pillars prone; and his hand
  encountered the boy,
And there sprang in the gloom of his soul a
  sudden lightning of joy.
'Him can I save!' he thought, 'if I were speedy
  enough.'   25
And he loosened the cloth from his loins, and
  swaddled the child in the stuff;
And about the strength of his neck he knotted
  the burden well.

There where the roof had fallen, it roared like
  the mouth of hell.
Thither Rahéro went, stumbling on senseless folk,
And grappled a post of the house, and began
  to climb in the smoke: 30
The last alive of Vaiau; and the son borne by the sire.
The post glowed in the grain with ulcers of eating fire,
And the fire bit to the blood and mangled his
  hands and thighs;
And the fumes sang in his head like wine and
  stung in his eyes;
And still he climbed, and came to the top, the
  place of proof,   35
And thrust a hand through the flame, and
  clambered alive on the roof.
But even as he did so, the wind, in a garment
  of flames and pain,
Wrapped him from head to heel; and the waistcloth
  parted in twain;
And the living fruit of his loins dropped in the
  fire below.

About the blazing feast-house clustered the
  eyes of the foe,   40
Watching, hand upon weapon, lest ever a soul
  should flee,

Shading the brow from the glare, straining the
    neck to see.
Only, to leeward, the flames in the wind swept
    far and wide,
And the forest sputtered on fire; and there might
    no man abide.
Thither Rahéro crept, and dropped from the
    burning eaves,   45
And crouching low to the ground, in a treble
    covert of leaves
And fire and volleying smoke, ran for the life
    of his soul
Unseen; and behind him under a furnace of
    ardent coal,
Cairned with a wonder of flame, and blotting the
    night with smoke,
Blazed and were smelted together the bones of
    all his folk.   50

He fled unguided at first; but hearing the breakers roar,
Thitherward shaped his way, and came at length
    to the shore.
Sound-limbed he was; dry-eyed; but smarted in
    every part;
And the mighty cage of his ribs heaved on his
    straining heart
With sorrow and rage. And 'Fools!' he cried, 'fools
    of Vaiau,   55
Heads of swine – gluttons – Alas! and where
    are they now?
Those that I played with, those that nursed me,
    those that I nursed?
God, and I outliving them! I, the least and the worst –
I, that thought myself crafty, snared by this
    herd of swine,
In the tortures of hell and desolate, stripped of
    all that was mine: 60
All! – my friends and my fathers – the silver
    heads of yore
That trooped to the council, the children that
    ran to the open door
Crying with innocent voices and clasping a father's knees!
And mine, my wife – my daughter – my sturdy
    climber of trees,
Ah, never to climb again!'   65

Thus in the dusk of the night,
(For clouds rolled in the sky and the moon was
    swallowed from sight,)
Pacing and gnawing his fists, Rahéro raged by
    the shore.
Vengeance: that must be his. But much was to
    do before;
And first a single life to be snatched from a
    deadly place,   70
A life, the root of revenge, surviving plant of
    the race:
And next the race to be raised anew, and the lands
    of the clan
Repeopled. So Rahéro designed, a prudent man
Even in wrath, and turned for the means of revenge
    and escape:
A boat to be sized by stealth, a wife to be taken
    by rape.   75

Still was the dark lagoon; beyond on the coral wall,
He saw the breakers shine, he heard them bellow
    and fall.
Alone, on the top of the reef, a man with a flaming
    brand
Walked, gazing and pausing, a fish-spear poised
    in his hand.
The foam boiled to his calf when the mightier
    breakers came,   80
And the torch shed in the wind scattering tufts
    of flame.
Afar on the dark lagoon a canoe lay idly at wait:
A figure dimly guiding it: surely the fisherman's mate.
Rahéro saw and he smiled. He straightened his
    mighty thews:
Naked, with never a weapon, and covered with
    scorch and bruise,   85
He straightened his arms, he filled the void of his
    body with breath,
And, strong as the wind in his manhood, doomed
    the fisher to death.
Silent he entered the water, and silently swam,
    and came
There where the fisher walked, holding on high
    the flame.

Loud on the pier of the reef volleyed the breach
    of the sea;   90
And hard at the back of the man, Rahéro crept to
    his knee
On the coral, and suddenly sprang and seized him,
    the elder hand
Clutching the joint of his throat, the other snatching
    the brand
Ere it had time to fall, and holding it steady and high.
Strong was the fisher, brave, and swift of mind
    and of eye –   95
Strongly he threw in the clutch; but Rahéro resisted
    the strain,
And jerked, and the spine of life snapped with a
    crack in twain,
And the man came slack in his hands and tumbled
    a lump at his feet.

One moment: and there, on the reef, where the
    breakers whitened and beat,
Rahéro was standing alone, glowing and scorched
    and bare,   100
A victor unknown of any, raising the torch in the air.
But once he drank of his breath, and instantly set
    him to fish
Like a man intent upon supper at home and a
    savory dish.
For what should the woman have seen? A man with
    a torch – and then
A moment's blur of the eyes – and a man with a torch
    again.   105
And the torch had scarcely been shaken. 'Ah, surely,'
    Rahéro said,
'She will deem it a trick of the eyes, a fancy born
    in the head;
But time must be given the fool to nourish a
    fool's belief.'
So for a while, a sedulous fisher, he walked the reef,
Pausing at times and gazing, striking at times with
    the spear: 110
– Lastly, uttered the call; and even as the boat
    drew near,
Like a man that was done with its use, tossed the
    torch in the sea.

Lightly he leaped on the boat beside the woman;
  and she
Lightly addressed him, and yielded the paddle and
  place to sit;
For now the torch was extinguished the night was
  black as the pit.   115
Rahéro set him to row, never a word he spoke,
And the boat sang in the water urged by his
  vigorous stroke.
— 'What ails you?' the woman asked, 'and why did
  you drop the brand?
We have only to kindle another as soon as we
  come to land.'
Never a word Rahéro replied, but urged the canoe.   120
And a chill fell on the woman. — 'Atta! speak! is
  it you?
Speak! Why are you silent? Why do you bend aside?
Wherefore steer to the seaward?' thus she panted
  and cried.
Never a word from the oarsman, toiling there in
  the dark;
But right for a gate of the reef he silently headed
  the bark,   125
And wielding the single paddle with passionate
  sweep on sweep,
Drove her, the little fitted, forth on the open deep.
And fear, there where she sat, froze the woman to stone:
Not fear of the crazy boat and the weltering deep alone;
But a keener fear of the night, the dark, and the
  ghostly hour,   130
And the thing that drove the canoe with more than
  a mortal's power
And more than a mortal's boldness. For much she
  knew of the dead
That haunt and fish upon reefs, toiling, like men,
  for bread,
And traffic with human fishers, or slay them and
  take their ware,
Till the hour when the star of the dead goes down,
  and the morning air   135
Blows, and the cocks are singing on shore. And surely
  she knew
The speechless thing at her side belonged to the grave.

                    It blew
All night from the south; all night, Rahéro contended
  and kept
The prow to the cresting sea; and, silent as though
  she slept,   140
The woman huddled and quaked. And now was the
  peep of day.
High and long on their left the mountainous island lay;
And over the peaks of Taiárapu arrows of sunlight struck.
On shore the birds were beginning to sing: the
  ghostly ruck
Of the buried had long ago returned to the covered
  grave;   145
Ad here on the sea, the woman, waxing suddenly brave,
Turned her swiftly about and looked in the face
  of the man.
And sure he was none that she knew, none of her
  country or clan:
A stranger, mother-naked, and marred with the marks
  of fire,
But comely and great of stature, a man to obey and
  admire.   150

And Rahéro regarded her also, fixed, with a frowning
  face,
Judging the woman's fitness to mother a warlike race.
Broad of shoulder, ample of girdle, long in the thigh,
Deep of bosom she was, and bravely supported his eye.

'Woman,' said he, 'last night the men of your folk –   155
Man, woman, and maid, smothered my race in smoke.
It was done like cowards; and I, a mighty man of my
  hands,
Escaped, a single life; and now to the empty lands
And smokeless hearths of my people, sail, with
  yourself, alone.
Before your mother was born, the die of to-day was
  thrown   160
And you selected: – your husband, vainly striving,
  to fall
Broken between these hands: – yourself to be severed
  from all,
The places, the people, you love – home, kindred,
  and clan –
And to dwell in a desert and bear the babes of a
  kinless man.'

Reading 8.5 Robert Louis Stevenson, 'Christmas at sea'

Source: Robert Louis Stevenson (1890) *Ballads*, **London, Chatto and Windus, Piccadilly, pp. 133–7.**

The sheets were frozen hard, and they cut the naked
   hand;
The decks were like a slide, where a seaman scarce
   could stand;
The wind was a nor'wester, blowing squally off the sea;
And cliffs and spouting breakers were the only
   things a-lee.

They heard the surf a-roaring before the break of day;   5
But 'twas only with the peep of light we saw how
   ill we lay.
We tumbled every hand on deck instanter, with
   a shout,
And we gave her the maintops'l, and stood by to
   go about.

All day we tacked and tacked between the South
   Head and the North;
All day we hauled the frozen sheets, and got no
   further forth;   10
All day as cold as charity, in bitter pain and dread,
For very life and nature we tacked from head to head.

We gave the South a wider berth, for there the
   tide-race roared;
But every tack we made we brought the North
   Head close aboard:
So 's we saw the cliffs and houses, and the breakers
   running high,   15
And the coastguard in his garden, with his glass
   against his eye.

The frost was on the village roofs as white as ocean
   foam;
The good red fires were burning bright in every
   'longshore home;
The windows sparkled clear, and the chimneys
   volleyed out;

And I vow we sniffed the victuals as the vessel
    went about.   20

The bells upon the church were rung with a mighty
    jovial cheer;
For it's just that I should tell you how (of all days
    in the year)
This day of our adversity was blessèd Christmas morn,
And the house above the coastguard's was the house
    where I was born.

O well I saw the pleasant room, the pleasant faces
    there,   25
My mother's silver spectacles, my father's silver hair;
And well I saw the firelight, like a flight of homely elves
Go dancing round the china-plates that stand upon
    the shelves.

And well I knew the talk they had, the talk that was
    of me
Of the shadow on the household and the son that
    went to sea;   30
And O the wicked fool I seemed, in every kind of way.
To be here and hauling frozen ropes on blessed
    Christmas Day.

They lit the high sea-light, and the dark began to fall.
'All hands to loose topgallant sails,' I heard the
    captain call.
'By the Lord, she'll never stand it,' our first mate,
    Jackson, cried.   35
… 'It's the one way or the other, Mr. Jackson,'
    he replied.

She staggered to her bearings, but the sails were new
    and good,
And the ship smelt up to windward just as though
    she understood.
As the winter's day was ending, in the entry of the
    night,
We cleared the weary headland, and passed below
    the light.   40

And they heaved a mighty breath, every soul on board
    but me,
As they saw her nose again pointing handsome out to sea;
But all that I could think of, in the darkness and the cold,
Was just that I was leaving home and my folks were
    growing old.

Glossary

alliteration

An example of the poetic patterning of sound, alliteration occurs when words that appear in close proximity to one another begin with the same letter or sound, as in Wordsworth's poem 'I wandered lonely as a cloud', which, in the fourth line, pairs 'dancing' and 'daffodils'.

allusion

With allusion a literary text invokes another, older literary text or author. Often this is done by direct quotation, correct or incorrect, and with or without attribution. There is another looser form of allusion, known as 'echo', where the literary text consciously or unconsciously repeats rhythms or words from another text.

apostrophe

A direct address made in the first person ('I') to someone or something which is characterised in the second person ('you', 'thee'). Wordsworth's poem 'To the Cuckoo' begins with an apostrophe to the bird that extends through the entire first stanza: 'O blithe New-comer! I have heard, / I hear thee and rejoice: / O Cuckoo! shall I call thee Bird, / Or but a wandering Voice!' De Quincey also makes extensive use of apostrophe for his grander effects, as in the address to opium in *Confessions of an English Opium-Eater*: 'O just, subtle, and mighty opium! … Thou only givest these gifts to man; and thou hast the keys of Paradise, oh just, subtle, and mighty opium!'

assonance

An example of the poetic patterning of sound, assonance occurs when words that appear in close proximity to one another contain the same or similar vowel sounds within them.

author

In popular usage, simply the writer of a text. However, the idea of the author carries greater cultural weight than that of writer, especially from the Romantic period onwards. It includes the notion that authors have an especially direct and privileged relation to an imaginative reality, and that this gives them a potentially prophetic power and voice. It implies too an increased sense of authorial celebrity, and carries the implication that the author's writings can be understood by appeal to his or her life, and that conversely his or her life can be read through their writings.

ballad metre

See **metre**.

blank verse

See **metre**.

broadsheet ballad

A ballad printed on a single sheet of paper (a broadsheet), sold on the streets. The subjects of such ballads varied from crimes and scandals, to political agitation and hard-luck war stories.

cadence

This term comes from the Latin 'cadere' (to fall). It denotes the final chord progression of a phrase of music, the music returning 'home', if you like. In literature, it describes the melodic pattern of a writer's voice, or denotes the closing of a poetic line with a fall in the rhythm, stress, or tone on the last word or syllable.

couplet

See **metre** and **rhyme**.

diction

The style characterised by a writer's vocabulary.

dramatic monologue

This is a device often used in poetry, in which an imaginary speaker addresses an imaginary audience. The dramatic monologue was particularly popular in nineteenth-century poetry, and draws upon the soliloquy in drama.

elegy

A mode of poetry derived from the ancient Greeks, and revived by English poets in the Romantic period. Elegiac writing is mournful, contemplative, and reflective, and is considered to be the most fitting mode of poetry to remember the dead. The most famous example of the elegy in English poetry is Thomas Gray's 'Elegy Written in a Country Churchyard' (1751).

empirical evidence

Evidence is empirical if it can be measured or recorded accurately, such as distance, weight, time or frequency, in standard units. Empirical evidence can be derived from observation alone, or from a controlled experiment, but it is always capable of being verified by repetition. For example, if I measure a table and find it to be 160 cm long, another person measuring its length should also come up with the same figure – this would prove that the length of the table is verifiable empirical evidence.

enjambement

A term describing the way a sentence in a poem runs over into the next line or lines without pausing because the grammatical unit is not yet complete, as in Wordsworth's poem, 'I wandered lonely as a cloud': 'The waves beside them danced, but they / Outdid the sparkling waves in glee'.

epic poetry

Epic was regarded as the 'highest' poetic form, and was therefore the most ambitious form to attempt. Descended from Homeric epic (specifically *The Iliad*), through to John Milton's *Paradise Lost* (1667), its ambitions are nothing less than to describe the ways of the cosmos and the place of man in it.

epistolary novel

A novel where the story is told in the form of letters between two or more people. The epistolary (from 'epistle', or letter) novel was particularly popular in the eighteenth century, because it gave readers a sense of the events being part of real life, rather than a fiction.

fantasy

In literary terms, fantasy, or the fantastic, is characterised by its interest in characters and events that have no place in the real, natural world.

first-person narrator

A first-person narrator is the 'I' who is telling the story, as in the opening of De Quincey's *Confessions of an English Opium-Eater*: 'I here present you, courteous reader, with the record of a remarkable period in my life'.

Gothic

Gothic writing is defined by anxiety about the unknown. It is characterised by its use of terror and suspense, often accompanied and heightened by elements of the supernatural. It specialises in the evocation of nightmarish repetition and a claustrophobic atmosphere.

half-rhyme

See **rhyme**.

hybrid

This term originally comes from biology, and means the offspring of cross-breeding between two different species or types. In literature, 'hybrid' is a term usually applied to writing that, like a biological hybrid, shows the characteristics of two or more literary traditions or forms. For example, *Wuthering Heights* demonstrates both gothic and realist qualities, and can be classified as a 'hybrid' because of this.

iambic metre

See **metre**.

iambic pentameter

See **metre**.

information economy

An information economy is one in which increasing numbers of people were literate, and had ready access to information, and where information itself had an intrinsic economic value. For example, the huge increase in the circulation of newspapers during the nineteenth century shows that news had a value, and that a large number of people were prepared to pay to access this valuable, up-to-date information.

insignificant detail

See ***significant and insignificant detail.***

irony

Generally speaking, irony involves implying something other than what is explicitly said; it requires readers to 'read between the lines' and, often, to perceive more than a fictional or dramatic character does. Romantic irony is a special kind of irony. It is a kind of literary self-consciousness in which an author signals his or her freedom from the limits of a given work by puncturing its fictional illusion and exposing its processes of composition as a matter of authorial whim.

lexicon

The vocabulary used by a writer.

lyric

A lyric – literally, a song – is a short poem devoted to expressing a single mood or moment of consciousness and which usually foregrounds the poet as a first-person speaker. It is typically deeply personal in mode, and specific to time and place. Prose can be described as lyrical when it adopts a strongly emotional and evocative way of describing seasons, landscape, or weather, or more generally when it aspires to poetic condensation and intensity.

metaphor

A type of figurative language that establishes an identity between two apparently dissimilar things, but without explicitly comparing them. The opening lines of Shelley's 'Lines written in the Vale of Chamouni', for example, establish an implicit comparison between 'the everlasting universe of things' and a river, and are therefore metaphorical: 'The everlasting universe of things / Flows through the mind, and rolls its rapid waves …' Metaphor is strictly distinguished from simile by the use of the words 'like' or 'as'. Shelley's 'To a Skylark' is structured as a string of similes: 'Like a poet hidden / In the light of thought, / Singing hymns unbidden …'

metonym

A form of metaphor where a comparison is made via a substitution of a part for the whole.

metre

The general technical term for the underlying regular rhythm or beat that a poem may adopt. There are a number of conventional metres, which include the iambic (an unstressed syllable followed by a stressed one) and the trochaic (a stressed syllable followed by an unstressed one). Wordsworth's line 'I dipped my oars into the silent Lake' (from *The Prelude*) is an example of iambic metre; Shelley's 'Hail to thee, blithe Spirit!' (the first line of 'To the Skylark') is an example of trochaic metre. Iambic pentameter is a line of ten syllables that falls into five iambic measures or 'feet'. Unrhymed iambic pentameter, the basic metre of Milton's *Paradise Lost* and Wordsworth's *The Prelude*, is also known as blank verse; for Romantic writers it carried connotations of 'freedom' because it did not rhyme. Ballad metre is trochaic feet, with four stresses in each line.

novella

A term for a work of sustained prose fiction between 20,000 and 40,000 words in length, that is longer than a short story, but shorter than a novel. The novella became more clearly identified as an intermediate literary form between the short story and the novel in a range of European literatures during the course of the nineteenth century. Unlike a full-length novel, a novella will rarely have a complicated sub-plot, or multiple narrators and numerous highly developed characters; instead, it typically depends on developing a single character or point of view. Unlike the short story, the novella is long enough to explore more than a single episode or point in time.

ode

An ode is a lyric poem, usually addressing a particular person or thing. It has two forms, the Pindaric (so called because it was written by the Greek poet Pindar, *c*.518–*c*.438 BCE) and the Horatian (invented by the Latin poet Horace in about 65 BCE). However, modern odes do not necessarily have a regular metre, fixed form, or prescribed rhyme scheme although they often adopt the lofty style associated with the form.

pastoral

A literary genre with a history dating back to classical times, pastoral describes poems, plays or novels set in the countryside. The conventional assumption of pastoral is of a rural innocence or purity that provides a moral reference point for the corruption, greed and decadence of cities.

persona

The mask and voice adopted explicitly or implicitly by an author whether in their own person or as some fictive narrator in order to tell a story, provide a description, or make an argument.

personification

A variety of metaphoric comparison in which human qualities are attributed to a non-human object, as in De Quincey's apostrophe in *Confessions of an English Opium-Eater*: 'Oxford-street, stony-hearted step-mother! Thou that listenest to the sighs of orphans, and drinkest the tears of children …'

prolepsis

The opposite of analepsis. Whereas analepsis is what is popularly called 'flashback', prolepsis can be termed 'flashforward'. Analepsis is a moment when the narrative leaps backwards in time, prolepsis is a moment when the narrative leaps forward in time, before returning to the original chronological sequence and pacing of events.

protagonist

The chief character in a literary work.

realism

A literary term used to describe modes of writing concerned with characters and events that would be plausible in the real, natural world.

reception

The reception history of literary texts refers to how they have been interpreted by different readers, audiences and critics over time. This might also include literary re-workings of the original text. Certain historical events written up in a particular way might also have a 'reception history', as they are re-written again and again at later historical moments.

register

A register is a particular type or style of language associated with a particular context. Thus, for example, we can talk about formal and informal registers, or registers associated with different occupational discourses (legal, medical, academic, religious and so on).

rhyme

An example of sound patterning in poetry. Rhyme may be 'end-rhyme', which is where the sound at the end of each line of poetry rhymes with another line. It may also be 'half-rhyme', where the sound at the end of each line is similar but not exact.

A rhyme scheme may be marked up, where the first rhyme is designated 'a', the second 'b', and so on. Certain verse forms, such as terza rima and the **sonnet**, have prescribed rhyme schemes. Two consecutive lines which rhyme are known as a rhyming couplet.

romance

A literary term used to describe a mode of writing that engages with the desires and imaginative lives of its characters and readers.

significant and insignificant detail

Small details in the narrative of detective fiction, such as objects, or pieces of information, that might be clues in helping to solve the crime. Often in detective fiction, significant and insignificant detail may appear to be interchangeable, i.e. something that appears to be important turns out to be irrelevant to the resolution of the plot, while a seemingly unimportant piece of information might prove central to solving the crime. The ability to distinguish between the two is often a test of the reader's attention and helps to keep our interest in the narrative to the end. Writers of detective fiction invariably scatter both significant and insignificant detail through their narratives.

sonnet

A 14-line lyric poem in iambic pentameter with a complex rhyme scheme which differs according to whether it belongs to the Petrarchan or the Shakespearean variant. The English sonnet conventionally adopts one of these variants, and typically involves a 'turn' from the argument of the first eight lines to the final six which serve as a conclusion. The Petrarchan scheme (abba abba cde cde) ends with a pair of **tercets**, that is to say, sets of three lines. The Shakespearean scheme (abab cdcd efef) ends with a clinching rhyming couplet, that's to say, two lines that rhyme with each other. The sonnet traditionally uses the **metre** known as iambic pentameter.

sublime

A key concept for eighteenth- and nineteenth-century thinking about the imagination, the divine, and nature. The experience of the sublime involves extreme landscapes or situations which elicit in the observer a state of awareness combining fear, admiration and awe. Although landscapes are often described as themselves sublime, the apprehension of sublimity arises in the observer's consciousness.

syntax

A technical term for sentence structure.

tercet

A three-line unit, characteristic of the form known as terza rima, which Dante pioneered in *The Divine Comedy*.

trochaic metre

See **metre**.

trope

A term for figurative language, or a motif.

vocabulary

A term for the writer's choice of language, closely related to 'diction' and 'lexicon'. Writers may consciously use 'low' or 'high', simple or complex, slang or formal language, and may mix the two for effect as De Quincey does here, in *Confessions of an English Opium-Eater*, by juxtaposing the word 'consternation' with the word 'bolt': 'I was struck with some little consternation when I saw him suddenly raise his hand to his mouth, and (in the school-boy phrase) bolt the whole [piece of opium]'.

voice

A term for the effect many texts give that the writer is speaking to you as the reader. It is a useful term, because it allows us to distinguish between the writer as a historically verifiable person, and the voice that they craft in a poem or a story. Thus we can speak of the voice De Quincey adopts in his *Confessions*, without presuming that it embodies De Quincey himself in a natural, comprehensive or unproblematic way.

Acknowledgements

Grateful acknowledgement is made to the following sources:

Reading 1.4

Darlington, B. (ed.) (1977) *William Wordsworth: Home at Grasmere*, Ithaca and London, Cornell University Press, pp. 38–106.

Readings 1.5 and 1.6

Wordsworth, J., Abrams, M.H., and Gill, S. (eds) (1979) *William Wordsworth: The Prelude 1799, 1805, 1850: Authoritative Texts; Context and Reception; Recent Critical Essays*, New York, W.W. Norton and Company, pp. 1–13.

Readings 2.1–2.8

Leader, Z. and O'Neill, M. (eds) (2003) *Percy Bysshe Shelley: The Major Works*, Oxford, Oxford University Press.

Reading 3.1

Lindop, G. (ed.) (1998) *Thomas De Quincey: Confessions of an English Opium-Eater and Other Writings*, Oxford, Oxford University Press, pp. 235–44. By permission of Oxford University Press.

Reading 4.1

Robertson, R. (trans.) (2008) *E.T.A. Hoffman: The Golden Pot and Other Tales*, Oxford, Oxford University Press, pp. 85–118 and 403. By permission of Oxford University Press.

Index

Page references in **bold** refer to figures